Expressions of the Heart

Daisy Worrell

Copyright © 2019 Deep Inkwell
All rights reserved.
www.deepinkwell.com
ISBN: 978-0-578-54487-8

Deep Inkwell

Dedication

Dedicated to the One I love.

Contents

Acknowledgements

I would like to thank my Mom and Dad for their love and support throughout the writing of this book, as well as throughout my life. I don't think I could have written this book without you. The both of you have been very great blessings in my life. I love you, and I thank the Lord for you.

Most of all, I would like to thank the Lord. Thank you for teaching me. Thank you for your guidance, love, and support throughout the writing of this book, as well as throughout my life. You are the only reason this book was written. Without you I could not have done it. We did it! I hope it is everything you wanted it to be. I love you.

Introduction

This book is a collection of personal lessons I've learned, thoughts, and insights. I thank the Lord for teaching me. If it weren't for Him, I would not have learned these things.

The great majority of the chapters were originally essays I wrote. They are candidly written – unsophisticated and plain. Each of them are on a different topic. When I wrote them, I did not intend to compile them into a book. They were only essays I wrote, as I was learning from the Lord, to document things I had learned, my thoughts, and insights. Later I felt led to make a book out of them.

While the reader can read the chapters of this book out of order, I would suggest reading them in order. As they have been arranged, they are mostly in chronological order. I feel that something is gained from reading them this way, because I was growing with each chapter I wrote. Many in the beginning are shorter and simpler, and they progressively become somewhat longer and more complex.

The goal of this book is to impart knowledge, wisdom, and understanding. It is titled *Expressions of the Heart*, because it expresses many things of the heart. Of God's heart, as well as mine, and I hope the shared feelings of other people.

I trust that this book, along with the Holy Spirit, will act as a harrow on the hearts of those who read it. A harrow, with each chapter acting as a disc or tine of that harrow on the heart, breaking up fallow ground.

The Lord is saying to the men of Judah and Jerusalem, Plow up the hardness of your hearts; otherwise the good seed will be wasted among the thorns. (Jeremiah 4:3 TLB)

Sow for yourselves righteousness; reap steadfast love; break up your fallow ground, for it is time to seek the LORD, that he may come and rain righteousness upon you. (Hosea 10:12 ESV)

Plant the good seeds of righteousness and you will reap a crop of my love; plow the hard ground of your hearts, for now is the time to seek the Lord, that he may come and shower salvation upon you. (Hosea 10:12 TLB)

Please be led by the Holy Spirit as you read. Listen to Him and let Him guide you in what is true. Take what is good, leave what you should.

I hope you are blessed by what I've written.

1

Appearance

My journal entry from July 6, 2011

In the Bible, I found this passage (1 Samuel 16:6-7 NASB):

When they entered, he looked at Eliab and thought, "Surely the LORD'S anointed is before Him." But the LORD said to Samuel, "Do not look at his appearance or at the height of his stature, because I have rejected him; for God sees not as man sees, for man looks at the outward appearance, but the LORD looks at the heart."

I also found this, that Jesus said (John 7:24 NASB):

"Do not judge according to appearance, but judge with righteous judgement."

I would so like to be able to see as the Lord sees. So much is placed on appearance. Instant judgements are made on appearance. I think there is something to be known by one's appearance, but I hope that I learn from it in a righteous way, or in the way the Lord would have me learn from it - not by my own mind. Even somewhere in Ecclesiastes it mentions you can see a fool by the way he walks.[1]

Wouldn't it be nice to see and meet people in the right way? To see and know their hearts rather than their appearance. If one judges by appearance it can be very deceitful. I don't want to be deceived. I think the truth is more important than I know. Not only should I not judge by appearance because it can be deceitful, but because the Lord instructs us not to, and I want to please Him by being obedient and faithful. Furthermore, we're supposed to be imitators of God.

the one who says he abides in Him ought himself to walk in the same manner as He walked. (1 John 2:6 NASB)

Of course, I need the Lord's help to be able to do anything, this included.

Living in the world, it is so easy to put importance on things the world puts importance on, without even realizing it. In fact, it seems perfectly "normal." But what is the truth of the matter? Here's another verse from the Bible that can relate to these things, among others.

For all that is in the world, the lust of the flesh and the lust of the eyes and the boastful pride of life, is not from the Father, but is from the world. (1 John 2:16 NASB)

So, so much of what is around us is of/from the world. Things we thought were "just life" or didn't even question are not things that are from the Lord.

May the Lord help us, give us wisdom and understanding and help us sift through what is of the world, and what is of Him. May we live in the things that are His.

2

Truth

My journal entry from November 1, 2011

Sometimes it seems like one of the most rare things in this world is truth. Truth is so important, and yet it is undervalued, hidden, or so mixed up and tainted by the world and its ways that it can hardly be perceived.

For example, if a person were to tell a joke that really isn't truth, is this to be valued or not? This can be a perplexing question, but the fact remains that it is not truth.

Is it then a lie? I would initially think that a lie is a falsehood with malicious intent. So, does that mean that a falsehood intended for good is not a lie? At the risk of being labeled a "stick in the mud" by the world (which really is no risk), I think both falsehoods, intended for good or not, could be called a lie.

I think it's best to always strive for truth in one's life - in every aspect - and to avoid falsehoods. This can certainly be a challenge, and a different way of living. But really, just try to think of what you speak. Is it really true? Or even what you think - your thoughts - are they true? It can be surprising to learn just how much is not true, but seems to have been accepted as truth, for some reason or another.

The world may say that "the truth hurts" or say that something is an expression of "tough love." I think much of the time these things are an excuse for abrupt, thoughtless, and hurtful behavior that is not done in love. But yes, at times the truth is so real and unshakable that hearing it, and realizing it, can hurt. As far as "tough love" goes, I suppose there are times when things must be done that may not seem nice, but are truly done in love.

It is amazing to examine the things around us, and see how true they are. Advertising in stores, magazines, on T.V. It is repulsive how misleading, how false they can be. The images that we see: how real are they? Even people, we can alter our appearance so much. The lives people lead. The lives the world says people live: is that really living? I mean, if a person were to live "differently" than the "ideal life" the world glorifies, does that mean that they are not truly living? So much falseness is exposed to people every day, all the time. Where are they to grow from? Where is their base, their rock to stand firm on?

It is important to sift the truth from what is false. To examine things accepted as true, and make sure that they are true. Even little things that don't seem significant enough to examine are things that are important to know the truth about.

So many times in the Bible the truth is referred to. I've often read these references to truth, but did not really take it seriously I think. However, I think the more one strives for truth in everyday things too, and lives in it, the better it will be. I'm not even sure how it will be better, but I believe it is what is best. Certainly, it is better than living in deceit and false things. What good are they? Furthermore, one is left blind and trying to grasp the air when believing and living in deceit.

Buy truth, and do not sell it, Get wisdom and instruction and understanding. (Proverbs 23:23 NASB)

And the Word became flesh, and dwelt among us, and we saw

His glory, glory as of the only begotten from the Father, full of grace and truth. (John 1:14 NASB)

So Jesus was saying to those Jews who had believed Him, "If you continue in My word, then you are truly disciples of Mine; and you will know the truth, and the truth will make you free." (John 8:31-32 NASB)

Jesus said to him, "I am the way, and the truth, and the life; no one comes to the Father but through Me." (John 14:6 NASB)

As a result, we are no longer to be children, tossed here and there by waves and carried about by every wind of doctrine, by the trickery of men, by craftiness in deceitful scheming; but speaking the truth in love, we are to grow up in all *aspects* into Him who is the head, *even* Christ, from whom the whole body, being fitted and held together by what every joint supplies, according to the proper working of each individual part, causes the growth of the body for the building up of itself in love. (Ephesians 4:14-16 NASB)

The John 14:6 verse is very striking. Jesus says He is "... the truth ..." Having read this verse in the past, I understood that He is "the way." The only way. Also, I understood how He is "the life." How He gives life to sinners and is life. He says He is "the truth," too. It is really something to think about.

Let us seek truth everywhere it can be had. I started out by saying the truth seemed like one of the rarest things in this world, but now I tend to think there is no real truth in the world.

3

Sin

My journal entry from August 25, 2011

It is never worth it - to sin. I think, if presented with the truth of a situation, where one is at the crossroads of choosing to sin or not and had the clarity to see it, more people would choose not to sin.

At that crossroads, it seems the enemy is trying to blur one's vision with thoughts that sinning is a better choice than not sinning. In the end, it truly was not "worth it."

Furthermore, the fact that the Lord doesn't want you to sin should be enough to keep one from sinning. Weighing out in your mind whether it would be worth it or not should not be the deciding factor. One's love and respect for the Lord would ideally be/should be what makes one choose not to sin.

It seems even the enemy himself knows it wasn't the thing to do. For, after one sins, he comes after you with thoughts that you're worthless, useless, good-for-nothing, a failure, and maybe even that the Lord loves you less as a result of your sin.

Even believers stumble. I'm not sure if I should put the word "even" at the beginning of the previous sentence. But sometimes I feel there is an idea that once you are born again or are a believer, or whatever one would call it, that the person is immune to sin. I think they see sin for what it is, and try (with God's help) to live and grow in their new nature. But going against the old nature, the flesh, is still a struggle. It's a struggle that is sometimes lost. I'm not sure what else to say but that they strive to win against sin and if there are losses to it, to confess and ask forgiveness from the Lord and for help to be able to not do it again.

I feel the Lord is not happy when one sins, but is loving, understanding, and forgiving. I feel He does not want us to beat ourselves up forever because of our sin, which can happen to those with a conscience and maybe a feeling of accountability, but to fully realize our mistake, learn from it, strive to not do it again and lift our heads up and move forward and grow in Him.

In the race we may have stumbled, but the race is not over yet. Don't stop because you have stumbled, but pick yourself up and continue, being careful to not stumble again.

4

Wretched

My journal entry from August 16, 2012

Why do I always do what I know I should not do? I must
change. I cannot go on doing over and over again what I shouldn't
do. It makes me feel very ashamed to ask God to forgive me for the
same things I've asked Him to forgive me for several times before. I
feel sincere, and yet insincere when I know I'm asking forgiveness
for repeat sins, and I knew it was the wrong thing to do!

The Lord has shown me so much and given me so much grace
and mercy. I feel like I disappoint Him when I sin. What a true
wretch I am. I don't want to sin and disappoint the Lord anymore.
He's the only One I have, and I want to make Him pleased with me.
Not disappointed or, heaven forbid, sorry that He chose me!

I know what I should do and deliberately don't do it.
Sometimes it's because I'm hearing, "Is it really a bad thing to do?"
or, "It's ok," or "Maybe it doesn't really matter." Sometimes I know
it's wrong right away, but sometimes I fall for these things and sin
anyway when in my heart I know it is sin. Or, at least something I
told the Lord I would not do anymore.

Again and again, it is never worth it to sin - never! No matter how sensible or insignificant it may seem.

Oh Lord, please help me to do what is right - always - and to cling to truth tightly and not be fooled into sinning, even if I really feel like sinning, Lord.

There seems to be a part of me that wants to and likes to sin. But there is another part of me that hates to. I want to foster and cultivate the part that hates to sin and kill off the part that wants to sin. Please help me, again and again, to do this Lord! And please forgive me again and again. How I wish I didn't have to ask you to forgive me for the same sins, or any at all, but I know I must ask you every day. Lord, help me to stop doing what is wrong and sinful, and to not be fooled into thinking it is all right to do something that is wrong. Please, forgive me Lord.

Please help me to be patient with myself Lord, but not so much that I give myself too much allowance for my seemingly inevitable, or truly inevitable sinning. However inevitable it is, please help me to keep my sins at a minimum, Lord, and help me always to strive to please you and do what is right. No matter how much that other part of me wants to sin, because there's still the part that really doesn't want to. I want to listen to that part, and make that part stronger and more and more dominant, while the other part gets weaker and less and less noticeable.

Oh Lord, I need your constant help, guidance, understanding, strength, and forgiveness so much. Please help me not to disappoint You anymore! I feel disappointed in myself when I disappoint You. Also, please help me to forgive myself as You forgive me. When You forgive me Lord, I want to forgive myself also.

Help me to realize where and what went wrong, and to move forward. Move forward and keep trying to follow the right path and not stray from it, even when there are nearly irresistible temptations along the path. Please help me to turn away, turn away quickly and keep moving forward Lord. Thank you, Lord for forgiving me - forgiving me and forgiving me and forgiving me. Please help me to be more and more like You Lord. To forgive, and do what is right, and not sin, but to turn from it, Lord. To turn from it and keep moving forward and growing from doing so too.

5

A Challenge to Love

Why is it difficult for me to love someone as much as I want to, when they have a fault (what I consider a fault) that bothers me so much? I see the fault clearly. I can sense when they're about to do it and I want to somehow hold them back from doing it, but it wouldn't be practical unless I got up and put my hand over their mouth.

It's hard to define exactly what this fault that I dislike in them is. I guess it's a kind of immaturity, or foolish talk, that I find unbecoming of them. The reaction it creates in me is less respect for them, or disappointment. I want them to be better than that. I want to respect them, not disrespect them. I want to love this person fully, even with this fault, but it bothers me so much!

By God's grace I know enough that there are many faults to overlook in someone when you love them. One must extend grace and allow people to be what they are, and not go and point out every shortcoming they have. I would want others to do the same for me. Also, it exercises my self-control.

I was struggling with this issue with this person, and I was puzzled as to why I was having such a hard time with it. I was thinking about it when the Lord told me, "It could be a challenge for you to love." I was surprised to hear this. "A challenge for me?" I thought. For a moment I felt defensive, but then I knew it was true. It was a challenge for me to love this person. I want to be more like Christ, and He loves me so much. I want to be that way toward others. He loves me with all my faults. How could I not do the same for this person?

With this in mind, I have learned to try to separate the person's faults from who they really are and love them anyway. Somehow, I found it easier to do this when it was defined as a challenge. Somehow this definition made it ok that it was a struggle for me. Beyond that, any success I've had in loving the person despite their fault has been because the Lord has helped me to do so. (Thank you!)

Dear friends, let us practice loving each other, for love comes from God and those who are loving and kind show that they are children of God, and that they are getting to know him better. (1 John 4:7 TLB)

Always be humble and gentle. Be patient with each other, making allowance for each other's faults because of your love. (Ephesians 4:2 NLT)

Most important of all, continue to show deep love for each other, for love makes up for many of your faults. (1 Peter 4:8 TLB)

6

He Loves to Be Merciful

Something I learned about the Lord is that He loves to be merciful. I found this verse:

Where is there another God like you, who pardons sins of the survivors among his people? You cannot stay angry with your people, for you love to be merciful. (Micah 7:18 TLB)

I just really took note of the last part, where it says He loves to be merciful. Loves to. That's what He loves to do. I have to spend some time thinking about that for it to sink in. (Definition of mercy: kindness shown toward someone whom you have the right or power to punish.[1]) How thankful I am that He's that way.

He is merciful and tender toward those who don't deserve it; he is slow to get angry and full of kindness and love. He never bears a grudge, nor remains angry forever. He has not punished us as we deserve for all our sins, for his mercy toward those who fear and honor him is as great as the height of the heavens above the earth. (Psalms 103:8-11 TLB)

7

Ever so Precious

They were taking pictures of the Cadillac. Sometimes they stood next to it or sat in the driver's seat. Someone suggested that he get in the picture too. But he said, "No, I would look like garbage next to that car!"

The words struck me. What are all the cars in the world compared to you, compared to a person, compared to a soul? How can a person ever be compared to a material thing? The worth of a person is beyond my comprehension. I really do not know how invaluable a person is. I don't think I'm able to know.

I am aware that it may have only been a hasty word, spoken without a second thought, but:

"... Whatever is in the heart overflows into speech." (Luke 6:45 TLB)

I believe the Lord taught me through this that He is grieved/hurt when people are self-deprecating and call themselves things like "garbage." This is not how the Lord views them. They are ever so precious.

You made all the delicate, inner parts of my body, and knit them together in my mother's womb. Thank you for making me so wonderfully complex! It is amazing to think about. Your workmanship is marvelous - and how well I know it! (Psalms 139:13-14 TLB)

God showed how much he loved us by sending his only Son into this wicked world to bring to us eternal life through his death. In this act we see what real love is: it is not our love for God, but his love for us when he sent his Son to satisfy God's anger against our sins. (1 John 4:9-10 TLB)

And what do you benefit if you gain the whole world but lose your own soul? Is anything worth more than your soul? (Matthew 16:26 NLT)

8

Meaning What You Say. Being True to What You Say.

It started when they said they were going to do something and then did not do it. Then this was repeated many times. Now when they begin to say, "I'm going to ... " I don't really listen to them anymore. I don't like that I do this, but when they say it and don't do it, what's the point of listening? If I do, I feel like I'm just setting myself up for disappointment when I believe them, only to be let down later. Also, I feel like I'm not respecting them as I should, which I really don't like. I would prefer for them not to say it at all, than to say it and then not do it. It's another one of those "faults" that I must overlook and love them anyway.

I know there are times when unforeseen circumstances arise, and one is unable to do what they said they were going to do.

I have said that I was going to do something, but then did not, too many times myself. What I learned is that it is important to be true to what you say and mean what you say.

It is far better not to say you'll do something than to say you will and then not do it. (Ecclesiastes 5:5 TLB)

I was able to see how it can negatively affect one's reputation as well.

If you must choose, take a good name rather than great riches; for to be held in loving esteem is better than silver and gold. (Proverbs 22:1 TLB)

(Definition of esteem: respect for or a high opinion of someone.[1])
In the Bible it says that the Lord does not behave this way, so I don't want to behave that way either.

The Lord's promise is sure. He speaks no careless word; all he says is purest truth, like silver seven times refined. (Psalms 12:6 TLB)

When trying to live in this way, I'm amazed at how many times I have to try and stop myself from saying things. Sometimes it makes a conversation awkward. Sometimes I have failed. Also, I can easily see how many would think I'm taking this too seriously. But I want to really try, and live in this way - being true to my words and really meaning what I say. By God's grace I will be able to grow in this.

9

Taming the Tongue

I have had those times when I'm talking to someone (it's almost always someone I know very well), and then a thought comes to me. I know if I say it, it will be kind of sharp. Like, it would stir them up or be like a jab at them. I try to put it away and not say it. But it's difficult and my mouth wants to speak it so badly I can hardly bear it!

Sometimes I'm talking and the same kind of thought comes to my mind and I say it. I knew I shouldn't have. It's such a strange thing. I wish I could reach out and grab the words as they are spoken out of my mouth and pull them back. But it's too late. Now I feel like I'm half an inch tall.

Then there are the few times when the same kind of thought comes to my mind and I don't let myself speak it. When I succeed I feel so happy! It was like I won a little battle inside of me.

So also the tongue is a small thing, but what enormous damage it can do. A great forest can be set on fire by one tiny spark. And the tongue is a flame of fire. It is full of wickedness, and poisons every part of the body. And the tongue is set on fire by hell itself, and can turn our whole lives into a blazing flame of destruction and disaster. (James 3:5-6 TLB)

Self-control means controlling the tongue! A quick retort can ruin everything. (Proverbs 13:3 TLB)

The heart of a righteous person carefully considers how to answer, but the mouths of wicked people pour out a flood of evil things. (Proverbs 15:28 GW)

Those who love to talk will suffer the consequences. Men have died for saying the wrong thing! (Proverbs 18:21 TLB)

... If anyone can control his tongue, it proves that he has perfect control over himself in every other way. (James 3:1-2 TLB)

10

Waiting

I've been thinking about waiting. At times it's easy for me, but at other times it's very difficult. Why?

Because sometimes the one waiting does not realize the reasons for their waiting. But much is going on during the waiting time, necessary things. It's because these things are not seen or known by the person waiting, as if they are waiting for no good purpose.

(Definition of wait: Stay where one is or delay action until a particular time or event.[1])

Who waits? Those who wait are waiting for the right time. The right time for themselves, the right time for someone else, or the time for circumstances to be right. If they did not wait, it would not be right.

Lately I've been learning more than ever to wait. To wait for the Lord, for healing, and for other things. It requires patience and trust, which is a challenge in itself, but especially when I don't understand or see everything that is ahead of me. If I saw everything that was in the future, then I wouldn't need to trust or have faith. It's most difficult to have faith and trust during those times when I find myself absolutely unable to understand the "why," "how," and "when." I'm thankful that the One I wait on sees and understands and is faithful and full of mercy.

Don't be impatient. Wait for the Lord, and he will come and save you! Be brave, stouthearted and courageous. Yes, wait and he will help you. (Psalms 27:14 TLB)

That is why I wait expectantly, trusting God to help, for he has promised. I long for him more than sentinels long for the dawn. (Psalms 130:5-6 TLB)

For since the world began no one has seen or heard of such a God as ours, who works for those who wait for him! (Isaiah 64:4 TLB)

We can rejoice, too, when we run into problems and trials for we know that they are good for us - they help us learn to be patient. And patience develops strength of character in us and helps us trust God more each time we use it until finally our hope and faith are strong and steady. Then, when that happens, we are able to hold our heads high no matter what happens and know that all is well, for we know how dearly God loves us, and we feel this warm love everywhere within us because God has given us the Holy Spirit to fill our hearts with his love. (Romans 5:3-5 TLB)

11

But I Want You

Long ago, even before he made the world, God chose us to be his very own, through what Christ would do for us; he decided then to make us holy in his eyes, without a single fault – we who stand before him covered with his love. His unchanging plan has always been to adopt us into his own family by sending Jesus Christ to die for us. And he did this because he wanted to! (Ephesians 1:4-5 TLB)

Wanting and needing are different. I think there is little dispute about that. But, which one (want or need) is more meaningful?

First things that come to my mind when I think of needs are shelter, water, and food. Needs can be things like these. In addition, I think of chores needing to be done. They usually aren't pleasant, but it is a kind of need. Needs most of the time seem to be associated with obligations.

First things that come to my mind when I think of wants are pleasing the Lord and knowing Him more, and becoming physically whole again (as of now). On a lower level, I think of wanting warmer weather, and all kinds of pleasant things. Wants most of the time seem to be associated with desires.

There are times when something wanted could also be needed, and something needed could be wanted. Nevertheless, there is a definite difference between the two. Sometimes I think people want something so much they identify it as a need. On the other hand, sometimes people dislike a need so much they don't want it.

In terms of relations between people, I wonder if I would rather be needed or wanted. It seems nice to be needed. It also seems nice to be wanted. But, the more I think about it, I would rather be wanted than needed. Wanting, to me, indicates liking, desiring. Needing someone seems like it's only because you're filling a need in your life, as if the person can give you something and fill this need.

Just interesting to think about the differences, but I do have a backstory on this subject. The other night I was very upset. I was ruminating about my current physical condition and thinking all kinds of things. Somehow I came to the low point in my thought processes and thought to myself, "Nobody needs me." Then I went to bed and slept. The next morning was less intense but the thought was still with me. I began to pray, talking to the Lord. Then I went down a mental list of all the people who don't need me. I came to the end of the list and then thought of the Lord, the One closest to me, and I told Him, "You don't need me!" Which is true. Then He told me, "But I want you. Is that not more than need?" Hearing this surprised me because I held a need in higher esteem than a want. The fact is the Lord doesn't need anything, but He wants me (and you) and I need and want Him.

12

Attributes of God Part 1: Jealous

Definition of jealous: fiercely protective or vigilant of one's rights or possessions. Intolerant of rivalry or unfaithfulness.[1]

In the Bible it describes God as being a jealous God. If I thought someone was jealous over me I would probably feel cared about. If I cared for them, I would not want to do anything that would give them cause to be jealous over me. To think that the Lord, set so high above all things, feels that way about you and I is amazing to me. He cares about who He loves like that.

In the definition of jealous, it says, "fiercely protective … of one's … possessions." There haven't been many times where I can remember feeling this in real life, but I can remember once someone spoke to my mom in a bad way and as a result I felt strangely protective over her. I remember it because it was a rare feeling like heat and energy rising up inside me, like I was angered and protective at the same time. I love her and don't want her treated like that. I guess this example doesn't fit the definition exactly because she's obviously not my possession, but I think it's along the same lines of what the definition means. Interesting to think that the Lord feels this way too.

God is jealous over those he loves; that is why he takes vengeance on those who hurt them. He furiously destroys their enemies. (Nahum 1:2 TLB)

The definition also says, "Intolerant of ... unfaithfulness." My dog Blitz (who has since passed away) was the best dog in the world to me. He would follow me around everywhere and paid the most attention to me. However, if anyone offered him food, he was their instant best friend. I remember him being completely fixated on someone with food, and I would call his name and it was like he didn't even hear me call. Although in this example it was humorous, it could be looked at as an example of unfaithfulness. I was tolerant of it, but it is a fearful thought to think that the Lord is not tolerant of unfaithfulness.

You must never bow to an image or worship it in any way; for I, the Lord your God, am very possessive. I will not share your affection with any other god! (Exodus 20:5 TLB)

You shall not bow down to any images nor worship them in any way, for I am the Lord your God. I am a jealous God ..." (Deuteronomy 5:9 TLB)

Finally, the definition says, "Intolerant of rivalry ..." Probably most people have had a time when they liked someone, and then saw them paying attention to someone else. The feeling is unmistakable. Could the Lord really feel like that toward me and those He loves?

Israel began to follow foreign gods, and Jehovah was very angry; He was jealous of his people. (Deuteronomy 32:16 TLB)

For the LORD your God is a consuming fire, a jealous God. (Deuteronomy 4:24 NIV)

I have read and heard over and over how the Lord loves you. I know it to be true, and I want to realize it more and more. But learning how He is a jealous God, jealous over those He loves, gives me a different perspective of how He really feels and who He is.

13

Personality vs. Character

Is there a difference between personality and character? I was wondering about this. I have heard the two terms used in similar ways, sometimes even as synonyms for each other. They are not the same. Confusion can arise because both personality and character contribute to making a unique individual. Additionally, it is common for each to influence the other, in different ways. This can portray that what is seen will automatically equal what it really is.

The term 'personality' is derived from the Latin word 'persona,' which means mask.[1] Definition of personality: The distinctive qualities and traits of an individual. 2. Social and personal traits that makes a person appealing.[2] It is generally associated with the outer appearance and behavior of an individual.[3]

The term character comes from the ancient Greek word kharasso, meaning "I engrave."[4] Definition of character: A distinguishing feature : characteristic. 2. The group of ethical and mental characteristics that mark a person or group. 3. Moral integrity.[5] Character can be described as a pattern of moral ... qualities of an individual.[6]

Both personality and character can make a person unique.

Personality is generally defined as illustrating a set of inborn traits. It is the way one carries oneself.[7] While there are aspects that are generally unchanging and are expressed by a person throughout their life, it can be inconsistent. A person can change their personality to fit different situations as well. Character is usually used to describe a person's level of integrity and encompasses one's moral values.[8] While it too can change, it tends to be more consistent and the changes are slower.

Character will frequently influence personality. For example, if the character of a person is good, it will often show in their personality. In difficult circumstances, this same person of good character may not show it in their personality. In such a circumstance, you may actually see more of their character. Personality does not influence one's character, but it can give an inaccurate perception of their character.

Personality is about persona and that ultimately comes down to the qualities and characteristics that we want to put across, but this may not always be the same as those which represent our true and consistent character. It's about 'outside' and 'indoor' behavior or, the public versus private persona.[9] Although personality can be a reflection of character, there are times when it is not a reflection, but actually a mask that covers character. An imperfect analogy could be that of a vehicle that looks like a Ferrari but it's chassis and powertrain are that of a Yugo. In contrast, there may be a vehicle that looks like an ordinary mid-1980s sedan, but it is sitting on a high performance chassis and powertrain. Then there are those vehicles that look like what they are.

Problems can arise when personality and character are confused with each other. When we stop mistaking personality for character, we stop mistaking the fact that aspects of a person for being an automatic precursor to shared core values and compatibility.[10] To continue with the car analogies, imagine purchasing that Ferrari with the Yugo insides. I guess it comes down to what people really want, but personally I would be extremely disappointed. Actually, I would probably feel cheated by whomever sold the car to me, and yet have no one to blame but myself for not inspecting the car first. If I bought the mid-1980s sedan and found out what it had, I would be thrilled. Presuming I paid what that car typically costs, I would probably feel like I stole it from whomever sold it to me. Finally, if I purchased a vehicle that looked like what it truly is, I imagine I would have no surprises and would feel satisfied.

The differences between personality and character are important to discern. Both play a part in making a person unique. Character can influence personality, and personality can obscure character. Once the differences and similarities are clearly understood, the opportunity of avoiding confusion and possible misconceptions are greatly improved.

14

Attributes of God Part 2: Omniscient

He determines the number of stars and calls them each by name. Great is our Lord and mighty in power; his understanding has no limit. (Psalms 147:4-5 NIV)

He knows about everyone, everywhere. Everything about us is bare and wide open to the all-seeing eyes of our living God; nothing can be hidden from him to whom we must explain all that we have done. (Hebrews 4:13 TLB)

In him lie hidden all the mighty, untapped treasures of wisdom and knowledge. (Colossians 2:3 TLB)

Definition of omniscient: knowing everything.[1]
God knows everything. I do not know of any other person or thing that knows everything. There is nothing else that does.

"With whom will you compare me? Who is my equal?" asks the Holy One. (Isaiah 40:25 TLB)

While His other attribute from part 1 (jealous) can be felt and experienced by people, the omniscient attribute is unique to Him.

He has all knowledge of everything. History, science, all of nature, all people, all information of every kind he knows. My mind is incapable of fully understanding the vastness of this. When I used to work at the library I would be standing in the aisles of books and think, "I wish I knew everything that are in these books." I was impressed by all the knowledge that was contained there. All of the knowledge contained in every book on earth is little compared to what God knows.

All ideas I have for attempting to compare this attribute with something in everyday life are insufficient. I try to imagine meeting someone who knows everything. Face to face with them, I would feel kind of self-conscious because they would know everything about me – every unsavory detail. The One who does know everything about me loves me! This is so hard to understand.

I am glad He knows everything. He knows me better than I do, and He knows things that I could never make other people understand. Sometimes when I pray I do not know what words to use. I cannot express in words what I want to say or what I am feeling. There are times when I simply do not know what to say to Him at all. But then I realize He knows and understands perfectly, and I am so glad!

I want to know more about Him who knows everything.

O Lord, you have examined my heart and know everything about me. You know when I sit or stand. When far away you know my every thought. You chart the path ahead of me, and tell me where to stop and rest. Every moment, you know where I am. You know what I am going to say before I even say it. You both precede and follow me, and place your hand of blessing on my head. (Psalms 139:1-5 TLB)

What is the price of five sparrows—two copper coins? Yet God does not forget a single one of them. And the very hairs on your head are all numbered. So don't be afraid; you are more valuable to

God than a whole flock of sparrows. (Luke 12:6-7 NLT)

For whenever our heart condemns us, God is greater than our heart, and he knows everything. (1 John 3:20 ESV)

15

Broken Heart

Definition of brokenhearted: crushed by sadness or grief.[1]

Sadness and grief can come upon you in so many ways. In smaller ways that cause sadness for a short time, and in ways so impacting that you are completely crushed and end up brokenhearted. The sadness and grief is so heavy it feels more like you are dying or drowning in misery and bitter anguish. Or, drowning in tears. Where is hope to be found at a time like this? Sometimes it is so disorienting and hurts so much you can barely think of hope.

And now, O Lord, for what do I wait? My hope is in you. (Psalms 39:7 ESV)

This friend of mine betrayed me – I who was at peace with him. He broke his promises. His words were oily smooth, but in his heart was war. His words were sweet, but underneath were daggers. Give your burdens to the Lord. He will carry them. He will not permit the godly to slip or fall. (Psalms 55:20-22 TLB)

Being rejected is painful. Particularly if the rejection was from someone you cared about. Even if it is done with some consideration of your feelings, it still means they do not want you. The cherished friendship, along with the hopes and dreams tied to it, evaporate in one moment. Confusion can follow, and then you question yourself a lot.

Hope deferred makes the heart sick; but when dreams come true at last, there is life and joy. (Proverbs 13:12 TLB)

The death of something you loved can make you brokenhearted too. I feel qualified to write only about something I loved, rather than someone. There is just emptiness and grief. A few things are regretted, but some comfort can be found in good memories.

The broken heart is so hurt it wants to find something to mend it as quickly as possible and will often find momentary comfort in the wrong things. Anything to numb it. "Just make this stop!" it screams.

Healing starts with forgiving those who hurt you, even when they were not sorry or did not ask to be forgiven. You deserve healing. Forgive yourself, too. I have asked the Lord to heal my heart. Many times I do not have elaborate words to pray. I just ask, "Please heal all the hurt, Lord." Or, at times all I can muster is, "God, help!" He understands, and my faith that He will help and heal is more than the words I say.

He heals the brokenhearted, binding up their wounds. (Psalms 147:3 TLB)

Yes, the Lord hears the good man when he calls to him for help, and saves him out of all his troubles. The Lord is close to those whose hearts are breaking; he rescues those who are humbly sorry for their sins. The good man does not escape all troubles – he has them too. But the Lord helps him in each and every one. (Psalms 34:17-19 TLB)

16

Attributes of God Part 3: Eternal

Everyone is going to spend eternity somewhere. What is eternity like? Eternity means all time without beginning or end. It is yet another thing that I cannot fully understand. Eternity is an amount of time that will never end – that attempt at a definition sounds like an oxymoron.

Everything around me will cease to exist at some point. The thought of something not ending I cannot comprehend. Add to that the thought of it never having a beginning and I am more perplexed.

God is so great that we cannot begin to know him. No one can begin to understand eternity. (Job 36:26 TLB)

I cannot take credit for this analogy, but I heard it somewhere and thought it was very good so I will use it. Take a grain of sand; that represents a person's lifetime. Drop it onto the Sahara Desert; that represents eternity. The contrast is vivid.

The terms eternal and everlasting have different meanings. Eternal means without beginning or end. Everlasting means lasting forever. The difference is that something everlasting had a beginning.

God is eternal. He did not have a beginning and will not have an end. Like His attribute from part 2 (omniscient) being eternal pertains only to Him.

Before the mountains were created, before the earth was formed, you are God without beginning or end. You speak, and man turns back to dust. A thousand years are but as yesterday to you! They are like a single hour! We glide along the tides of time as swiftly as a racing river, and vanish as quickly as a dream. We are like grass that is green in the morning but mowed down and withered before the evening shadows fall. (Psalms 90:2-6 TLB)

From eternity to eternity I am God. No one can oppose what I do. (Isaiah 43:13 TLB)

I am the A and the Z, the Beginning and the Ending of all things," says God, who is the Lord, the All Powerful One who is, and was, and is coming again! (Revelation 1:8 TLB)

Glory and honor to God forever and ever. He is the King of the ages, the unseen one who never dies; he alone is God, and full of wisdom. Amen. (1 Timothy 1:17 TLB)

17

Exploring Proverbs 15:16-17

16: Better a little with reverence for God, than great treasure and trouble with it. 17: It is better to eat soup with someone you love than steak with someone you hate. (Proverbs 15:16-17 TLB)

Verse 16 says that a little is better than great treasure with trouble. What makes having little, better, is reverence for God. It takes some time for this to sink in as truth. What does it really mean?

Definition of reverence: honor or respect that is felt for or shown [to someone or something]. The state of being revered.[1]

Definition of revere: to have great respect for (someone or something): to show devotion and honor to (someone or something).[2]

Definition of trouble: distress, affliction, danger, or need.[3]

So, it is better to have little with honor and respect for God, than to have great treasure with distress.

I think verse 17 emphasizes verse 16. It explains that a humble meal with someone you love is better than a special meal with someone you hate.

I imagine sitting at a table with someone I love and enjoying a simple meal. To me that would be just fine. I would probably like being with them more than focusing on the simplicity of the meal. Then I imagine sitting at a table with someone I hate and trying to enjoy a steak. I would probably feel troubled, be preoccupied with that, and not enjoy the steak at all.

This does not say that great treasure or steak is bad. The difference shown in these verses, that which makes something less actually better, is reverence for God and love. It is drawing an illustration of what is most valuable. It is amazing that the addition of those two things (reverence for God and love) to something small, can increase it to the point where it is superior to what was originally greater.

Can this be expressed using math?

(reverence for God and/or love) + something little > something great + trouble

or

something great + trouble < something little + (reverence for God and/or love)

Here are the same verses in another version of the Bible:

Better a little with the fear of the LORD than great wealth with turmoil. Better a small serving of vegetables with love than a fattened calf with hatred. (Proverbs 15:16-17 NIV)

18

Attributes of God Part 4: Holiness

In a great antiphonal chorus they sang, "Holy, holy, holy is the Lord of Hosts; the whole earth is filled with his glory." (Isaiah 6:3 TLB)

The holiness of God transcends any idea that we have of holiness and any aspect of holiness that anyone might reflect.

Definition of holy: 1. Belonging to, derived from, or associated with a divine power: sacred. 2. Regarded with or deserving of worship or veneration: revered. 3. Spiritually perfect: saintly.[1]

He is morally perfect. Not only good, but perfect. He is separated from all things and creatures that are not morally perfect, because He cannot tolerate anything that opposes His nature. Not a single sin can He tolerate.[2]

I know you get no pleasure from wickedness and cannot tolerate the slightest sin. (Psalms 5:4 TLB)

It is impossible for me to understand holiness, because it is foreign to sinful mankind.

"For my thoughts are not your thoughts, neither are your ways my ways," declares the Lord. "As the heavens are higher than the earth, so are my ways higher than your ways and my thoughts than your thoughts." (Isaiah 55:8-9 NIV)

There are times for joyful closeness to Him and knowing Him as Father, but right now I want to study His attribute of holiness. He is not to be taken as casual, common, or ordinary. He is not the, "Big Guy upstairs."[3]

Serve the Lord with reverent fear; rejoice with trembling. (Psalms 2:11 TLB)

I try to imagine being in the presence of a king. First, I would enter his palace. Walking down massive hallways lined with columns, I would be in awe of the exquisite details put into this magnificent structure. "Am I really allowed to be here?" I would think. I would go into his throne room. There, surrounded by splendor, dignitaries would bow and worship him. He would be powerful, have all authority, his grandeur would be tremendous, and he would seem untouchable. If I were standing there in front of him, I might feel his gaze rest upon me and I would not want to look into his eyes. The immensity of his righteousness and nobility would be disarming. I would realize what and who he is.

The Old Testament tells about the temple that was built for God to come and live in. It goes into detail about how it was to be constructed. Many verses tell about the requirements of the priests who worked in the temple, and how the Ark of the Covenant was not to be touched, but moved by poles.

For I want the people of Israel to make me a sacred Temple where I can live among them. (Exodus 25:8 TLB)

When Aaron and his sons have finished packing the sanctuary and all the utensils, the clan of Kohath shall come and carry the units to wherever the camp is traveling; but they must not touch the holy items, lest they die. This, then, is the sacred work of the sons of Kohath. (Numbers 4:15 TLB)

Make poles from acacia wood overlaid with gold, and fit the poles into the rings at the sides of the Ark, to carry it. (Exodus 25:13-14 TLB)

We are shown an example of the fearful nature of the holiness of God by a man named Uzza in the Old Testament. King David and his troops were transporting the Ark to Jerusalem. It was placed on a cart pulled by oxen, and Uzza and his brother Ahio drove the oxen ...

But as they arrived at the threshing-floor of Chidon, the oxen stumbled and Uzza reached out his hand to steady the Ark. Then the anger of the Lord blazed out against Uzza, and killed him because he had touched the Ark. And so he died there before God. (1 Chronicles 13:9-10 TLB)

Why? Wasn't Uzza trying to do good? Uzza presumed something. He presumed his hand was holier than the ground, and he was wrong. The ground has never disobeyed God.[4]

Definition of presume: to take for granted, assume, or suppose. To undertake with unwarrantable boldness. To undertake (to do something) without right or permission.[5]

Another example found in Leviticus 10:1-3 TLB:

But Nadab and Abihu, the sons of Aaron, placed unholy fire in their censers, laid incense on the fire, and offered the incense before the Lord – contrary to what the Lord had just commanded them! So fire blazed forth from the presence of the Lord and destroyed them. Then Moses said to Aaron, "This is what the Lord meant when he said, 'I will show myself holy among those who approach me, and I will be glorified before all the people.'" And Aaron was speechless.

Interestingly, speaking to Ezekiel about His temple, God said, "And this is the basic law of the Temple: Holiness! The entire top of the hill where the Temple is built is holy. Yes, this is the primary law concerning it." (Ezekiel 43:12 TLB)

So we see that God is holy. Where He resides must also be holy. More Bible verses telling about the holiness of God:

... but the Lord of Hosts is exalted above all, for he alone is holy, just and good. (Isaiah 5:16 TLB)

The high and lofty one who inhabits eternity, the Holy One, says this: I live in that high and holy place where those with contrite, humble spirits dwell; and I refresh the humble and give new courage to those with repentant hearts. (Isaiah 57:15 TLB)

Who else is like the Lord among the gods? Who is glorious in holiness like him? Who is so awesome in splendor, a wonder-working God? (Exodus 15:11 TLB)

"With whom will you compare me? Who is my equal?" asks the Holy One. (Isaiah 40:25 TLB)

19

On Being Sensitive

I feel like most people notice a characteristic about themselves that they do not like. They may go through their life disliking it continually, come to accept it, or come to value that characteristic.

When I was younger I noticed about myself that I was sensitive, and I did not like it. I felt it was a weakness. Experiences would seem a lot more profound or affecting than it seemed they should be.

I remember once as a kid I had a pet frog. For some reason, it was obviously dying. I held it in my hand and I knew it was dying and I began to cry. I could logically see that I had not even had the frog very long, and I did not connect with it in a way that I would another kind of animal like a dog or something. Nevertheless, that was my reaction. It was actually embarrassing.

I got a little older and I noticed how I was sensitive to other circumstances in life. Perhaps it was not just being sensitive, but I felt like I noticed too much. I wished I just did not notice some things at all. I absolutely disliked this about myself. I prayed to God, "Please, help me not to be so sensitive, Lord. Make me less sensitive. Make me callous and not let things affect me so much." I saw nothing good about this characteristic.

Years passed. It did not happen overnight and I do not exactly remember what happened, but my perspective changed. One day I was praying and at one point I was thanking the Lord for making me sensitive. Suddenly I remembered when I had prayed years before, asking the Lord to make me the opposite of this. I was glad He did not answer my prayer the way I wanted Him to before.

One thing I learned is that when you are callous you cannot feel. You will not notice. There are good and bad points about this. I write primarily about being sensitive psychologically, but there are correlations in physical ways. For some, when you start shoveling dirt and have no gloves on, you can feel the rough wood-grain of the shovel's handle. One does not have to work very long and you get blisters. Conversely, if you had really tough hands you might not feel fine things like a cat's fur or sewing thread.

I think there is a price to be paid whether you are tough or sensitive. Aspects can be missed or perceived, and there are gains and losses in this. I came to realize the Lord made people with different characteristics for His own good reasons.

20

New

Don't copy the behavior and customs of this world, but be a new and different person with a fresh newness in all you do and think. Then you will learn from your own experience how his ways will really satisfy you. (Romans 12:2 TLB)

Don't copy the behavior and customs of this world, but let God transform you into a new person by changing the way you think. Then you will learn to know God's will for you, which is good and pleasing and perfect. (Romans 12:2 NLT)

Do not conform to the pattern of this world, but be transformed by the renewing of your mind. Then you will be able to test and approve what God's will is--his good, pleasing and perfect will. (Romans 12:2 NIV)

Definition of custom: 1. An accepted practice or convention followed by tradition. 2. A habitual course of action of an individual.[1]

I find this verse exciting and relieving. To me it is exciting because we are to be something new – something that we were not originally. The very way we think is to be changed and the result of this is transformation. We are told not to conform ourselves to the world. It brings relief because I am not to concern myself with being acceptable to the world. Appearing a certain way, knowing how to use the latest slang, behaving in a way the world likes, or being tied down to the customs of the world are not to be a concern for me.

The result of being transformed is that we will be able to know God's will.

he saved us, not because of righteous things we had done, but because of his mercy. He saved us through the washing of rebirth and renewal by the Holy Spirit, (Titus 3:5 NIV)

he saved us, not because of the righteous things we had done, but because of his mercy. He washed away our sins, giving us a new birth and new life through the Holy Spirit. (Titus 3:5 NLT)

This verse from Titus tells us that renewal and new life is accomplished by the Holy Spirit. It is He who does this supernatural work of renewal and transformation in a person. We are being transformed into the image of the Lord Jesus Christ.

This is an ongoing process in life. It is amazing what Holy Spirit does! It is wonderful to recognize the changes He has made and is currently making in you. It is excellent, but often difficult.

Therefore, if anyone is in Christ, he is a new creation. The old has passed away; behold, the new has come. (2 Corinthians 5:17 ESV)

And we all, who with unveiled faces contemplate the Lord's glory, are being transformed into his image with ever-increasing glory, which comes from the Lord, who is the Spirit. (2 Corinthians 3:18 NIV)

And I am certain that God, who began the good work within

you, will continue his work until it is finally finished on the day when Christ Jesus returns. (Philippians 1:6 NLT)

21

"She's a Foreigner."

As a visitor in a foreign country I do not know their customs and traditions. I do not know the ways that are common to them. Perhaps I would look different from the native people as well. In behavior and/or appearance I would stand out as someone who does not live in that country.

Maybe someone would notice this and say, "She's a foreigner." I imagine I would probably not find this complementary. If possible, I might try to change whatever it was that made me obviously different. Studying some guide books on the culture or country may be profitable.

Interesting to read that the Bible says we are foreigners in this world. In addition, it does not say to study the ways of the world so you can fit in. We are supposed to stay away from the ways of the world; the sinful things. We were not always foreigners. Receiving salvation through faith in Jesus Christ has made us foreigners.

Once you were less than nothing; now you are God's own. Once you knew very little of God's kindness; now your very lives have been changed by it. Dear brothers, you are only visitors here. Since your real home is in heaven I beg you to keep away from the evil pleasures of this world; they are not for you, for they fight against your very souls. (1 Peter 10-11 TLB)

Once you were not a people, but now you are the people of God; once you had not received mercy, but now you have received mercy. Dear friends, I urge you, as foreigners and exiles, to abstain from sinful desires, which wage war against your soul. (1 Peter 2:10-11 NIV)

22

Safety

One day I was working in the library and I observed two small children playing tag. One was running away from the other, and she ran to her father. When she reached him she said, "Safety zone!" to the child that was chasing her. She could not be touched because she was in the safety zone next to her father.

I was able to see how this situation can be compared to our relationship with God. Outside God's will, and not following His directions, one is open to get "tagged" so to speak. By God's grace, they will see their susceptibility to being tagged, and will run back to Him for safety.

Like sheep you wandered away from God, but now you have returned to your Shepherd, the Guardian of your souls who keeps you safe from all attacks. (1 Peter 2:25 TLB)

This verse describes God as the Guardian of your soul. The soul is one's mind, will, and emotions.

Unfortunately, I have done things outside of God's will. I wandered away, as this verse says. Sometimes I have wandered and did not feel in danger of being tagged. I think I was simply unaware of the risk. Then there were times where I wandered away and later understood how alarmingly close I was to being tagged. Or, in keeping with the verse, I understood how alarmingly close I was to being devoured by a wolf. Takes my breath away how close I was. Finally, there were times I wandered away and got attacked and wounded, resulting in my hobbling back to the Shepherd, crying for Him to help.

How invaluable it is to have the wisdom to stay close to God and follow His instructions. To have this wisdom is by His mercy and grace.

23

Proverbs 30:7-9

O God, I beg two favors from you before I die: First, help me never to tell a lie. Second, give me neither poverty or riches! Give me just enough to satisfy my needs! For if I grow rich, I may become content without God. And if I am too poor, I may steal, and thus insult God's holy name. (Proverbs 30:7-9 TLB)

Two things I ask of you, LORD; do not refuse me before I die: Keep falsehood and lies far from me; give me neither poverty nor riches, but give me only my daily bread. Otherwise, I may have too much and disown you and say, 'Who is the LORD?' Or I may become poor and steal, and so dishonor the name of my God. (Proverbs 30:7-9 NIV)

I think these verses are fascinating. The man speaking here does not want poverty or riches. I believe it shows what he does want.

It seems the comfort that can come with being rich is capable of luring one into reliance on things other than God. Perhaps it can cause one to think they do not need God because they feel secure already.

The desperation that can come with poverty can lead one to do things that dishonor God.

I think these verses are speaking about this man's desire to stay in a right place with God. To be kept in a station in life that lends itself to being as free from temptations as possible.

But as for me, my contentment is not in wealth but in seeing you and knowing all is well between us. And when I awake in heaven, I will be fully satisfied, for I will see you face to face. (Psalms 17:15 TLB)

As for me, I shall behold Your face in righteousness; I will be satisfied with Your likeness when I awake. (Psalms 17:15 NASB)

24

Attributes of God Part 5: Omnipresent

You both precede and follow me, and place your hand of blessing on my head. This is too glorious, too wonderful to believe! I can never be lost to your Spirit! I can never get away from my God! If I go up to heaven, you are there; if I go down to the place of the dead, you are there. If I ride the morning winds to the farthest oceans, even there your hand will guide me, your strength will support me. (Psalms 139:5-10 TLB)

Definition of omnipresence: The fact of being present everywhere.[1]

There are many ways to consider God's omnipresence.

One way I was thinking about is how He is not confined by time. I go through life, living out each day as it comes because I am confined by time. But God is not taking each day as it comes because He is above the limits of time. He is already in tomorrow. He is everywhere. This thought is beyond my understanding, but so much of God is.

Where shall I go from your Spirit? Or where shall I flee from your presence? If I ascend to heaven, you are there! If I make my bed in Sheol, you are there! If I take the wings of the morning and dwell in the uttermost parts of the sea, even there your hand shall lead me, and your right hand shall hold me. (Psalms 139:7-10 ESV)

Can a man hide himself in secret places so that I cannot see him? declares the LORD. Do I not fill heaven and earth? declares the LORD. (Jeremiah 23:24 ESV)

Who is like you, LORD God Almighty? You, LORD, are mighty, and your faithfulness surrounds you. (Psalms 89:8 NIV)

25

Please Keep Off Grass

A graceful, bright green blade of grass grows up through the earth. Fresh and new, it reaches to the sun.

An intricate spider's web sparkles; the morning light highlighting the drops of dew.

A friendly greeting is offered to a stranger.

Tender, curious, tentative things. What is hidden in a person's heart? Many things are kept there. Some have never been audibly spoken. Some resided there in the heart of a person and were not known until someone touched it and it came to life.

I cannot write about what is in the hearts of men, but I will write about what I have observed in the hearts of women. Not all women, but I think a remarkably high number of them.

I have seen glimpses of very deep hopes, ideas, and dreams in the hearts of women. Ingrained, strong, tender, and sentimental are some words that could describe them. It is not easy to write about. Basically they are desires and hopes of becoming married and having a family. I imagine this may sound old fashioned. Nonetheless, it is very real.

It is there. Clearly seen in some, and quite buried in others. I just know it is very close to the heart and the incredible lengths some women will go to try to fulfill them show the strength of this desire.

As a teenager I would have the typical sleepover with a friend. She would go on and on about how she was not going to get married or have kids. She was adamant. She had other plans. Years later she tells me how she wants to get married etc., even prefacing that with, "Remember how I always said I didn't want to get married?"

I have personally experienced the strange unearthing of these sentiments in myself. Once I met a man and we were getting to know each other. We were talking and asking lots of questions. He asked me a question no one had ever asked me before, or since. He asked me if I would like to have kids. Apparently he wanted to. First of all, it took me by surprise and I thought it was too personal a question to be asking so soon. I had never considered this question openly before, and after some loss for words my answer was something like, "Well, yes, I guess nearly every girl wants to …" Further topics in this discussion were worldviews, family, and marriage. It was a very unusual conversation and after it was over I felt like things I did not know existed in my heart had been revealed.

The point is I have seen these aspirations in the hearts of women. It amazes me a little how widespread these hopes are. I have heard them expressed to me by others. They are so hopeful and sincere that as I listen I want to somehow protect these dreams of theirs, and I want them to happen for them.

It is an awful thing to see these dreams either knowingly or unknowingly mishandled by people. I think this can happen by saying they will never happen, or that they are crazy. Or, by believing the idea that these goals are inferior to having a career. Also, people may deliberately play on these desires to their own advantage. The main issue I am getting at is, it is an awful shame when these heartfelt dreams are trampled on.

My advice in an analogy: be careful to not trample on the grass or let it be trampled on. One cannot always trust others to be conscientious. Guard and protect those cherished dreams.

26

God Loves You Part 1: Will You Be My Child?

I know God loves me. I know He loves others. I want to realize more and more how much He loves me. To really know it, and live life accordingly. I think it would change how I live – especially my thoughts.

I found these verses and they helped me understand how much the Lord loves.

Obey God because you are his children; don't slip back into your old ways – doing evil because you knew no better. But be holy now in everything you do, just as the Lord is holy, who invited you to be his child. (1 Peter 1:14-15 TLB)

It says that He "invited you to be his child." Just try and imagine what that means. Imagine a person here on earth inviting you, wanting you, to be their child. They would love you and care for you very much. They would not mind you being associated with them. You would be thought of and seen as their child.

The same verses in two other translations:

As obedient children, do not be conformed to the former lusts *which were yours* in your ignorance, but like the Holy One who called you, be holy yourselves also in all *your* behavior; (1 Peter 1:14-15 NASB)

As obedient children, do not conform to the evil desires you had when you lived in ignorance. But just as he who called you is holy, so be holy in all you do; (1 Peter 1:14-15 NIV)

More verses about being God's children:

See how very much our Father loves us, for he calls us his children, and that is what we are! But the people who belong to this world don't recognize that we are God's children because they don't know him. (1 John 3:1 NLT)

For those who are led by the Spirit of God are the children of God. (Romans 8:14 NIV)

But to all who believed him and accepted him, he gave the right to become children of God. (John 1:12 NLT)

In addition to being invited by God to be His child, it is important to observe that the label is not only an expression of affection. These verses say that we literally become the children of God when we believe and accept Him.

27

Attributes of God Part 6: Faithfulness

Definition of faithful: 1. Strict or thorough in the performance of duty. 2. True to one's word, promises, vows, etc. 3. Steady in allegiance or affection; loyal, constant. 4. Reliable, trusted, or believed. 5. Adhering or true to fact, a standard, or an original; accurate.[1]

It seems to me that faithfulness is universally accepted as a good and commendable attribute. It denotes trustworthiness, and reliability.

Faithfulness can be found in people, animals, brands, cars, appliances, and the list could continue. People can be faithful employees or be known to be true to their word. The faithfulness of a dog to its master is a common concept. Then there are brands of products that people know and trust. The same idea goes for cars and appliances.

Do I trust in God's faithfulness as much as I trust in the faithfulness of these things? There is no safer place to put my trust than in God. His faithfulness never fails.

I remember once I was round dancing at a square dance festival with a stranger. I cannot remember what figure was being cued, but it was understood that the lady would allow some of her weight to rest on the man's hand, which was at her back, for the sake of keeping her balance. However, I balanced myself and did not rest upon his hand. He felt this and told me, "Trust me, trust me ..." Which meant to go ahead and allow him to help me balance. I did not do it.

This memory came to mind as I was contemplating the faithfulness of God. It is like the Lord says to me, "Trust me, trust me ..." In this case, I want to trust Him because He tells me to, it is better for me (than trying to "balance myself"), and because I can do so in complete safety. In addition, I think it is easier to trust someone when you know them.

There are many verses telling about the faithfulness of God. I found that reading them not only built up my trust in Him, but helped me know Him more. He always keeps His promises.

Even when we are too weak to have any faith left, he remains faithful to us and will help us, for he cannot disown us who are part of himself, and he will always carry out his promises to us. (2 Timothy 2:13 TLB)

the God who made both earth and heaven, the seas and everything in them. He is the God who keeps every promise, (Psalms 146:6 TLB)

Every good thing the Lord had promised them came true. (Joshua 21:45 TLB)

Understand, therefore, that the Lord your God is the faithful God who for a thousand generations keeps his promises and constantly loves those who love him and who obey his commands. (Deuteronomy 7:9 TLB)

Blessed be the Lord who has fulfilled his promise and given rest to his people Israel; not one word has failed of all the wonderful promises proclaimed by his servant Moses. (1 Kings 8:56 TLB)

O Lord, I will honor and praise your name, for you are my God; you do such wonderful things! You planned them long ago, and now you have accomplished them, just as you said! (Isaiah 25:1 TLB)

Of course not! Though everyone else in the world is a liar, God is not. Do you remember what the book of Psalms says about this? That God's words will always prove true and right, no matter who questions them. (Romans 3:4 TLB)

He has given us both his promise and his oath, two things we can completely count on, for it is impossible for God to tell a lie. Now all those who flee to him to save them can take new courage when they hear such assurances from God; now they can know without doubt that he will give them the salvation he has promised them. (Hebrews 7:18 TLB)

Now we can look forward to the salvation God has promised us. There is no longer any room for doubt, and we can tell others that salvation is ours, for there is no question that he will do what he says. (Hebrews 10:23 TLB)

Sarah, too, had faith, and because of this she was able to become a mother in spite of her old age, for she realized that God, who gave her his promise, would certainly do what he said. (Hebrews 11:11 TLB)

28

Strong Enough for Patience?

Definition of patient: 1. Enduring affliction or pain without anger or complaint. 2. Understanding : tolerant. 3. Persevering : steadfast.[1]

Endure: 1. To carry on through : undergo successfully. 2. To tolerate : bear. 3. To continue in existence.[2]

Understanding: adj. Disposed to kindness, compassion, tolerance, etc.[3]

Tolerance: 1. Recognition of and respect for the opinions, beliefs, or actions of others. 3. Capacity to withstand pain or hardship.[4]

Persevere: To persist in an idea, purpose, or task despite obstacles.[5]

Steadfast: 1. Not moving : fixed. 2. Unyieldingly firm in purpose, faith, or attachment : loyal.[6]

Patience: 1. The fact, quality, or habit of being patient.[7]

The other day I looked up the definition of patience. After reading it, and looking up the definitions of all the other words used to define patience, I was amazed.

What does being patient mean? It can mean waiting 3 to 5

minutes while the microwave heats up leftovers. It can mean waiting for commercials to end. Or, waiting for hot water. It can mean these things, but there is so much more depth to being patient.

I think someone who is truly patient must be incredibly strong. Just take one of the words that describes patience, like persevere. In part, it means to persist in a purpose despite obstacles. It can be very easy to get discouraged and give up. But to get discouraged and not give up – that takes perseverance and strength.

Take the word steadfast. In part I think it means to stay firm in a belief, and not wavering. It almost speaks about integrity. It can be difficult to keep believing something that you do not see, even when you know it is true.

An aspect of patience is tolerance. Part of being tolerant is the capacity to withstand pain or hardship. Just thinking about that makes me uncomfortable. Yet, I would like to be able to withstand those things without caving in to bad compromises.

These are just some aspects of what it means to be patient. I begin to understand why so seemingly few people are patient.

I will hear people shamelessly say, "I'm not a patient person," maybe with an added, "at all." Is this meant to be laughed at? Or is it a warning? Seems to me it would not be a shortcoming of mine I would like to divulge. Besides, the fault would become obvious eventually and one might not even have to wait very long to see it; no need for patience there.

Events and circumstances happen every day that test one's patience. Again, I think someone who is truly patient must be incredibly strong. Where does this strength come from? I know I am not strong enough to meet the standards of being patient on my own. I am not capable of anything on my own. Holy Spirit helps me to be patient.

But when the Holy Spirit controls our lives he will produce this kind of fruit in us: love, joy, peace, patience, kindness, goodness, faithfulness, gentleness and self-control; ... (Galatians 5:22-23 TLB)

But the fruit of the Spirit is love, joy, peace, longsuffering, gentleness, goodness, faith, Meekness, temperance: ... (Galatians 5:22 KJV)

These verses say "he will produce this kind of fruit in us" and "the fruit of the Spirit is ..." It does not say maybe he will.

Interesting that the King James version of Galatians 5:22 uses the word longsuffering rather than patience.

Longsuffering: Patiently bearing difficulties or wrongs.[8]

Patiently bearing difficulties is one thing, but patiently bearing wrongs? Yes, this too.

I think patience is a beautiful thing, and rare. Kind of like a pearl in an oyster. It is an impressive and exquisite quality to observe in a person.

29

Mysterious

Oh, the depth of the riches and wisdom and knowledge of God! How unsearchable are his judgements and how inscrutable his ways! (Romans 11:33 ESV)

"Can you fathom the mysteries of God? Can you probe the limits of the Almighty? (Job 11:7 NIV)

God's voice thunders in marvelous ways; he does great things beyond our understanding. (Job 37:5 NIV)

As much as I try to know God and understand His ways, there are always going to be mysteries about Him. There are many times where I must accept that I do not understand what His plans are and why He does things the way He does. This requires humility and faith.

It is easier to have faith in Him when you know that His ways are always good, just, and wise.

Perhaps it is part of my nature, but I like to know why things are the way they are. When someone tells me something, it is not uncommon for me to ask, "How do you know?" I do not mean it in an insolent way. I want to know if this information is true and useful. I ask the Lord questions, and I am humbled and thankful when He answers. I do not have to ask Him, "How do you know?"

Somewhat off-topic, nevertheless: recently I have come to the shameful realization that sometimes when I ask, I just want His answer to be an affirmation of what I want. I have learned that sometimes I have not been willing to hear "No" from Him. What is the point of asking Him when I am not willing to hear His answer? My unwillingness is even more absurd because I know His answer is always best. While getting "my way" rather than His way may seem ideal, it can quickly become painfully apparent that it is not.

One way I was thinking about how His ways are mysterious and thus unknown to me, is to compare it to making a strawberry-rhubarb pie. I imagine the Lord being the Baker, and I am the rhubarb. He knows what He is doing, and He has the recipe. As the rhubarb, it would be ridiculous for me to look up at Him and say, "Are you sure you know what you're doing? I strongly feel that you chopped me up too fine. Furthermore, I think you are adding too many strawberries ..."

I am tired out, O God, and ready to die. I am too stupid even to call myself a human being! I cannot understand man, let alone God. (Proverbs 30:2-3 TLB)

The LORD is righteous in all His ways And kind in all His deeds. (Psalm 145:17 NASB)

He is the Rock, his works are perfect, and all his ways are just. A faithful God who does no wrong, upright and just is he. (Deuteronomy 32:4 NIV)

30

A Primer on the Devil

It is important to know the methods and goals of the devil. Like in football, it would be to a team's great advantage to know what plays the other team was planning on using. Banishing ignorance in the ways of the devil helps one to avoid being deceived and the following consequences.

In the Bible Jesus tells us what satan's plan is and in fact, all that he does:

The thief comes only to steal and kill and destroy. I came that they may have life and have it abundantly. (John 10:10 ESV)

I believe he steals, kills, and destroys anything that is good; anything that is the way God meant it to be. The scope is very broad. I know I will not cover a great deal of it, but I will try to give some examples. Some very basic things like air and water have been affected by evil. Chemtrails in the air and fluoride in the water. Additives that are not good to consume are added to products.

While you can see the effects of evil in elements and products, I believe a main target of satan is the human race. Something that

God loves dearly. Something that was created in His image (Genesis 1:27) and where His very Spirit can dwell. The elements and products I mentioned: what can they negatively affect? Among other living things, people.

Another condition I have noticed, that is used to its greatest potential by the devil, is being distracted. This can happen in many ways. I know people love to be entertained. The devil knows it too. Internet, movies, music, phones that seem to have become an added member of the human body, other people, and hobbies are very entertaining. At home I could be listening to music. If I am in the car there is music. If neither of those are happening I could be found in front of some kind of screen, being social with other people, or doing something that entertains me and occupies time. Not a moment is unfilled. While these things in themselves are not bad, I am pointing out how they can be used by the devil to distract people to the point that they do not consider why they exist; the purpose of their life and the things of God. It is as if the devil thinks, "Let me divert them with entertainment. They enjoy that. They'll be so distracted they won't have time to think about God."

I have noticed the saddening theft, death, and destruction of beauty. I think it starts with influencing perceptions and standards of what is beautiful. Then in terms of what is beautiful, what is acceptable, popular and admirable. For example, art. There is a difference between art and filth. But, anything can be art now. Also, the beauty of women has been an excellent target. There is more to being beautiful than what is seen outwardly. But even that which is seen outwardly has deteriorated in my opinion. For that matter, the beauty of men has been dismantled as well. Why are men portrayed as unrespectable and unintelligent slobs? While these examples show some of the destruction of beauty, thankfully by God's grace it has not perished completely. Not everyone has accepted these perceptions and standards.

One fact to bear in mind is that the devil has no mercy. At a person's weakest points in life, he is right there to try and take advantage of it. Nothing is too innocent, or too pitiable for him to destroy.

As I mentioned before, I believe he steals, kills, and destroys anything that is good; anything that is the way God meant it to be. One thing I have noticed is that he is particularly sensitive to anything that brings the kingdom of God to Earth. Anything that is God's will, and when God is working in a person's life and drawing them to Him. Just watch the fit the devil is thrown into when a person begins to consider God or do His will. He will try anything to keep these things from happening.

I think it is very important to be aware of satan's ways. I do not want to be ignorant of them so that I am not deceived. It is important to know the truth. In that way one can keep from being deceived as well.

There is more ground to cover on the schemes and designs of the devil and there are ways to combat them.

31

Meriting Love

Definition of merit: n. 1. A usually high level of superiority : worth. v. To deserve : earn.[1]

Love is not given only because of merit. This goes against one's natural inclinations. But as children of God we now have a new nature. (The new nature being given when one trusts in Jesus for the forgiveness of their sins.)

"There is a saying, 'Love your friends and hate your enemies.' But I say: Love your enemies! Pray for those who persecute you! In that way you will be acting as true sons of your Father in heaven. For he gives his sunlight to both the evil and the good, and sends rain on the just and on the unjust too. If you love only those who love you, what good is that? Even scoundrels do that much. If you are friendly only to your friends, how are you different from anyone else? Even the heathen do that. But you are to be perfect, even as your Father in heaven is perfect. (Matthew 5:43-48 TLB)

While one may not feel they have actual enemies to love, we have daily opportunities to love. There is the person who treats you unkindly at work, and the person who cut you off while driving. One reaction might be to curse the so-and-so who cut you off, but that is not what we are supposed to do. Instead of harboring a grudge and thinking of how bad that person at work is, we are to love and pray for them.

These beliefs are scoffed at by the world, but it is what we are instructed to do by our Lord Jesus. Consequently, I want to try my best to obey. I know that I am only able to do so with His help and not because of my own strength.

Funny, even the single word "obey" in the previous paragraph my old nature does not like. Let alone what is to be obeyed. Some synonyms of obey: submit, follow, observe, conform. Indeed, all these words describe my new nature's behavior toward God. Antonyms of those words: disobey, lead, resist, ignore, rebel. All of these words describe my old nature's behavior toward God.

When we were utterly helpless with no way of escape, Christ came at just the right time and died for us sinners who had no use for him. Even if we were good, we really wouldn't expect anyone to die for us, though, of course, that might be barely possible. But God showed his great love for us by sending Christ to die for us while we were still sinners. (Romans 5:6-8 TLB)

32

See or Believe

I practiced the song. As usual I did not practice my scales as much as I should have, but I did practice the song. But now at my piano lesson, in front of my teacher, I was unsuccessful in playing it without errors. As I sat on the piano bench and gazed unhappily at the keys I said, "Practice makes perfect," to reassure and console myself. To which my teacher responded, "Perfect practice makes perfect."

I remembered this when I was thinking about the saying, "seeing is believing." Seeing is not believing. Believing is believing.

Long ago when I was in summer camp, we had this activity where you would stand blindfolded and let yourself fall backwards. You would trust other campers to catch you rather than let you fall to the floor. You had to believe you would be caught because you definitely did not see. Some people were really hesitant to fall backwards, and some were quite trusting.

Shifting to spiritual matters, it is unfortunate how much I can rely on sight rather than faith. In the Bible we are told:

For we live by faith, not by sight. (2 Corinthians 5:7 NIV)

For we live by believing and not by seeing. (2 Corinthians 5:7 NLT)

Faith is the confidence that what we hope for will actually happen; it gives us assurance about things we cannot see. (Hebrews 11:1 NLT)

Faith is contrary to the mind and to the eyes. Faith is understood by our new nature but not by the old.

Definition of contrary: 1. Completely opposite, as in direction or character. 2. Unfavorable : adverse. 3. Recalcitrant : willful. 4. Counter : opposed.[1]

In part, I think my old nature wants to rely on sight because it placates my mind; my own knowledge. It nourishes the ego and makes it seem that one is in control to a degree. Also, it surprises me how unreliable sight can be. It is not always the test for truth. In the Bible we are told:

Trust in the LORD with all your heart; do not depend on your own understanding. (Proverbs 3:5 NLT)

Sometimes I think about that time when Jesus spat on the ground to make mud, and then applied it to a blind man's eyes and healed him (John 9:6). The way this was done does not make sense to my mind, nor to my eyes, had I seen this take place. Setting aside the making of mud, if Jesus just touched the man's eyes or spoke to him and healed him, I still would not be able to understand this with my mind though my eyes would see it. I mean, this miracle happened because of the power of God and faith, not because it made sense to the mind. If Jesus relied on what made sense, on human knowledge, I think this miracle would not have happened at all.

The necessity of trusting the Lord despite what you see and beyond what you understand is vitally important. How is growing in the Lord possible without it? It is necessary for even the smallest baby-steps of growth.

And without faith it is impossible to please God, because anyone who comes to him must believe that he exists and that he rewards those who earnestly seek him. (Hebrews 11:6 NIV)

"I tell you the truth, anyone who believes in me will do the same works I have done, and even greater works ..." (John 14:12 NLT)

Believing - having faith - in God is needed. It can grow by His grace, and with time and experiences. I think it helps to identify and understand that it is normal for your mind, eyes, and old nature to be at odds with your faith. Hopefully this "normal" state diminishes more and more. Away with all attempts by the mind and eyes to convince that faith is futile. I want to hold tightly to faith in God, not on what I can understand or see. To trust Him relentlessly.

For our light and momentary troubles are achieving for us an eternal glory that far outweighs them all. So we fix our eyes not on what is seen, but on what is unseen, since what is seen is temporary, but what is unseen is eternal. (2 Corinthians 4:17-18 NIV)

Though you have not seen him, you love him; and even though you do not see him now, you believe in him and are filled with an inexpressible and glorious joy, (1 Peter 1:8 NIV)

Then Jesus told him, "You believe because you have seen me. Blessed are those who believe without seeing me." (John 20:29 NLT)

33

The Most Important Thing in Life

Timothy, guard what has been entrusted to your care. Turn
away from godless chatter and the opposing ideas of what is falsely
called knowledge, which some have professed and in so doing have
departed from the faith. Grace be with you all. (1 Timothy 6:20-21
NIV)

Oh, Timothy, don't fail to do these things that God entrusted to
you. Keep out of foolish arguments with those who boast of their
"knowledge" and thus prove their lack of it. Some of these people
have missed the most important thing in life – they don't know
God. May God's mercy be upon you. (1 Timothy 6:20-21 TLB)

What is the most important thing in life to you?
I noticed a tendency in myself that, with the help of God and
these verses, I have been learning to relax. This tendency is about
feeling that I am never where I should, need, or want to be. As if I
am forever looking ahead to something not yet attained and think
that when it is attained, I will then feel complete. A feeling of
restlessness. Like a dog constantly pulling at a leash, ready to move

ahead rather than being content walking beside its master.

One could live through their entire life with this sort of mindset, and I am not willing to do that. I learned that I already have the most important thing in life, and that is knowing God. Having this perspective allows me to have peace and rest. I do not mean I have no trials. I mean I can be as that dog walking contentedly beside my Master. In the rain or sun. Or, like the contentment one may feel while being with someone they love regardless of what they are doing. While I want to know Him more and keep growing and maturing as He would want me to, I do not need to feel anxious about it.

I was thinking about how if I did not know God, I would unconsciously be looking for something to fill His place in my life. All of which would not fill the position. Possessions, status, abilities, achievements, and other people would never fulfill my need or desire of Him. But, I am sure it would not keep me from expecting them to.

Maybe for a limited time these things would satisfy, but many problems arise when people look for replacements of God. Disappointment, disillusionment, and a lack of peace can result. I cringe a little inside when I hear people speak of their significant other as someone who "completes" them or who they would "die without." May I never speak such words! Only God completes me, and only without Him would I die. (I do not mean to express these statements in a proud, self-sufficient way that makes me seem like I do not need other people, or in a way that makes marriage seem insignificant.)

To me, the idea of someone "completing" you is unfair and brings false expectations. It is asking too much. It is like asking someone to be what only God can be to you. Perhaps one of those false expectations is unconditional love. People love with conditions. God loves unconditionally. I think the more we become like God, the closer we get to loving unconditionally.

When no one else loves, understands, or knows you, He does and always will.

Yet they say, "My Lord deserted us; he has forgotten us."
"Never! Can a mother forget her little child and not have love for
her own son? Yet even if that should be, I will not forget you."
(Isaiah 49:14-15 TLB)

Even if my father and mother abandon me, the LORD will hold
me close. (Psalm 27:10 NLT)

I pray that out of his glorious riches he may strengthen you
with power through his Spirit in your inner being, so that Christ
may dwell in your hearts through faith. And I pray that you, being
rooted and established in love, may have power, together with all
the Lord's holy people, to grasp how wide and long and high and
deep is the love of Christ, and to know this love that surpasses
knowledge—that you may be filled to the measure of all the fullness
of God. (Ephesians 3:17-19 NIV)

34

Love by Bearing Burdens and Being Considerate

Share each other's troubles and problems, and so obey our Lord's command. (Galatians 6:2 TLB)

Bear one another's burdens, and so fulfill the law of Christ. (Galatians 6:2 ESV)

When others are happy, by happy with them. If they are sad, share their sorrow. (Romans 12:15 TLB)

These verses come to mind as I try, with successes and failures, to live them. Bearing each other's troubles, problems, and burdens can feel like hard work. Like an actual weight has been placed on your shoulders.

For me, I have put these verses into action in a few different ways. One of them is when I hear someone complaining. At first, I do not want to hear it. I just feel like it is a bother. Like, I was doing ok and then someone bothers me with complaints. Also, the complaint seems to have no beneficial result. There is really nothing I can do to alleviate the complaint; it is just said and left there for me to feel bad about. However, I have been learning to be more empathetic and to show love in such a circumstance. Whatever the complaint was about, it came from someone who was distressed. I must be considerate of that and help to "bear" their trouble. Even when there is nothing I can do about it, I can offer something. Many times I have noticed the person does not really want you to do anything about it. They just want to vent, and have you listen and understand.

Other times I have put these verses into use is when someone is having a bad day, and I am having a good day. I am feeling pretty good. I can enjoy the fact that I am alive and then someone around me does not share the same feelings. I can take this situation two ways. First, the route I do not want to take: I can think, "Well, I'm not going to let them bring me down." Then I go on to disregard their situation. The route I do want to take: I want to pause my idyllic day (yes, old nature, make this huge sacrifice) and be considerate of their situation. I want to listen to what they are saying and help to bear their burden.

My old nature is completely selfish. I know that when I take these actions, my old nature must surrender; it must die. I feel a tug-of-war inside me at these times. The old nature fighting against the new nature. Bearing one another's burdens takes Holy Spirit's help, grace, love, strength, and patience.

I have experienced my own burdens being shared by others as well as not being shared by others. I compare it to struggling to carry a 5 gallon bucket full of water and someone comes up beside you and lends a hand. I feel loved and cared for. In my experiences, they cannot take your burden from you completely, but can lighten your load. When they are not shared by others, I feel alone and unloved. However, I have learned that there are some difficulties in life that other people just cannot share with you. Even if they want to and/or you want them to. You must take some journeys alone, but with God.

On the flipside, I am learning that you can show love and consideration in another way. For example, if I have a complaint, there are times when I should not express it, for the benefit of others. Or if I am having a bad day, perhaps I should not share every discouraging detail about it to someone who I can see is feeling cheerful. If I do not have a complaint of any kind, but simply have something to say and see that the one I intend to speak to is not in a state to receive it well, I will try to keep it to myself.

To me, it should go both ways. I think it is about loving others.

Don't think only of yourself. Try to think of the other fellow, too, and what is best for him. (1 Corinthians 10:24 TLB)

Being happy-go-lucky around a person whose heart is heavy is as bad as stealing his jacket in cold weather, or rubbing salt in his wounds. (Proverbs 25:20 TLB)

If you shout a pleasant greeting to a friend too early in the morning, he will count it as a curse! (Proverbs 27:14 TLB)

35

Romans 8:28

Romans 8:28 is well known and one of the most encouraging verses in the Bible. Its promise provides comfort and reassurance in difficult times that seem to have no good purpose or reason.

And we know that God causes everything to work together for the good of those who love God and are called according to his purpose for them. (Romans 8:28 NLT)

In the past I understood it to mean that everything, whether it is good or bad, is actually made into something beneficial by God for the Christian. I found this very encouraging, but what was this "good" that everything worked together for? It seemed somewhat ambiguous. Like everything worked together for some good, whatever that was. The reason for this ambiguity was probably because this "good" was defined by me, and it changed so often.

Then I listened to a preacher and he said that the Romans 8:28 verse should never be used without the following verse. Verse 29 defines for us what this "good" is.

For God knew his people in advance, and he chose them to become like his Son, so that his Son would be the firstborn among many brothers and sisters. (Romans 8:29 NLT)

So, the "good" that all things work together for is that we become more like Jesus.

Sometimes reading the same verses in different Bible versions helps me to understand their meaning better. The same two verses in the TLB and ESV Bible versions:

And we know that all that happens to us is working for our good if we love God and are fitting into his plans. For from the very beginning God decided that those who came to him – and all along he knew who would – should become like his Son, so that his Son would be the First, with many brothers. (Romans 8:28-29 TLB)

And we know that for those who love God all things work together for good, for those who are called according to his purpose. For those whom he foreknew he also predestined to be conformed to the image of his Son, in order that he might be the firstborn among many brothers. (Romans 8:28-29 ESV)

Again, this "good" that all things are worked together for by God, is that we become like Jesus. Ultimately, for His glory.

Is finding this out a disappointment? Does it seem like a catch to a promise that seemed ideal? When I first learned this, I reacted with some of these feelings. This just shows how I liked my own will better than God's. I was not thinking of God's definition of good (true good) and His will. I was thinking of my definition of good (self-centered good) and my will.

This knowledge of Romans 8:28-29 should not be a disappointment. Is there really anything better for the Christian than becoming more like Jesus? It is God's will. When we become more like Jesus it brings glory to God.

And we know that for those who love God all things work

together for good, for those who are called according to his purpose. For those whom he foreknew he also predestined to be conformed to the image of his Son, in order that he might be the firstborn among many brothers. And those whom he predestined he also called, and those whom he called he also justified, and those whom he justified he also glorified. (Romans 8:28-30 ESV)

And we all, with unveiled face, beholding the glory of the Lord, are being transformed into the same image from one degree of glory to another. For this comes from the Lord who is the Spirit. (2 Corinthians 3:18 ESV)

Bring all who claim me as their God, for I have made them for my glory. It was I who created them.'" (Isaiah 43:7 NLT)

36

Death and Life. Leading and Following.

Then Jesus said to his disciples, "If anyone wishes to come after Me, he must deny himself, and take up his cross and follow Me. For whoever wishes to save his life will lose it; but whoever loses his life for My sake will find it. (Matthew 16:24-25 NASB)

Truly, truly, I say to you, unless a grain of wheat falls into the earth and dies, it remains alone; but if it dies, it bears much fruit. Whoever loves his life loses it, and whoever hates his life in this world will keep it for eternal life. (John 12:24-25 ESV)

In the past, these verses were not easy for me to understand. But, when Holy Spirit helped me understand, and certain events happened in my life, they became clearer.

Jesus was an example for us to follow.

But whoever keeps His word, in him the love of God has been truly perfected. By this we know that we are in Him: the one who says he abides in Him ought himself to walk in the same manner as He walked. (1 John 2:5-6 NASB)

For to this you have been called, because Christ also suffered for you, leaving you an example, so that you might follow in his steps. (1 Peter 2:21 ESV)

He gave His will and His life in exchange for the will of the Father. We are to do the same.

So Jesus explained, "I tell you the truth, the Son can do nothing by himself. He does only what he sees the Father doing. Whatever the Father does, the Son also does. (John 5:19 NLT)

I don't speak on my own authority. The Father who sent me has commanded me what to say and how to say it. And I know his commands lead to eternal life; so I say whatever the Father tells me to say." (John 12:49-50 NLT)

I can do nothing on my own. I judge as God tells me. Therefore, my judgement is just, because I carry out the will of the one who sent me, not my own will. (John 5:30 NLT)

For I have come down from heaven, not to do my own will but the will of him who sent me. (John 6:38 ESV)

Just as the living Father sent me and I live because of the Father, so the one who feeds on me will live because of me. (John 6:57 NIV)

Jesus says that coming after Him takes denial of self, taking up your cross, and following Him. Also, He says that if you love and save your life you will lose it. There is the analogy of a grain of wheat falling into the earth and dying to produce fruit. I think all of these point to the denial and death of your will in exchange for God's good and perfect will.

When you die to your own will for God's will, it produces spiritual growth, goodness, and life. This affects your life and the lives of those around you. The grain of wheat that dies produces more wheat. If it does not die, it remains only one grain by itself.

I know this can be difficult to understand, and actually disagreeable. It is absolutely disagreeable to my self-centered old nature. If it spoke it would say, "What? What do you mean die? I have things to do. I've got plans and this is my life." However, Jesus bought the Christian and he no longer belongs to himself. Additionally, when one becomes a Christian they no longer live for themselves.

Don't you realize that your body is the temple of the Holy Spirit, who lives in you and was given to you by God? You do not belong to yourself, for God bought you with a high price. So you must honor God with your body. (1 Corinthians 6:19-20 NLT)

He died for everyone so that those who receive his new life will no longer live for themselves. Instead, they will live for Christ, who died and was raised for them. So we have stopped evaluating others from a human point of view. At one time we thought of Christ merely from a human point of view. How differently we know him now! This means that anyone who belongs to Christ has become a new person. The old life is gone; a new life has begun! (2 Corinthians 5:15-17 NLT)

Sometimes it takes a lot to get to the point where one realizes this, accepts it as truth, and lives it. It always takes Holy Spirit. Personally, I had to get to the point where I felt like there was not much left in life for me. It was necessary for me to be broken before I accepted this truth. Shamefully, it was easier to let God have my life in greater and increasing measure when I had no use for it anymore, and let God control things when I could not.

As I thought about this whole subject of dying to self (denial, submission) and living for the purposes of God, it made me think of leading and following. Like the leading and following that happens in dancing. I do not know very much about leading and following in dancing. Nevertheless, the amount I know helped me to understand this subject better. When I have danced, being the girl, I followed. I waited to feel direction – where to move, fast or slow, stop or go. In a way, I submitted to who I was dancing with and let them lead. So, it made me think of submitting to God; letting Him lead. Does he want me to do this? Go here or there? Do this or that?

I want to do what He wants me to do, even if I do not want to do it. This conflict exists because I have the new nature given to me by God, but still live with the old nature. My new nature desires to do God's will, but my old nature does not. How am I able to do what He wants me to even when I don't want to? I am enabled to by Holy Spirit. Further motivations to do this are because God is always right and good, I belong to Him, and He loves me.

There are many ways that one dies. For example, it could be saying "I love you" when you do not feel like saying it. Conversely, it could be not saying things. Maybe it is something as big as giving up (or accepting) a job or friendship. Or, moving somewhere else to live. On the other hand, it could be something as small as picking up a piece of litter from the floor. Actions that your old nature recoils from and despises, but your new nature enjoys and desires to do if it is God's will.

A personal experience of my "dying" was when I was listening to this song. I liked the song, but the lyrics were not good. But I liked the sound of the song so I continued listening to it. Each time I would listen to it I felt a slight uneasiness. Holy Spirit was nudging me, telling me that it was not pleasing to Him for me to be listening to it. Excuses immediately came to mind like, "But I don't agree with the lyrics, I just like the rest of the song." Finally, after many nudges, I asked the Lord if He wanted me to listen to the song. He said no. So even though I wanted to keep listening to the song, I denied this desire and stopped listening to it. It was minor, such a small thing. But my old nature did not like this denial one bit. It struggled but had to die; lose, and not get its way. This is a very small example of "dying."

In this instance I could understand, in part, why I should not continue listening to the song. Because it was not good. There are times when one must submit to the will of God when they do not understand why.

Throughout his life Jesus submitted to the Father. Continually putting His own will aside for the will of the Father. To the point of physically dying on the cross as part of God's will. Life and goodness beyond expression was the result.

So remember, there is a purpose in dying. You are following Jesus' example and are being conformed to His image. When your will dies, God's will lives in and through you; His kingdom is brought to Earth. This not only affects your life, but the lives of others as well. It produces spiritual growth, life, and brings glory to God. The single grain of wheat dies and produces more wheat.

always carrying about in the body the dying of Jesus, so that the life of Jesus also may be manifested in our body. For we who live are constantly being delivered over to death for Jesus' sake, so that the life of Jesus also may be manifested in our mortal flesh. (2 Corinthians 4:10-11 NASB)

37

Seeking Holiness: Motives

As obedient children, do not conform to the evil desires you had when you lived in ignorance. But just as he who called you is holy, so be holy in all you do; for it is written: "Be holy, because I am holy." (1 Peter 1:14-16 NIV)

People may be pure in their own eyes, but the LORD examines their motives. (Proverbs 16:2 NLT)

Recently, I thought I should update my profile picture on Facebook. I began to think about what kind of picture of myself I should take. Like, what kind of background, lighting, angles, etc. As I thought about this, I felt like Holy Spirit gave me insight about myself by presenting me with the question, "Why?" This made me examine my motives.

I could have deceived myself by thinking it was purely to update my profile picture. But I could not get away with that. I had to get to the roots; my true motives. They were not pretty. They were ugly things like pride, conceit, finding self-worth from others' opinions, and stirring emotion in others.

Those who belong to Christ Jesus have nailed the passions and desires of their sinful nature to his cross and crucified them there. Since we are living by the Spirit, let us follow the Spirit's leading in every part of our lives. Let us not become conceited, or provoke one another, or be jealous of one another. (Galatians 5:24-26 NLT)

The depravity of the ever-present old nature is surprising sometimes. Although, at this point in my life I should not really be surprised.

"The human heart is the most deceitful of all things, and desperately wicked. Who really knows how bad it is? But I, the LORD, search all hearts and examine secret motives. I give all people their due rewards, according to what their actions deserve." (Jeremiah 17:9-10 NLT)

All this brought me to thinking about motives and examining them. Are my motives pleasing to God? Or are they seeking to satisfy my old nature?

For am I now seeking the approval of man, or of God? Or am I trying to please man? If I were still trying to please man, I would not be a servant of Christ. (Galatians 1:10 ESV)

And whatever you do or say, do it as a representative of the Lord Jesus, giving thanks through him to God the Father. (Colossians 3:17 NLT)

So whether you eat or drink, or whatever you do, do it all for the glory of God. (1 Corinthians 10:31 NLT)

What motivates me to do or say things? I discovered that identifying my motives is an effective way to check myself and decide whether to do something or not.

In the past I would have rarely thought of my motives. Lately I feel like, while I have the liberty to do things, not all of them are good.

All things are lawful, but not all things are profitable. All things are lawful, but not all things edify. (1 Corinthians 10:23 NASB)

Since I want to please God, become more like Him, and keep growing spiritually, why should I bother with things that I want nothing in common with? Things that are of a former way of life. It would be kind of like driving an old car with filthy seat covers. Then buying a new car and deciding to use the same filthy seat covers you had in the old car. It does not make sense to me. Forget about the old and move on to better things.

You were taught, with regard to your former way of life, to put off your old self, which is being corrupted by its deceitful desires; to be made new in the attitude of your minds; and to put on the new self, created to be like God in true righteousness and holiness. (Ephesians 4:22-24 NIV)

This means that anyone who belongs to Christ has become a new person. The old life is gone; a new life has begun! (2 Corinthians 5:17 NLT)

Those who are dominated by the sinful nature think about sinful things, but those who are controlled by the Holy Spirit think about things that please the Spirit. So letting your sinful nature control your mind leads to death. But letting the Spirit control your mind leads to life and peace. For the sinful nature is always hostile toward God. It never did obey God's laws, and it never will. That's why those who are still under the control of their sinful nature can never please God. But you are not controlled by your sinful nature. You are controlled by the Spirit if you have the Spirit of God living in you (And remember that those who do not have the Spirit of Christ living in them do not belong to him at all.) (Romans 8:5-9 NLT)

"Beware of practicing your righteousness before men to be noticed by them; otherwise you have no reward with your Father who is in heaven. "So when you give to the poor, do not sound a trumpet before you, as the hypocrites do in the synagogues and in the streets, so that they may be honored by men. Truly I say to you, they have their reward in full. (Matthew 6:1-2 NASB)

My conscience is clear, but that doesn't prove I'm right. It is the Lord himself who will examine me and decide. So don't make judgements about anyone ahead of time--before the Lord returns. For he will bring our darkest secrets to light and will reveal our private motives. Then God will give to each one whatever praise is due. (1 Corinthians 4:4-5 NLT)

38

God Loves You Part 2: Not Performance Based

I would not go to the extreme of saying it was love. There were qualities I thought were very attractive. Other areas were definitely lacking, but did not matter. I saw potential. I was let down several times and thought it was over. It was difficult to see past being let down, sometimes at critical moments in life when I was in need. But my affection for my 1978 Chevrolet Monte Carlo was not performance based.

It is easy for me to see my reasons for liking this car. But, could I ever imagine someone feeling this way toward me? I am sure I have as many flaws as the car, probably more.

I have noticed that most merit is based on performance. Keeping or losing a job often depends on one's performance. Winning or losing usually depends on performance. Being wary around a dog that has bitten you is caused by your thoughts of its past performance. Some judgements based on performance are simply common sense.

From a very early age people learn that if they do something wrong there are consequences. Discipline is necessary. Doing right and not wrong needs to be learned.

Particularly for children, there is a Christmas song called "Santa Claus Is Comin' To Town." Although its lyrics do not say outright that if you are not good you will not receive a gift, I feel like that is what it's getting at. The first part of the song is, "You better watch out, you better not cry, you better not pout I'm telling you why, Santa Claus is coming to town." The not-so-subtle message that I see here is that I must behave in a certain way to deserve a gift.

After years of growing up learning these things, by being taught and through personal experiences, the idea of earning things becomes ingrained. I think the problem is when this mindset is transferred to the idea of being loved.

I believe when this happens people are wrongly influenced by it. They try to earn love. It is a frightening thought to me. The thought of trying anything and everything to have someone love you. The thought itself is alarming to me, let alone actually doing it.

Instead, I think if you are truly loved by someone you will want to please them as a result of that. Not in order to be loved.

I hope everyone has experienced the amazing moments of paradox when love encounters the ingrained performance-based mindset. Moments in life when you did everything completely wrong, but it was basically nullified because of love. So conflicting to everything "normal" and expected, it's confounding.

Love is not earned. It is given. If somehow it was earned, I just hope that whoever earned it has the strength to keep earning it and whoever is giving it happens to be placated enough to keep giving it. In such a case it seems so fragile and miserable. Is it really love?

Love is patient, love is kind. It does not envy, it does not boast, it is not proud. It does not dishonor others, it is not self-seeking, it is not easily angered, it keeps no record of wrongs. Love does not delight in evil but rejoices with the truth. It always protects, always trusts, always hopes, always perseveres. (1 Corinthians 13:4-7 NIV)

The best example of love that was given, not earned and not based on one's performance, is God's love for us demonstrated through the sacrifice of His only Son Jesus.

Very rarely will anyone die for a righteous person, though for a good person someone might possibly dare to die. But God demonstrates his own love for us in this: While we were still sinners, Christ died for us. (Romans 5:7-8 NIV)

At one time we too were foolish, disobedient, deceived and enslaved by all kinds of passions and pleasures. We lived in malice and envy, being hated and hating one another. But when the kindness and love of God our Savior appeared, he saved us, not because of righteous things we had done, but because of his mercy. He saved us through the washing of rebirth and renewal by the Holy Spirit, (Titus 3:3-5 NIV)

God saved you by his grace when you believed. And you can't take credit for this; it is a gift from God. Salvation is not a reward for the good things we have done, so none of us can boast about it. (Ephesians 2:8-9 NLT)

For I am sure that neither death nor life, nor angels nor rulers, nor things present nor things to come, nor powers, nor height nor depth, nor anything else in all creation, will be able to separate us from the love of God in Christ Jesus our Lord. (Romans 8:38-39 ESV)

Additionally, because of God's love and His Spirit living in us, we have a new life. Part of that new life is no longer being slaves to sin and unrighteousness. We are able, by His Spirit, to obey Him and love others as He loves us.

Therefore be imitators of God, as beloved children; and walk in love, just as Christ also loved you and gave Himself up for us, an offering and a sacrifice to God as a fragrant aroma. (Ephesians 5:1-2 NASB)

A new commandment I give to you, that you love one another: just as I have loved you, you also are to love one another. (John 13:34 ESV)

This is how love is made complete among us so that we will have confidence on the day of judgment: In this world we are like Jesus. There is no fear in love. But perfect love drives out fear, because fear has to do with punishment. The one who fears is not made perfect in love. We love because he first loved us. (1 John 4:17-19 NIV)

39

Worse Than a Fool

I don't have a favorite book of the Bible, but the book of Proverbs is one of my favorites. I like it because it's so full of wisdom. If you read it, you may notice that it contains a lot of information about fools. You can quickly and clearly understand that it isn't good to be a fool.

A fool:
1. Has fun in being bad.
2. Thinks he needs no advice.
3. Is quick-tempered.
4. Gets into constant fights.
5. Endangers himself with his words. His mouth is his undoing.
6. Insists on quarreling.

A fool's fun is being bad; a wise man's fun is being wise. (Proverbs 10:23 TLB)

A fool thinks he needs no advice, but a wise man listens to

others. (Proverbs 12:15 TLB)

A fool is quick-tempered; a wise man stays cool when insulted. (Proverbs 12:16 TLB)

A fool gets into constant fights. His mouth is his undoing! His words endanger him. (Proverbs 18:7 TLB)

It is an honor for a man to stay out of a fight. Only fools insist on quarreling. (Proverbs 20:3 TLB)

Definition of fool: n. 1. One deficient in good sense or judgement. 3. One who can easily be tricked : dupe.[1]
These are just some of the characteristics of a fool. There are many other verses in Proverbs that describe him/her. So it got my attention when I read a verse that says there is something worse than being a fool.

There is one thing worse than a fool, and that is a man who is conceited. (Proverbs 26:12 TLB)

Definition of conceited: 1. Unduly proud of oneself : vain.[2]
All of this information was very interesting to me. It is more than that, too. By God's grace, it is knowledge that can be formed into wisdom.

Blessed is the one who finds wisdom, and the one who gets understanding, for the gain from her is better than gain from silver and her profit better than gold. She is more precious than jewels, and nothing you desire can compare with her. Long life is in her right hand; in her left hand are riches and honor. Her ways are ways of pleasantness, and all her paths are peace. She is a tree of life to those who lay hold of her; those who hold her fast are called blessed. (Proverbs 3:13-18 ESV)

Do not speak in the hearing of a fool, for he will despise the good sense of your words. (Proverbs 23:9 ESV)

Leave the presence of a fool, for there you do not meet words of knowledge. (Proverbs 14:7 ESV)

If any of you lacks wisdom, let him ask God, who gives generously to all without reproach, and it will be given him. (James 1:5 ESV)

40

Humility vs. Pride

Pride ends in destruction; humility ends in honor. (Proverbs 18:12 TLB)

But he gives us more and more strength to stand against all such evil longings. As the Scripture says, God gives strength to the humble, but sets himself against the proud and haughty. (James 4:6 TLB)

Humility is necessary in our walk with God, and so is the absence of pride.

Humility: The quality or state of being humble.[1]

Humble: adj. 1. Marked by modesty or meekness. 2. Respectfully deferential. 3. Lowly and unpretentious.[2]

Jesus is our Lord and an example to follow. He humbled Himself, and this resulted in honor.

Your attitude should be the kind that was shown us by Jesus Christ, who, though he was God, did not demand and cling to his rights as God, but laid aside his mighty power and glory, taking the disguise of a slave and becoming like men. And he humbled himself even further, going so far as actually to die a criminal's death on a cross. Yet it was because of this that God raised him up to the heights of heaven and gave him a name which is above every other name, that at the name of Jesus every knee shall bow in heaven and on earth and under the earth, and every tongue shall confess that Jesus Christ is Lord, to the glory of God the Father. (Philippians 2:5-11 TLB)

Pride: Excessive self-esteem : conceit.[3]
Conceit: An exaggerated opinion of oneself : vanity.[4]
The devil is our enemy. He became proud, and this resulted in his destruction.

How you are fallen from heaven, O Day Star, son of Dawn! How you are cut down to the ground, you who laid the nations low! You said in your heart, 'I will ascend to heaven; above the stars of God I will set my throne on high; I will sit on the mount of assembly in the far reaches of the north; I will ascend above the heights of the clouds; I will make myself like the Most High.' But you are brought down to Sheol, to the far reaches of the pit. (Isaiah 14:12-15 ESV)

"Son of man, raise a lamentation over the king of Tyre, and say to him, Thus says the Lord GOD: "You were the signet of perfection, full of wisdom and perfect in beauty. You were in Eden, the garden of God; every precious stone was your covering, sardius, topaz, and diamond, beryl, onyx, and jasper, sapphire, emerald, and carbuncle; and crafted in gold were your settings and your engravings. On the day that you were created they were prepared. You were an anointed guardian cherub. I placed you; you were on the holy mountain of God; in the midst of the stones of fire you walked. You were blameless in your ways from the day you were created, till unrighteousness was found in you. In the abundance of your trade you were filled with violence in your midst, and you sinned; so I cast you as a profane thing from the mountain of God, and I destroyed you, O guardian cherub, from the midst of the stones of fire. Your heart was proud because of your beauty; you corrupted your wisdom for the sake of your splendor. I cast you to the ground; I exposed you before kings, to feast their eyes on you. (Ezekiel 28:12-17 ESV)

I think the contrast between humility and pride is plain to see. They are like opposites. The results of humility and pride are very different from each other too. How Jesus lived as opposed to how the devil did, and their results, speak for themselves.

I feel that sometimes I have not noticed these things as much as I should. I think they are very important to take note of.

Another thing I find notable is that Jesus did not cling to His rights as God; He laid them aside. It makes me think about what "rights" I have that I should lay aside in order to be humble.

The Bible says that the devil was proud because of his beauty. A trait that he should not have taken credit for, because he was created that way by God. Also, it says he corrupted his wisdom for the sake of his splendor. Sounds like he valued his splendor, or impressiveness, more than his wisdom. It makes me think about avoiding taking credit for things that I have no right to, and cautions me not to undervalue or trade wisdom.

I notice that Jesus descended when he humbled Himself, and the devil wanted to ascend and be like God.

To me, these are important things to consider and be aware of. Learning more about humility and pride definitely makes me not want to be proud.

Particularly sobering is the James 4:6 verse that says God "sets himself against the proud ... " Try to imagine that! That God sets Himself against proud people. On the other hand, it says He "gives strength to the humble ... "

There are many examples throughout the Bible showing that humility is necessary in living the Christian life. One of those examples is shown in this verse from Proverbs:

Trust in the LORD with all your heart, and do not lean on your own understanding. (Proverbs 3:5 ESV)

One cannot choose to depend on God with all their heart, and forgo their own understanding without humility.

Pride disgusts the Lord. Take my word for it – *proud men shall be punished.* (Proverbs 16:5 TLB)

Pride ends in a fall, while humility brings honor. (Proverbs 29:23 TLB)

Then he told this story to some who boasted of their virtue and scorned everyone else: "Two men went to the Temple to pray. One was a proud, self-righteous Pharisee, and the other a cheating tax collector. The proud Pharisee 'prayed' this prayer: 'Thank God, I am not a sinner like everyone else, especially like that tax collector over there! For I never cheat, I don't commit adultery, I go without food twice a week, and I give to God a tenth of everything I earn.' But the corrupt tax collector stood at a distance and dared not even lift his eyes to heaven as he prayed, but beat upon his chest in sorrow, exclaiming, 'God, be merciful to me, a sinner.' I tell you, this sinner, not the Pharisee, returned home forgiven! For the proud shall be humbled, but the humble shall be honored." (Luke 18:9-13 TLB)

41

Trust!

Scenario 1

She peered at the speedometer. "You're going too slow. Speed up." She strummed her fingers on the armrest. "Are we there yet? We should be taking a right turn soon." She was very tired but would not dare close her eyes to rest. "Do you know where we're going? I really think you should let me drive." He slowed and pulled the car over to the side of the road. As she hastily grabbed at her seatbelt to unbuckle it she said, "Great. Let's switch places and then we'll really be on our way." But he said, "No. I pulled over to tell you to trust me."

Take 2

She looked out the window enjoying the scenery as he drove. "I'm glad you know where we're going," she said. His driving abilities were not doubted by her. She really didn't think about it at all. Except in cases where his skills exceeded her expectations. Like the time they travelled through a snow storm safely. Or, when he navigated through heavy traffic. At complete peace, she closed her eyes and fell asleep.

Definition of trust: n. 1. Firm reliance in the honesty, dependability, strength, or character of someone or something. 2. One in which faith or confidence is placed. 3. Care : custody. 5. Reliance on something in the future : hope.[1]

A degree of trust is exercised in many areas of life. Sometimes I think I trust in things and I am not really conscious that I'm doing so. I trust that the mail will be delivered, and I trust that my car will run.

In these examples, I am not anxious or concerned about them happening. I trust that they will happen. Why? Because based on their histories, they almost always happen. They faithfully occur.

I long to trust the Lord more. The scenario I wrote in the beginning came to mind as I thought about trusting the Lord. I don't want to be like that "backseat driver" that does not trust the one who is driving. The driver, or the Lord, knows what he's doing. He knows everything. His plans for His people are good. He's my Father and I should trust Him as His child.

For I know the plans I have for you, declares the LORD, plans for welfare and not for evil, to give you a future and a hope. (Jeremiah 29:11 ESV)

So, what is keeping me from trusting Him more? I have a few reasons. I think it is because I do not see what He sees. Or maybe I do not fully comprehend His faithfulness. Also, I have this incorrect idea that if I trust Him completely, I am being lazy. Like, I feel that I'm not doing enough on my own if I trust Him fully. I guess it could be like a passenger in a car. Because I am sitting there letting someone else drive, I feel like I'm not doing enough. I don't feel that way in real life as a passenger in a car, but somehow I can feel that way when it comes to trusting the Lord.

I don't see the whole picture of my life and what will be. But it doesn't matter because He does and I trust Him. Only with Holy

Spirit's help and with humility will I learn to trust Him more.

Many times I do not see the "why" of things, or "how," or "when." When this happens I might wallow in my blindness for a while, perhaps whine and feel weak about it, but finally return to quietly trusting in the Lord which strengthens me.

For thus said the Lord GOD, the Holy One of Israel, "In returning and rest you shall be saved; in quietness and in trust shall be your strength." ... (Isaiah 30:15 ESV)

I find that trusting in the Lord is easier when it becomes a necessity. When all the usual things you used to trust do not sustain you anymore. Or, do not even exist anymore.

Painful as it may be, it is actually a good thing when you are compelled to trust the Lord. I can look at it as practicing. When you practice something like playing a musical instrument, you get better at it over time. By the way, practicing is usually not fun. I can compare it to building up muscles in the body, too. With repeated use your muscles get stronger. Although, there are times when they're sore. So, again with Holy Spirit's help, as I practice trusting the Lord over and over I will get better at it. Hopefully, it will become easier as well.

Knowing the consistent and faithful histories of the mail being delivered and my car running causes me to trust in them. Likewise, one can look to the history of the Lord to know He can be trusted. Look in the Bible for the history of His faithfulness. Look at the past things He's done in your own life. Know that He keeps all His promises.

the God who made both earth and heaven, the seas and everything in them. He is the God who keeps every promise, (Psalms 146:6 TLB)

I must remember to trust Him when I do not see, and rely on Him when I do not know. Remembering His faithfulness and wisdom will help me to trust Him more too.

The Lord says: Cursed is the man who puts his trust in mortal man and turns his heart away from God. He is like a stunted shrub in the desert, with no hope for the future; he lives on the salt-encrusted plains in the barren wilderness; good times pass him by forever. But blessed is the man who trusts in the Lord and has made the Lord his hope and confidence. He is like a tree planted along a riverbank, with its roots reaching deep into the water – a tree not bothered by the heat nor worried by long months of drought. Its leaves stay green and it goes right on producing all its luscious fruit. (Jeremiah 17:5-8 TLB)

I like these verses. The tree that is compared to the man who trusts in the Lord experiences heat and long months of drought, but is not bothered or worried by them. I notice it doesn't say that it's free from heat and drought, but that it is able to endure it and actually stay green and keep producing fruit.

I like this passage from the Bible too. Right before David fought Goliath:

"Come over here and I'll give your flesh to the birds and wild animals," Goliath yelled. David shouted in reply, "You come to me with a sword and a spear, but I come to you in the name of the Lord of the armies of heaven and of Israel – the very God whom you have defied. Today the Lord will conquer you and I will kill you and cut off your head; and then I will give the dead bodies of your men to the birds and wild animals, and the whole world will know that there is a God in Israel! And Israel will learn that the Lord does not depend on weapons to fulfill his plans – he works without regard to human means! He will give you to us!" (1 Samuel 17:44-47 TLB)

In the face of seemingly impossible odds, David showed such confidence and trust in the Lord. It is amazing.

He will keep in perfect peace all those who trust in him, whose thoughts turn often to the Lord! Trust in the Lord God always, for in the Lord Jehovah is your everlasting strength. (Isaiah 26:3-4 TLB)

It is better to trust the Lord than to put confidence in men. (Psalms 118:8 TLB)

Who among you fears the Lord and obeys his Servant? If such men walk in darkness, without one ray of light, let them trust the Lord, let them rely upon their God. But see here, you who live in your own light, and warm yourselves from your own fires and not from God's; you will live among sorrows. (Isaiah 50:10-11 TLB)

If you want favor with both God and man, and a reputation for good judgement and common sense, then trust the Lord completely; don't ever trust yourself. (Proverbs 3:4-5 TLB)

When I am afraid, I put my trust in you. (Psalm 56:3 ESV)

My protection and success come from God alone. He is my refuge, a Rock where no enemy can reach me. O my people, trust him all the time. Pour out your longings before him, for he can help! (Psalms 62:7-8 TLB)

O my soul, why be so gloomy and discouraged? Trust in God! I shall again praise him for his wondrous help; he will make me smile again, *for he is my God!* (Psalms 43:5 TLB)

All those who know your mercy, Lord, will count on you for help. For you have never yet forsaken those who trust in you. (Psalms 9:10 TLB)

42

Worry

Trust and worry seem closely related. Without trust, worry has a place to thrive. Without ladybugs, aphids thrive. Aphids suck the sap out of plants, making the plants languish in various ways. Worrying can have the same effects on people.

Definition of worry: v. 1. To feel or cause to feel anxious or distressed. n. 1. Mental anxiety or distress.[1]

This issue has been one of the most challenging things for me to overcome. For years the Lord has told me, "don't worry." By His grace, I am doing better at this.

I did not take His instruction seriously enough. Usually when I say "don't worry" to someone, or I hear it said to me, I take it as an expression intended to console rather than a command to obey. If He said to me, "don't lie" I would take it seriously. So when He says, "don't worry" I want to take it seriously too.

I am aware of a few reasons for my worrying. I think it is related to how much I trust God. Also, pride makes me think I can better control a situation if I worry about it; better than God can. Which is untrue. Another reason is when I am not worried, I feel like I'm being lazy. Perhaps I feel like I'm accomplishing something worthwhile when I worry. Which is untrue. Let it go.

Can any one of you by worrying add a single hour to your life? (Matthew 6:27 NIV)

There is a saying, "God helps those who help themselves." I was surprised to discover that this is not in the Bible. I believe this saying is false. Believing wrong things such as this cause people, like me, to get caught in deception which is a terrible thing. Deception can be subtle.

If this saying were true, it would be just too bad for anyone who can't help themselves. Also, one could believe that they must help themselves in order for God to help them. Or, they might become proud in thinking that they were able to help themselves, so then God helped or blessed them as a result.

I hope I am not alluding that people should do nothing at all. Among other things, we are instructed to trust the Lord.

There are many verses in the Bible addressing laziness and the like, but that is another subject.

Here are a few Bible verses that I think counter "God helps those who help themselves":

When we were utterly helpless, Christ came at just the right time and died for us sinners. (Romans 5:6 NLT)

We felt we were doomed to die and saw how powerless we were to help ourselves; but that was good, for then we put everything into the hands of God, who alone could save us, for he can even raise the dead. (2 Corinthians 1:9 TLB)

Even when we are too weak to have any faith left, he remains faithful to us and will help us, for he cannot disown us who are part of himself, and he will always carry out his promises to us. (2 Timothy 2:13 TLB)

I bring the deception of this saying to light because I think the truth of the matter alleviates worry. This is a burden we do not have to carry.

Cast your burden on the LORD, and he will sustain you; he will never permit the righteous to be moved. (Psalm 55:22 ESV)

Give all your worries and cares to God, for he cares about you. (1 Peter 5:7 NLT)

So do not worry, saying, 'What shall we eat?' or 'What shall we drink?' or 'What shall we wear?' For the pagans run after all these things, and your heavenly Father knows that you need them. But seek first his kingdom and his righteousness, and all these things will be given to you as well. Therefore do not worry about tomorrow, for tomorrow will worry about itself. Each day has enough trouble of its own. (Matthew 6:31-34 NIV)

Be anxious for nothing, but in everything by prayer and supplication with thanksgiving let your requests be made known to God. And the peace of God, which surpasses all comprehension, will guard your hearts and your minds in Christ Jesus. (Philippians 4:6-7 NASB)

O my soul, why be so gloomy and discouraged? Trust in God! I shall again praise him for his wondrous help; he will make me smile again, for he is my God! (Psalms 43:5 TLB)

A psalm of David. The LORD is my shepherd; I have all that I need. He lets me rest in green meadows; he leads me beside peaceful streams. He renews my strength. He guides me along right paths, bringing honor to his name. Even though I walk through the valley of the shadow of death, I will fear no evil, for you are with me; your rod and your staff, they comfort me. You prepare a feast for me in the presence of my enemies. You honor me by anointing my head with oil. My cup overflows with blessings. Surely your goodness and unfailing love will pursue me all the days of my life, and I will live in the house of the LORD forever. (Psalm 23 NLT)

43

Beauty Is Vain

Charm is deceitful, and beauty is vain, but a woman who fears the LORD is to be praised. (Proverbs 31:30 ESV)

Definition of vain: 1. Having or showing undue or excessive pride in one's appearance or achievements : conceited. 2. Marked by futility or ineffectualness : unsuccessful, useless. 3. Having no real value : idle, worthless. 4. archaic : foolish, silly.[1]

I try to keep an open mind, but there are people I disagree with. There are some I disagree with repeatedly; we disagree on practically everything. Based strictly on this fact, if they agree with something I am very likely to choose the opposite.

Having this outlook is probably faulty to hold true to completely. But when it is applied to what the world values and what God values, having such a perspective can be very helpful. The world and God consistently disagree with each other.

Do not love this world nor the things it offers you, for when you love the world, you do not have the love of the Father in you. For the world offers only a craving for physical pleasure, a craving for everything we see, and pride in our achievements and possessions. These are not from the Father, but are from this world. (1 John 2:15-16 NLT)

So I have noticed how much attention the world gives to a person's physical beauty. It highly values it. This gives me cause to think the opposite.

People will choose what they value.

When presented with a box of chocolates, which one will you choose? What are they filled with? Personally, I think the kind with a cherry inside are disgusting. No matter how beautiful the outside is, I will not choose it. What is on the outside is not enough.

However, it is tempting. My first instinct would be to choose the prettiest one. How horrible it is to select it without using wisdom, bite into it and taste its sickening filling.

The Bible tells us that beauty is vain, but a woman who fears the Lord is to be praised. I would say the same pertains to a man. The Bible lets us know that beauty has no real value; it is useless, worthless, and futile. This is important to me because I believe the Bible is true, and in life I would like to value things that are truly valuable.

I realize this truth can be difficult to accept. Especially when the world we live in believes differently and so do our eyes. It is natural – to our old nature. We are called to more than that. This is where Holy Spirit must renew our minds and enable us to be different. We have received a new nature when we put our faith and trust in Jesus and received the Holy Spirit.

Death and Destruction are never satisfied, and neither are human eyes. (Proverbs 27:20 NIV)

The sinful nature wants to do evil, which is just the opposite of what the Spirit wants. And the Spirit gives us desires that are the opposite of what the sinful nature desires. These two forces are constantly fighting each other, so you are not free to carry out your good intentions. (Galatians 5:17 NLT)

Thank God! The answer is in Jesus Christ our Lord. So you see how it is: In my mind I really want to obey God's law, but because of my sinful nature I am a slave to sin. So now there is no condemnation for those who belong to Christ Jesus. And because you belong to him, the power of the life-giving Spirit has freed you from the power of sin that leads to death. The law of Moses was unable to save us because of the weakness of our sinful nature. So God did what the law could not do. He sent his own Son in a body like the bodies we sinners have. And in that body God declared an end to sin's control over us by giving his Son as a sacrifice for our sins. He did this so that the just requirement of the law would be fully satisfied for us, who no longer follow our sinful nature but instead follow the Spirit. Those who are dominated by the sinful nature think about sinful things, but those who are controlled by the Holy Spirit think about things that please the Spirit. So letting your sinful nature control your mind leads to death. But letting the Spirit control your mind leads to life and peace. For the sinful nature is always hostile to God. It never did obey God's laws, and it never will. (Romans 7:25-8:7 NLT)

Finding out that beauty is vain is an unhappy road for those who must travel it to understand it is true. This unhappy road can take different forms. It can mean striving for, and trying to maintain, physical beauty in order to be "loved." Or, missing opportunities because one is so shallow. It can even be realizing you married someone for the wrong reasons.

Do not let your adorning be external – the braiding of hair and the putting on of gold jewelry, or the clothing you wear – but let your adorning be the hidden person of the heart with the imperishable beauty of a gentle and quiet spirit, which in God's sight is very precious. (1 Peter 3:3-4 ESV)

I think these verses should be taken with wisdom and

discernment. For example, I don't believe it means one should never braid their hair. I believe it's saying that the heart is what matters, rather than the external. So let that be what is focused on.

Years ago, I was visiting my grandparents in the Philippines. I was staying at their home, and one day a lady came to visit them. I think I greeted her when she arrived and that's all. She saw me and apparently started to think about her son. She sat in the living room and called him on her phone. The point of her conversation was to see if he was interested in meeting me. His response was, "As long as she's pretty."

Without truth, guidance, and wisdom a girl could be satisfied with this. Or be beyond satisfied and think she was lucky someone was "interested." With truth, guidance, and wisdom a girl would know this is not right.

Again, people will choose what they value. We can see what the world values, and what we are told in the Bible is of no value. We can see what the world thinks is worthless, and what is precious to God. Which will you choose?

By Holy Spirit living in us, let us choose to disregard the ways of the world and our sinful natures, and instead regard the ways of God.

That's why those who are still under the control of their sinful nature can never please God. But you are not controlled by your sinful nature. You are controlled by the Spirit if you have the Spirit of God living in you. (And remember that those who do not have the Spirit of Christ living in them do not belong to him at all.) (Romans 8:8-9 NLT)

As a face is reflected in water, so the heart reflects the real person. (Proverbs 27:19 NLT)

When they arrived, Samuel took one look at Eliab and thought, "Surely this is the LORD's anointed!" But the LORD said to Samuel, "Don't judge by his appearance or height, for I have rejected him. The LORD doesn't see things the way you see them. People judge by outward appearance, but the LORD looks at the heart." (1 Samuel 16:6-7 NLT)

44

The Perspective of Love

A few months ago I got a puppy. His name is Cooper and he's a small, brown, mixed-breed dog.

The dog I had previously was named Blitz. He was a mixed-breed too, but primarily Jack Russell Terrier. He was the best dog in the world to me.

So, I did not expect Cooper to live up to my opinion of Blitz. Not just because of my high opinion of Blitz, but because I did not want to hold Cooper to that standard. I wanted him to have the freedom of being himself, so to speak. I wanted to value him individually; for his own character.

Blitz exhibited terrier qualities to the extreme. He was very smart, high-energy, and fearless.

Over these few months of having Cooper, I have noticed that he's very different from Blitz. He's sensitive and careful, but also very smart.

As I was contemplating the differences between the two dogs, the Lord taught me something. It is this: I valued both dogs independently from each other. I cared for them as they were. I saw that they were different, but that did not result in my feelings changing toward either of them. The Lord was teaching me that He loves and values people in the same way. Not on a scale of who is "better" than another, but individually.

This means something to me because I have wondered why the Lord would love me. In my way of thinking, there are a lot of other people that would be easier for Him to love. Then I remember that He purposely created each person and created them differently. This was no mistake because He doesn't make mistakes. He could have made everyone the same but did not.

I have observed a variety of birds at the bird feeder. I've noticed the behavior of Steller's Jays. (I call them blue jays.) They're quirky, loud, and they hop. With their tails flicking and the crest on the top of their heads rising and falling, they're almost always in motion. Then there are the Mourning Doves. Their little legs move one at a time when they walk; like a person. They seem docile because they don't chase other birds away from the feeder. Basically, they are very different from the blue jays in manner and appearance.

Obviously birds are different than people, but bear with me and let us imagine this: The dove is not concerned that it isn't like the blue jay. It doesn't pay it any attention, but goes about its business. Likewise, the blue jay doesn't go around wishing it were like the dove. They're different and it is good.

As a result of God using these observations, I've learned a few things. First, that God purposely created each person differently and it was no mistake. He loves and values each individually, as he made them. Also, I've learned to not compare myself to others. This isn't something I have decided on one occasion. I have to refrain from doing it each time I catch myself starting to compare.

One more analogy. Imagine an artist created two different paintings. One is a painting of a boat and the other a flower. The artist is very pleased with both of them. One day he sees the boat painting crying. "What's wrong?" he asks it. "Why did you make me like this? There must be something wrong with me. I'm not anything like the flower! Not at all!" The artist replies, "Because I planned a special purpose for you. You're going to a maritime art show. You will win a prize for me. I cannot use the flower there."

For we are God's masterpiece. He has created us anew in Christ Jesus, so we can do the good things he planned for us long ago. (Ephesians 2:10 NLT)

You made all the delicate, inner parts of my body, and knit them together in my mother's womb. Thank you for making me so wonderfully complex! It is amazing to think about. Your workmanship is marvelous – and how well I know it. You were there while I was being formed in utter seclusion! You saw me before I was born and scheduled each day of my life before I began to breathe. Every day was recorded in your Book! How precious it is, Lord, to realize that you are thinking about me constantly! I can't even count how many times a day your thoughts turn towards me. And when I waken in the morning, you are still thinking of me! (Psalms 139:13-18 TLB)

45

Asking

The subject of asking has been on my mind lately.

When one does not ask for something outright, the sincerity of their desire is in question.

One could be completely ready to give, is ready and waiting to give, but are simply waiting to be asked. That is all.

You will not always get it, but if you really want something you will ask for it.

Recently I happened to meet a guy I used to know. I had not seen or talked to him for months. We caught up with each other a little - talking about what has been going on in our lives. He said, "I should get your phone number again. I don't have it anymore." Over the course of the conversation this was repeated a few times. At the time I didn't really think about what I was saying, but each time he said that, I replied, "Yeah, you should." The conversation continued for a while and then we parted ways.

Looking back, I see why I did not give him my number. Because he did not ask. If he had asked me, I would have. I was not intentionally waiting to be asked. I was responding to him candidly, in the moment. Perhaps my communication skills were unsophisticated.

Yet, if I was intentionally waiting to be asked, would it have been wrong? Show me just a little more determination, if you are sincere, by asking instead of stating.

I understand there might have been some insecurity or pride involved. I mean, asking someone, "Can I have your number?" makes one more vulnerable than saying, "I should get your number," and then waiting for a response. Maybe that was his way of asking. Who is to know? Nevertheless, I believe if you really want something you will ask for it.

Many times, I was aware someone wanted something, but they did not ask me outright. But I was pleased to give them what they wanted if I could.

So, I bring the subject of asking over to spiritual matters. Is it important to ask God for things? I think it is. I certainly don't want to miss something simply because I do not ask Him.

Ask and it will be given to you; seek and you will find; knock and the door will be opened to you. For everyone who asks receives; the one who seeks finds; and to the one who knocks, the door will be opened. Which of you, if your son asks for bread, will give him a stone? Or if he asks for a fish, will give him a snake? If you, then, though you are evil, know how to give good gifts to your children, how much more will your Father in heaven give good gifts to those who ask him! (Matthew 7:7-11 NIV)

If any of you lacks wisdom, let him ask God, who gives generously to all without reproach, and it will be given him. But let him ask in faith, with no doubting, for the one who doubts is like a wave of the sea that is driven and tossed by the wind. For that person must not suppose that he will receive anything from the Lord; he is a double-minded man, unstable in all his ways. (James 1:5-8 ESV)

What causes fights and quarrels among you? Don't they come from your desires that battle within you? You desire but do not have, so you kill. You covet but you cannot get what you want, so you quarrel and fight. You do not have because you do not ask God. When you ask, you do not receive, because you ask with wrong motives, that you may spend what you get on your pleasures. (James 4:1-3 NIV)

This is the confidence we have in approaching God: that if we ask anything according to his will, he hears us. And if we know that he hears us--whatever we ask--we know that we have what we asked of him. (1 John 5:14-15 NIV)

It is good to ask God for spiritual and material things, remembering to always hold His will above our own. I believe we are to focus primarily on seeking God Himself, and asking for spiritual things. All our other needs will follow. We're told:

Seek the Kingdom of God above all else, and live righteously, and he will give you everything you need. (Matthew 6:33 NLT)

But seek first the kingdom of God and his righteousness, and all these things will be added to you. (Matthew 6:33 ESV)

It's important to be careful what you ask for. I've realized that sometimes I wasn't careful, and did not fully understand what I was asking for. Once I prayed that I would never take anything for granted. I think it was a good thing to ask for, but I did not expect what would happen for me to receive it. Try to count the cost of what you're asking for before you ask, and see if you really want it.

I think it's appropriate to add that the Lord can give without being asked. He knows what you need before you ask, and He knows your heart's desires.

Take delight in the LORD, and he will give you your heart's desires. (Psalm 37:4 NLT)

You know what I long for, Lord; you hear my every sigh.

(Psalm 38:9 NLT)

Do not be like them, for your Father knows what you need before you ask him. (Matthew 6:8 NIV)

The Lord was pleased that Solomon had asked for wisdom. So God replied, "Because you have asked for wisdom in governing my people with justice and have not asked for a long life or wealth or the death of your enemies--I will give you what you asked for! I will give you a wise and understanding heart such as no one else has had or ever will have! And I will also give you what you did not ask for--riches and fame! No other king in all the world will be compared to you for the rest of your life! (1 Kings 3:10-13 NLT)

I will share two experiences when I have found this to be true; two material things I have received from the Lord without asking.

I'm not a fan of mushrooms, but once about a year ago I felt like eating mushrooms. I think I thought about mushrooms for days. I did not tell anyone about it because it was unimportant. I had the opportunity to go purchase some, but I thought it was unnecessary so I did not. Shortly thereafter I came home to find a box of mushrooms on the kitchen counter. My dad bought them. This was very unusual. We rarely buy mushrooms, maybe once a year.

My second receiving-without-asking experience has to do with the pillow I sleep on. I'm involuntarily particular about pillows; it's a matter of what makes my neck hurt or not. I've tried many different pillows, only to find they make my neck hurt. Long story, but I finally found a pillow and it felt like I had found the only pillow in the world that would work for me. It was a decorative pillow, meant to be put on a couch or something, rather than be used in one's bed. It made my neck feel fine, but it was not ideal. It was oversized so I had to fit two pillowcases over it. Additionally, because of its size I was positioned farther away from the headboard when I slept, so my feet would be uncomfortably close to the end of the mattress. I had used it for a long time. One night I looked at the pillow discontentedly and thought, "I might have to live with this pillow the rest of my life."

Months later I'm in a store. I had no intention of looking for a pillow, but I found myself in the pillow aisle. I looked them over with some resentment, and hesitated to choose one. There were various ones to pick from. I did ask the Lord if I should get one, and if so, which one. So I left the store with a new pillow. I was not overflowing with hope that I would like it, but I had some hope about it.

The new pillow is actually more comfortable than the one I had been using. It's normal in size, so no more trouble with two pillowcases, etc.

I know some would say these experiences were just coincidences of life. But I know that they were not, and I thank the Lord for them.

Returning to our primary focus. Sometimes I think the Lord waits, and would like to see if we really want Him. Are we determined and sincere enough to ask Him? To pursue Him?

46

It's Gonna Happen

Chapter 11 of the book of Hebrews in the Bible is encouraging and thought-provoking to read. It helps one to persevere in faith. Listed there are wonderful examples of people's faith in God.

What is faith? It is the confident assurance that something we want is going to happen. It is the certainty that what we hope for is waiting for us, even though we cannot see it up ahead. Men of God in days of old were famous for their faith. (Hebrews 11:1-2 TLB)

Here I'll list some of the examples:

1. By faith – by believing God – we know that the world and the stars – in fact, all things – were made at God's command; and that they were all made from things that can't be seen (verse 3).

2. By faith Abel obeyed God and brought an offering that pleased God more than Cain's did. God accepted Abel and proved this by accepting his gift (verse 4).

3. Noah believed God's warning about the future even though there was no sign of a flood (verse 7).

4. Abraham trusted and obeyed God when God told him to leave home and go far away to another land which He promised to give him. So he went, not even knowing where he was going (verse 8).

5. Sarah had faith and because of this had a child despite her old age, because she realized that God, who gave her his promise, would certainly do what he said (verse 11).

6. Even while God was testing him, Abraham still trusted in God and his promises. He was ready to slay even Isaac, through whom God had promised to give Abraham a whole nation of descendants. He believed that if Isaac died, God would bring him back to life again (verse 17-19).

7. It was by faith that Joseph, as he neared the end of his life, confidently spoke of God bringing the people of Israel out of Egypt. He was so sure that he made them promise to carry his bones with them when they left! (verse 22).

I see that faith in God is believing that what God says is going to happen, is going to happen. It's gonna happen. What God says is truth; it is reality.

Faith is even more blind than I thought. I say that because the people in the listed examples did not see what was ahead. They did not have "proof," but believed God anyway.

It does not matter to God what seems impossible or improbable to people. It does not matter to Him what seems probable or a "sure thing" in mankind's point of view. What He does, and the faith we have in Him, do not depend on those things.

Again, faith is even more blind than I thought. Do I trust Him with my hopes that depend upon Him? Do I trust His word regardless of everything else?

Maintaining one's faith is essential. It always precedes seeing.

If sight or feelings support a person more than they depend on God in faith, what becomes stronger? Their dependence on sight and feelings. If one must cling to faith alone, faith becomes stronger, and that is what God wants for His people.

47

Hypocrisy

How can you think of saying to your friend, 'Let me help you get rid of that speck in your eye,' when you can't see past the log in your own eye? Hypocrite! First get rid of the log in your own eye; then you will see well enough to deal with the speck in your friend's eye. (Matthew 7:4-5 NLT)

Definition of hypocrisy: The feigning of qualities and beliefs that one does not actually possess or hold, esp. a pretense of piety or moral superiority.[1]

Everyone should avoid being hypocritical. Christians especially should be careful because we are supposed to be representatives of Jesus.

And whatever you do or say, do it as a representative of the Lord Jesus, giving thanks through him to God the Father. (Colossians 3:17 NLT)

When a Christian is being hypocritical, I believe they are lacking humility and fear of God. In addition, they may have forgotten that the good things they received were given; they did not earn them.

Being humble will help you to evaluate yourself accurately. With the fear of the Lord you will know that you are ultimately accountable to Someone who knows all things.

I must always remember not to be proud about anything good that I have, but be humbly thankful to God. The One who gave it to me. Without God, I am not good. God is good.

Holy Spirit's help, along with all these things, will enable a Christian to avoid being hypocritical.

Can you remember a time when you were criticizing a behavior of someone, and as you finish speaking you feel convicted? You know you're criticizing a behavior you have done, or still do. I have, and it is not an enjoyable moment to realize I was being hypocritical. On the other hand, I'm grateful that Holy Spirit works on my conscience like that. Being convicted is beneficial, if one is not too blind to see where they're wrong and not too stubborn to receive correction.

Fear of the LORD is the foundation of wisdom. Knowledge of the Holy One results in good judgement. (Proverbs 9:10 NLT)

Do you suppose, O man—you who judge those who practice such things and yet do them yourself—that you will escape the judgment of God? (Romans 2:3 ESV)

For what gives you the right to make such a judgment? What do you have that God hasn't given you? And if everything you have is from God, why boast as though it were not a gift? (1 Corinthians 4:7 NLT)

Not a single person on earth is always good and never sins. (Ecclesiastes 7:20 NLT)

48

You Are Mine

But now the Lord who created you, O Israel, says, Don't be afraid, for I have ransomed you; I have called you by name; you are mine. When you go through rivers of difficulty, you will not drown! When you walk through the fire of oppression, you will not be burned up–the flames will not consume you. For I am the Lord your God, your Savior, the Holy One of Israel, I gave Egypt and Ethiopia and Seba [to Cyrus] in exchange for your freedom, as your ransom. Others died that you might live; I traded their lives for yours because you are precious to me and honored, and I love you. Don't be afraid, for I am with you … (Isaiah 43:1-5 TLB)

I like these verses. The part where God says, "you are mine" is meaningful to me.

I've tried to imagine myself speaking those words to something or someone. To say those particular words, I would have to feel deep love. Whoever or whatever I was speaking to would be very cherished to me. To know that God speaks those words to His people means a lot.

These verses list various troubles that a person could go

through. Like, rivers of difficulty, and fire of oppression. We are able to survive these things because He is our God. Because He is our God. That alone is the reason.

I grew some peas in the garden this year. Before harvesting the pea pods, I tied a ribbon around the stem of each pod I wanted to keep for their seeds. This way, I would know not to harvest those ones. They would be left on the plant to fully mature and dry out. I could collect them later and plant them next year.

When I was harvesting the peas, sometimes I would mistakenly reach for one with a ribbon on it, see the ribbon, then let it remain on the plant. This made me think about how when we belong to the Lord, that simple fact (like the ribbon) can result in things happening or not happening in our lives. It's kind of like me reaching for a pea pod, seeing the ribbon, and then thinking, "Oh, nope. Hands off."

A little different angle on the same subject: think of the cars in Jay Leno's collection of vehicles. With his resources, I would expect a car in his collection is very well taken care of. I believe this because of his appreciation for vehicles, and his ability to take care of them. When we're in the Lord's collection, we too can expect similar things.

The Lord calls us His; "you are mine." He calls us precious, and honored. He loves us!

I guess I'd be pretty thrilled if someone told me they loved me, and I was precious and honored to them. Why not feel the same, if not more, when God says it? He calls us these things, and it means more than words.

49

Making Mistakes

I was praying and my mind began to wander. I thought about things that had nothing to do with praying. I realized what I did and felt bad about it. After all, here I am, able to have the amazing privilege of talking to God and I get distracted. What if I was talking with someone and I began to ignore them as my mind wandered? It's kind of rude. So I felt bad about it and said I was sorry to God and asked Him to forgive me.

He taught me something here. Something concerning more than one's mind wandering in prayer, but many other shortcomings, mistakes, and sins a person could do. He forgives and wants you to continue on without being burdened by your wrongdoing.

He does not love you only when you're doing everything right, and when you do something wrong ceases to love you. To believe this makes Him no better than man, and even less than that. His love is continuous and without variation. He doesn't change.

Whatever is good and perfect comes down to us from God our Father, who created all the lights in the heavens. He never changes or casts a shifting shadow. (James 1:17 NLT)

I am the LORD, and I do not change. That is why you descendants of Jacob are not already destroyed. (Malachi 3:6 NLT)

Jesus Christ is the same yesterday and today and forever. (Hebrews 13:8 NIV)

When you do something wrong, repent, ask for forgiveness, and know that He has indeed forgiven you. When I've done something wrong, and confess it to Him and ask for forgiveness, sometimes I still feel guilty for a while before I think He's not upset with me anymore. I hope initial remorse does exist and sins are not taken lightly, but after we're forgiven let us move forward without being weighed down. Don't take it unnecessarily hard. He wants us to keep progressing.

Note that He does more than forgive.

If we confess our sins, he is faithful and just to forgive us our sins and to cleanse us from all unrighteousness. (1 John 1:9 ESV)

Love keeps no record of wrongs.

It does not dishonor others, it is not self-seeking, it is not easily angered, it keeps no record of wrongs. (1 Corinthians 13:5 NIV)

God is not unloving, ever. Remember He's patient and understanding. Like a loving parent, He wants and helps His children to grow in necessary ways.

For the LORD corrects those he loves, just as a father corrects a child in whom he delights. (Proverbs 3:12 NLT)

He will not always chide, nor will he keep his anger forever. He does not deal with us according to our sins, nor repay us according to our iniquities. For as high as the heavens are above the earth, so great is his steadfast love toward those who fear him; as far as the east is from the west, so far does he remove our transgressions from us. As a father shows compassion to his children, so the LORD shows compassion to those who fear him. For he knows our frame; he remembers that we are dust. (Psalm 103:9-14 ESV)

50

Remembering Eternity

From time to time I observe things that go on around me and feel saddened. These things are world events, the ways people live, wrong becoming right - the general deterioration of morality that is manifested in many ways.

This not only makes me feel sad at times, but want to see goodness preserved and restored. I found these verses reassuring:

"Blessed are those who hunger and thirst for righteousness, for they shall be satisfied. (Matthew 5:6 NASB)

"Blessed are those who mourn, for they shall be comforted. (Matthew 5:4 NASB)

Living in the world can make one fixated on their brief life on earth. We may lose our focus on what it most important, and forget eternity.

The unrighteousness in the world can slowly skew our perspectives. For example, one knows what is right, but they see it disregarded by the world. Their friends and family do not follow it, so the question may come to their mind, "Does it really matter?" The conviction to live righteously begins to wear off. Right and wrong become blurred.

Adjust your perspective by remembering Who and what we're living for.

These verses from Hebrews 11 are referring to the men of God in days of old:

If they had wanted to, they could have gone back to the good things of this world. But they didn't want to. They were living for heaven. And now God is not ashamed to be called their God, for he has made a heavenly city for them. (Hebrews 11:15-16 TLB)

We're living for God now, and for eternity. This world is not our home.

But we are citizens of heaven, where the Lord Jesus Christ lives. And we are eagerly waiting for him to return as our Savior. (Philippians 3:20 NLT)

Wherever your treasure is, there the desires of your heart will also be. (Luke 12:34 NLT)

"But when these things begin to take place, straighten up and lift up your heads, because your redemption is drawing near." (Luke 21:28 NASB)

As we wait for Christ's return, let us be diligent to do His will. Hold tightly to the things God has taught you. Don't let the tentacles of the world touch you, no matter how subtly they come. Be free as a bird from those things. You belong to God, not to this world. Don't compromise right for wrong.

He who is steadfast in righteousness will attain to life, And he who pursues evil will bring about his own death. (Proverbs 11:19 NASB)

With all the appealing things the world has to offer, and the momentum of the frenzied crowds racing toward those things, living the Christian life can feel like you are walking against strong winds. Press forward. The enticing things of the world - don't even turn your head to look. You're living for eternity.

But you are a chosen race, a royal priesthood, a holy nation, a people for his own possession, that you may proclaim the excellencies of him who called you out of darkness into his marvelous light. (1 Peter 2:9 ESV)

"You are the salt of the earth. But what good is salt if it has lost its flavor? Can you make it salty again? It will be thrown out and trampled underfoot as worthless. (Matthew 5:13 NLT)

Therefore, since we are surrounded by such a huge crowd of witnesses to the life of faith, let us strip off every weight that slows us down, especially the sin that so easily trips us up. And let us run with endurance the race God has set before us. (Hebrews 12:1 NLT)

Endure suffering along with me, as a good soldier of Christ Jesus. Soldiers don't get tied up in the affairs of civilian life, for then they cannot please the officer who enlisted them. (2 Timothy 2:3-4 NLT)

Heaven and earth will pass away, but my words will never pass away. (Luke 21:33 NIV)

51

Love Letter

Beloved,

How are you today? I'm writing to remind you that I love you. My love for you is very strong, it never weakens. I've always loved you – from the very beginning. Before you even knew Me.

I know everything about you. I know all your struggles and hardships, joys and sorrows. My eyes are never off of you. When everyone else is looking the other way, My eyes are focused on you. I've never stopped thinking about you.

Sometimes when difficulties come, I know you doubt My love for you. Believe that I love you; don't try to feel it. My love for you never fails.

I see all the things you do. I know you're trying. Beloved, I love you perfectly – now. I never loved you more or less. I love you as much right now as when we meet in heaven.

My child, My love for you is so great. It cannot be expressed in words. I wish you knew just how much I love you. You are Mine, My very own.

52

It's a Trap

Fear of man is a dangerous trap, but to trust in God means safety. (Proverbs 29:25 TLB)

Definition of fear: n. 1. Alarm and agitation caused by expectation or realization of danger. 2. Reverence : awe. 3. A state of dread or apprehension.[1]

I think this verse can be interpreted a couple different ways. First, it can mean being afraid of man is a trap. Second, it can mean revering or regarding man is a trap. The second way is what I'll write about.

Stop trusting in mere humans, who have but a breath in their nostrils. Why hold them in esteem? (Isaiah 2:22 NIV)

Don't be concerned with meeting the obligations or expectations of people. Their opinions are very fickle, changeable, and of no worth. It is a trap, and can ensnare a person in many ways. Focus on pleasing God instead. His ways are steady, sure,

and pure. His love is given truly.

I want to make clear that I'm not writing about not loving others. We're supposed to love others. There is a difference between loving others, and endeavoring to win their approval. It's trying to win their approval that is a trap.

Also, I don't mean to ignore advice, constructive criticism, or correction from other people.

I want to concentrate on regarding the approval or disapproval of people above the approval of God and above what can ensnare your soul. Don't be selfish, but don't be deceived - protecting your soul does not equal selfishness. A person's soul is their mind, will, and emotions.

Meeting obligations created by people (others or yourself) can mean sacrificing too much. An example I can share has to do with someone I know. I will call him Peter. His brother lives many miles away. When he comes to town there is the opportunity to see him. However, based on a lifetime of experiences, Peter does not enjoy taking this opportunity. With the intention of making him ignore his own reasons for feeling this way, this reason was given: "But he's your brother." Sometimes, being related to someone is not enough reason.

It is what it is, but don't sacrifice too much for meeting obligations. A person's soul suffers for it. One could be swayed to and fro, meeting the obligations of everyone their whole life and end up living for other people. I feel like I'm speaking more to myself than anyone else when I say this, but you have to learn how to say "no."

I think expectations are very similar to obligations, especially to someone who is sensitive to others. Sometimes a person's health is sacrificed when they try to meet expectations – expectations that they do not have to meet. In addition, a person's self can be sacrificed when trying to meet expectations. Soon, you don't recognize yourself because you've been trying to become who someone else would like you to be.

One personal example comes from when I used to work at the library. I was minding my business, putting books away, when a

stranger came up to me and told me to smile. I obliged, but I cannot say it was genuine.

Laughter can conceal a heavy heart, but when the laughter ends, the grief remains. (Proverbs 14:13 NLT)

I think it is so annoying when people tell me to smile. It's bad enough telling someone how they should look. On top of that, this is like someone's telling me how to feel on command and that bugs me. I think to myself, "Please leave me alone. If my face displeases you, just don't look." It has happened to me more than once and it has always come from a man. I do not understand what logic they use to decide this is appropriate to say to someone. Especially someone they don't know. If they think telling me to smile accomplishes anything positive for me, they're deluded. I will restrain myself from ranting more about this pet peeve of mine, because I would go further off topic for too long.

Despite this, when I would see this stranger again in the library, I would feel slightly self-conscious of my smile-less face. As if his expectation of me mattered.

If I continued to let this feeling of someone's expectation affect me, it could result in two things that aren't good. I could become self-conscious of my face whenever I'm not smiling in the presence of others, which is an unnecessary burden for anyone. Also, I could make myself smile, and become something I'm not. Similar snares and the creation of mental baggage to a person's soul could follow conformity to other kinds of expectations. This really is a trap.

People's opinions are very fickle, changeable, and of no worth. I can see this when I go to a car show. Someone will think a car is absolutely stunning, and the next person will not be impressed at all. How is either opinion worth anything? It doesn't change what the car is.

Another example from my time working at the library: I was putting books away, as usual, and this guy complimented me on what I was wearing. It was a nice compliment. Months later at the library, the same man tells me, "You look downright slovenly." I

had to consult a dictionary to know what that meant. I admit I was not dressed like I was going out for afternoon tea, but it wasn't that bad in my opinion. So, people's opinions are changeable, and they are opinions.

Just because something is of no worth definitely doesn't mean people will treat it as such. I think part of the problem is that people have a need to be loved and valued. If they feel like they're loved and valued based on these things that have no value (meeting obligations and expectations and receiving approval by people), it may not matter to them. They're getting the high, so why does genuine contentment matter? A counterfeit is never better than the real thing, but it will be embraced when a person thinks they have nothing else.

Fear of man is described as a dangerous trap. It catches a person. Sometimes it can be like something you drag around with you through life.

Revere and regard God instead. His approval has value. His ways are unchanging and pure. There is no flaw in his motives. He is always loving. I believe He doesn't have opinions because He is truth.

Desire His approval. Even if you're surrounded by people with smiling faces, nodding their heads in approval of you, don't be satisfied with that. Or, possibly deceived by it. Look to Him and see if He approves. That's what matters. It's kind of like if you're in a group of people and they agree with you on something, but somehow that doesn't matter because you're looking at the one you love and want to see what they think.

For they loved human praise more than the praise of God. (John 12:43 NLT)

"Your approval or disapproval means nothing to me, for as I know so well, you don't have God's love within you. I know, because I have come to you representing my Father and you refuse to welcome me, though you readily enough receive those who aren't sent from him, but represent only themselves! No wonder

you can't believe! For you gladly honor each other, but you don't care about the honor that comes from the only God!" (John 5:41-44 TLB)

I think it's very interesting that when Jesus spoke in the previous verses, He said, "Your approval or disapproval means nothing to me, for as I know so well, you don't have God's love within you." It makes me think that I should especially disregard the approval or disapproval of those who don't have God's love in them. Additionally, I believe I should pay more attention to what someone who has God's love within them says.

but just as we have been approved by God to be entrusted with the gospel, so we speak, not as pleasing men, but God who examines our hearts. (1 Thessalonians 2:4 NASB)

But Peter and the apostles answered, "We must obey God rather than men. (Acts 5:29 ESV)

53

Working Out

"Physical training is good, but training for godliness is much better, promising benefits in this life and in the life to come." (1 Timothy 4:8 NLT)

I am grateful that I have learned this lesson in part, and I'm continuing to learn it. It's been another epiphany of what is best in life. It definitely wasn't one I expected to learn.

It is kind of sad to see muscles, formerly developed and strong, slowly decrease and become weaker. How much more it is to see spiritual muscles decline!

There are obvious benefits to building physical muscles. There are greater and lasting benefits to developing spiritual muscles. Build those muscles of faith and trust!

How do you build up spiritual muscles? Feed yourself properly. I would suggest a diet of prayer (not just talking but listening too), reading the Bible, fellowship with other Christians, and other ways of learning about and knowing God.

An essential step to muscle strength is Holy Spirit baptism.

"And now I will send the Holy Spirit, just as my Father promised. But stay here in the city until the Holy Spirit comes and fills you with power from heaven." (Luke 24:49 NLT)

Once when he was eating with them, he commanded them, "Do not leave Jerusalem until the Father sends you the gift he promised, as I told you before. John baptized with water, but in just a few days you will be baptized with the Holy Spirit." (Acts 1:4-5 NLT)

Another way to build up spiritual muscles is to use them. Many times I've done this because I felt I had to. For example, I've had to exercise faith. It has usually not been fun to do this. It's hard! Especially if it hasn't been used and tested so much before. But with God's grace and time, it grows in strength.

Take a look at this verse:

Dear brothers, is your life full of difficulties and temptations? Then be happy, for when the way is rough, your patience has a chance to grow. So let it grow, and don't try to squirm out of your problems. For when your patience is finally in full bloom, then you will be ready for anything, strong in character, full and complete. (James 1:2-4 TLB)

This is a challenging thing to do – to be happy when the way is rough. But, look at the outcome. The end result is that you will be, "strong in character, full and complete." You will be ready for anything. I like that.

That particular word "squirm" was striking to me. It is exactly what my first reactions have been to my problems. I think, "How can I get out of this?" Then I've tried various ways to get out; squirming here and there to find a way out. It isn't easy to recognize your problem, and purposefully be still and let God run its course in your life. The point is to exercise your patience and faith in God. Also, this often acts as refinement in one's life; burning away the rubbish.

The "purposefully be still" part that I mentioned can sometimes

feel as though you are purposefully being still in flames. Your new nature knows this is beneficial, but your old nature wants to get out of the fire.

Remove the impurities from silver, and the sterling will be ready for the silversmith. (Proverbs 25:4 NLT)

Behold, I have refined you, but not as silver; I have tried you in the furnace of affliction. (Isaiah 48:10 ESV)

I can only thank God for teaching me this. It was only after many failed attempts to squirm out of my problems that I became still and trusted completely in God. As I wait, my patience and faith in Him are being exercised and are growing. Refinement is happening, too.

The NLT version of James 1:2 says: "Dear brothers and sisters, when troubles of any kind come your way, consider it an opportunity for great joy."

By God's grace, I have been able to do this from time to time. Sometimes this surprises me. When I'm faced with a difficult issue, I've actually been able to see it as an opportunity for building up trust in God. I have not really felt like myself when I am able to do this. I don't recognize myself; it's really not in my nature to do that. It's probably because it isn't my old nature, but my new one. Also, Holy Spirit enables me to see a problem as an opportunity for joy. There is no way I could do that on my own. It is encouraging to notice that I don't recognize myself in a situation such as this, because it shows me that I'm changing from what I used to be.

Imagine the effort and strain a person goes through to work out and develop physical muscles. Persistence and a lot of sweat goes into it. There are probably times when they feel they've reached their limit and want to stop. Similar things happen to a person when spiritual muscles are developed.

The day comes when a person has worked out long enough and are able to lift 50 lbs. easily. They could look at a 10 lb. weight and not be intimidated at the prospect of lifting it. The same could go for a person who has, by God's grace, developed spiritual muscles. They've gone through tests and trials. Now, when faced with another trial, they can overcome it with little difficulty. To God be the glory!

There are other spiritual muscles to grow and develop besides patience, faith, and trust.

We can rejoice, too, when we run into problems and trials for we know that they are good for us – they help us learn to be patient. And patience develops strength of character in us and helps us trust God more each time we use it until finally our hope and faith are strong and steady. Then, when that happens, we are able to hold our heads high no matter what happens and know that all is well, for we know how dearly God loves us, and we feel this warm love everywhere within us because God has given us the Holy Spirit to fill our hearts with his love. (Romans 5:3-5 TLB)

For you, O God, have tested us; you have tried us as silver is tried. You brought us into the net; you laid a crushing burden on our backs; you let men ride over our heads; we went through fire and through water; yet you have brought us out to a place of abundance. (Psalm 66:10-12 ESV)

So be truly glad. There is wonderful joy ahead, even though you have to endure many trials for a little while. These trials will show that your faith is genuine. It is being tested as fire tests and purifies gold--though your faith is far more precious than mere gold. So when your faith remains strong through many trials, it will bring you much praise and glory and honor on the day when Jesus Christ is revealed to the whole world. (1 Peter 1:6-7 NLT)

Moving to a somewhat related yet different subject, perhaps this verse is most meaningful and understood to those who have had physical problems:

That is why we never give up. Though our bodies are dying,

our spirits are being renewed every day. For our present troubles are small and won't last very long. Yet they produce for us a glory that vastly outweighs them and will last forever! (2 Corinthians 4:16-17 NLT)

It's true our physical bodies are dying; they're decaying. But, our spirit is being renewed each day. That is something to be thankful for, and is actually exciting. Despite the body, we can enjoy new growth and newness through revelations and relationship with God each day.

I heard someone talk about this once, and it is something to consider. I've heard the common, wistful wish, "Oh, to be young again!" I understand what is meant by that, but I believe there is a profit to growing older.

When a person grows old, what is there to look forward to anymore? I mean really? Yes, there are definite blessings to enjoy like retirement and grandkids. But, personally, I don't want to think that when you reach a certain age you just suffer with physical ailments, aimlessly exist, and wish you were young again until you die.

I think there is something more to sincerely look forward to, and that is knowing God more and more. In ways you just didn't when you were younger. Growing and functioning as He intends you to. Learning new things you never knew before, and having a closer relationship with Him. After all, becoming a Christian isn't a one-time thing you did and now you're done. That was the starting point.

But the godly will flourish like palm trees and grow strong like the cedars of Lebanon. For they are transplanted to the LORD's own house. They flourish in the courts of our God. Even in old age they will still produce fruit; they will remain vital and green. They will declare, "The LORD is just! He is my rock! There is no evil in him!" (Psalm 92:12-15 NLT)

I will be your God throughout your lifetime--until your hair is white with age. I made you, and I will care for you. I will carry you along and save you. (Isaiah 46:4 NLT)

54

The Vine

Remain in me, and I will remain in you. For a branch cannot produce fruit if it is severed from the vine, and you cannot be fruitful unless you remain in me. "Yes, I am the vine; you are the branches. Those who remain in me, and I in them, will produce much fruit. For apart from me you can do nothing. Anyone who does not remain in me is thrown away like a useless branch and withers. Such branches are gathered into a pile to be burned. (John 15:4-6 NLT)

When a person does things the Lord wants them to do, they are likened to a branch that bears fruit. The things He may have you do are so various I hesitate to give examples because I don't want to limit the possibilities. But for example, it could be preaching, teaching, pastoring, being a prophet, or becoming a missionary. Or, producing fruit in many other ways like being a "light" in your workplace or wherever you are, influencing for good, even speaking the right words to someone at the right time. It may seem big, or it may seem small. Whatever it is the Lord wants you to do, and you doing it can be called "fruit."

Sometimes the fruit itself can become the center of one's attention. It's appealing, and producing it can become a goal that unfortunately surpasses what should be the priority.

Bearing fruit for God is excellent and what He wants, but don't become so focused on the fruit you bear that you forget your fundamental attachment to the Vine. Apart from Him you can do nothing. If one's focus and pursuit is the work they're doing for God more than their relationship with God, it's like the connection between the branch and the Vine is compromised.

One's relationship with God is from which all these fruit come. He's the Vine, and we are branches.

Furthermore, don't work for the Lord only like He's your employer. Employee-employer relationships are sometimes cold. Also, they're often based on how well you work.

The Lord is so much more than that. Our relationship with Him is to be more than that too.

Enjoy your relationship with Him as your Father, or someone very close. An intimate friend.

It is a wonderful thing to enjoy the Lord, and not feel like your relationship with Him is some sort of obligation.

Don't lose that wisdom – to enjoy Him.

55

Why Do You Believe as You Do?

Quietly trust yourself to Christ your Lord and if anybody asks
why you believe as you do, be ready to tell him, and do it in a
gentle and respectful way. (1 Peter 3:15 TLB)

I read this verse and it made me consider what answer I would
give, if someone asked me why I believe as I do. The first reason
that came to my mind is it's so I can go to heaven.

What I believe is that Jesus was (and is) God's Son and He came
to earth to die and was resurrected. He died to pay for our sins, so
that when we believe in Him we have right standing with God and
eternal life.

Another reason why I believe as I do is because I want my life
to have meaning and purpose. Without receiving His salvation, I
could not know God. If I did not know God, my life would be
pointless. I would be spiritually dead. It would be like I was just
walking around on earth, doing some good things and some bad
things, but with no real or lasting reason for being here. Knowing
the One who created me gives purpose for my existence.

If I didn't know God I feel like I would be searching for

something more in life. I think some people feel that way inside themselves – that there is something more to life – and there is. I want to have that intended relationship with Him. Knowing the One who created me is fulfilling in a way nothing else can be. He is why I was created. Not for other people or for myself, but for Him.

The most logical reason for believing as I do is because it's such an awesome gift and opportunity. How could I refuse it? I cannot adequately compare it to anything, but I will give it a try anyway. Let's say someone wanted to give you a brand new car. In this imagination, choose whatever car would be most appealing to you. Would you refuse it? I hope I would not.

This comparison makes me think of when people win or are given a new car on T.V. shows and the like. They seem very excited about it. Perhaps I would react similarly, but I just notice the disparity in the appreciation of a car as opposed to salvation. How can anything be greater than the gift of life and right standing with God?

The gift of salvation that God offers us is undeserved; it's because of his mercy, love, and kindness that we can have it. This gift is peace between us and God, renewed relationship, as well as going to heaven. It's a gift of life rather than death; like being pardoned from death row. What a humbling and amazing gift this is. I think that's why in the Bible it's referred to as "Good News."

... I came that they may have life and have it abundantly. (John 10:10 ESV)

This Good News tells us that God makes us ready for heaven–makes us right in God's sight–when we put our faith and trust in Christ to save us. This is accomplished from start to finish by faith. As the Scripture says it, "The man who finds life will find it through trusting God." (Romans 1:17 TLB)

Therefore, since we have been made right in God's sight by faith, we have peace with God because of what Jesus Christ our Lord has done for us. Because of our faith, Christ has brought us into this place of undeserved privilege where we now stand, and we confidently and joyfully look forward to sharing God's glory. (Romans 5:1-2 NLT)

For Moses wrote that if a person could be perfectly good and hold out against temptation all his life and never sin once, only then could he be pardoned and saved. But the salvation that comes through faith says, "You don't need to search the heavens to find Christ and bring him down to help you," and "You don't need to go among the dead to bring Christ back to life again." For salvation that comes from trusting Christ–which is what we preach–is already within easy reach of each of us; in fact, it is as near as our own hearts and mouths. For if you tell others with your own mouth that Jesus Christ is your Lord, and believe in your own heart that God has raised him from the dead, you will be saved. For it is by believing in his heart that a man becomes right with God; and with his mouth he tells others of his faith, confirming his salvation. (Romans 10:5-10 TLB)

As for you, you were dead in your transgressions and sins, in which you used to live when you followed the ways of this world and of the ruler of the kingdom of the air, the spirit who is now at work in those who are disobedient. All of us also lived among them at one time, gratifying the cravings of our flesh and following its desires and thoughts. Like the rest, we were by nature deserving of wrath. But because of his great love for us, God, who is rich in mercy, made us alive with Christ even when we were dead in transgressions—it is by grace you have been saved. And God raised us up with Christ and seated us with him in the heavenly realms in Christ Jesus, in order that in the coming ages he might show the incomparable riches of his grace, expressed in his kindness to us in Christ Jesus. For it is by grace you have been saved, through faith— and this is not from yourselves, it is the gift of God— not by works, so that no one can boast. For we are God's handiwork, created in Christ Jesus to do good works, which God prepared in advance for us to do. (Ephesians 2:1-10 NIV)

56

Love

Love is patient, love is kind. It does not envy, it does not boast, it is not proud. It does not dishonor others, it is not self-seeking, it is not easily angered, it keeps no record of wrongs. Love does not delight in evil but rejoices with the truth. It always protects, always trusts, always hopes, always perseveres. (1 Corinthians 13:4-7 NIV)

The epitome of a high standard is the goal to love. Reading the attributes of love shows how difficult it is. It's a goal that just cannot be met without God.

The one who does not love does not know God, for God is love. (1 John 4:8 NASB)

We know how much God loves us, and we have put our trust in his love. God is love, and all who live in love live in God, and God lives in them. (1 John 4:16 NLT)

It is a shame that the mere mention of the word "love" can stir up bitterness in people. It can bring up memories of past experiences. Cynicism is expressed. If it's not shown outwardly, it can be felt inside; an internal eye-roll.

Unfortunately, people have reason to feel that way. How can words and actions attributed to love be reconciled to being hurt? They don't go together. Maybe it's better put this way: there is love and then there are imitations of it. The imitation hurts. People can become disillusioned with love because of their experiences with the imitation of it or their idea of it. Love is perverted by mankind, the world, sin, and evil.

In addition, people fail. A person with the greatest of intentions, who know and love God, and try their best to love still fail at times.

Love really does not equal torture. It is one of the most beautiful things there is, if not the most beautiful.

If you love someone, you'll want what is best for them. It's remarkable how often "love" suddenly disappears when it means one has to sacrifice something. Or, wait for something. I think it's actually pretty easy to tell if someone loves you when you learn what love is.

Showing love can be difficult because it may make one feel vulnerable or weak. It's kind of scary to express love and not have it returned or even received. However, there is no strength in being cold or surrounded by one's emotional barriers in the hope of being protected. That shows where one is weak or hurt.

Also, it stifles life. I believe love allows growth and forward movement. When there is no love, it's like there is nowhere to go from there.

Lookout for your soul, but don't become hardhearted despite how others behave. Don't become something other than what God created you to be. Be wise at the same time as you keep your love from growing cold.

Jesus mentioned one of the events that will signal his return is that people's love will be cooled because of sin.

Sin will be rampant everywhere and will cool the love of many. (Matthew 24:12 TLB)

I think it is fairly easy to see that happening now. Let's not let that happen to us.

Sometimes communicating with someone can be like a test of psychological gymnastics. There are so many underlying pains and insecurities that surface in different ways. It's amazing. It's just a fact that people have "stuff." What I have a choice in is how I handle it. With God's grace, I will handle it with love.

It can hurt first. When someone says something hurtful to me, my initial reaction is to write them off. That is closely followed by me wondering if I did something wrong. If that is ruled out and I get over myself, I see that there was more to it. I see that they were hurting inside in some way, and to soothe or protect themselves they spoke that way to me. It still hurt, but that feeling subsides and something between feeling sorry for them and sincerely wishing they didn't hurt takes its place.

Loving others takes humility and sacrifice. It's necessary in even the smallest, daily dealings with people. For example, someone is irritable and impatient. I cannot respond to that by matching their irritability and impatience. If I do, it causes strife. There's just something that you have to give to others; it's love and understanding. Another example is when you find yourself in a position where you can rightly say to someone, "I told you so!" I don't mean that you should never say that to someone. I suppose there are times when that could be beneficial, but most of the time it just makes one feel superior and highlights the fact that someone else was wrong. That does not seem edifying or loving to me. Final example: you hear someone expressing some sort of suffering they went through. Like, "I had a tooth pulled today. I hate going to the dentist ..." One could respond with, "That's nothing. Once I had two wisdom teeth extracted and the anesthetic was barely working!" The one-upping in this situation is not loving. It makes the person who was one-upped feel like what they went through was irrelevant. Sometimes I have to stop thinking of myself so much and extend a little consideration.

By the way, love doesn't always equate to making everyone

happy.

Something I noticed about loving others is that your old nature must die in order to love. This must die: I want, I will, I have a right, me first. Sometimes when I feel broken inside is when it seems easiest to love. Perhaps I'm able to be more compassionate at those times. When I feel "strong" and self-satisfied is when it's the hardest. It takes incredible surrender and real strength to love. So I must try my best, but ultimately depend on Holy Spirit (God) in me to show Himself (love) through me.

If you love your neighbor as much as you love yourself you will not want to harm or cheat him, or kill him or steal from him. And you won't sin with his wife or want what is his, or do anything else the Ten Commandments say is wrong. All ten are wrapped up in this one, to love your neighbor as you love yourself. Love does no wrong to anyone. That's why it fully satisfies all of God's requirements. It is the only law you need. (Romans 13:9-10 TLB)

57

Hearing His Voice

After he has gathered his own flock, he walks ahead of them, and they follow him because they know his voice. They won't follow a stranger; they will run from him because they don't know his voice." (John 10:4-5 NLT)

My sheep hear my voice, and I know them, and they follow me. (John 10:27 ESV)

So I wanted to hear the voice of God. I really wanted to.

I read these verses and learned that God's people know His voice. I was a Christian and had been baptized in His Spirit, so how come it seemed I did not just "know" His voice? This troubled me. It can be frustrating to want to understand or know something so much, but feel like you don't have all the answers.

I wanted to know His voice; I didn't want to hear just any voice and think that was God when it wasn't.

Perhaps the journey of others to knowing God's voice differs from mine, but for me it took some time. There were occasions where I knew I heard God's voice, and there was no other explanation for knowing this than that unexplainable "knowing." Other than those occasions, it has taken me some time to know His voice and I'm still learning about this. I have not yet heard His voice audibly. So far it's been inside.

I realize sharing this subject to most people would make me seem mentally unwell. That's understandable. But, it is undeniable that much of the Christian life is supernatural and cannot be confined to human understanding.

Spend time with Him to know His voice. Pray and be quiet so you can listen for His voice. When I do this I have to make a conscious effort to quiet the thoughts in my mind. Sometimes it takes a while before I can quiet my mind. If I'm upset in some way, it can be harder to hear. Being at peace helps open your spiritual ears. I've heard that fasting helps too. With His help, over time you can distinguish your own thoughts from His voice, as well as from the enemy's. His voice will never contradict the Bible.

Don't be surprised as you try to learn and discern God's voice, that the enemy or your own old nature will make you question your sanity. You may think, "What am I doing? Am I actually listening to voices? This is what insane people do. I couldn't share this with anyone because they would think I'm crazy." Or, you may be spoken to in the first person, "I'm going crazy." This could be an ideal tactic to make you stop what you're doing and miss a wonderful thing.

Remember that God has given us a sound mind. Recall this Scripture and believe it to dispel such thoughts:

For God hath not given us the spirit of fear; but of power, and of love, and of a sound mind. (2 Timothy 1:7 KJV)

Here's a tip. I've noticed it isn't unusual for the enemy to say accusatory things. Like, "You always do that. You never listen." In contrast, when the Lord corrects me I feel like an inner unrest; like my conscience is being touched or pulled. Also, sometimes when the enemy says things it's as if he's labeling you; you've got certain bad habits and always will be that type of person. With the Lord, it's like He knows your issues but wants to help you change.

It always takes faith to know His voice, and it takes God from start to finish. I can do my part, spending time with Him etc., but it's always Him who really enables all of this to happen.

It is a precious thing to hear His voice. Some things He will say to you will touch your very heart and leave you completely disarmed. I believe He wants His people to hear His voice on a personal level. He loves you. Would he not want you to hear His voice?

In addition to the things I mentioned before, if you would like to hear God's voice I encourage you to ask Him to speak to you and help you know His voice. Ask for discernment too. Take those verses from the book of John as a fact or a promise; that His own know and hear His voice. That includes you. Remember, hearing His voice is for all who are His. Not just some; He has no favorites.

I feel I must add that God can speak to whoever He wants to – even those who don't know Him. The apostle Paul was eagerly persecuting Christians when the Lord spoke to him and changed his life.

58

"It's Just a Joke."

This is a perspective of mine. I know it is not for everyone, but I hope that anything true I've written is retained and anything untrue is rejected.

If someone had the skill of telling jokes that did not insinuate, demean, or deceive, I would be impressed.

So many times saying "it's just a joke" is an excuse to cover up something wrong that was said, or an excuse to say something wrong. It's code for, "What I said was wrong but you should be ok with it because I called it a joke." In addition, many times it shows that a person was not straightforward enough to say what they meant, so they masked it in a "joke."

When a person has to tell you what they said was a joke indicates it really wasn't. (Or, on rare occasions, it was simply a bad one.) They may even say, "You can laugh. It was a joke." Instantly, I look inward and think: "It must be me. Did I miss something? But what they said wasn't right. I must not have a sense of humor ..." It's not a matter of lacking a sense of humor at all. It's just that the "joke" was garbage.

I used to feel obliged to feign a laugh at someone's unfunny joke, and still do sometimes. If I didn't laugh, I felt like I was letting them down. Because I knew they wanted me to laugh, and if I didn't I felt like I was making them uncomfortable. By God's grace I'm learning things, and I should feel no guilt in letting someone's joke fall flat. Especially if it insinuates, demeans, or deceives.

I know I may be encouraged to "lighten up." But, I will not lighten up if it means truth, righteousness, and love is compromised.

To honestly believe what someone is telling you, and then be told "it's just a joke" initially makes one feel naïve and gullible. But, instead of hearing them say "it's just a joke," it's more like hearing them say, "what I just told you isn't true." Don't feel bad that you respected them enough to believe they meant what they said.

This makes me think of when I hear people telling children lies. Also known as fairy tales, manipulation techniques, and the catch-all: "joking around." I can see on the child's face that they are fully believing what this "adult" is telling them. Their interest is piqued and they're all ears. The adult may think this is amusing, but when the truth is finally revealed, the child realizes they were told lies.

Just as damaging as a madman shooting a deadly weapon is someone who lies to a friend and then says, "I was only joking." (Proverbs 26:18-19 NLT)

Sometimes I wonder if people think or care about what they say. If they don't care about how it can affect others, perhaps they might care about how it effects their own reputation.

How many people love the truth spoken in love? Some love speaking the truth, but wield it like wrecking ball, without love. Personally, I want my love of truth to increase. With love, I would like to prefer truth over my people-pleasing tendencies.

I hope I'm not inferring that it's right to be offended. Don't get stuck in being offended. One must forgive and overlook an offense. I'm trying to explain that there is importance to truth with love, and jokes often get a free pass in observing truth with love simply because it is called a "joke." The label doesn't change what it is. Also, I'm expressing my disappointment in seeing that this doesn't matter to many people.

A person's wisdom yields patience; it is to one's glory to overlook an offense. (Proverbs 19:11 NIV)

Whoever forgives an offense seeks love, but whoever keeps bringing up the issue separates the closest of friends. (Proverbs 17:9 GWT)

Indeed, we all make many mistakes. For if we could control our tongues, we would be perfect and could also control ourselves in every other way. (James 3:2 NLT)

Make allowance for each other's faults, and forgive anyone who offends you. Remember, the Lord forgave you, so you must forgive others. (Colossians 3:13 NLT)

I don't expect people who don't have God's Spirit living in them to care about the truth of most jokes, but I do expect Christians to give this some consideration.

Obscene stories, foolish talk, and coarse jokes--these are not for you. Instead, let there be thankfulness to God. (Ephesians 5:4 NLT)

You brood of snakes! How could evil men like you speak what is good and right? For whatever is in your heart determines what you say. A good person produces good things from the treasury of a good heart, and an evil person produces evil things from the treasury of an evil heart. And I tell you this, you must give an account on judgment day for every idle word you speak. (Matthew 12:34-36 NLT)

Instead, we will speak the truth in love, growing in every way more and more like Christ, who is the head of his body, the church.

(Ephesians 4:15 NLT)

59

Dangers of Idealism, Self-Worth, and Pleasing God

Definition of ideal: n. 1. A conception or standard of perfection. 2. One considered a perfect model. 3. An ultimate objective : goal. 4. An honorable principle or motive.[1]

Definition of idealism: n. 1. The practice of seeing things in ideal form. 2. Pursuit of high-minded or worthy goals.[2]

Recently the Lord has been teaching me about a serious flaw of mine. I'm very grateful for that, because I don't want to experience any more damaging results from it. With His help, I can change my ways now.

It took a while to figure out what it was. It's not perfectionism. I don't believe perfection is attainable. Also, I'm not the kind of person that cares about keeping my room spotless, or cares if items are precisely arranged in my closet. Many times I will look at something and decide, "It's good enough." What I've been learning is that I have been an idealist toward myself.

When I get an idea in my mind, I get too determined to accomplish it. It has been at my own expense. I set standards for myself that were too high, but have failed to see that despite the many signs. Until recently, I was not aware I did this.

I looked at my past and saw how this flaw has been repeatedly harmful to me. One example is when I used to work at a library. I worked as a Page, otherwise known as the one who shelves the stuff that people return. When I was a new employee, I took my time with shelving. But, I became bored quickly. To interest myself I increased my speed to see how fast I could shelve and remain accurate. My efficiency was noticed by my supervisor and others, and it kind of became my new standard or expectation of work. I know pride was a factor, but I had it in my mind to achieve a certain level of work. This had zero benefit to me because I was paid by the hour. Nevertheless, I was determined so I pushed myself. After all, working at my optimum capacity seemed like a great ideal. Every day my body was saying this is too much. It doesn't seem like this job would be physically demanding, but it was. I was pushing 100 lb.+ carts of books, squatting approximately 40 times an hour for multiple hours, and lifting books – all as quickly as I could. Near the end of my employment at the library I was extremely unhappy, feeling burned out, and I truly believe I hated books. In the end, I injured myself and I'm still recovering nearly a year later.

This idealistic flaw of mine goes beyond how I have pushed my body. It has affected certain relationships. Again, I would have an idea in my mind and I was intensely focused to achieve it. I could easily see all the things that seemed ideal for me to do. I would try too hard and do too much. Although it probably did not show in my words or facial expressions, it showed in my actions. I did things I hated, but in my mind it didn't matter because the sacrifices were worth it. But, I'm learning that certain things should not be sacrificed. With the Lord's help, I will not make these mistakes again.

I can see this flaw evident in many other past experiences.

I would try too hard and then suffer for it. I would get fixated on reaching my idealistic goals. It can be difficult for me to see what I think is ideal, and purposely achieve less than that. But, that is what I'm learning I should do for my sake. I cannot forfeit common sense and my well-being for idealistic goals.

The more I think about idealism, the more senseless it seems. To make a mockery out of it, it would be like sacrificing oneself on an altar of idealism. Lying pathetically upon the altar, with their dying breath they would whisper, "I did it. I was an ideal employee." It's senseless!

One of the deceptions of idealism is the idealist thinks what they're doing is right. It makes sense to them. Being the ideal employee or the ideal friend seems very good and commendable, but not at any cost.

Idealism is a heavy burden to bear. The ideal is rarely met. As one tries to reach it, there is a lot of suffering. The first thing to be disregarded in the pursuit of the ideal is myself. I see that I did not regard myself as I would other people. I wasn't even kind to myself like I would be to others. For instance, if I failed at something I would think, "How could I do that? Why? What was I thinking?" But, if someone else failed at the same thing, I would think, "It's ok. They'll do better next time." When one is idealistic toward themselves they live with anxiousness, futile obligations, harsh self-criticism, and a feeling like you haven't been good enough.

This makes me think of the commandment in the Bible about loving your neighbor as much as you love yourself. Here's a question: do I love myself as much as I love my neighbor?

There are byproducts of idealism. There is pride. The idea that, "I can do this. I can achieve this when others would have given up." Also, there's the desire to control. Basically, to control the process to reaching the ideal, so I feel more assured I can actually reach it.

That saying I've heard about never giving up does not help the idealist at all. There are times when you must give up.

Another thing that doesn't help the idealist are the results they enjoy from reaching the ideal. There is praise from others, even acceptance. Perhaps there is a rare moment of feeling satisfied with themselves. Reaching an ideal is one struggle, but it's a greater struggle to feel the need to consistently maintain an ideal. Like my work at the library.

So I was wondering, what caused me to think in this dysfunctional, idealistic way? Where did it originate? I have to retrace my history. First, it comes from feeling I need to prove myself. Why? Because I don't feel adequate. Why? Because of various perspectives resulting from life experiences. What life experiences?

I don't bring up these experiences to relay a sob story or place blame anywhere. I bring them up in the hope that it will be beneficial to people, including me. It goes back to my childhood. I know that's a cliché. Nevertheless, I feel like a lot of dysfunction can begin in one's childhood because children are so impressionable. They have no preset worldview or even a definition of who they are, unless they are told or it's formed from personal experiences. It's like their perceptions and identity are formed by others at that age. Often, it stays with them and affects their lives as adults.

Going back to my life experiences and why I felt inadequate – the beginnings of idealism for me. One example I remember is as a kid, under the age of seven I guess, I would like to draw. I'd draw typical pictures of trees and birds, etc. Pleased with what I drew, I would show it to a family member. My childish drawing would be critiqued. "This line could be straighter. Why don't you color in the trees?" Then it's like I'd go back to the drawing board and improve on what I already thought was good. I didn't do good enough. This memory seems like a silly little thing – almost nothing - but it effects. Also, the enemy will try to use anything to bring people into dysfunction, and the earlier the better.

A big factor in feeling inadequate comes from how I am. I'm normally a reserved person. Shy, introverted, whatever terms that accurately describe it, that's my nature. It's how I am. I've always been that way. As a small child, I was oblivious to the fact that I was different from most people in this way until it was made clear through many experiences. Then, I was very aware of it. For an impressionable youth, the simple fact that they aren't like most people makes them feel like there's probably something wrong with them. After all, if the majority are a certain way, it should follow that that is normal and the minority is not normal … not true. Also, the extroverted/entertainer type is more admirable in society than the introverted/observing type, especially for a girl. Somehow, quiet, reserved behavior is more acceptable for a man. "He's the strong, silent type." While a talkative, "bubbly" girl is more acceptable. If she's quiet and reserved, there's a tendency to think she's aloof and stuck-up. But, that's not how I am. I care and I probably care too much. Just my thoughts and opinions. Back on topic: various things were said to me that basically made me feel like I wasn't enough; people wanted more from me. More talk, more outward shows of emotion, or something. "You're so quiet." "She's so quiet." "Just be yourself!" In the past, I would take this seriously. I felt I was displeasing to people, and I wasn't enough.

What was I doing that was so wrong? It's as if I was never meeting even the normal standard, so perhaps this resulted in me trying too hard in various situations later on in life.

When getting to know someone, I have actually taken it upon myself to warn them I am different.

By God's grace I know better now. I don't have to feel apologetic for how I am. In response to "Just be yourself!" I think, "I am being myself. Apparently that's not who you think I am, or what you really want." I'm going to be a little cynical here, but sometimes when I hear, "Just be yourself!" I think it's more like, "Just be how I want you to be. Be something I understand and something that makes me comfortable." Also, I've learned that being myself simply isn't pleasing to some people. That's all. Knowing the truth brings freedom.

So, recently my idealistic mindset was changed when it converged upon my relationship with the Lord. I have it fixed in my mind that I want to please Him. I began to take it upon myself to achieve my "ideal." My own idea of what would please Him. I thought, "I should read the Bible more. I need to listen to this audio sermon. I have to pray more." I feel like I was trying to make His will happen in my life (a.k.a. what would please Him) and be "enough." To continue with this mindset would make me feel burned out.

My idealism hindered the Lord's leading in my life and complicated matters. It made it all more difficult.

I don't have to be enough for Him. I never was or ever will be, anyway. That's why His love means so much. He loves me regardless. Think of that! He loves me as I am, right now. Someone loves me completely and perfectly. Figuratively, it doesn't matter if the lines in my childish drawing aren't straight. In His love, He covered my inadequacies at the cross. He made me perfectly acceptable to Him. He is the ideal.

That doesn't mean I can do anything I want because He made up for it at the cross; I don't want to take advantage of His grace. It means I don't need to achieve an ideal version of myself for Him. I couldn't if I tried, and He knows that.

In terms of His will happening in your life, there is something valuable to learn in letting Him lead you. It's necessary that He leads. Part of letting Him lead is making sure you're not trying to lead. He knows how to lead, and if I try to interfere it makes things complicated. Very rarely have I danced with someone following their lead completely; without cues like in round dancing. When I have, there is a certain amount of rest that I've experienced. Relying on someone else to lead was easy and restful to me. I didn't really need to think, but I followed. I believe it is like this with the Lord. There's a certain amount of rest when one trusts and relies on Him to lead. Take a breath and know He's got it handled.

That saying about doing it yourself if you want it done right or done at all isn't always true. A prime example of that is God's will. If anyone but Him starts and finishes it, it isn't right. He must be the leader; the dominant One. I have a part to play in it, but I don't take it upon myself to determine it or accomplish it. Also, how can I be expected to reach a destination I do not know? He knows the destination, so I should let Him get me there.

I think part of pleasing Him is to count on Him to lead you into doing what is pleasing to Him. It's your part to follow and obey. I feel like if one is not led and motivated by Him to do something for Him, they're doing it from themselves and it's not good. Look at this:

"Not everyone who says to me, 'Lord, Lord!' will enter the kingdom of heaven, but only the person who does what my Father in heaven wants. Many will say to me on that day, 'Lord, Lord, didn't we prophesy in your name? Didn't we force out demons and do many miracles by the power and authority of your name?' Then I will tell them publicly, 'I've never known you. Get away from me, you evil people.' (Matthew 7:21-23 GWT)

All of the things they did seem like amazing ways to please God. It makes sense. But, the things some people will do - prophesying, casting out demons, doing miracles - are not led by God and the Lord will even say He didn't know them! He will actually call them evil. Of course I believe God does lead and work through people to prophesy, cast out demons, and perform miracles. The difference lies in being led by God or by themselves. In following His will or yours. Another difference I see here is God knowing someone or not.

Before I continue I want to include this:

All Scripture is inspired by God and is useful to teach us what is true and to make us realize what is wrong in our lives. It corrects us when we are wrong and teaches us to do what is right. God uses it to prepare and equip his people to do every good work. (2 Timothy 3:16-17 NLT)

Do your best to present yourself to God as one approved, a worker who has no need to be ashamed, rightly handling the word of truth. (2 Timothy 2:15 ESV)

The Bible, given to us by God, is excellent and provides innumerable and tremendous benefits. I believe a part of "rightly handling the word of truth" as it says in 2 Timothy 2:15, means that we should study and know what is in the Bible. Also, the Lord can speak to a person through the Scriptures; leading them to certain verses or making things known to them as they read. I do not mean to say a word against it.

My own ideas of what please Him may not be what He wants me to do. For instance, I may think that reading the Bible every day is pleasing to Him. That makes sense. But, I would suggest that it is possible He may have someone refrain from reading the Bible for a time. Does this seem like a radical, un-Christian suggestion? He may want you to refrain from reading for a while for His own reasons. Maybe simply to rest. Maybe it's so you learn to come to Him directly in Spirit rather than making the Scriptures your God.

"You search the Scriptures because you think they give you eternal life. But the Scriptures point to me! Yet you refuse to come to me to receive this life. (John 5:39-40 NLT)

Furthermore, it is possible that a person could study the Bible all their lives and not know God. This could be compared to knowing all about the mechanical aspects of a car, but never drive it.

With all I've written taken into account, I believe I need to learn to expect more from Him. Expect more from Him and not from me. Depend and rely on Him more, instead of somehow relying on my own efforts. I must remember that He is faithful. I want to please Him, and I think an essential part of that is trusting Him to work things out in my life. I can't be the one that makes His will happen. He has to do it.

For God is working in you, giving you the desire and the power to do what pleases him. (Philippians 2:13 NLT)

For I am confident of this very thing, that He who began a good work in you will perfect it until the day of Christ Jesus. (Philippians 1:6 NASB)

The LORD will work out his plans for my life--for your faithful love, O LORD, endures forever. Don't abandon me, for you made me. (Psalm 138:8 NLT)

But by the grace of God I am what I am, and his grace to me was not without effect. No, I worked harder than all of them--yet not I, but the grace of God that was with me. (1 Corinthians 15:10 NIV)

Now may the God of peace, who through the blood of the eternal covenant brought back from the dead our Lord Jesus, the great Shepherd of the sheep, equip you with every good thing to do His will. And may He accomplish in us what is pleasing in His sight through Jesus Christ, to whom be glory forever and ever. Amen. (Hebrews 13:20-21 BSB)

60

Contentment

I would like a simple life. I would like simplicity and peace.

Does that not sound opposite of what the world offers and applauds? I feel like the world pushes being sophisticated over being simple. Complex ideas and theologies over the simplicity of truth. Hustling and stress (with all the "good" reasons for it) over peace.

Definition of contentment: n. Satisfaction : happiness.[1]

Is there another word so foreign to our culture? The word itself seems unfamiliar, let alone experiencing the condition of contentment.

In one way of thinking, the word and the condition would best be extinguished. For the sake of making money. Many businesses live off of discontentment. Why should I purchase that product or service if I'm content without it?

There are many factors that create discontentment in a person so they buy a product, service, or idea. One doesn't have to be very smart to see this is true. One example is advertising. Notice how it's suggested that if you don't buy a product, you will be unhappy, or be disapproved of by others. Discontentment makes money.

Beyond the monetary benefits of discontentment, the devil would like to use it to enslave the soul. This can be accomplished by first creating discontentment in one way or another. Then, one could become so focused on their discontentment and trying to remedy it, that they make bad choices. These choices can affect them throughout their life.

Material possessions are not truly fulfilling. Neither is being in need. To know and obey God, have enough, and be content with that is being rich to me. Add health to that, and what more could you want?

Material possessions may bring happiness for a while, but they do not lead to a fulfilling life. It's better to learn that now. Imagine working and chasing after money, making it one's life purpose. Thinking it will satisfy only to realize it doesn't. That would be a tragic lesson to learn. Can their riches save them? Will the money love them back? There's nothing wrong with money or being rich, but when money becomes your god there is something wrong. I only mention all this because I believe a lot of discontentment can come from this issue.

But people who long to be rich fall into temptation and are trapped by many foolish and harmful desires that plunge them into ruin and destruction. For the love of money is the root of all kinds of evil. And some people, craving money, have wandered from the true faith and pierced themselves with many sorrows. But you, Timothy, are a man of God; so run from all these evil things. Pursue righteousness and a godly life, along with faith, love, perseverance, and gentleness. (1 Timothy 6:9-11 NLT)

Take note that it says the love of money is the root of all kinds of evil, not money.

If you are content, other people may be bothered by this. For example, if you are unmarried, single, and content with it, other people can be discontented at your contentment. The conversation goes kind of like this.

"Do you have a boyfriend?"

"No."

"What?" (With an almost pained facial expression.)

"No, I don't."

"You have to meet some people. I'll get you out."

"No, it's ok."

I feel like I have disrupted their mental peace by my confession of singleness. I actually think they don't believe that I'm content about it. I don't mean that I'm not open to it changing at some point, but I'm not going to allow myself to be discontent about it and live as if my life revolves around meeting "the one."

On the other hand, I've experienced becoming discontented because someone else is. I see they're concerned about something, or are driven to obtain something. Then I think maybe I should be feeling the same way about it too. But, I realized I should not judge what I "should" be doing by what others are doing because that outlook is faulty and brings discontent.

The other day I had the opportunity of going on a trip to Seattle. I had no reason to go, but my parents were going and I could go with them if I wanted to. I tried to find a reason for going. I thought I could take the opportunity to go shopping at some of the stores that are not around where I live. Then I thought, "But I don't need anything. I don't even want anything." So I did not go to Seattle.

Of course, I could easily go to the mall and find things I might want, but what's the point? I typically don't find satisfaction in buying things I don't need. There are always pretty things to buy, but I've lost interest. It just isn't appealing to me. Not because I'm so loaded with material items, but because I just don't care. I do not care about name brands or if my handbag is on trend. I will buy a handbag if I need one, can afford it, and like it. Not always in that order.

The things I want cannot be bought. I'm kind of glad they cannot be bought because if they could, I know I would not be able to afford them. Despite wanting things that cannot be bought, I can still find contentment. I find it by looking to the Lord and knowing He's my God, remembering His promises and attributes, and trusting Him.

I was praying the other day, and I was saying to the Lord with great earnestness and turmoil in my heart, "I wish I understood!" Basically, I wish I understood everything – understood Him, understood why things happened the way they did, and much more. Afterwards, I thought to myself that I really don't want to need to understand. Instead, I want to trust the Lord. That way, understanding something or not won't determine whether I'm content or not. I can find contentment in trusting the Lord. I remember that He understands what I do not. If I only found contentment when I understood something, I may never find contentment because there are some things I will not understand.

What a wonderful thing it is when that red hot, burning question, "why?" cools into pure trust in God. Thank God for God.

To close, here are various verses from the Bible that I think relate to being content:

Better is a handful of quietness than two hands full of toil and a striving after wind. (Ecclesiastes 4:6 ESV)

Better a little with the fear of the LORD than great wealth with turmoil. (Proverbs 15:16 NIV)

Rich men are conceited, but their real poverty is evident to the poor. (Proverbs 28:11 TLB)

He fed you with manna in the wilderness (it was a kind of bread unknown before) so that you would become humble and so that your trust in him would grow, and he could do you good. He did it so that you would never feel that it was your own power and might that made you wealthy. Always remember that it is the Lord your God who gives you power to become rich, and he does it to fulfill his promise to your ancestors. (Deuteronomy 8:16-18 TLB)

Since the Lord is directing our steps, why try to understand everything that happens along the way? (Proverbs 20:24 TLB)

Trust in the LORD with all your heart; do not depend on your own understanding. (Proverbs 3:5 NLT)

Keep your life free from love of money, and be content with what you have, for he has said, "I will never leave you nor forsake you." So we can confidently say, "The Lord is my helper; I will not fear; what can man do to me?" (Hebrews 13:5-6 ESV)

"I am leaving you with a gift--peace of mind and heart. And the peace I give is a gift the world cannot give. So don't be troubled or afraid. (John 14:27 NLT)

And he said to them, "Take care, and be on your guard against all covetousness, for one's life does not consist in the abundance of his possessions." (Luke 12:15 ESV)

These people always cause trouble. Their minds are corrupt, and they have turned their backs on the truth. To them, a show of godliness is just a way to become wealthy. Yet true godliness with contentment is itself great wealth. After all, we brought nothing with us when we came into the world, and we can't take anything with us when we leave it. So if we have enough food and clothing, let us be content. (1 Timothy 6:5-8 NLT)

I am not saying this because I am in need, for I have learned to be content whatever the circumstances. I know what it is to be in need, and I know what it is to have plenty. I have learned the secret of being content in any and every situation, whether well fed or hungry, whether living in plenty or in want. I can do all this through him who gives me strength. (Philippians 4:11-13 NIV)

This should be your ambition: to live a quiet life, minding your own business and doing your own work, just as we told you before. (1 Thessalonians 4:11 TLB)

61

Speed

I write this from the perspective of a recovering idealist.

I'm learning that because of my previous mindset (idealism), functioning in my new mindset is an adjustment. I need to allow myself time to adjust.

While some may struggle with being motivated for further growth in the Christian life, I'm learning that I need to tame my "motivation" which isn't really motivation but the remnants of idealism. I must remember that I am not the one who makes God's will happen, He does. Also, I am not the one that sets the pace of that, God does. I need to dial down my motor.

Although this life is fleeting compared to eternity, it is not to be lived in a fleeting way. Things take time. Learning and growing take time. Do not be discouraged in the time it takes to learn. Don't rush through life.

Here's an analogy. A child is eating too fast, and a parent or someone tells them to slow down, "enjoy your food." I feel like I'm the child that's eating too fast; in trying to learn and grow. I need to slow down, and as much as I can, learn to enjoy each thing in life as it comes.

My dog, Blitz, would eat too fast. He would basically inhale food. I wondered if he even tasted what he ate or knew what it was.

There is a speed of living and activity in the world that inhibits introspection, growth, and even time with God. There's barely time to think. Often, when a person does have time to think, they're too tired to do so. I understand that. A lot of good can come from thinking, while at the same time not overthinking.

I observed something in the garden. While it may not be true across the board, I think it's worth mentioning. This is what I noticed: vegetables that are more substantial, like winter squash and root vegetables, take a significant amount of time to grow. In contrast, less substantial vegetables like lettuce, and summer squash don't take as much time. I have noticed this with flowers too. The flowers that spring up and bloom right away are often less impressive than flowers that take more time to grow. The flowers that grow quickly are still very attractive, I don't mean that they aren't. It's kind of hard to express what I mean. A Bachelor's Button flower seed doesn't take long to germinate and produce blooms. I'm guessing 2 to 3 months. An orchid from seed to bloom would take much longer, maybe years. So, it is an interesting observation to me that substantial vegetables and flowers seem to take more time to grow.

Can this be applied to the speed of growth for people? That the longer it takes a person to grow in different ways means there will be more impressive results? I cannot say, but people grow at different rates of speed and if one grows slower than another it does not necessarily mean it is wrong.

I'm not sure what my point is in all of this, except to say to allow yourself time to grow and learn. It is a process; enjoy it as much as you can. Be patient with yourself. Again, don't become discouraged in the time it takes to learn. Faster isn't always better.

Do not be anxious about anything, but in every situation, by prayer and petition, with thanksgiving, present your requests to God. (Philippians 4:6 NIV)

Besides being wise, the spokesman also taught the people what he knew. He very carefully thought about it, studied it, and arranged it in many proverbs. The spokesman tried to find just the right words. He wrote the words of truth very carefully. Words from wise people are like spurs. Their collected sayings are like nails that have been driven in firmly. They come from one shepherd. Be warned, my children, against anything more than these. People never stop writing books. Too much studying will wear out your body. (Ecclesiastes 12:9-12 GWT)

62

Value Systems

I like the way a value system is described in the article, "Have a Personal Value System" by Z. Hereford:

A personal value system is a set of principles or ideals that drive and/or guide your behavior.

Your personal value system gives you structure and purpose by helping you determine what is meaningful and important to you.

It helps you express who you are and what you stand for.

If you are unaware of, or become disconnected with your values, you end up making choices out of impulse or instant gratification rather than on solid reasoning and responsible decision-making.

Your values define your character. They impact every aspect of your life including:

- personal and work behaviors
- your interactions with family, friends and co-workers
- your decision-making processes
- the direction you take in life.

This is why it is so important to know what you value, why you value it and what precedence it takes in your life.[1]

What is your value system? What do you live by?

The value systems of the world and mankind are skewed and even opposite of God's value system, which is truth. His ways bring life and freedom. The other value systems are deceptive. One thinks they're endeavoring in something of value, or that they are placing value on things accurately.

The Bible gives us God's value system. It guides us in how we should live. There are many straightforward truths to be found there. They show us wisdom and what God values.

It's really a great blessing that God has given us the right value system. On my own, using limited knowledge, I would not want to create something so important as a value system for life.

God gave Solomon very great wisdom and understanding, and knowledge as vast as the sands of the seashore. In fact, his wisdom exceeded that of all the wise men of the East and the wise men of Egypt. He was wiser than anyone else, including Ethan the Ezrahite and the sons of Mahol--Heman, Calcol, and Darda. His fame spread throughout all the surrounding nations. He composed some 3,000 proverbs and wrote 1,005 songs. He could speak with authority about all kinds of plants, from the great cedar of Lebanon to the tiny hyssop that grows from cracks in a wall. He could also speak about animals, birds, small creatures, and fish. And kings from every nation sent their ambassadors to listen to the wisdom of Solomon. (1 Kings 4:29-34 NLT)

I've often thought of Solomon, and all that he was able to do and experience in life. Much of it is listed in chapter 2 of the book of Ecclesiastes in the Bible. He did many things others could only dream of. Also, he had power and wealth that were so great it is not easy to comprehend. I notice many of these things fit very nicely into the value systems of the world as ways to find fulfillment. But, for Solomon they did not. They were futile. At the end of Ecclesiastes Solomon says, "Here is my final conclusion: fear God and obey his commandments, for this is the entire duty of man. For God will judge us for everything we do, including every hidden thing, good or bad." (Ecclesiastes 12:13-14 TLB)

God's value system is composed of important truths. Basics that God intends us to live by. They're not just rules for the sake of having rules. They are for our own good. However, they can be overlooked. When they are overlooked, the focus and trajectory of a person's life is misguided.

Living by the wrong value system is like trying to bake something with an incorrect recipe. The ingredients in the recipe are carefully measured and the instructions are followed. It seems to make sense and may feel right during the whole process. But, the final result is not what was wanted or expected.

Here's another way to look at it. God created people. He knows what is best for them and how things should work. Compare that to a car being designed and manufactured. A workshop manual and owner's manual are written for the car. That's what should be used in the care and use of the car, not manuals for a truck or motorcycle.

Notice the urgency and plain sense in calling out to a person to tell them they are going the wrong way. "Not that way, this way!" Even if they're heading the wrong way to something as simple as a certain street. How much more does the Lord call out to people to tell them they're going the wrong way in life, and with serious, life-altering consequences?

Choices in life are often decided by values. Choosing what is truly of value vs. what a person values more. God's way, or one's own way. If a person chooses a way other than God's way, that's their choice. God does not force a person to choose His way. He calls out, instructs, directs, suggests, warns, but many go their own way. I have chosen my own way plenty of times and it is not the right way to go.

One must trust that He knows the right way. His ways are always best. If that is not immediately apparent, it will be.

Let us choose God's value system as our own. When God's value system becomes a person's value system, much of the battle is won.

Do not become weary in doing good, obeying God, and seeking after Him and truth. So much of the other things in life on earth are meaningless. Like Solomon said – to obey God and keep His commandments, that is the duty of man. The Lord didn't tell man to achieve all these requirements that other value systems would demand. He said to seek first His Kingdom and His righteousness; give Him first place in your life and live as He wants you to.

… Teach these truths, Timothy, and encourage all to obey them. Some may deny these things, but they are the sound, wholesome teachings of the Lord Jesus Christ and are the foundation for a godly life. (1 Timothy 6:2-3 TLB)

Oh, that their hearts would be inclined to fear me and keep all my commands always, so that it might go well with them and their children forever! (Deuteronomy 5:29 NIV)

63

You

People weren't created to be robots for God. They don't carry out His will for their lives without any feeling or unique qualities. I believe when a person serves God their God-given individuality is expressed in the most beautiful way.

In the endeavor of serving God and living in His will, part of our selves are inevitably expressed as well as God Himself. I don't believe we were meant to lose our unique qualities in the process. God purposely made us different and that is utilized, not lost.

The Lord created people specifically. You are something special and cherished to God in a way nobody else is. You're not common. You're rare. If you were to die, God would not think, "Oh well, it's no loss. I'll just create another one" or, "It doesn't matter, Jane or John is about the same anyway." No one is like you, and there will never be another person like you! You may think, "That's a relief" that there is only one of you. But, think of someone who you admire or someone you think is better than you. God created only one of them, and determined that one was enough in that case as well.

Who knows and appreciates this more than God? I think most people who have owned a dog even know this. That each is special and there will never be another that is the same. When they're gone it's an irreplaceable loss. Nothing can bring them back.

I cannot emphasize the value of your uniqueness enough. Also, your talents, skills, and perspectives are important. Don't try to mimic others thinking you'll be more valuable that way. I think the different ways people function in the body of Christ is exquisite. The different perspectives of the same topic that God can give people is one example. Take a verse from the Bible and ask someone what they have learned from it. Then ask another person and they'll have learned something different from the same verse. Both can be true and the different perspectives edify. The differences God created in people contribute to His church and the Kingdom of God. The individual qualities of each person are needed.

The ways and venues in which God would have people fulfill His purpose for their lives are so diverse. Not everyone is meant to be in full-time ministry (like a missionary or pastor), but to be a godly influence in your particular sphere of influence.

God is not limited by what one thinks is likely or usual. He may use you in the music industry, in medicine, as a clerk in a store, as a fisherman, farmer, car salesperson, craftsman, or in painting pictures.

I would be careful not to be condescending toward a particular occupation that may seem lowly to the world. If that is where God wants you to be, that's the best place to be. For example, I would not scoff at someone who God chose to glorify Him through the growing and selling of flowers, and being an influence in their certain sphere. They would achieve more for the Kingdom of God doing that, rather than in any other occupation if that is what God wants them to do.

The Lord cares more about who you are than what you do for Him. It's the condition of one's heart that is most important, and the good "fruits" of that will naturally follow. He's interested in you more than your work for Him.

God sees your heart's desires and everything you think about. He sees all your dreams and hopes. All of them. Don't you think they mean something to Him? When you love someone you care about their hopes and dreams. You care about what they think.

You think about them all the time. You hear their name and your heart jumps. Your eyes scan the crowd looking for them, and everyone else is just a blur. You replay over and over again in your mind what they said to you and how they said it. You think of the things they like and don't have to try to remember them because they were seared into your psyche the moment you learned them. You remember their birthday. You know their middle name and why they were given it. You're out in public and out of the corner of your eye you think you see them, but it's only someone who kind of looks like them. You know and care about their perspectives on various subjects. You value what they think. You know the way they speak, walk, move, and the color of their eyes. When they smile at you, it feels like your backbone has disappeared, as did your peripheral vision. You see them speaking to someone and wish they were speaking to you. You see them treated unjustly and feel like taking the offender outside. You're uninterested in going to an event and ask, "Who's going to be there?" "There's Joe, Mary, Nathan, Anne …" and then they speak their name and it suddenly seems totally worth going. You're interested in this person like no one else. You're smitten and captivated. You love this person.

This person is you. All of this and more is all about you.

God loves you like this and so much more. Nobody will care for you and love you like He does. You're His own creation. He'll never abandon you. Nobody will understand you like He does. He knows you better than you know yourself.

O Lord, you have examined my heart and know everything about me. You know when I sit or stand. When far away you know my every thought. You chart the path ahead of me, and tell me where to stop and rest. Every moment, you know where I am. You know what I am going to say before I even say it. You both precede and follow me, and place your hand of blessing on my head. This is too glorious, too wonderful to believe! I can never be lost to your Spirit! I can never get away from my God! If I go up to heaven, you are there; if I go down to the place of the dead, you are there. If I ride the morning winds to the farthest oceans, even there your hand will guide me, your strength will support me. If I try to hide in the darkness, the night becomes light around me. For even darkness cannot hide from God; to you the night shines as bright as day. Darkness and light are both alike to you. You made all the delicate, inner parts of my body, and knit them together in my mother's womb. Thank you for making me so wonderfully complex! It is amazing to think about. Your workmanship is marvelous – and how well I know it. You were there while I was being formed in utter seclusion! You saw me before I was born and scheduled each day of my life before I began to breathe. Every day was recorded in your Book! How precious it is, Lord, to realize that you are thinking about me constantly! I can't even count how many times a day your thoughts turn towards me. And when I waken in the morning, you are still thinking of me! (Psalms 139:1-18 TLB)

Now God gives us many kinds of special abilities, but it is the same Holy Spirit who is the source of them all. There are different kinds of service to God, but it is the same Lord we are serving. There are many ways in which God works in our lives, but it is the same God who does the work in and through all of us who are his. The Holy Spirit displays God's power through each of us as a means of helping the entire church. (1 Corinthians 12:4-7 TLB)

I like how the following verses describe each believer as a part of the church, or the "body" of Christ. Every part is necessary and valued.

Our bodies have many parts, but the many parts make up only one body when they are all put together. So it is with the "body" of Christ. Each of us is part of the one body of Christ. Some of us are Jews, some are Gentiles, some are slaves and some are free. But the Holy Spirit has fitted us all together into one body. We have been baptized into Christ's body by the one Spirit, and have all been given that same Holy Spirit. Yes, the body has many parts, not just one part. If the foot says, "I am not a part of the body because I am not a hand," that does not make it any less a part of the body. And what would you think if you heard an ear say, "I am an ear, and not an eye"? Would that make it any less a part of the body? Suppose the whole body were an eye – then how would you hear? Or if your whole body were just one big ear, how could you smell anything? But that isn't the way God has made us. He has made many parts for our bodies and has put each part just where he wants it. What a strange thing a body would be if it had only one part! So he has made many parts, but still there is only one body. The eye can never say to the hand, "I don't need you." The head can't say to the feet, "I don't need you." And some of the parts that seem weakest and least important are really the most necessary. Yes, we are especially glad to have some parts that seem rather odd! And we carefully protect from the eyes of others those parts that should not be seen, while of course the parts that may be seen do not require this special care. So God has put the body together in such a way that extra honor and care are given to those parts that might otherwise seem less important. This makes for happiness among the parts, so that the parts have the same care for each other that they do for themselves. If one part suffers, all parts suffer with it, and if one part is honored, all the parts are glad. Now here is what I am trying to say: All of you together are the one body of Christ and each one of you is a separate and necessary part of it. (1 Corinthians 12:12-27 TLB)

God has given each of you some special abilities; be sure to use them to help each other, passing on to others God's many kinds of blessings. (1 Peter 4:10 TLB)

He is merciful and tender toward those who don't deserve it; he is slow to get angry and full of kindness and love. (Psalms 103:8 TLB)

The LORD appeared to me in a faraway place and said, "I love you with an everlasting love … (Jeremiah 31:3 GWT)

64

The Power of Truth

Truth destroys deception. Therefore, it destroys the ways that people are held from freedom and an abundant life.

It is a terrible thing when a person believes a lie, something false, a deception, fib, or whatever one wants to call it. The scope of consequences to this are vast. It can be as minor as believing that tomatoes are poisonous and so one lives their life avoiding tomatoes. Not because they wouldn't enjoy them, although they'd never know, but because what they believe is false. Or, it can be as life-altering as believing a form of abuse you suffered was your fault. One could go around their whole life carrying the baggage of guilt and shame and be unable to live freely.

Sin started in the Garden of Eden through believing a lie.

The serpent was the shrewdest of all the wild animals the LORD God had made. One day he asked the woman, "Did God really say you must not eat the fruit from any of the trees in the garden?" "Of course we may eat fruit from the trees in the garden," the woman replied. "It's only the fruit from the tree in the middle of the garden that we are not allowed to eat. God said, 'You must not eat it or even touch it; if you do, you will die.'" "You won't die!" the serpent replied to the woman. "God knows that your eyes will be opened as soon as you eat it, and you will be like God, knowing both good and evil." The woman was convinced ... (Genesis 3:1-6 NLT)

Lies may be presented to us in a way that seems somewhat reasonable at first. They come from oneself, others, or the devil. Don't think the devil is stupid. He'll approach you in a clever way. He wants you to listen to him, not scare you away or make his scheme obvious. Sometimes these deceptions first come through thoughts that question truth. This can then lead one to disbelief of truth and belief of the deception. Notice how the serpent began the conversation with Eve with the question, "Did God really say you must not eat the fruit from any of the trees in the garden?" before he spoke the lie, "You won't die!"

Some time ago I made some flash cards to help myself learn (and hopefully memorize) certain truths that combat certain deceptions. If a doubt/question leading to disbelief or a lie would come to my mind, I would remember the truth that specifically opposes it. I would read or rehearse the memorized truth in my mind to dispel the lie. So, on one side of a card I wrote a lie, and on the other side a truth (Bible verse) to counter it. For example:

One side would have the lie/question leading to disbelief: "Do your prayers really matter?"

If/when that question comes to my mind, I can fight it off by remembering this verse:

Confess your sins to each other and pray for each other so that you may be healed. The earnest prayer of a righteous person has great power and produces wonderful results. (James 5:16 NLT) (This truth would be written on the other side of the card.)

On another card, the lie: "I'll never change." (Struggling with sin.)

On the other side the truth: If we confess our sins, He is faithful and righteous to forgive us our sins and to cleanse us from all unrighteousness. (1 John 1:9 NASB)

It's encouraging to know that when Jesus was tempted in the wilderness (Matthew 4:1-11), He successfully resisted the temptations of Satan with Scriptures, with truth.

Pursue truth. Perhaps it isn't easy at first to keep rejecting the lies and holding fast to truth. It can feel like an effort and you might feel silly resisting deception. You can speak the truth out loud if you like. You may feel even more silly doing that. The devil would like you to feel silly resisting deception so that you don't do it. But, this is a very important issue and I would rather feel silly for a while and have truth, than feel practical and believe deception. Sometimes the deceptive thought isn't dispelled the first time you counter it with truth, but keep resisting. Don't allow yourself to be fooled.

So humble yourselves before God. Resist the devil, and he will flee from you. (James 4:7 NLT)

One aspect of the Bible I have appreciated, among many others, is that it is true. It is enjoyable to read something that is completely true, and does not contain misinformation.

Though I know it's full of truth, I have questioned myself, "Do I really believe the Bible is true?" I mean, how much? To what extent? Sometimes I skim over what I read and fail to realize the depth of truth. For example, these verses:

Joyful is the person who finds wisdom, the one who gains understanding. For wisdom is more profitable than silver, and her wages are better than gold. Wisdom is more precious than rubies; nothing you desire can compare with her. (Proverbs 3:13-15 NLT)

Do I really believe this is true about wisdom, or is it just some nice sentiment? I believe it is completely true. It is true, literally. Wisdom is worth more than silver, gold, and rubies. If a person had silver, gold, and rubies without wisdom, I imagine they would squander them. Also, how can rubies, gold, and silver keep a person from making the wrong choices?

More pertinent to the topic of this essay:

Jesus said to the people who believed in him, "You are truly my disciples if you remain faithful to my teachings. And you will know the truth, and the truth will set you free." (John 8:31-32 NLT)

Jesus said the truth will set you free. Again, this is not some amusing sentiment, but it is absolute truth.

There are many parables, analogies, metaphors, symbolism, etc. in the Bible. However, in many ways I believe I should take the Bible more literally.

When a person learns the truth it can change so much in their lives. Knowing the truth does set you free. Being "set free" can happen in many different ways. It can happen by knowing the truth of Jesus, or knowing the truth about various matters in your own life. Resulting in living an abundant life in freedom from baggage and slavery to sin. It can happen by knowing the truth about what the Lord has made available to us through Jesus and the Holy Spirit, and taking advantage of these needed and amazing things. As a result, living a life full of His Spirit, and being able to receive the gifts of the Spirit and use them as He intended. (1 Corinthians, chapters 12-14)

For you are the children of your father the devil, and you love to do the evil things he does. He was a murderer from the beginning. He has always hated the truth, because there is no truth in him. When he lies, it is consistent with his character; for he is a liar and the father of lies. (John 8:44 NLT)

Jesus answered, "I am the way and the truth and the life. No one comes to the Father except through me. (John 14:6 NIV)

They don't belong to the world, just as I don't belong to the world. "Sanctify them by the truth. Your word is truth. (John 17:16-17 ISV)

Then Pilate said to him, "So you are a king?" Jesus answered,

"You say that I am a king. For this purpose I was born and for this purpose I have come into the world—to bear witness to the truth. Everyone who is of the truth listens to my voice." (John 18:37 ESV)

See how I love your precepts; preserve my life, LORD, in accordance with your love. All your words are true; all your righteous laws are eternal. (Psalm 119:159-160 NIV)

Teach me your ways, O LORD, that I may live according to your truth! Grant me purity of heart, so that I may honor you. (Psalm 86:11 NLT)

Little children, let us not love in word or talk but in deed and in truth. (1 John 3:18 ESV)

65

Things Noticed

This is a list of various things I've noticed/lived. I hope it's not too unhappy to read, but I list these things purposely. There are some burdensome things people may notice and wish they weren't the only ones to notice. They wish someone else would notice too, so they would not be alone with these observations. Someone else to share in the same things they experience, and to understand. Some of them can seem too heavy to handle alone.

I suppose these things are not just noticed, but felt. I suppose if they were not felt in some way, it wouldn't matter that they were noticed. It's the emotions involved that are not enjoyable to bear, especially alone.

Some of them are not burdensome at all. They're just things I've noticed or thought about and wonder if anyone else does.

Some of them are semi-burdensome. Like, having a minor but annoying ache or pain, but not feeling like sharing it with anyone so they wouldn't be bothered, so you bear it by yourself.

It can feel lonesome to be alone with feelings, emotions, and observations. Yet, someone else does share in all these noticed and felt things. In a way nobody else can.

God is that someone else. I may feel like I notice a lot, but He notices everything. Things I do not notice. There is nothing He doesn't know. He doesn't miss a thing. There is no part or place on earth that His eyes do not see. Nothing goes unnoticed by Him in one's daily life, or in any secret place in their heart. Things even they do not know reside there. Nothing is hidden or unknown to Him. He really knows! I find great comfort in that. I can share things with Him and He doesn't get impatient or weary. If I don't share them with Him, He still knows. If there are things I cannot adequately share through words, He still understands. Furthermore, He understands what I do not.

So, here's the list.

Laughing to the point of tears turns to crying in a matter of seconds. Nobody else notices though, because it seems like you're still laughing.

Someone is subtly but intentionally left out of a group.

A person's words hurt someone but nobody else seems to notice.

A letter carefully written and addressed, but then purposely never mailed.

Realizing someone will never know how much you think/thought of them.

The thrill of being understood.

Realizing someone else was misunderstood.

Knowing someone so well, during a conversation you're 2 steps ahead of them, like in chess or something.

Knowing someone so well, you get a feeling from their body

language and tone of voice that they're about to say something you don't want them to say. Sometimes this situation is funny and sometimes it's not.

When someone is listening to you, or not.

When someone is doing more than their fair share of the work.

When you're the one who cared the most.

When you lost a material item you cared about.

Something so wonderful it seems unreal, so you try not to think about it very much in case it somehow disappears from reality.

The one waiting at the end of the line.

The purpose behind someone's line of questioning.

The delight of someone helping you or showing you kindness when you really needed it.

When you can see your actual reflection in someone else's eyes.

What a kind touch accomplishes in moment, words would have taken a lot longer.

When you know someone so well, body language is used to communicate and it happens to work seamlessly.

Picking up and throwing away a piece of trash that you did not drop there, and nobody seeing you throw it away.

Taking the blame and not shifting it.

Good and bad things left unsaid.

A wrong overlooked because of love.

Dreams that are not foolish and some that are.

When someone finishes your sentence better than you could.

When you are instantly happier knowing someone is where you will be.

When you know someone so well, by the velocity of their closing doors, drawers, cupboards, or by their uncharacteristic carelessness in handling objects, you know they're upset.

Favoritism.

Things only you and God know.

When your tears combine with the water as you shower, and it seems like you're bathing in tears.

When you cry yourself to sleep, and feel like it will be better in the morning. But you wake up the next morning and resume crying.

When someone you don't really know treats you how you wish someone you know treated you.

Looking at the moon and thinking of all the people in the past who have looked at the same moon.

Observing your eyes in the mirror and wondering what kinds of things these very eyes will see in the future.

When applying lip balm or some other product to your lips, you think about how they've never kissed anyone or been kissed.

Looking at other people and wondering what wonderful plans God has designed specifically for them.

The simple joy of running and laughing like a child.

The pretty spiral cowlicks in a dog's fur.

Realizing the hidden meaning behind why they repeatedly wanted to take you swimming.

Those sometimes private, unpleasant moments when you realize you were being a fool.

He knows all that we see and think. He knows all our dreams and desires. He knows all the intricacies of you; all and every complexity. None of them are a puzzle to Him.

You know what I am going to say before I even say it. (Psalms 139:4 TLB)

He knows about everyone, everywhere. Everything about us is bare and wide open to the all-seeing eyes of our living God; nothing can be hidden from him to whom we must explain all that we have done. (Hebrews 4:13 TLB)

This is my command--be strong and courageous! Do not be afraid or discouraged. For the LORD your God is with you wherever you go." (Joshua 1:9 NLT)

He determines the number of the stars; he gives to all of them their names. Great is our Lord, and abundant in power; his understanding is beyond measure. (Psalm 147:4-5 ESV)

The LORD looks down from heaven and sees the whole human race. From his throne he observes all who live on the earth. He made their hearts, so he understands everything they do. (Psalm

33:13-15 NLT)

Not one sparrow (What do they cost? Two for a penny?) can fall to the ground without your Father knowing it. And the very hairs of your head are all numbered. (Matthew 10:29-30 TLB)

You know when I sit and when I rise; you perceive my thoughts from afar. You discern my going out and my lying down; you are familiar with all my ways. (Psalm 139:2-3 NIV)

But Jesus the Son of God is our great High Priest who has gone to heaven itself to help us; therefore let us never stop trusting him. This High Priest of ours understands our weaknesses, since he had the same temptations we do, though he never once gave way to them and sinned. So let us come boldly to the very throne of God and stay there to receive his mercy and to find grace to help us in our times of need. (Hebrews 4:14-16 TLB)

66

Attributes of God Part 7: Mercy, Goodness, and Love

Definition of mercy: 1. Kind and compassionate treatment : clemency. 2. A disposition to be benevolent and forgiving. 3. Something to be thankful for.[1]

Clement: adj. 1. Merciful : lenient. 2. Mild, as weather : temperate. clemency – n.[2]

Lenient: adj. 1. Inclined to be forgiving and mild : merciful. 2. Not demanding : tolerant.[3]

Benevolence: n. 1. An inclination to do charitable or kind acts. 2. A charitable act.[4]

Mercy is truly something to be thankful for, as the definition says. I remember once I got a ticket for driving with expired license tabs. I was not aware they were expired when I drove the car. It wasn't even my car, but I didn't bother arguing with the officer. There was nothing to be argued and no excuse to be given, it was completely clear they were expired. Along with the ticket, there was the option to appear in court or write to the judge to contest it. I chose to write. Not to contest it, but to basically ask for mercy. I waited for a response from the judge and wondered if they were the kind who was strict or lenient. Eventually I received their answer in the mail; the ticket was waived. I was very thankful! I felt indebted somehow, because there was nothing good I did to merit this. The outcome was based on the judge's decision.

In my point of view, I feel it is easiest to show mercy towards someone who acknowledges that they've done something wrong. Yet, it can be shown when a wrong is not acknowledged.

They refused to obey and didn't pay any attention to the miracles you did for them; instead, they rebelled and appointed a leader to take them back into slavery in Egypt! But you are a God of forgiveness, always ready to pardon, gracious and merciful, slow to become angry, and full of love and mercy; you didn't abandon them, even though they made a calf-idol and proclaimed, 'This is our God! He brought us out of Egypt!' They sinned in so many ways, but in your great mercy you didn't abandon them to die in the wilderness! ... (Nehemiah 9:17-19 TLB)

"But the Lord our God is merciful, and pardons even those who have rebelled against him. (Daniel 9:9 TLB)

Let your remorse tear at your hearts and not your garments." Return to the Lord your God, for he is gracious and merciful. He is not easily angered; he is full of kindness, and anxious not to punish you. (Joel 2:13 TLB)

Therefore go and say to Israel, O Israel, my sinful people, come home to me again, for I am merciful; I will not be forever angry with you. Only acknowledge your guilt; admit that you rebelled against the Lord your God and committed adultery against him by worshipping idols under every tree; confess that you refused to follow me. O sinful children, come home, for I am your Master and I will bring you again to the land of Israel—one from here and two from there, wherever you are scattered. And I will give you leaders after my own heart, who will guide you with wisdom and understanding. (Jeremiah 3:12-15 TLB)

"This is a hard decision," David replied, "but it is better to fall into the hand of the Lord (for his mercy is great) than into the hands of men." (2 Samuel 24:14 TLB)

"O my God, bend down your ear and listen to my plea. Open your eyes and see our wretchedness, how your city lies in ruins–for everyone knows that it is yours. We don't ask because we merit help, but because you are so merciful despite our grievous sins. (Daniel 9:18 TLB)

Definition of good: 1. adj. Having desirable or favorable qualities. 2. a. Suitable : appropriate. b. Convenient. 3. Whole : sound. 4. Superior to the average : satisfactory. 5. Discriminating. 6. Salutary : beneficial. 7. Competent : skilled. 8. a. Sure : safe. b. Valid or sound. c. Genuine : real. 9. a. Ample : considerable. b. Bountiful. 10. Full. 11. Pleasant : enjoyable. 12. a. Virtuous : upright. b. Benevolent : cheerful. c. Loyal : staunch. 13. a. Well-behaved. b. Socially correct : proper. n. Something that is good. 2. Welfare : benefit. 3. Goodness.[5]

Although good is observed in people, no person is good all the time. People are always fallible. I believe when goodness is observed in someone, whether they believe in Jesus or not, it is a reflection of God's character. Since man was created in His image, there are similarities between God and man. Even evil people know how to give good gifts to their children.

If you, then, though you are evil, know how to give good gifts to your children, how much more will your Father in heaven give good gifts to those who ask him! (Matthew 7:11 NIV)

For the Lord is always good. He is always loving and kind, and his faithfulness goes on and on to each succeeding generation. (Psalms 100:5 TLB)

"When you call me good you are calling me God," Jesus replied, "for God alone is truly good ..." (Matthew 19:17 TLB)

In that way you will be acting as true sons of your Father in heaven. For he gives his sunlight to both the evil and the good, and sends rain on the just and on the unjust too. (Matthew 5:45 TLB)

"Love your *enemies!* Do good to *them!* Lend to *them!* And don't be concerned about the fact that they won't repay. Then your reward from heaven will be very great, and you will truly be acting as sons of God: for he is kind to the *unthankful* and to those who are *very wicked.* (Luke 6:35 TLB)

The Lord is good. When trouble comes, he is the place to go! And he knows everyone who trusts in him! (Nahum 1:7 TLB)

He isn't really being slow about his promised return, even though it sometimes seems that way. But he is waiting, for the good reason that he is not willing that any should perish, and he is giving more time for sinners to repent. (2 Peter 3:9 TLB)

Definition of love: n. 1. Intense affection. 3. Enthusiasm or fondness. v. 1. To feel love for. 2. To enjoy enthusiastically.[6]
Affection: n. A fond or tender feeling toward another.[7]
Fond: adj. 1. Affectionate : loving. 2. Having a liking or affection. 3. Immoderately affectionate : doting. 4. Deeply felt : cherished.[8]
Immoderate: adj. Exceeding normal bounds : extreme.[9]
I kind of like that word: immoderate. Exceeding normal bounds. Depending on what it is, I like it when something exceeds the norm. Part of the definition of love is "intense affection." All right, so what is affection? It's a fond feeling toward another. What is fond? Immoderate affection. So we go back to the definition of love: "intense affection." According to these definitions, love is an intense degree of immoderate (exceeding normal bounds) affection. I don't understand it perfectly, but I get the idea that it is a very

high, extreme amount of affection towards someone.

What can I really compare God's love to? Is it like the love between a parent and child? Or like the love between a husband and wife? In the Bible, God's love for His people is compared to these things. I think one could compare God's love to them, but in every earthly example there are failures and corruptions. God's love never fails and is not corruptible. He didn't love us because we loved Him first, or because we had something to give Him. His love is whole, pure, and perfect.

Is God's love explainable when it is just given? Love is explainable when it is given by someone because someone else, in their view, merits it. For example, because a person is talented, because they are accomplished, because they are wealthy, because they are attractive, or because they have enough good things going for them to merit their love. The "because" is accounted for in some way, but not when God loves.

How priceless is your unfailing love, O God! People take refuge in the shadow of your wings. (Psalm 36:7 NIV)

He didn't choose you and pour out his love upon you because you were a larger nation than any other, for you were the smallest of all! It was just because he loves you, and because he kept his promise to your ancestors. That is why he brought you out of slavery in Egypt with such amazing power and mighty miracles. (Deuteronomy 7:7-8 TLB)

But the Lord wouldn't listen to Balaam, instead, he turned the intended curse into a blessing for you, because the Lord loves you. (Deuteronomy 23:5 TLB)

Dear friends, let us practice loving each other, for love comes from God and those who are loving and kind show that they are the children of God, and that they are getting to know him better. But if a person isn't loving and kind, it shows that he doesn't know God– for God is love. God showed how much he loved us by sending his only Son into this wicked world to bring to us eternal life through his death. In this act we see what real love is: it is not our love for God, but his love for us when he sent his Son to satisfy God's anger against our sins. (1 John 4:7-10 TLB)

The lyrics of this hymn from 1917, The Love of God, speak in a moving way about God's love.

The love of God is greater far, than tongue or pen can ever tell
It goes beyond the highest star, and reaches to the lowest hell
The guilty pair, bowed down with care, God gave his Son to win
His erring child He reconciled, and pardoned from his sin

O love of God, how rich and pure!
How measureless and strong!
It shall forevermore endure
The saints' and angels' song

When hoary time shall pass away, and earthly thrones and kingdoms fall
When men, who here refuse to pray, on rocks and hills and mountains call
God's love so sure shall still endure, all measureless and strong
Redeeming grace to Adam's race, the saints' and angels' song

O love of God, how rich and pure!
How measureless and strong!
It shall forevermore endure
The saints and angels' song

Could we with ink the ocean fill, and were the skies of parchment made
Were ev'ry stalk on earth a quill, and ev'ry man a scribe by trade
To write the love of God above, would drain the ocean dry

Nor could the scroll contain the whole, tho stretched from sky
to sky

O love of God, how rich and pure!
How measureless and strong!
It shall forevermore endure
The saints' and angels' song

67

"I'm a Christian."

Ok, I've heard this statement before. I've said it about myself as well. I've learned that it doesn't always mean what I think it does.

Once, when I didn't know any better, I happened to meet a guy at a square dance. He seemed nice enough. Though he wasn't physically unattractive, I did not find him attractive. He was around my age and another solo dancer. He was obviously interested in me. Actually, probably not in me, but in eligible women. After recent past mistakes in giving out my phone number to people, I had already made up my mind that there was no way I was going to give him my number, should he ask. Near the end of the evening, he asked if I was a Christian and I told him yes. Then he told me he was too. When he said that, because I didn't know any better, it was like almost everything changed in my mind. As if one big, all-encompassing check mark was made on an imaginary list of requirements a prospective significant other should have. Suddenly he seemed a little attractive.

Well, I was sadly mistaken - sadly mistaken. Because I thought when someone said they were a Christian it automatically meant x,y, and z. It took me a painfully long time to learn that it doesn't automatically mean anything. One ironic realization was that he behaved worse, in my opinion, than some people who don't claim to be Christians. I wonder how many girlish tears have been spilled with this pitiful phrase on the lips or on the mind: "But he said he was _____ !" Fill in the blank. I wish that blank could never be filled with "a Christian."

Wake up and stop being a fool! I see here another example of how unfortunate it is to lack wisdom and knowledge. In particular, to disregard or be ignorant of what the Bible says. I feel if I had more wisdom and been better educated in what the Bible says, and actually followed it, I would have known that when someone says they're a Christian it doesn't necessarily mean anything. In fact, it can be a lie. Also, I would have known better ways to see someone for who they really are. Of course I have looked back on this unhappy chapter in my life and feel like I was awfully naïve. I dislike that very much.

My people are destroyed for lack of knowledge. Because you have rejected knowledge, I also will reject you from being My priest. Since you have forgotten the law of your God, I also will forget your children. (Hosea 4:6 NASB)

I think it's interesting to notice in this verse that the Lord is saying His people are destroyed for lack of knowledge. It's interesting to me because it shows that His own people can lack knowledge to the point of being destroyed because of it. I believe this destruction can be death, or different kinds of suffering in life.

I don't want to be foolish or lack knowledge. Perhaps I have tended/tend to believe what people say too much. Perhaps I tend to gloss over someone's actions because of what they say. There are some subjects people talk about that I have an easier time being skeptical toward. But, I feel like I was at a disadvantage when it came to him telling me he was a Christian. I have several reasons for feeling that way. First, there are several connotations to being a Christian that create specific expectations for me. For example, being truthful, doing what's right, and being loving. So, these were some of my expectations. Kind of like if I were to drive a Prius. I would have certain expectations. I would expect above average miles per gallon, a reliable vehicle, etc. Second, I feel that being a Christian is such a personal and meaningful part of one's life; a part of themselves. An inseparable part of their life. I did not expect it to be used falsely or not taken seriously. To me, it could be compared to telling someone you're not married, but you are. I mean, how can you be deceitful and/or flippant with something so meaningful like that? The fact is people can and do. Another factor that I feel put me at a disadvantage in this situation is when he told me he was a Christian, he hit my softest spot.

I thought of two possible explanations to why someone says they are Christian, but don't show it in their behavior. First, it can be that they are not a Christian at all. Second, they could be an immature Christian - a baby one.

One may ask, "But, how can you know what's in a person's heart? How can you judge if they are a Christian or not? Besides, Christians aren't supposed to judge." My answers are in these verses:

"Beware of false teachers who come disguised as harmless sheep, but are wolves and will tear you apart. You can detect them by the way they act, just as you can identify a tree by its fruit. You need never confuse grapevines with thorn bushes or figs with thistles. Different kinds of fruit trees can quickly be identified by examining their fruit. A variety that produces delicious fruit never produces an inedible kind. And a tree producing an inedible kind can't produce what is good. So the trees having the inedible fruit are chopped down and thrown on the fire. Yes, the way to identify a tree or a person is by the kind of fruit produced. Not all who sound religious are really godly people. They may refer to me as 'Lord,' but still won't get to heaven. For the decisive question is whether they obey my Father in heaven. (Matthew 7:15-21 TLB)

You brood of vipers, how can you who are evil say anything good? For the mouth speaks what the heart is full of. (Matthew

12:34 NIV)

When I wrote to you before I said not to mix with evil people. But when I said that I wasn't talking about unbelievers who live in sexual sin, or are greedy cheats and thieves and idol worshipers. For you can't live in this world without being with people like that. What I meant was that you are not to keep company with anyone who claims to be a brother Christian but indulges in sexual sins, or is greedy, or is a swindler, or worships idols, or is a drunkard, or abusive. Don't even eat lunch with such a person. It isn't our job to judge outsiders. But it certainly is our job to judge and deal strongly with those who are members of the church, and who are sinning in these ways. God alone is the Judge of those on the outside. But you yourselves must deal with this man and put him out of your church. (1 Corinthians 5:9-13 TLB)

Dear brothers, what's the use of saying that you have faith and are Christians if you aren't proving it by helping others? Will that kind of faith save anyone? If you have a friend who is in need of food and clothing, and you say to him, "Well, good-bye and God bless you; stay warm and eat hearty," and then don't give him clothes or food, what good does that do? So you see, it isn't enough just to have faith. You must also do good to prove that you have it. Faith that doesn't show itself by good works is no faith at all–it is dead and useless. But someone may well argue, "You say the way to God is by faith alone, plus nothing; well, I say that good works are important too, for without good works you can't prove whether you have faith or not; but anyone can see that I have faith by the way I act." Are there still some among you who hold that "only believing" is enough? Believing in one God? Well, remember that the demons believe this too–so strongly that they tremble in terror! Fool! When will you ever learn that "believing" is useless without doing what God wants you to? Faith that does not result in good deeds is not real faith. (James 2:14-20 TLB)

This passage from the book of James was a little hard for me to understand at first. The very mention of something other than believing being an important, if not vital, aspect in regard to the way to God was disturbing. But, notice the quotation marks around "believing." What I get from these verses is that true believing, as opposed to untrue "believing," will show itself in outward acts. So, these outward acts are described as a way to prove that you have faith.

There have been times when I've met someone, and because of how they behave I've suspected they were a Christian. Later, I find out that they are. I like that. To be known as a Christian because of your life and how you conduct it, and because you say you are. Rather than because one says they are and depending on how they live, that's the only evidence of their "faith." How sad it would be to know someone well, be told they identify themselves as a Christian, and be surprised by that because there was no clue that they were. I don't want to be that kind of person.

I am grateful for this important lesson. I value it not only because it is so important, but because it came at a very high price personally. Now when I hear someone say, "I'm a Christian," in my mind I wonder what they mean by that. I'm hopeful, but basically I have an I'll-wait-and-see attitude. Or, at worst, a prove-it-to-me attitude. I think the prove-it-to-me attitude isn't quite right. I think I feel that way because I was hurt, but I don't want to be resentful about it. Makes me think of all the very unfortunate times people say they are Christians but then go on to treat people badly, giving Christians a bad name. I've considered using a different way to describe what I believe. Like, instead of saying "I'm a Christian," perhaps I could say "I'm a follower of Jesus," "I believe in Jesus," or "I believe Jesus is Lord." Yet, a person could say those things and not really mean them either. I wish it were always true that when I hear a person say, "I'm a Christian" it means what it should mean. But then, I wish a lot of things. Truth can be like icy-cold water on one's face, but I prefer that over living in deception.

For salvation that comes from trusting Christ–which is what we preach–is already within easy reach of each of us; in fact, it is as near as our own hearts and mouths. For if you tell others with your own mouth that Jesus Christ is your Lord, and believe in your own heart that God has raised him from the dead, you will be saved. For it is by believing in his heart that a man becomes right with God; and with his mouth he tells others of his faith, confirming his salvation. (Romans 10:8-10 TLB)

And how can we be sure that we belong to him? By looking within ourselves; are we really trying to do what he wants us to? Someone may say, "I am a Christian; I am on my way to heaven; I belong to Christ." But if he doesn't do what Christ tells him to, he is a liar. But those who do what Christ tells them to will learn to love God more and more. That is the way to know whether or not you are a Christian. Anyone who says he is a Christian should live as Christ did. (1 John 2:3-6 TLB)

You will remember that before you became Christians you went around from one idol to another, not one of which could speak a single word. But now you are meeting people who claim to speak messages from the Spirit of God. How can you know whether they are really inspired by God or whether they are fakes? Here is the test: no one speaking by the power of the Spirit of God can curse Jesus, and no one can say, "Jesus is Lord," and really mean it, unless the Holy Spirit is helping him. (1 Corinthians 12:2-3 TLB)

68

Thought-Life

For though we live in the world, we do not wage war as the world does. The weapons we fight with are not the weapons of the world. On the contrary, they have divine power to demolish strongholds. We demolish arguments and every pretension that sets itself up against the knowledge of God, and we take captive every thought to make it obedient to Christ. (2 Corinthians 10:3-5 NIV)

It is important to be aware of our thoughts. Being able to discern which thoughts agree with truth is key. In addition, not every thought you have was originated by you; not every thought is your own.

This truth that one's thoughts should agree with is God's truth: what He says, how He sees things, what He's given to us in the Bible.

The main point I want to focus on from these verses from 2 Corinthians is the part that says "… and we take captive every thought to make it obedient to Christ." What does that mean? I will try my best to explain what I believe it means.

First, I believe we are responsible for what we think about. For example, when I wake up in the morning consciousness quickly comes to me and I begin to think. My thoughts race and I think about a lot of things that do not matter. I haven't even gotten out of bed yet and my head feels sore because I'm thinking so hard. I know the cause is thinking; I can choose to stop thinking and my head feels fine. What I've learned is that I can choose to be quiet in my mind and I do not have to think about things that do not matter. I will not accept that I have no control over my thoughts.

Refocusing on "… and we take captive every thought to make it obedient to Christ." Notice what thoughts you have. Do they agree with God's truth? Or do they disagree? Are they obedient to Truth, or disobedient?

A couple weeks ago I was feeling ill. To the point where I was actually willing/wanting to see a doctor. The types of symptoms I was having made me afraid. Afraid of what the symptoms could mean, and if they would get worse. I hate being afraid. Nevertheless, that's how I felt and many of my thoughts corresponded to that. A couple days after I saw the doctor I was still having symptoms. I just happened to be at the Home Depot when I felt the fear (and corresponding thoughts) strangely increasing. The fear began to outweigh the symptoms. I just knew it wasn't right. By God's grace I remembered this verse:

For God hath not given us the spirit of fear; but of power, and of love, and of a sound mind. (2 Timothy 1:7 KJV)

I rehearsed this verse over and over again in my mind. Specifically, the part that says, "… God hath not given us the spirit of fear; but of power …" I felt like I had a grip on not much else other than that truth. I had to reject the fearful thoughts and replace them with truth. "He hasn't given me a spirit of fear, but of power." After about 5 to 7 minutes I felt much better. My physical symptoms were still there, but the fear was gone. It was replaced with kind of a steady feeling. Like the increasing chaos in my mind was subdued and settled. I don't want anything God hasn't given me, and He hasn't given me fear.

Another experience I can share happened just yesterday. I was in Wal-Mart. I was minding my business walking through the store. I happened to walk through the area where they sell baby stuff. Like, little clothes, diapers, etc. Then a thought came to me: "You won't ever have a baby." By God's grace, I had enough discernment to notice that thought. It was intrusive. I thought, "Whoa. Where did that come from?" Where it came from was hell.

Babies are a blessing, truly. But I do not have baby fever. I did some questionable baby-sitting a few times in my life, but never really wanted to. (I say questionable because I am doubtful that it counts as baby-sitting. I was probably 10 or 11 years old, the kid was around 5, and his parents did not leave their house. They were simply not available to watch him for a few hours.) Every time I've held a baby (not ever by my request) it made me uncomfortable. Mainly because I felt like I was holding someone's dearest in my arms, and what if I dropped it? Or, if it were to cry as I held it I would probably look like a villain. I didn't think they were cute until I was in my 20s, and I don't want one right now. I'm not in the proper circumstances for such a thing anyway. But, maybe someday. So, this thought that intruded into my mind was not my own and I knew it. At the time, my reaction toward the thought ended with "Where did that come from?" I did not reject the thought. I was slacking and just allowed myself to wallow in the hopelessness it brought to my mind. This is not what I should have done. I should have rejected that thought. I do not need to suffer with wallowing in it. Also, wallowing can turn into believing. I do not want to believe a lie, or any thoughts that are not good. Children are a blessing. God could very well bless me like that someday.

Children are a gift from the LORD; they are a reward from him. (Psalm 127:3 NLT)

Sometimes these deceitful thoughts come at the worst times. When you're feeling weak for some reason, these thoughts can come and want to make you despair. They're like attacks. Like wild animals attacking weak prey. An opportunity for making a kill is observed and that opportunity is taken. It can feel like a fight. A fight that's unseen; in your mind. If one is feeling weak, it can be harder to reject these thoughts. A person can be lured into believing them.

Sometimes I have not realized I've believed a lie until later. Sometimes years later.

I think it's very sad when a person believes a lie.

In the last experience I shared, I said I wallowed in the unpleasant result of that thought instead of rejecting it. It takes diligence to take one's thoughts captive. If I'm not paying attention, or if I'm feeling sorry for myself I can let a thought get by and believe it for awhile. I don't want to be lazy about taking my thoughts captive. It certainly takes some discipline, but it is worth it.

Value truth and the benefits of it occupying your mind. And because you value it, protect it. Think of it as if you are a sentry or guard. You've got your armor on, and you have a shield and spear. You're to guard the entrance to someplace. Someone wants to enter, but you hold your spear across the threshold so they cannot come in. You make sure they're safe first, then lift the spear and let them pass. Another person comes up and you check them out too. They're an intruder that wants to enter, but you don't let them. They don't belong in this place you're guarding. Taking your thoughts captive to make them obedient to Christ is like this. The place you're guarding is your mind. To make your thoughts obedient to Christ is like making sure they are in agreement with His truth. If they're not, they're not allowed in your mind.

At times I have felt guilty because an ugly thought has come to my mind. I think an ugly thought could and certainly has been originated by me, but not always. I don't know if anyone else has had this happen, but an ugly thought has come to my mind out of the blue. Then I realize it's not a good thought and feel bad that I even thought it. Let me suggest something. Sometimes that thought was not originated by you, but was spoken to you in your thoughts. By who? The devil or his associates. I have learned that if an ugly thought comes to me out of the blue like that, I will not feel guilty.

I'll reject the thought and think, "No. That's all you. I will have nothing to do with that" and place the blame where it belongs. Just because it came to your mind doesn't mean it was yours. Just like if someone speaks to you. You comprehend what they said in your mind, but the words were not yours. The words were theirs.

A little off topic, but sometimes these lies or bad thoughts are not thoughts, but words actual people speak to you. Regardless of the way they're delivered, or how they come to you, reject them.

A difference I've noticed between thoughts that agree with God's truth and thoughts that don't is that one provides hope and the other doesn't. The deceiving thoughts (whether they come from the devil, other people, or from oneself) provide no forward movement, direction, or hope. They just bring you down. Thoughts that line up with God's truth give a person hope, and a place to grow from. It's like they brighten you up, or are like a "chin-up." Sometimes that "chin-up" can be more like slowly lifting your head up in resolve and persistence, rather than an I-feel-awesome-everything-is-great type of reaction.

Some examples of deceitful thoughts a person should reject:

"You're a failure." No, you're not because God has plans for you - a future. (I know the plans that I have for you, declares the LORD. They are plans for peace and not disaster, plans to give you a future filled with hope. Jeremiah 29:11 GWT)

"You probably won't live very long." (I shall not die, but live, and declare the works of the LORD. Psalm 118:17 KJV)

"God doesn't care about you." (Don't be afraid, for I am with you. Don't be discouraged, for I am your God. I will strengthen you and help you. I will hold you up with my victorious right hand. Isaiah 41:10 NLT)

"God doesn't care about me." (At times it can sound like you're thinking the thought about yourself, rather than someone speaking to you).

"I'm nothing." You're God's beloved one. (The LORD your God is with you. He is a hero who saves you. He happily rejoices over you, renews you with his love, and celebrates over you with shouts of joy. Zephaniah 3:17 GWT)

"I'm not good at anything." (In his grace, God has given us different gifts for doing certain things well. So if God has given you the ability to prophesy, speak out with as much faith as God has given you. Romans 12:6 NLT)

"God loves other people, but not me." (Then Peter began to speak: "I now realize how true it is that God does not show favoritism. Acts 10:34 NIV. The one who is righteous and mighty does not grant special favors to princes or prefer important people over poor people because his hands made them all. Job 34:19 GWT)

"I was a big mistake." God doesn't create mistakes. (Your hands have made and fashioned me; give me understanding that I may learn your commandments. Psalm 119:73 ESV)

"I'm just taking up room." I notice many ungodly thoughts just want to make a person feel worthless. This is not true! (Now here is what I am trying to say: All of you together are the one body of Christ and each one of you is a separate and necessary part of it. 1 Corinthians 12:27 TLB)

"You're not good enough." True about the past, but because of Jesus, what He did, and our belief in Him, we are good enough. (Therefore, since we have been made right in God's sight by faith, we have peace with God because of what Jesus Christ our Lord has done for us. Romans 5:1 NLT)

Reject lies by countering them with truth. If you have a deceitful thought, just think or speak the truth against it. If you think, "I was a big mistake." Just say or think, "No, I reject that thought. God doesn't create mistakes," and back it up with Bible verses. Find God's truth; verses in the Bible that are opposed to these thoughts. Other Bible verses could be used instead of the ones I've included here. There are probably some verses that contradict these deceitful thoughts better. Remember what the devil does. He steals, kills, and destroys. Are your thoughts stealing things from you, killing off your hope, or destroying you? If I can't think of a verse immediately to counter a bad thought I may have, I can still choose to reject it. For instance, I get a bad thought. Then in my mind I'll just think, "No," and refuse to think about it. The thought may repeat itself. I will still react by thinking, "No" and choose not to spend any time thinking about the thought. Instead of just "No" sometimes I'll reject a thought by thinking, "I will not think that, in Jesus' name." (Speaking of babies) This makes me think of a child sitting in a high-chair, being fed. A spoonful of food comes at them, but they shut their mouth tight and turn their head away. The spoon is moved to the left and then to the right, but the child resists and is not going to be convinced to open their mouth. I want to be like that when someone (even myself) tries to feed me a bad thought or lie. I don't care if it's making train sounds or is flying around like a simulated plane.

So, what is the purpose of taking captive every thought to make it obedient to Christ? To keep yourself from believing lies. To me, believing a lie is like living in a prison when you don't have to live there. Living like a prisoner when you are really free to go, if you only knew it. Or, like someone (stronger than you) gripping your wrist. You may try to reach out for something, but you're unable to. Or, you may try to pull away and be free, but you're stuck. It's something that controls you in a bad way. For example, take that lie, "I'm not good enough." If a person believed that, they may feel unqualified to even approach God in prayer. Looking at it from a different angle, believing that lie could make them feel they're not good enough to be loved by anyone.

Again, value truth and your mind. I value my car. If I saw a thief in it I would be angry and have a right to remove them. (I don't know the exact laws on this specific issue, but I hope you get what I mean.) Value your mind more than that. I have a right to throw out anything that doesn't belong there, and with indignant violence. Stand your ground like a diligent guard. When a thought comes to me that wants to steal, kill, or destroy I will not let it have its way.

With the Lord's help you will learn to discern your thoughts. Sometimes they are cleverly deceptive. They may target your most vulnerable or weak point. But, if you are aware of your vulnerable or weak point you can be sure to guard it especially well. At other times, a bad thought will seem like a very poor attempt at bringing you down; you will recognize it immediately for what it is.

There have been times when I have to reject thought, after thought, after thought. No, it's not always easy. Is the Christian life supposed to be easy? It can be a fight, but one that we can be assured of winning. Jesus is greater than the power of Satan. Instead of fighting like I'm not sure if I'll win, I think of it as maintaining occupied territory and rightfully claiming what Jesus bought. He's given us freedom, truth, and a Spirit of power.

For though we walk in the flesh, we do not war after the flesh: (For the weapons of our warfare *are* not carnal, but mighty through God to the pulling down of strong holds;) Casting down imaginations, and every high thing that exalteth itself against the knowledge of God, and bringing into captivity every thought to the obedience of Christ; (2 Corinthians 10:3-5 KJV)

A final word: Be strong in the Lord and in his mighty power. Put on all of God's armor so that you will be able to stand firm against all strategies of the devil. For we are not fighting against flesh-and-blood enemies, but against evil rulers and authorities of the unseen world, against mighty powers in this dark world, and against evil spirits in the heavenly places. Therefore, put on every piece of God's armor so you will be able to resist the enemy in the time of evil. Then after the battle you will still be standing firm. Stand your ground, putting on the belt of truth and the body armor of God's righteousness. For shoes, put on the peace that comes from the Good News so that you will be fully prepared. In addition to all of these, hold up the shield of faith to stop the fiery arrows of the devil. Put on salvation as your helmet, and take the sword of the Spirit, which is the word of God. Pray in the Spirit at all times and on every occasion. Stay alert and be persistent in your prayers for all believers everywhere. (Ephesians 6:10-18 NLT)

69

Attributes of God Part 8: Justice

Because God does not punish sinners instantly, people feel it is safe to do wrong. (Ecclesiastes 8:11 TLB)

Definition of justice: n. 1. The principle of ideal or moral rightness. 2. The upholding of what is right : fairness. 3. The administration of law. 4. A judge.[1]

Knowing God is just gives me hope and assurance. I hear about various injustices and can rely on God to rightly punish the offenders. I wonder about the injustices that are not known about, and can still rely that justice will be served. If not by our courts, then by God. No person will be able to hide, lie, or bribe their way out of what punishment they deserve.

I was thinking about criminals that are caught and punished for nightmarish crimes. When I read or hear about their punishment, or the amount of years they must spend in jail, I sometimes think they deserved worse punishment. I can be left feeling like justice wasn't really served at all. I try not to think about it too much, but I think about the awful torture they inflicted upon the innocent and the victim's families. Lives they've taken away or years from a person's life stolen. How can justice be adequately served? If I relied wholly on our courts and laws to serve justice, I would not have hope or assurance in that truly happening.

I don't have all the answers. But, I know God is just. He can do anything. He can create or may already have ways to make someone experience for themselves all the pain and suffering they inflicted on others. He could make a criminal relive the very crime they committed, except this time they feel the pain times 10. I don't know how God will judge, but it will be just and nothing will be missed. The death of someone will not free them from still being judged by God.

I remember something that happened a couple years ago. We used to have one pet chicken, a hen. I did not particularly like it. One day I was in the house and I heard some vague squawking outside. I figured it was laying an egg or something. But the sounds persisted and sounded a little different than usual, so I looked out the window. I saw the chicken running for its life across the lawn with our neighbor's three dogs chasing it. I ran outside toward the chicken who had just been caught by one of the dogs. The dog was pulling the hen's feathers out and it looked like it was having a great time. I was angry. I yelled at the dogs and a couple ran away. The last dog left reluctantly. The chicken was missing some feathers, but survived. I was so angry at those dogs because of what they did to the chicken, and yet I did not love the chicken. I barely liked it. If I can feel that way towards a bird, I cannot imagine how God feels when people and innocents are hurt by others.

For we know him who said, "Vengeance is mine; I will repay." And again, "The Lord will judge his people." It is a fearful thing to fall into the hands of the living God. (Hebrews 10:30-31 ESV)

And do not fear those who kill the body but cannot kill the soul. Rather fear him who can destroy both soul and body in hell. (Matthew 10:28 ESV)

"Jehovah your God is God of gods and Lord of lords. He is the great and mighty God, the God of terror who shows no partiality and takes no bribes. He gives justice to the fatherless and widows. He loves foreigners and gives them food and clothing. (Deuteronomy 10:17-18 TLB)

He appointed judges throughout the nation in all the larger cities, and instructed them: "Watch your step – I have not appointed you – God has and he will stand beside you and help you give justice in each case that comes before you. Be very much afraid to give any other decision than what God tells you to. For there must be no injustice among God's judges, no partiality, no taking of bribes." (2 Chronicles 19:5-7 TLB)

"Listen to me, you with understanding. Surely everyone knows that *God doesn't sin!* Rather, he punishes the sinners. There is no truer statement that this: *God is never wicked or unjust.* He alone has authority over the earth and dispenses justice for the world. If God were to withdraw his Spirit, all life would disappear and mankind would turn again to dust. (Job 34:10-15 TLB)

"Must God tailor his justice to your demands? Must he change the order of the universe to suit your whims? The answer must be obvious even to you! (Job 34:33 TLB)

You can be very sure that the evil man will not go unpunished forever. And you can also be very sure that God will rescue the children of the godly. (Proverbs 11:21 TLB)

For he has set a day for judging the world with justice by the man he has appointed, and he proved to everyone who this is by raising him from the dead." (Acts 17:31 NLT)

You have wearied the Lord with your words. "Wearied him?" you ask in fake surprise. "How have we wearied him?" By saying that evil is good, that it pleases the Lord! Or by saying that God won't punish us – he doesn't care. (Malachi 2:17 TLB)

"Watch now," the Lord of Hosts declares, "the day of judgement is coming, burning like a furnace. The proud and wicked will be burned up like straw; like a tree, they will be consumed – roots and all. But for you who fear my name, the Sun of Righteousness will rise with healing in his wings. And you will go free, leaping with joy like calves let out to pasture. (Malachi 4:1-2 TLB)

He will give each one whatever his deeds deserve. He will give eternal life to those who patiently do the will of God, seeking for the unseen glory and honor and eternal life that he offers. But he will terribly punish those who fight against the truth of God and walk in evil ways – God's anger will be poured out upon them. There will be sorrow and suffering for Jews and Gentiles alike who keep on sinning. But there will be glory and honor and peace from God for all who obey him, whether they are Jews or Gentiles. For God treats everyone the same. (Romans 2:6-11 TLB)

70

Growing Up

One of the first things I learned as a Christian, and in fact, before I was one, is that Jesus died for our sins. I feel this is a fairly well-known fact. Every Christian believes this, and I think some people who are not Christians are aware of this belief of Christianity.

In the recent past, when I thought about the fact that Jesus died for my sins it was difficult for me to really comprehend what that meant. Jesus dying for my sins was foreign to me, even though I believed it. It was too distant a thought for me to appreciate.

Lately, as I read more of the Old Testament and understand how I am in relation to God, I have grown to appreciate the fact that Jesus' death atoned for my sins much more. It has become more precious to me and I see how much I depend on it every day. I believe as time goes on I will understand and appreciate it more and more.

I see Jesus' death and resurrection as more than covering my sins so I can go to heaven. I see it as the way of having a restored relationship between myself and God.

Now we rejoice in our wonderful new relationship with God –
all because of what our Lord Jesus Christ has done in dying for our
sins – making us friends of God. (Romans 5:11 TLB)

Jesus' death for the payment of our sins was not the end goal in
itself. Yes, He came to die for our sins, but for a reason. It was for
our new life and restoring our relationship with God that was
broken when Adam sinned. Also, His payment was in full; nothing
can be added to it for our salvation. The atonement of our sins was
the essential beginning to knowing God. It's kind of like getting into
a car is not the end goal. A person typically gets into a car so they
can go somewhere. It's the essential beginning.

Yes, Adam's one sin brings condemnation for everyone, but
Christ's one act of righteousness brings a right relationship with
God and new life for everyone. (Romans 5:18 NLT)

Imagine a couple got married. For awhile, friends and family
would hear from them, "We got married!" That would be the news
they would share. I don't know how long this would be "news."
Maybe for a year, and depending on who they see. Let's imagine 3
years later, someone would ask them, "So, how's it going? How are
you?" And they would reply, "We got married!" 6 years later, again
they would be asked, "How're you doing? What have you been up
to?" And they would reply, "We got married!" But, what else? I
mean, yes we all know you got married, but there is more to being
married than getting married, isn't there? It goes without question.
The covenant relationship began when you got married, but that
wasn't all there was to it. Life goes on after getting married, surely
there is something new to talk about.

So, I compare this imperfect illustration to becoming a
Christian. A new Christian would say, "Jesus died for my sins." For
awhile this would be their news. 3 years later, "Jesus died for my
sins." 6 years later, "Jesus died for my sins." Yes, but what else? The
relationship began years ago, has anything happened since then?

I do not mean that we should not share the Good News with

others, or that we should ever forget that Jesus died for our sins. I do not mean to diminish its importance in the least. I'm trying to explain that there is more to the Christian life.

I have heard people teaching to a congregation of Christians that Jesus died for our sins. This is wonderful, but it is repeated over and over again to people who already know it. Perhaps not every Sunday, but frequently. I think everyone there already knows that inexpressibly wonderful fact. There may be a few listening who do not know the Good News, but for this essay I'm focusing on people who are already Christians. For people who are already Christians I think this is where Christianity becomes boring. To hear the same elementary facts of Christianity repeated as though one didn't know them already. At least I will speak for myself and say that this is where it gets boring for me. How can it be otherwise, when I am taught what I already know, over and over again? If I were going to an art class that taught me what the primary colors are and did not teach me more than that, I would become bored.

I want more. The awareness I have that there is more I attribute to the grace of God and reading in the Bible that there is more beyond receiving salvation. Like there is more beyond getting married. Jesus dying for our sins (and our belief in Him) created the way to having a relationship with God.

Many years ago I knew, according to the Bible, that it is good to obey God and do the things He wants you to do. Honestly, even as a Christian I recognized I had little desire to do this. It's kind of difficult to explain, but it's like I recognized I had little desire to obey God, and at the same time I had a great desire to obey Him. I think that's my old nature vs. my new nature. So, I prayed that God would help me want to do His will. To help me love Him more. To want Him. To even want the "more" that I have mentioned.

For God is working in you, giving you the desire and the power to do what pleases him. (Philippians 2:13 NLT)

When I learned that there was more beyond receiving salvation, I wanted it. What is "it"? There are many things. Many of them I'm sure I don't know about. One of them is being filled with the Holy Spirit like the believers in the book of Acts were. Then, there are many spiritual gifts to learn about and find out which ones God has given to you. Growing in these spiritual gifts I think is a lifelong endeavor. Then there is finding out what God's will for your life is, and what He wants to do. I've thought about these things a lot, but I'm learning that along with all these, what I really want is God Himself. To know Him personally, not just know about Him. To know His voice and hear what He has to say. To learn what He likes and doesn't like. To learn what He thinks. To learn what He would like to teach me. God is so vast and endless there are always new things to learn about Him. There are mysteries to find out. I want the kind of relationship that Jesus' death and resurrection has allowed us to have.

I would like to learn about these things in practical, understandable ways. I really dislike trying to learn something in ambiguous ways that leave me wondering about the subject as much as I was before. But, I can understand that sometimes it is difficult to explain these subjects in practical ways. Especially when they are subjects that are not explainable purely through human logic. In contrast, the mechanics of a car can be explained logically and every part can be seen. So, how do you find out what spiritual gifts God has given you? How do you learn to hear His voice? What is God's will for my life? It is a blessed, wonderful thing to have people teaching other Christians clearly about these things; helping them to grow up. Holy Spirit, God Himself, will also teach a person about these things.

I've been a Christian since I was about 10 years old. A few years ago (over 10 years after I had become a Christian), I felt a marked increase in "hunger" for God. I would say I don't know why I felt that way, because there was no particular event that resulted in this feeling. But I won't say I don't know why, because I know it was sparked by God. Not because of a particular event or by me consciously deciding, "Hmmm, I think I'll hunger for God." No, it wasn't like that. It came upon me – this hunger for God. I felt there must be more to knowing God; not only having a distant knowledge of Him. I desired to know Him, to reach out and touch Him if I could. I didn't know what I was really wanting with Him, just something more. I contemplated literally packing up a tent and going far into the woods by myself and camping out for the purpose of getting completely alone and to focus on finding out more about God. To get alone, seek Him, and nothing else. Shortly thereafter this marked increase in hunger for God, I learned about being filled with the Holy Spirit like the believers in the book of Acts were. I learned that this is different than receiving salvation. Then I realized I did not have this "Holy Spirit baptism," but I did receive salvation. When I realized this I was so unhappy. Because I didn't like that I didn't have it. I was missing something important. I doubt I've ever felt so unhappy before. It was a different kind of unhappiness; an awful type of yearning and hunger for something. I wanted this Holy Spirit baptism and the speaking in tongues that goes with it. So, I prayed for it and thank God that He gave it to me! It doesn't have to be complicated. If you're a Christian and you want this, ask God for it. I won't try to go into what it means for a person, but I give it as an example of there being more to this Christian life.

The other day I noticed in myself again a feeling of hunger for God; to really know Him personally. It is a process, getting to know a Person. It takes time. Although hunger isn't a delightful feeling, I was very thankful for it. Because, without it I realized I might be content with less than what Jesus made the way for us to have. I might be content in knowing God as an acquaintance, rather than a close friend.

So get rid of all evil behavior. Be done with all deceit, hypocrisy, jealousy, and all unkind speech. Like newborn babies, you must crave pure spiritual milk so that you will grow into a full experience of salvation. Cry out for this nourishment, now that you have had a taste of the Lord's kindness … (1 Peter 2:1-3 NLT)

Going further with this theme of hunger, sometimes the world and its ways will satisfy you. Then there comes a time when it doesn't and never will again. When that happens in the life of a Christian, they've hit a major milestone in their growth. Have you ever had a craving for something? So, you eat something but it just did not satisfy. It's like that. Some things you know will not satisfy even before you eat it. What kinds of things does the world offer for satisfaction? Popularity, wealth, personal accomplishments, possessions, experiences. What does God offer for satisfaction? Relationship with Him, fulfillment of your purpose, an abundant new life, helping others. One offers the temporary, and He offers what lasts. We're living in two worlds simultaneously. Separate yourself from the ways and values of the world. They are not for you.

You are living a brand new kind of life that is continually learning more and more of what is right, and trying constantly to be more and more like Christ who created this new life within you. In this new life one's nationality or race or education or social position is unimportant; such things mean nothing. Whether a person has Christ is what matters, and he is equally available to all. (Colossians 3:10 TLB)

You have been Christians a long time now, and you ought to be teaching others, but instead you have dropped back to the place where you need someone to teach you all over again the very first principles in God's Word. You are like babies who can drink only milk, not old enough for solid food. And when a person is still living on milk it shows he isn't very far along in the Christian life, and doesn't know much about the difference between right and wrong. He is still a baby-Christian! You will never be able to eat solid spiritual food and understand the deeper things of God's Word until you become better Christians and learn right from wrong by practicing doing right. (Hebrews 5:12-14 TLB)

I like the illustration of milk vs. solid food. I would not like to live on milk. I would probably be hungry for something more substantial. I can only imagine the physical condition of someone who lived solely on milk. I wouldn't like to live solely on "milk" spiritually either. To me, spiritual "milk" would be like learning and believing Jesus died for our sins. While absolutely wonderful and necessary, as milk is for a baby, the baby grows up and it is normal that it should eat solid food. Actually the more I think about it, the moment of believing Jesus died for our sins is more like being born ("born again") rather than it being like spiritual "milk." It practically comes before any intake of milk. So, perhaps believing Jesus died for our sins would not really be like "milk" a baby Christian drinks, but precedes even that. Food for thought. I wonder how many people are hungry for solid food, spiritually speaking.

I imagine myself sitting down to a table, along with others, about to partake in a meal. We eagerly anticipate this meal, because we're all hungry. Then we're each served a glass of milk and only a glass of milk. More than that was wanted, but it's ok we'll take it. This is repeated 3 times a day for a month. By the end of the month we're all starving for real food and sick of milk. When presented with another glass of milk some people leave the table in disgust, some dash the glass of milk across the table in contempt, others cry in misery as they look at the milk, and some drink the milk as they have nothing else for nourishment. I think a person living solely on milk is as unnatural as a Christian living solely on spiritual "milk."

I don't want to be a baby Christian forever. I want to grow up and be all that the Lord wants me to be. Always and only with the Lord's help, I am trying, and I am learning and growing.

I believe God, as our Father, would like His children to grow. I know in this earthly life, it is normal for a baby to grow up. I imagine it would be a joy to see them grow and learn new things. So, I think our Heavenly Father would like His children to grow too.

Let us stop going over the same old ground again and again, always teaching those first lessons about Christ. Let us go on instead to other things and become mature in our understanding, as strong Christians ought to be. Surely we don't need to speak further about the foolishness of trying to be saved by being good, or about the necessity of faith in God; you don't need further instruction about baptism and spiritual gifts and the resurrection of the dead and eternal judgement. The Lord willing, we will go on now to other things. (Hebrews 6:1-3 TLB)

Dear brothers, I have been talking to you as though you were still just babies in the Christian life, who are not following the Lord, but your own desires; I cannot talk to you as I would to healthy Christians, who are filled with the Spirit. I have had to feed you with milk and not with solid food, because you couldn't digest anything stronger. And even now you still have to be fed on milk. For you are still only baby Christians, controlled by your own desires, not God's. When you are jealous of one another and divide up into quarreling groups, doesn't that prove you are still babies, wanting your own way? In fact, you are acting like people who don't belong to the Lord at all. (1 Corinthians 3:1-3 TLB)

Dear friends, let us practice loving each other, for love comes from God and those who are loving and kind show that they are the children of God, and that they are getting to know him better. (1 John 4:7 TLB)

I close my letter with these last words: Be happy. Grow in Christ. Pay attention to what I have said. Live in harmony and peace. And may the God of love and peace be with you. (2 Corinthians 13:11 TLB)

We all, with unveiled face, beholding the glory of the Lord, are being changed into his likeness from one degree of glory to another; for this comes from the Lord who is the Spirit. (2 Corinthians 3:18 RSV)

May your growth in knowing the fullness of our Lord continue with the patient nurture of the Holy Spirit as He transforms us into His image. Amen!

71

"As Long as You're Happy."

Before I begin, I just want to warn you that this is going to be a chapter you may not want to read. It contains a lot of my opinions and what goes through my mind. I've spent a lot of time thinking about things, and it shows. There will be considerable amounts of rambling and ranting. If reading about someone's feelings is boring to you, definitely don't read this because there will be lots of that. If you are feeling cheerful, please don't read this. I want you to stay cheerful. The content is heavy. If you don't want to read about someone's personal difficulties, don't read this. If you get squeamish at the thought of blood/girl issues, don't read this.

I am sincere. There is a lot of personal subject matter, and I understand it isn't what people want to read sometimes. I just want to warn you so you have a chance at avoiding regretting reading it. Actually, I wonder how much anyone will benefit from reading this. Perhaps it is I who will benefit from writing it out.

Finally, I know other people have suffered much, much worse things than I have. This is just my story.

I have divided this into 7 sections, because it is lengthy. I hope that helps provide some structure and ease in reading.

1

Have you ever heard someone make a statement like, "As long as you're happy"? I think there are a few variations of it. Like, "Do whatever makes you happy," or, "Well, as long as you're happy. That's what matters."

I have caught myself saying or thinking statements like these. I think they are shallow and terribly subjective things to say. They are so subjective, they're practically useless. They mean nothing. What if what made someone happy was committing crimes? Would all that mattered be that they were happy? I know such statements are generally meant to encourage. But, if I take such statements seriously, they are meaningless.

2015 was the worst year of my life so far. It was the most stressful, painful, and difficult year.

2015 started well. It seemed so bright and brimming with hope. However, in early September things started to crumble. My dog, the best dog in the world to me, died. It was in an unexpected and violent way. He was let outside at night, which had happened countless times before without any trouble. This time he was attacked by a coyote and his back was broken. I still remember his white fur stained with blood, and the scared look in his glazed over eyes. I had never seen him look like that before. He was suffering and had to be put to sleep. He had been my cherished companion for 15 years.

Earlier in the year I had met a man who I liked. I didn't like him more than any other person until he opened his mouth and spoke. In other words, it wasn't because of how he looked, though his appearance was fine to me. I can notice someone is physically attractive, but not be attracted to them. It's a matter of character first, for me.

Some of the things I liked about him: His worldview was old-fashioned. Many of his viewpoints were the same as my own. Some of his moral standards were higher than mine, which was a pleasant surprise. It was such a surprise, I wondered if it were true. He was caring and kind. He would walk me to me door, or to my car, or would want me to call him when I got home.

Some of the kindness he showed reminded me of what a parent or guardian would do, which was a bit awkward (considering he was only a year older than me) but endearing too. For instance, telling me I'd better keep my coat on because it was cold. Or, appreciating small accomplishments of mine. Accomplishments that were so nominal, they might not be termed "accomplishments" and are generally only appreciated by people who care about you. He offered to pay my cell phone bill, because we would talk so much. I appreciated the offer and thought that was considerate, but I declined because I didn't want to become unnecessarily attached at that point or cost him money.

He seemed like a leader. One reason why I liked that was because I didn't have to initiate everything. He seemed like a leader and as a result, he seemed more like a "man," however bad that sounds. That was attractive.

I guess I don't agree with every aspect of feminism. I believe there are differences between men and women that are beyond the physical and I appreciate those differences. Men and women aren't the same, but equal. However, that's a topic I won't go into any further here.

In this day and age, to me he seemed like a very rare sort of person.

He had some ideas I didn't completely like. He had his whole life planned. Get married, buy a house, have kids, grow old, and die. I'm slightly exaggerating that, but to me it was too planned. It felt rigid, a little boring, and almost confining. I like to approach the future a little more ambiguously; with more flexibility and freedom in various outcomes being possible. Yes, I would like to have those things that he had planned, but I guess it's not in my nature to be so … planned. If find it uninspiring. Maybe I'm being unrealistic and impractical, but this issue showed how different we were.

It's like this. Imagine planting a flower seed, and then waiting for it to grow. Before it even sprouts, someone has planned its stages of growth: Week 2, sprout will emerge. Week 4, buds will form. Week 5, flowers will bloom and be blue in color. Week 6, flowers will die. It's as if everything is known beforehand. The good kind of "unknowns" are eliminated. The anticipation and wonder of watching the plant grow is diminished because its stages of growth have already been revealed. Or it could be compared to this. You're about to watch a movie, and someone tells you how it ends. It makes watching the movie less interesting.

I know life is not a plant or movie. I drew those illustrations to describe how I felt. I suppose I am a bit of a dreamer. Maybe I'm being childish. I know a prudent and sensible person makes plans in life. They're necessary. I'm not saying anything against plans, but he had his life planned planned. I wondered if something didn't go as he had planned, would he be able to handle that well? One thing I learned is that it's difficult to be sure of any plans, especially when they involve people.

He often expressed his displeasure over the fact that he wasn't already married. He said his parents met in high school, and he wished he could've met someone when he was that age. He spoke of how his grandmother wanted grandkids. I felt he was unhappy that despite him being the eldest child, his younger brother had already started a family. It seemed like he was stressed over all this, and like he felt pressured to get married. I thought it may be true that his family (through one way or another) created pressure for him to be married, but what did he want? His family may want one thing, but what did he want? I wondered if he was the kind of person who is unduly influenced by the desires of their family. I thought that could be a problem.

One time I was talking to him about the Lord. He identified himself as a Christian. I was telling him that I wanted to find out what God's will for my life was; what He really wants me to do. At that time, I didn't know that He wanted His people to become like Christ. I was just vaguely aware that the Lord has different purposes for different people, and I wanted to find out what my purpose was. I was just sharing this desire in conversation. He responded by saying, "I know what God's will for my life is … to enjoy it." I really didn't know what to say, because I wasn't sure if he was correct or not. I just had a feeling that he wasn't correct. I mean, yes, God wants his people to enjoy things, but there must be a greater reason for why we're here. And there is, I just didn't know it then.

In this exchange I realized he was not on the same page as I was, in terms of spiritual aspirations. He sounded content to believe in Jesus as Lord, and then enjoy life. I believed in Jesus too, but I wanted to grow up spiritually and know Him more.

Some other things I disliked are trivial, I will admit. I'd known him for about 1 or 2 weeks when out of the blue he said, "I bet you couldn't cook for me." First of all, the presumption in the statement startled me. We had not previously discussed cooking in any way. What information was he using to come to that conclusion? Second, it showed just how old-fashioned he was. Like, because I'm the girl, I do the cooking. I know that's how it typically works out, which is fine with me. It is expected, but I prefer that it isn't expected tactlessly. I don't mind cooking for other people. Enjoyed or hated, I believe knowing how to cook is really a necessity of life. Third, if asked in a normal fashion I would cook for a person. If not asked at all, I would still cook. However, if you approach me in that manner I probably won't be cooking for you. I didn't say anything in response. I continued the conversation as if I never heard it.

Frequently I felt he was trying to get a rise out of me. The problem was I couldn't tell if he was joking or being serious because he sounded serious. If I knew he was joking, it wouldn't be a problem. For example, the cooking statement. It didn't seem to be spoken in a playful, teasing way, but as a fact. It sounded like he had somehow come to that conclusion and was dissatisfied. If he were just playing, it would be all right with me. I think that's one problem of getting to know someone primarily over the phone vs. in person. Meanings are more difficult to understand and body language isn't observed. Also, some people behave differently on the phone than in person. Besides that, I highly dislike talking on the phone.

Whenever it seemed he was trying to get a rise out of me it

didn't achieve anything positive. It would be ineffective, especially if I knew in that moment he meant to get a rise out of me. I would feel like we were in some kind of subtle competition with each other, instead of being more like a team. I don't want to compete with someone I like, I want to work together.

I had a hard time understanding why he did this. I got the impression it was a result of pain he endured from a past relationship that he was taking out on me. A couple times he spoke of a past relationship as if he had not fully healed from it. I thought to myself, "I'm not the person who hurt you."

Various mind games were employed, and it was very stressful. They're called mind games, but they don't feel like games. They aren't fun at all. I felt like I was being tested repeatedly. He'd say something semi-hurtful just to see how I would react. From judging my reaction, he could get a sense of how I felt about something. This never worked properly because if it bothered me I didn't convey it or I could decipher what he was trying to do and didn't take the bait.

If I didn't catch on immediately, I took it at face value which resulted in me being very confused. I'd think about the situation more and begin to see what the motive was. Then I'd end up feeling a bit sad. Sad because it was a little hurtful to me, and sad for him because it showed me he wasn't secure.

Because of all this, trust wasn't fostered. I felt like I was being trained to question what he said and wonder about his motives. I couldn't trust as much as I wanted to.

I think immature and insecure people play mind games. If I liked someone, I wouldn't want to put them through mind games and all that exhausting psychological exercise. Why is all that trouble necessary? Why must it be so complicated? How is it beneficial? Again, it felt as if we were somehow in a competition with each other, instead of being on the same side. If you want to know how I feel about something, ask me instead of trying to find out through obscure tests and mind games.

Since cars are an interest of mine, a few times I talked to him about this subject. He asked me a few questions about my car and I answered. I could sense something happened after I said my Cadillac had radial tires and not the original bias-ply type. He got kind of quiet and softly said, "It sounds like you know about cars." I paused and then just continued talking.

In the few times I brought up the subject of cars, the same kind of thing would happen. He would get quiet, and he usually wasn't that way. Maybe he wasn't interested in cars. However, I thought that was unlikely as he said he used to have a classic car, and would like to own one again in the future. So, then I thought the subject of cars was not one he was very knowledgeable in. He didn't talk much about them. Maybe he just didn't know much about them. Perhaps he thought I knew more about them than he did and was uncomfortable with that.

This basically alerted me to the fact that he had an ego. I guess everyone does, but I saw that his was sensitive. Then I wondered how deep it went. Like, does this extend to any and every subject? Is there any subject I can know more about than he does, without him feeling a bad way about it? Or, must he always know more than I do in order to feel unbruised?

I suppose it could have been embarrassing to have a girl know more about cars than he did. But, I'm not a mechanic in the broadest sense of the word and I know less about cars than a lot of other people. I'm truly not that knowledgeable about cars. I would like to learn more about them. I wasn't throwing around car lingo, pretending I knew more than I did. I decided not to talk about cars anymore, in case it made him feel uncomfortable.

Another trivial thing I disliked was that he talked about his height frequently. I didn't talk about it, but he often did. I couldn't tell if he was either proud or insecure about it. To me, he shouldn't be proud about it because, like all of us, we're born that way. If he was insecure about it, I felt sorry for him because he shouldn't have to suffer with that.

I tried not to get too attached too quickly, but it is difficult when the other person isn't cooperating. For example, he spoke of marriage several times, saying things like, "In a year we'll either be good friends or be married." He'd call me pet names. Part of me thought it was kind of appealing, but another part of me was thinking, "I really don't know you that well." He told me how much he earned. Why did I need to know that? He brought up a baby name he liked, and how many kids each of us wanted. At that time these were subjects I rarely thought about in the privacy of my mind, let alone discussing it with a man. There were many more instances of premature dialogue.

He had charm, enough for two people I think. I failed at not getting too attached.

Although there were things I didn't like, what I did like mattered to me more. I brushed off the things I didn't like. I had an excuse or reason for each. If he had his life planned, perhaps I should stop being an unrealistic dreamer and get practical too. If I thought he was under pressure by his family to get married, maybe he truly wanted that for himself as well. If he didn't have a desire to pursue God, at least he was a Christian. If my cooking abilities failed to meet his standards, I could learn to be a better cook. If he wanted to get a rise out of me or play mind games, perhaps I should just get over it. If his ego was sensitive when cars were discussed, I could stop talking about them. And, if he was proud or insecure about his height, I should probably get over that too. I thought, "I can adapt. I can compromise. I can accept who he is." In some ways I began to change to suit him. Because I liked him, I was willing to do that. Besides, I'm sure I have disagreeable traits too.

Now it was September, a few days after my dog died. He called me and ended the "relationship." He said I was good-looking enough, but my personality was too different from his and his family's. In terms of premature dialogue, he acknowledged, "Sometimes I say too much." He said he didn't know, and that we could still be friends.

I admit we were like opposites in terms of our personalities, but I still liked him and thought you didn't have to have similar personalities. Now, I feel that perhaps two people should have similar personalities, or should at least be able to appreciate and understand the differences. I would be miserable if I expressed myself - how I see or feel about something - and have the other person always fail to understand me.

It was the worst phone conversation ever. I was trying to process everything I was hearing and felt like I was dying inside, but I thanked him for being straightforward and tried to encourage him in that he will find someone else. Meanwhile, a part of me wondered why I was even thanking and encouraging him. On the phone, I probably sounded like I wasn't very affected and like I didn't care very much. The truth is I was very affected and I cared a lot. I cared too much.

I had failed so badly at not getting too attached that I had thought this was the person I was going to marry. I cannot describe how intensely I dislike that I allowed that to happen. I felt mortified. How could I have become such a fool? I felt like I must not have been good enough to be loved. My best wasn't good enough. I guess I felt all the usual emotions when something like this happens.

Never before had I felt the incredible pain that rejection like that could bring. It hurt me so much I didn't shed a tear over it until weeks later. It is upsetting when something I cared about falls apart. I know now that I put way, way too much effort into it. It is upsetting to see that I liked him more than he liked me. To see how much I was willing to do/invest, but he wasn't. Also, the reason he gave me (personality differences) focused on the core of who I am. It was probably my biggest insecurity at that time - the fact that I'm reserved/introverted. Even so, it would have hurt no matter what the reason was.

I don't like cutting people off, but it would be very difficult for me if not impossible to go from knowing someone as more than a friend and then switching to having them as just a friend. So, that ended that.

About 1 hour after that happened I attended the first square dance lesson of the season that the square dance club I'm a part of was giving. It's the time for anyone who is interested in learning how to square dance to start to learn. The lessons last for about 6 months I think. For weeks prior to this I had painted signs and made flyers to promote this event and to try to help out the club. In other words, I cared about this event; it mattered to me. It mattered to me because the people in the club matter to me. I like them, all of them. So, I was looking forward to it and had worked towards its success (along with everyone else). Now the day had come, but I felt emotionally numb. The event went wonderfully well, but I just couldn't appreciate it as much as would have liked to. The contrast between the successful event and my relationship failure was so stark. Happiness and a broken heart at the same time, but the broken-hearted feeling dominated. The timing was bitterly ironic.

A couple weeks later I got my period. I hadn't had it for 2 or 3 months, which was abnormal. So, I was kind of glad it came. For me it typically lasts about 1 week. When 2 weeks had passed and I was still bleeding I became concerned. Also, it was significantly heavier bleeding than usual. I would bleed onto the driver's seat in my car and onto furniture at home. It was gory. 3 long weeks went by and I thought I might bleed to death. Still raw and reeling from the end of the "relationship," with the addition of this problem I felt less than human.

I was into week 4 of bleeding and began feeling sick, like light-headed. It was a scary situation, to say the least. At this time I was still working at the library. One day while working I injured myself near my right hip. When it happened I could feel a linear sort of pain and like a pulling apart of fibers inside me. Maybe it was a muscle or ligament, I don't know. I mentioned sustaining this injury in one of the other chapters.

After that I did my best to work for a couple more days, but ultimately could not continue working. I still remember hobbling to my boss' office and telling her I had to quit. Of course, she asked me why. I didn't know what was wrong with me, so I just said I wasn't well. I didn't even say I got injured. I wasn't thinking of workman's compensation for occupational injuries or anything like that. Looking back, at that time I probably wasn't thinking very sensibly in general. It was an awful conversation for me. A lot of pride died there. It was humbling to have my body overrule my will and for me to admit it. I was glad I didn't cry in front of her, although it almost happened. There were plenty of tears on the drive home.

Now that I wasn't working I rested in bed and the bleeding started to slack off, eventually stopping in about a week. I believe this issue happened because I was so stressed. The doctor I saw gave me no explanation. I found out I was now anemic. So, I began taking iron pills which can be an ordeal in itself.

2

For the work-related injury I went to multiple doctors trying to find out what it was; to get a diagnosis. I guess I won't go into every detail of all I went through. A low point was when one Physical Therapist not-so-gently implied that my emotional state was the cause of my pain after I got emotional in front of her. As a result, I felt that I was misunderstood, I wasn't being believed or taken seriously, that I was stupid, and that my emotions were unwarranted, which hurt. Especially when I went to her hoping for help.

I already hate to cry in front of people, especially strangers, but hate it even more when I do cry (despite every effort to hold it back) and I'm judged. In that most vulnerable moment, I'm judged. I'm aware of the fact that a person is often judged negatively if they cry in the presence of others. That's partly why I try to avoid it. I only cried in front of her when I began to explain what activities I couldn't do anymore. Besides that, I was feeling emotional because of the physical pain I was in, the frustration from the lack of a diagnosis, and because my life had just been turned upside down. To me, these are good reasons to cry. She didn't know what I was going through. That's a good reason to not judge someone.

Sadness is just as legitimate an emotion as happiness.

If I happen to cry in front of another person I must really be hurting because I hate to do that. I guess if that happens I just want to be comforted in any little way, rather than be told it's because of my emotions that I have pain. That made me feel worse than if she hadn't said anything at all.

I dislike when medical professionals speak to you like they know everything and you know nothing. By God's grace, I'm really not a stupid person. I try not to be. I was aware that a person's emotions/mental state can manifest themselves in physical ailments. I know it's true. I've experienced it for myself. In this particular case, the Physical Therapist was just plain incorrect. The injury was the cause of my pain. I just wanted to know what kind of injury I had and what, if anything, could be done about it.

Another point of irritation that I encountered with 3 different medical people is when they said something like, "At your age you shouldn't have to move like that," or "You're so young, you shouldn't be that way." I understand that their intentions in saying these things were good, but I did not receive them well. Again, I felt like they thought I was stupid. I am aware that I am not moving normally and that I am in pain and that it is not normal. Why would I even be there trying to get help if I thought I should be that way? I think I am aware of it more than anyone else because I am personally living it. It is the stating of the painfully obvious to me, as if I were ignorant of it, that I don't like. Furthermore, I feel like it just rubs it in – the fact that I'm not physically well "at my age." I am fully aware of it. Literally painfully aware of it, without being told. These kinds of statements do not help me at all. They make me feel worse.

On a different topic: I think it is presumptuous to believe that because a person is a certain age, that they are a certain way. For exaggerated example, believing that because a person is younger it means they're without a sorrow and that their life is carefree and perfect. I think every child's life should be carefree, but not every child's is. Thank God my childhood was carefree, and looking back at my life even a couple years ago I feel that I was blissfully ignorant of many things. I'm learning a lot pretty darn fast now, but I think a year from now I may look back at this time in my life and think I was still ignorant.

I do respect my elders, but occasionally they sure don't seem like elders. It bugs me that if I happen to be younger than someone, I can get the feeling that they're patronizing toward me for no other reasons than because they've made assumptions and they're older. I get this sense from them: "You've got a lot to learn. I've been through the school of hard knocks. I know more than you. You'll have to learn the hard way too, and just you wait and see what life is really like." They may very well know more than I do, but they don't have to be proud and condescending about it.

First of all, people just don't know what other people are going through unless they ask and get to know them. People go through all kinds of life experiences at different ages. If I were older and had been through hard experiences and saw someone younger who I assumed had not experienced those hardships, I would be glad for them. I'd hope they would be smarter than I was, and/or could go through life not having to learn things the hard way.

Why do some people feel that others should learn things with as much difficulty as they did? If possible, why not help others along and share some knowledge with them, instead of doing nothing, sitting back and letting them suffer through the same things you did? I understand that some things must be learned through personal experience and I don't mean people should be coddled. Is it coddling a person to help them avoid an unnecessary hardship? I don't know … maybe my idealistic mindset still exists to a degree. Or, maybe I'm simply being sensible.

Additionally, maturity does not always have to do with how old a person is. I've known people who are old and think like teenagers. I've known teenagers who think like old people. I won't say age doesn't matter at all, but it matters less than some people think it does.

All that said, I do not blame the medical professionals I saw. I know they were trying to help and not harm me. I imagine it can be difficult to find a diagnosis for some patients. That can be frustrating for them too. And, I know that a person in pain (for example, me) can blow things out of proportion.

Going from doctor to doctor was a roller coaster of emotions for me. Before going to an appointment, I would recall and rehearse the nature of my injury in order to describe it accurately to the doctor. How it happened, when it happened, how I felt, what movements make it worse, etc. I would try to keep my level of hope in check. Not too hopeful so I wouldn't be disappointed if no answer was found, and not too hopeless because I shouldn't be hopeless.

It was very distressing to look into the faces of doctors and the like, and realize they didn't know what was wrong with me. Despite not knowing, some of them thought they knew how to make me better. "4 to 6 weeks of Physical Therapy and you should be well." They would prescribe various treatments, but I felt like we weren't on the right track. I understand that sometimes treatment is administered and it's basically to see if a person gets better as a result of it. But, some of those treatments made me worse. Whatever the injury was, it wasn't the kind where you work through the pain to get better. Attempting that made it worse, and I know because I tried it on my own, and with the approval of professionals. I began to think that any method of treatment was a shot in the dark without first having a diagnosis.

I got tired of trying to find answers but getting none, so I decided I would not see another doctor.

3

At home I coped with the state of my life. It had changed radically. I went from being as active as I pleased, to now being in pain every day and not being able to walk normally. I could walk, thank God, but only for moving awkwardly around the house because of the injury/pain. Not for the simple joy of walking, like going for a walk outside. All these unhappy events I've described happened in about a month and a half.

I cannot adequately portray how life was for me. There's so much I'm not including in this essay. I could not move without pain, and if I didn't move, I still had pain. I was not able to find any mental comfort in a diagnosis, because I didn't have one. I thought of and tried to research many possible explanations. I would almost constantly wonder what was wrong with me, but never really know. I didn't know what to think, let alone what to do.

I realized now I could not exercise and hoped I would not gain too much weight. I thought (according to what the man who had just ended the "relationship" said) that that was one good point about me – that I was good-looking enough. I feared that since I could not exercise I might gain too much weight and lose that one good point about me. I thought if I were good-looking enough maybe someone could put up with the way my personality is and still love me because of how I looked. Of course, I see this completely differently now. But, that's how low I was feeling then.

I enjoyed square dancing and round dancing, but now I couldn't participate in these activities. That was heartbreaking to me. Like most people, I very much enjoyed being active and now it was just gone.

I felt so trapped in my body. No job, no ability for normal physical activity, living with constant physical pain, the end of a relationship - I felt so much anguish. Life as I knew it was over. It's a hard place when all your tears, all your effort, everything, does not change your situation. I felt trapped. I felt the grief of all I had lost. Who could ever love me now, in this condition? I felt like I was worth nothing. Now what was I going to do with my life? Or rather, my existence? I thought of killing myself. I distinctly remember the night I thought about it. I thought I could just shoot myself in the head with a gun and be done with it. But, I thought if I was somehow "unsuccessful" I might end up alive and in worse physical condition, which I did not want. Also, I didn't want to hurt the people who would be left behind, who love and care about me, if I had done such a thing. At that time I didn't even know that Bible verse (Psalm 118:17 KJV - I shall not die, but live, and declare the works of the LORD) to combat the devil and these thoughts with. What a dark time in my life that was!

Some months passed, and I saw that I was not recovering from the work-related injury as quickly as I would have liked. I was still struggling with believing that everything really happened the way they did. I began to question my belief in God, the One dearest to me. I wondered if it was worth believing in Him and living as a Christian. I couldn't understand why God would let this happen to me. Doesn't He love me? How could He be so unjust, when He's not unjust? What did I do wrong? With the choice of not believing in Him anymore before me, I thought, "Where else would I go?

Who else would I turn to?" My answer was that there was nowhere else for me to go, and nobody else to turn to. He is my God. That was "rock-bottom" for me, or as close to it as I've ever been.

4

More time passed and I realized I had to forgive God, although He did nothing wrong and never does. I had to forgive the man I knew, too. I had to forgive because I was holding a grudge with God and with this person.

For a long time all that had happened seemed bad, and nothing but bad. Recently, by God's grace I have been able to see it differently. Because I was so physically limited, I did what I could do and many of them were positive things I would have never done otherwise. I read, studied, wrote, prayed, and became closer to God. I could not indulge in things to distract myself from my situation. I had to face them directly, without the "drugs" of fun activities, other people, or my job.

One thing I've noticed about suffering (physically and emotionally) is that you feel alone. Even people who are very close to you seem so far away. Because they aren't experiencing what you are. When I felt alone, I gravitated toward God. He understood how I was feeling and comforted me.

The story of Job in the Bible took on a whole new meaning for me. I dare not compare what I've been through with what he went through. What he went through is almost unbelievable. The Lord said Job was blameless (Job 1:8) and look at all the suffering he went through! The Lord said there was no one on earth like him (same verse) and I believe it. To live what he lived through and not forsake the Lord was extraordinary.

The Lord is merciful and gracious. He is kind and has taught me so many important lessons during this seemingly too long time of recovery. Necessary lessons I would have not learned otherwise. I have come to know the Lord better. I learned what is truly important in life. I learned things about myself. The good and bad things about me and what I should change or not change. I now value how I am and if someone doesn't like it, it's not necessarily because there is something wrong with me. And, I don't need to worry about who appreciates the way I am or not. You want others to know your true self, and not be pleased, placated, and entertained by a façade. I learned that I want to try to be careful in how I interact with other people. I want to be considerate of people. I don't want to speak unnecessary or premature words that could lead a person on or play with their feelings. I knew that before, but I know it better now because I know how it can hurt. At times, I need to communicate better and plainly say to someone that I do not like what they're saying or how they're acting. I've gained much more empathy for people who are suffering physically, as well as emotionally. Someone's health problems are not who they are. Pride has been greatly destroyed in my life, and I hope it has been completely. I learned that most of my problems, if not all of them, were my own fault. I learned about the signs I ignored. There are many more lessons I've learned. Most of all, I am grateful for the growth in my relationship with the Lord.

I have been able to see that all the difficulties happening to me at once was useful. If I had suffered only one of them, I would not have been brought so low. I would have still felt strong enough on my own. I wouldn't have changed. I would not have felt like I needed the Lord so much. I needed to become broken, so the Lord could have His way and build me back up the way He wants me to be. The crumbling of my life is exactly what needed to happen. It was imperative. From the rubble, the Lord is rebuilding it properly and with the right Foundation. I don't mean the Lord made the difficulties happen in my life. I mean He used them and made beautiful things come from them. Everything happening at once, as well as the length of time recovery has been taking, accomplished the breaking of me. My job, my physical ability/health, activities I enjoy, another person, all had to be stripped away as things I "leaned on" for my self-worth and reasons for living. They were replaced with God Himself, and who or what is better than Him? There is stability and security in God. He doesn't change, and will never cease to be.

I believe God's people must find their identity with Him and not in their occupation, talents, activities, or in other people. God can use those things in a person's life, but it is not their identity. Generally, I think you can tell how much a person identified themselves in these things by how much pain they go through when these things are taken away.

I don't know much about horses. Basically, just what I've seen in western movies. What I meant by my needing to become broken compares nicely I think to breaking a horse. It's the self-will/old nature that has to be broken in a person. In the process of being broken there is a fight. Perhaps depending on the person, the severity of the fight varies. I visualize a horse being lassoed and it resisting. For me, it took a lot of suffering to be broken. I don't know what it takes for other Christians. I think the speed of this happening can vary in people, and their willingness has a lot to do with it. How long will they want their own way? How stubborn are they? Will the horse be easy or difficult to break? Through the suffering I experienced, I got to the point where I didn't want to fight anymore. I wanted God to have His way and do whatever He pleased with me. It was like, "God, I can't. I don't want to fight anymore. There's nothing I can do. I give up," and what follows is surrendering to God. Brokenness in a person is a kind of submission to God, where the natural self-will is not strong anymore. It has now surrendered and is obedient to God. I know that I wouldn't have been as surrendered to God without these things happening and breaking me. I was a Christian before all this, and somewhat surrendered, but not to the degree I am now.

I wonder if being "somewhat surrendered" is actually an oxymoron … how can one be partially surrendered? I suppose when some people become Christians they're surrendered to God pretty much from the start. Maybe others learn slower and give themselves over to God a part at a time.

I remember one day I was feeling really broken, but more in a sorrowful kind of way than the way I just described. I was thinking to myself, "I feel so broken." Then I heard the Lord say to me, "Stay broken." It surprised me. I thought maybe I misheard Him. Surely,

He wouldn't want me to stay broken. I did not mishear Him. I need to stay "broken," but not necessarily in a sorrowful way. I need to stay broken in terms of my self-will/old nature, stay surrendered to Him, so that He can have His way in my life. Lord willing, I will heal, but the self-will/old nature should remain broken. Like a person's arm, there are some "broken" points; the joints that flex and move. If they fused, one might say the arm was very strong, though virtually useless. There must be broken points for the arm to be used, move, and function properly.

It seems Paul had a physical problem that he asked the Lord to take away, but He didn't. Paul accepted this gladly. Why? The power of Christ worked through his weakness. He valued that more than being rid of the problem.

If I wanted to boast, I would be no fool in doing so, because I would be telling the truth. But I won't do it, because I don't want anyone to give me credit beyond what they can see in my life or hear in my message, even though I have received such wonderful revelations from God. So to keep me from becoming proud, I was given a thorn in my flesh, a messenger from Satan to torment me and keep me from becoming proud. Three different times I begged the Lord to take it away. Each time he said, "My grace is all you need. My power works best in weakness." So now I am glad to boast about my weaknesses, so that the power of Christ can work through me. That's why I take pleasure in my weaknesses, and in the insults, hardships, persecutions, and troubles that I suffer for Christ. For when I am weak, then I am strong. (2 Corinthians 12:6-10 NLT)

I don't mean to compare myself to Paul. I wanted to point out how his weakness was something he suffered from, and was unhappy about. However, his weakness helped in allowing the Lord to work wonderfully through him. It seems to me Paul saw this benefit from his weakness. As a result, he accepted it gladly. This makes me wonder if I would be willing to accept such a thing. Whatever form a weakness could take in a person's life, would I be willing to accept it, in order that so much good would come from it? It's a sacrifice, but one that cannot really be compared to the good it can bring.

It's taken me time to get over things, and I still am. At times when I am struggling with not being as physically able and pain-free as I used to be, I have a strange and intense dislike for anyone I see who seems to be walking normally. People I don't even know or truly dislike. I just dislike that I'm not able to walk like they do. I know it doesn't make sense. I just get that way sometimes. I have no idea what they're going through in their lives. For a long time after that period issue, I had fear every time I would get my period again. I wondered if I would stop bleeding at the appropriate time or not. I used to feel uneasy every time I'd see a library, because I got injured in one and I would remember that. I met the man I've mentioned at a square dance. Sometimes when I've been at a square dance, see the people dancing, hear the caller and the music, I get a sad feeling because I have memories. It's such a paradox to associate sad memories with something I enjoy, like dancing. So many other things I could include here.

Over 6 months after that relationship ended, I happened to meet him again. It was unavoidable because we were at the same event. As I said before, I had chosen to forgive him because I had been holding a grudge. I believe when you forgive someone, it's a choice not a feeling. Feelings may take more time to heal. Choices can be made in seconds. You can choose to forgive, then feelings will heal and you can move on. I believe if I don't forgive, the grudge will remain and so will adverse feelings.

It was weird to see someone who had meant something special to me, but now was kind of like a stranger. I was neither super friendly nor antagonistic. I was friendly, but I felt neutral. He said he hadn't met anyone else and seemed distressed about it. I said, "You don't have to worry about that." And, I meant it. He doesn't need to become worried over not finding someone. If it had not happened yet, it will happen. He was a nice enough person and I think many girls could like him.

I still cared about him, but not in the same way as before. We talked for awhile. I felt like we were on different planets. So much had happened to me since I spoke to him last. I had changed. In some ways I had changed, and in other ways I was who I was before, but more so. I perceived he had not changed. He had the same charm. He wanted to renew the "relationship." To him, it was as if nothing had transpired before (example: learning that my personality was too different than his). At least, he acted like nothing had happened. He said, "I wasn't ready before … but I'm ready now." That may be true, but now I was the one who wasn't ready. I wasn't ready before either, though I thought I was.

Mostly, I just listened to what he was saying. I sincerely find it fascinating how proficient some people are at talking. It is fascinating and sometimes impressive to see/hear people skilled at something that I'm not.

Essentially, I felt he didn't have some epiphany that made him think I was someone special. Instead, I was like the necessary female component needed to complete the plans he had made for his life. I was just someone. I wasn't interested in renewing anything.

He happened to meet my Dad that day. After introducing himself, the first thing he said to my dad was something like, "My grandma's been saying it's about time I settle down and have a couple kids." My Dad didn't think that was amusing. I thought it was funny, in both the odd and humorous sense. And, it made me question my former judgement. I wondered, "Who says that? Who says that right after meeting someone's Dad? Is this the person I liked so much?"

This meeting somehow helped me in getting over things. I saw that when I had the chance of being in a "relationship" with him again, now I was the one who wasn't interested. I don't mean that in a spiteful sort of way, as if to say, "Look at that. Look who came crawling back. Well, now he can have a taste of his own medicine!" followed by a "door slam" of sorts. No, not like that. I mean that I saw in myself that I had grown and changed, and now I could walk away from something I used to want.

Like I alluded to before, as a result of all that's happened I've gained so much. I know if I had recovered quickly, I would have missed very important lessons. If I had recovered quickly, I would have been busy with activities or distracted in some way from learning these important lessons. If I could somehow remove the fact that I've been unhappy from the equation of all that has happened, what remains is nothing but good. Good things that I would not have had, otherwise.

I see now that I would have continued to lead a mediocre Christian life. I would have lived my life, paying homage to the Lord now and then. I would be overly distracted by work, occupied with activities, and busy doing what I wanted to do. I would have been self-focused. The Lord would mean something to me, but not as deeply as He does now. I wouldn't have known Him as God, but as Someone I pay my respects to once in a while.

I've seen the difference between being happy and gaining in ways that do not typically come from being happy. These gains are mainly related to growing up and growing up spiritually too. Since as a Christian it is the Lord's will that I be transformed into His image and be holy, I will and must value that above being happy. I can see how through things I've suffered I have grown closer to Him. I can see how if I were always happy, I would remain shallow-minded and weak. I would be dependent upon circumstances in life going the way I want them to, to make me feel secure and strong. I am weak, but find my strength and security in the Lord.

Here I am a year and two months after all this started, and I am still recovering. By God's grace, I am still gaining things too. I started out by saying 2015 was the worst year of my life so far. It was the worst year. Yet, now I feel it was the year I hit a "jackpot" of sorts. Because it was the beginning of a closer walk with the Lord, and because I've learned invaluable lessons. I can write that and mean it, even now as I'm in pain.

5

I think it's important to learn that happiness is not the goal of being a Christian. Being happy is not the standard by which a

Christian should evaluate their life, and then determine if it is going well or not. When you learn that, you won't think that being unhappy means something is wrong. You won't think that when a difficulty comes, it necessarily means you did something wrong. It may be the opposite. Also, you will be able to see difficulties as opportunities for growth. For me, this revelation has brought relief. It has brought clarity too. I don't mean to say that being a Christian is constant unhappiness. It is not. The times I've felt the most happy and content are some of my times with the Lord. I mean that the goal is to become like Christ and if some unhappiness makes you more like Him, then it is beneficial.

I realize this is not always comforting to hear. If someone told me this when the events I've described first happened, I would not find it comforting. At that time, I would just want all the suffering to stop. Who cares about all the good things I would gain from it?

My old nature can see nothing but the bad things from this time in my life. It utterly hates every moment of it and wishes it never happened. But, my new nature is glad it happened. It is grateful and delighted to see all the priceless treasures that have come from it.

"All that matters is that you're happy." I know people mean well when they say things like that. But, if I really take what is said seriously, my being happy is not all that matters. All that really matters is that I'm becoming more like Christ. I don't value being happy above everything else.

Remember what the Lord desires to accomplish in the lives of His people – to make them holy like Him. So much of what happens in life are ways and means to get people where He wants them to be. The events are secondary to the hearts He wants to mold and make.

Look at life as a continuum. Not chopped up into good days and bad days, into moments of feelings, but as a continuing whole. The whole is a process towards a goal. The goal of being like Him. I think this perspective helps make sense of things. The bad days will have purpose as much as the good days. In addition, this perspective gives a person a wider view of life, rather than focusing on how they may be feeling one day. I don't mean to completely discount how someone feels day to day, but to try to help people look beyond what is immediately before them and know that there are greater purposes for it.

I would venture to say that if I wanted to be happy in this life on earth, in this world, I wouldn't be a Christian. I know that no matter what you believe, it doesn't guarantee a happy life. However, if I wanted to be happy in this life on earth, in this world, I would not be a Christian. I would do the things I had to do in life, be a generally good citizen, and other than that I would endeavor to find happiness in whatever way I could have it. That would be my goal. I wouldn't believe in Him or follow Him. He would mean nothing to me. And, since everyone who isn't a "bad person" goes to heaven, I could just avoid being a "bad person" (you know, murderers and extra bad people), believe and live as I please otherwise, and be assured of going to heaven anyway. There's practically nothing to lose. As a result, I think I would be an awfully self-centered person. I would also go to hell.

As I said before, I know that no matter what you believe, it doesn't guarantee a happy/easy life. Why is this true for other beliefs and manners of life, but when applied to Christianity it isn't talked about? Probably because it's unappealing.

I think it's a terrible misconception to believe that being a Christian should/must equal happiness in this earthly life. In my opinion, when that is believed, a Christian focuses more on the state of their happiness than on Jesus. It creates this kind of mindset: "I'll become a Christian so I can live a happy life." Instead of, "I'll become a Christian because Jesus is Lord." The moment a difficulty comes along it indicates something wrong must be happening. If enough difficulties come, there would be a logical tendency to think, "This Christian-thing isn't working out for me." It creates weaker Christians. This misconception sets people up for a harder fall when the difficulties do come.

What about all the suffering the Apostles went through? What about all the Christian martyrs in history? Were they following the same Jesus we are today? Or, is the Christianity of the past different from the Christianity of today? The reality that being a Christian does not always equal ease and happiness in this life is a hard truth. One that is quite unpalatable to our old nature. So much so, that it seems like it must not be true.

I believe another misconception is the idea that following Jesus is free. That it's free of cost. You believe in Jesus as Lord, become a Christian, and that's it. There is nothing else to do, just believe in Jesus and then live your life as you please. Without doing sinful things, of course.

Salvation is a free. There is nothing we did or can do to earn it. It was given. When you believe in your heart that Jesus is Lord, and as a result have been born again by His Spirit, you have salvation. However, following Jesus and growing up into all God wants you to be will cost you your life. There is a price to be paid. What do you think these verses mean?

Then Jesus said to his disciples, "If any of you wants to be my follower, you must give up your own way, take up your cross, and follow me. If you try to hang on to your life, you will lose it. But if you give up your life for my sake, you will save it. (Matthew 16:24-25 NLT)

Those who love their life in this world will lose it. Those who care nothing for their life in this world will keep it for eternity. (John 12:25 NLT)

"Anyone who wants to be my follower must love me far more than he does his own father, mother, wife, children, brothers, or sisters – yes, more than his own life – otherwise he cannot be my disciple. And no one can be my disciple who does not carry his own cross and follow me. But don't begin until you count the cost. For who would begin construction of a building without first getting estimates and then checking to see if he has enough money to pay the bills? Otherwise he might complete only the foundation before running out of funds. And then how everyone would laugh! 'See that fellow there?' they would mock. 'He started that building and ran out of money before it was finished!' Or what king would ever dream of going to war without first sitting down with his counselors and discussing whether his army of 10,000 is strong enough to defeat the 20,000 men who are marching against him? If the decision is negative, then while the enemy troops are still far away, he will send a truce team to discuss terms of peace. So no one can become my disciple unless he first sits down and counts his blessings – and then renounces them all for me. (Luke 14:26:33 TLB)

There is a choice in wanting to become all God wants you to be, or not. It is His will that we all become full grown.

Now these are the gifts Christ gave to the church: the apostles, the prophets, the evangelists, and the pastors and teachers. Their responsibility is to equip God's people to do his work and build up the church, the body of Christ. This will continue until we all come to such unity in our faith and knowledge of God's Son that we will be mature in the Lord, measuring up to the full and complete standard of Christ. (Ephesians 4:11-13 NLT)

A person who has received salvation, therefore a Christian, may not become all God wants them to be. Some of God's people will remain baby Christians, but they are still His.

If I were not following after Jesus, happiness is about all I would desire to have. It would be my goal in life. It's all I would want. And, it wouldn't really matter to me how I would get it as long as I wasn't a "bad person." Indeed, if a person is not following Jesus, they should pursue all the happiness they can have now. That is all they have.

A Christian doesn't live for all the happiness they can have now. They are living for Jesus and for the eternity ahead. The happy things this world offers can be enjoyed only for the time a person lives on earth. A Christian lays down their earthly life for Jesus and what lies ahead in eternity. I would rather enjoy happy things for eternity, than happy things for the timespan of my life here on earth.

I compare it to giving the Lord a penny, which represents my life. In exchange, He gives me back a bar of gold.

Know that being a Christian does not always equal happiness, and sometimes that is a direct result of our faith.

6

Lately I've been thinking that this Christian life is like a kamikaze mission. You've got to be all in. It may not mean physical death for every Christian, although it could happen, but it should mean the death of every Christian's old nature/self-will. It's like there is nothing you would withhold from God. Nothing you're holding onto or keeping for yourself. Instead, you have let it all go, and God has you completely. It can be hard to accept this. God can have 50% of me, or maybe 75%, but 100%? Surely, I can have a small part of me for myself. No, it must be 100%.

What I mean by there is nothing in your life that you would withhold from God is that it is His will that rules your life, not your own. Another way to put it is to be led by Holy Spirit rather than by your old nature/self-will. I think there are different examples of this. Perhaps my examples are not the best, but I will give them anyway. If I were listening to a song I liked but the lyrics were bad, I might feel Holy Spirit telling me that I shouldn't listen to it; that He doesn't want me to. Now, I have the choice of following my own will or His. I want to listen to the song because I like it, but I know He doesn't want me to. Am I willing to give up even something as small as one song, or is my own will still too strong to submit? Will I obey or not? One thing I learned is that obeying God is always the better choice. He doesn't ask you to do something for no reason, and the reason is always good. Another example: I say something unkind to someone. I know my motive behind what I said was not love. I may be pressed by Holy Spirit to say I'm sorry to that person. Again, my own will does not want to do that and will come up with a multitude of excuses for why I don't need to. But, in my heart I know Holy Spirit wants me to. So, am I willing to obey, humble myself, and apologize? These are small examples, but there could be bigger issues like giving up friendships, jobs, money, or many other things. It may not always be giving up things, but it's when God's will is obeyed rather than your own.

I think this becomes easier when you understand how good God's will always is. And, you'll want to obey Him because you love and trust Him. Since the goal is to become more like Christ, why cling to anything (like what your old nature/self-will wants) that is holding you back from the goal?

A vital aspect in this is that it's led by Holy Spirit. I cannot take it upon myself, take the lead, and go do things I know are good thinking I'm earning points with God.

We are all infected and impure with sin. When we display our righteous deeds, they are nothing but filthy rags. Like autumn leaves, we wither and fall, and our sins sweep us away like the wind. (Isaiah 64:6 NLT)

So I say, let the Holy Spirit guide your lives. Then you won't be doing what your sinful nature craves. (Galatians 5:16 NLT)

I know the death of your old nature/self-will, and giving your life to God is not always pleasant to think about. With God and time, I think a person will learn to delight in obeying God, and not themselves. Especially when they want to grow up and be all God wants them to be.

I'm kind of embarrassed to admit that surrendering and giving my life to God was much easier to me when it was useless to me. That's been another benefit of the difficulties I've had. Life didn't seem to be going so well anymore, so I didn't care about keeping it. If it was "going well," I would have liked it and would want to keep it for myself. Through this experience, I can see that even when I'm all better again, it is best to give 100% of myself to God. To not only give Him 50%, or parts of my life that don't affect me too much or that I deem appropriate to give, but to be wholly devoted to Him. I've got to take this life seriously at some point. It's so fragile and fleeting. It's not a test run. Is He my God or not? There is nothing better I can do with my life than give it to God.

By God's grace, if a person can learn this lesson without going through deep suffering, that would be wonderful. If a person must learn this lesson through deep suffering, it is unfortunate that they had to suffer, but a necessary lesson was learned.

My old self has been crucified with Christ. It is no longer I who live, but Christ lives in me. So I live in this earthly body by trusting in the Son of God, who loved me and gave himself for me. (Galatians 2:20 NLT)

In a race, everyone runs but only one person gets first prize. So run your race to win. To win the contest you must deny yourselves many things that would keep you from doing your best. An athlete goes to all this trouble just to win a blue ribbon or a silver cup, but we do it for a heavenly reward that never disappears. So I run straight to the goal with purpose in every step. I fight to win. I'm not just shadow-boxing or playing around. Like an athlete I punish my body, treating it roughly, training it to do what it should, not what it wants to. Otherwise I fear that after enlisting others for the race, I myself might be declared unfit and ordered to stand aside. (1 Corinthians 9:24-27 TLB)

Remember we are living out part of eternity right now. Eternal life is secured for all who believe in the Lord Jesus - for all who have put their faith and trust in Him. This life is a limited time on earth devoted to Him and to His will. This time on earth is very limited. If a person were to live to be 100 years old, it is still a very short time compared to eternity. Each person will spend eternity somewhere.

There certainly are happy, wonderful times for the Christian in this earthly life. Thoroughly enjoy those times. There typically are the usual joys people have in life. They're just not what is lived for or what is most important.

There is another side to being a Christian. There are times of happiness that have nothing to do with this world and everything to do with God. There is a truly abundant life. There is joy in solitary communion with God that cannot be well explained unless you've experienced it for yourself, or someone who is a better writer than I am explains it. No analogy will do. There are beautiful experiences when as a part of the church you are functioning as the Lord intended you to, and so are others. There are wonderful times when the Lord uses you to help others. Most of all, it is awesome God Himself who will take your breath away. These kinds of happiness make the typical joys in life pale in comparison.

7

The Lord is faithful and has put up with a lot from me in the past year and 2 months. I am thankful. Throughout that time, He never loved me less. Even when I was angry with Him or thought I was worthless, He didn't love me less and never will. He is gentle and loving toward me. He's helped me through the darkest times, and given me hope. He's always been with me. He's encouraged me and made me smile.

Because of the Lord, when doctors, others, and myself all failed to know what my physical problem was and thus a prognosis of my future, I wasn't hopeless. Even when I felt hopeless, I wasn't. I still had a shred of hope. Sometimes, a microscopic speck of hope. Not because of any other reason than because I knew who my God was. It was because of Him. Even the fact that I knew who He was I attribute to His mercy, not my intelligence. I knew that He is able to heal. He can heal people when doctors can do nothing more for them. For that matter, He can raise the dead. I really don't know what I would have done without the Lord, and I don't want to know.

I've learned that the times in my life when things are "going well" are times I need the Lord just as much as when things aren't "going well." I just feel I need Him more desperately when I'm suffering. In reality, I need Him just as desperately when I'm not suffering. Perhaps, even more at those times because I could become deceived into thinking I'm self-sufficient.

The times I begged Him to just make all the suffering stop at that moment, His answer was no. He was strong and patient to say no and I'm glad He did because there was still more to be gained. I doubt I would be strong enough to say no. I imagine if someone was suffering terribly and begged me to make their suffering stop and I had the power to do it, I would probably stop their suffering. Even if I knew they would gain invaluable things if they would endure it longer. It seems like it takes a strong kind of love to say no in such a circumstance.

He has better plans for me than I do. I don't know all that is ahead, but I trust Him. It's not always easy to do that. Sometimes it's very hard. That's another lesson I've learned and I'm still learning it through all this - to trust Him. I learned it mostly through the times when there has been nothing else I can do but trust Him, and it took a lot of suffering to get me to that point. Some lessons continue through life. They're not just learned and then you're done with them. Like, learning to and continuing to trust Him. They continue.

It is amazing how much growth takes place out of pain. Kind of like when a fruit tree is pruned.

Though I have a very long way to go, I can say that my unhappiness has truly made me more Christ-like. And, I attribute that to God working on me through my unhappiness, not the unhappiness alone. I don't mean that like, "Look at me, I'm so holy!" No, I just mean that I've made progress in holiness, thank God. He's made beautiful things come from horrible things. I know this may not make sense to some people, but anyone who has experienced this will know precisely what I mean.

And we know that God causes everything to work together for the good of those who love God and are called according to his purpose for them. For God knew his people in advance, and he chose them to become like his Son, so that his Son would be the firstborn among many brothers and sisters. (Romans 8:28-29 NLT)

But all these things that I once thought very worthwhile – now I've thrown them all away so that I can put my trust and hope in Christ alone. Yes, everything else is worthless when compared with the priceless gain of knowing Christ Jesus my Lord. I have put aside all else, counting it worth less than nothing, in order that I can have Christ, and become one with him, no longer counting on being saved by being good enough or by obeying God's laws, but by trusting Christ to save me; for God's way of making us right with himself depends on faith – counting on Christ alone. Now I have given up everything else – I have found it to be the only way to really know Christ and to experience the mighty power that brought him back to life again, and to find out what it means to suffer and to die with him. So, whatever it takes, I will be one who lives in the fresh newness of life of those who are alive from the dead. I don't mean to say I am perfect. I haven't learned all I should even yet, but I keep working toward that day when I will finally be all that Christ saved me for and wants me to be. (Philippians 3:7-12 TLB)

Yea doubtless, and I count all things *but* loss for the excellency of the knowledge of Christ Jesus my Lord: for whom I have suffered the loss of all things, and do count them *but* dung, that I may win Christ, And be found in him, not having mine own righteousness, which is of the law, but that which is through the faith of Christ, the righteousness which is of God by faith: That I may know him, and the power of his resurrection, and the fellowship of his sufferings, being made conformable unto his death; If by any means I might attain unto the resurrection of the dead. Not as though I had already attained, either were already perfect: but I follow after, if that I may apprehend that for which also I am apprehended of Christ Jesus. Brethren, I count not myself to have apprehended: but *this* one thing *I do*, forgetting those things which are behind, and reaching forth unto those things which are before, I press toward the mark for the prize of the high calling of God in Christ Jesus. (Philippians 3:8-14 KJV)

There is a right time for everything: A time to be born, a time to die; a time to plant; a time to harvest; a time to kill; a time to heal; a time to destroy; a time to rebuild; a time to cry; a time to laugh; a time to grieve; a time to dance; (Ecclesiastes 3:1-4 TLB)

Dear brothers, is your life full of difficulties and temptations? Then be happy, for when the way is rough, your patience has a chance to grow. So let it grow, and don't try to squirm out of your problems. For when your patience is finally in full bloom, then you will be ready for anything, strong in character, full and complete. (James 1:2-4 TLB)

Count it all joy, my brothers, when you meet trials of various kinds, for you know that the testing of your faith produces steadfastness. And let steadfastness have its full effect, that you may be perfect and complete, lacking in nothing. (James 1:2-4 ESV)

Dear friends, don't be surprised at the fiery trials you are going through, as if something strange were happening to you. Instead, be very glad--for these trials make you partners with Christ in his suffering, so that you will have the wonderful joy of seeing his glory when it is revealed to all the world. (1 Peter 4:12-13 NLT)

I have refined you, but not as silver is refined. Rather, I have refined you in the furnace of suffering. (Isaiah 48:10 NLT)

What a wonderful God we have – he is the Father of our Lord Jesus Christ, the source of every mercy, and the one who so wonderfully comforts and strengthens us in our hardships and trials. And why does he do this? So that when others are troubled, needing our sympathy and encouragement, we can pass on to them this same help and comfort God has given us. You can be sure that the more we undergo sufferings for Christ, the more he will shower us with his comfort and encouragement. We are in deep trouble for bringing you God's comfort and salvation. But in our trouble God has comforted us - and this, too, to help you: to show you from our personal experience how God will tenderly comfort you when you undergo these same sufferings. He will give you the strength to endure. (2 Corinthians 1:3-7 TLB)

The Spirit of the Lord God is upon me, because the Lord has anointed me to bring good news to the suffering and afflicted. He has sent me to comfort the broken-hearted, to announce liberty to captives and to open the eyes of the blind. He has sent me to tell those who mourn that the time of God's favor to them has come, and the day of his wrath to their enemies. To all who mourn in Israel he will give:

>Beauty for ashes;
>Joy instead of mourning;
>Praise instead of heaviness.

For God has planted them like strong and graceful oaks for his own glory. (Isaiah 61:1-3 TLB)

72

Words You Speak

Death and life are in the power of the tongue, and those who love it will eat its fruits. (Proverbs 18:21 ESV)

Death, life, and power are intense words. Their meanings are strong.

power: n. 1. The capacity or ability to do or accomplish something. 2. A particular ability, capability, or skill. 3. a. Strength, force, or might. b. Forceful impact : effectiveness.[1]

life: 1. The property or quality by which living organisms are distinguished from dead organisms or inanimate matter, esp. as shown in the ability to grow, carry on metabolism, respond to stimuli, and reproduce.[2]

death: n. 1. The cessation of life.[3]

Using these definitions with the verse from Proverbs would indicate that the tongue has capacities in death and life. There is power in what you speak. That's amazing to me.

I remember the saying, "Sticks and stones may break my bones, but words will never hurt me." Or, "Sticks and stones may break my bones, but names will never harm me." I think both versions of this saying are untrue. I think I understand what is meant by them. I think they are meant to console a person by saying that words will never hurt them. Or, maybe it could be a sort of personal creed, like determining for yourself that words will never hurt you. Nevertheless, it implies that physical injury may hurt a person, but words don't. Words have a greater impact than this saying suggests.

It is saddening to me how some dismiss the obvious, to their own detriment. I can understand why. Sometimes it is dismissed because it is too painful to face as truth. There have been times I have been reluctant to accept the truth. But, to me, it must be accepted for any progress to be made.

Words can hurt. Acknowledging this is acknowledging fact, not weakness. As the verse Proverbs 18:21 indicates, words can do more than hurt a person. They have power in things as serious as death and life. Words can help people, too.

There is one who speaks rashly like the thrusts of a sword, But the tongue of the wise brings healing. (Proverbs 12:18 NASB)

Imagine that. "Thrusts of a sword" … sounds violent, brutal, and deadly. That can be the effect of what a person speaks. On the other hand, words can bring healing. That is wonderful. I remember one time someone said something nice to me, and it truly felt like something inside me was mended. I noticed it. I wondered why something relatively small, like one sentence, affected me so positively. It's because words do have power. Also, at that moment I felt like a withering plant dying of thirst and someone came along and gave me water. The words brought life.

When a person realizes the power in spoken words, it can make them more careful of what they say. The seriousness of their words will become so real, they will want to speak carefully. They may consciously choose to speak good words toward themselves and others, rather than bad words.

Personally, there are some phrases I would avoid using toward myself. Particularly in a negative way. For instance, "I can't live without _____ ," "I'll never _____ ." There are statements I wouldn't choose to use toward others, like "You'll never amount to anything," "You never do that right," "Just wait. Someday this will happen to you," "You'll never understand," and other statements like these that are basically like curses against someone. It doesn't matter to me if they're done in "fun" or not. It's spoken negatively, and not in an edifying way.

If a person doesn't want what they speak to become reality or remain a reality, they shouldn't say it.

I understand that it's not enjoyable to watch what you say. It can feel like a chore, and a loss of fun. For some, not watching what they say is fun. But as I said before, I believe when a person really understands the power in their words they'll want to speak carefully.

On November 3, 2016, I started an experiment to test the power of words. I encourage others to try it too. It was educational, and it made the power of words undeniably real to me. It wasn't really scientific. I got the idea from others who have tried it, and I believe they got it from Dr. Emoto's experiments with water crystals. His experiments are fascinating, if you want to look into it.

In my experiment, I put the same amount of freshly cooked white rice in two jars. I labeled each jar with sticky notes. On one I wrote "love" and on the other one I wrote "hate." For 41 days I spoke nice things to the love jar, and bad things to the hate jar. I wasn't consistent in doing this each day. It felt kind of funny to be speaking to jars of rice, but for the sake of the experiment I did it anyway. Some of the things I said to the love jar were, "You're appreciated," "You're loved," "You have a future," and "You're good." Some of the things I said to the hate jar were, "No one loves you," "You're disgusting," "You have no future," and "No one wants you." When I began the experiment, both jars of rice were the same. After 41 days the rice in the love jar had a small amount of mold, while the rice in the hate jar was covered with mold. The difference between the two was obvious.

To me, the results were more than interesting. The results were serious. The Bible already indicates that there is power in the words you speak, but here before my eyes was evidence. The evidence before me was so clear, it was amazing. Yet, it only supported what the Lord has already said in the Bible.

It made me feel kind of somber, to see how words really affect. It made me think of the things I've spoken. And, if mere rice is affected by words, what about living, breathing things, like people? It made me consider what I say more than I do already.

Before this experiment I rarely said grace. Like, giving thanks to the Lord or saying a blessing over a meal before eating. Now, I feel motivated to say grace. My main motive should be to simply express my thankfulness to God, but another motive is to ask for His blessing over the food I'm about to consume. I saw how my words over the rice affected it (positively and negatively), so I wanted to take advantage of that with food I eat.

Moving to a somewhat different subject:

When there are many words, transgression is unavoidable, But he who restrains his lips is wise. (Proverbs 10:19 NASB)

In the multitude of words there wanteth not sin: but he that refraineth his lips *is* wise. (Proverbs 10:19 KJV)

I've had occasions recently to experience these verses in real life. With the holidays we've just been through, there were social events I attended. I'm not usually talkative, but at these events I talked more than usual. During conversations I would say things that weren't what I wanted to say, or even believed. I don't mean to say I lied, but I expressed myself wrong. For instance, I'd begin a segment of my talking with, "One of my problems is …" When in fact, if I think about it, I do not believe it is one of my problems. I just said it that way because it's something I'm dealing with, but it's not something I would really call a problem. Or, if someone else was talking, I would say, "Yeah" as if I agreed with what they said. When in fact, I did not agree with what they said, it just came out that way. I realized I spoke words I did not choose carefully. Sometimes I said "yeah" just to let the other person know I was listening, but if I scrutinize what I said it was like I was agreeing with them when that was not my intention. Sometimes I said the wrong thing because the conversation was so fast, to keep the pace I chose the first word that came to me, though it wasn't a very accurate one.

I would know I said the wrong thing in the middle of conversations I had, or after the event when I got home. Then I would talk to the Lord about them and say that I didn't mean those things, and I would take them back. I'd say I was sorry and ask for His forgiveness and for His help that I wouldn't do that anymore.

Basically, this verse (Proverbs 10:19) is so real to me. At these social events I would talk more, and there would be transgressions made. From the sheer quantity of words I spoke (and not choosing them carefully), transgressions were made. At every one of them I said things I didn't want to say, and it just happened that way because of not being careful enough. The chance of saying the wrong thing increased as the amount of words increased. I thought to myself, "The more I talk the more mistakes I make." I don't want to give myself any excuses for it, either. It doesn't matter if I was so engaged in the conversation that I was careless with my words. And, it doesn't matter if I need to take an awkwardly long pause in the conversation to choose better words. I would like to be responsible for the words I choose to speak, and speak the right ones.

The answer to this dilemma is not to cease from talking. A person could go to the extreme and think that they'd better not say anything to avoid making mistakes. Generally, I believe it's true that the more a person talks, the more chance there is of saying the wrong things. However, I think the answer is to simply be careful and consider one's words. And, to ask the Lord for help with this and for self-control.

As I thought more about the whole subject of the power of one's words, it came to my mind that I tell Cooper (my dog) that he's a good dog at least 10 times a day. I say it as I'm playing with him, or just when he looks up at me. It makes me wonder about the effect it has on him. There have been times that because of his behavior, someone else will disapprovingly say to him, "You're so fickle!" So I say, "He's not fickle!" To make sure a bad word didn't have an effect on him.

In frustration, when a parent says to their child, "You never listen!" I understand why that is said. However, I wonder if they understand the power of what they're pronouncing over their child.

Be aware of what others say to you. If you hear them speaking to you in a way that isn't right, do not accept it. For example, if someone says to you, "You're not smart enough," don't accept that. First, don't believe what they say. You could respond with, "I am smart enough," or, "No, I don't accept that." If in fun someone says to you, "You're crazy!" I would not accept that either. The statements a person should not accept can come subtly too. For instance, someone saying in a soft and soothing voice, "Dear, you're just not the kind of person who can get a job like that," don't believe it or accept it. In addition, an unacceptable statement could sound good: "You're perfect!" Absolutely not, that is just false. Someone could actually be praying over you. Regardless of that, if they're not saying right and true things, you are not obligated to accept it. Not accepting bad words will help a person protect themselves from being affected.

Remember, there is power in words to influence for good as well. As I'm sure we all know, words can be used to encourage, support, love, show kindness and sympathy, and help others. Speak in good ways.

Words have power. I think that understanding this helps a person to be more careful. We have the choice of saying good things or bad things toward ourselves and others. While it takes discipline and self-control, it is wise to choose good words.

The tongue has the power of life and death, and those who love it will eat its fruit. (Proverbs 18:21 NIV)

He who guards his mouth and tongue, Guards his soul from troubles. (Proverbs 21:23 NASB)

Set a guard, O LORD, over my mouth; Keep watch over the door of my lips. Do not incline my heart to any evil thing, To practice deeds of wickedness With men who do iniquity; And do not let me eat of their delicacies. (Psalm 141:3-4 NASB)

A gentle tongue is a tree of life, but perverseness in it breaks the spirit. (Proverbs 15:4 ESV)

Kind words are like honey – sweet to the soul and healthy for the body. (Proverbs 16:24 NLT)

73

Alone with God

I wanted to write a little about the importance of being alone with God. When I say "being alone with God," I mean talking with/praying to Him. I mean setting aside a time to be away from distractions and focus on communicating with Him. This is simple, but it is an effort. It takes discipline, time, and concentration. But it is so important and the benefits are beyond words.

To begin, I don't mean to say anything against being in church/being with other Christians, reading the Bible or other spiritual books, or listening to teachings and preaching. I just want to focus on being alone with God.

Being alone with God helps a person to get to know Him. Not through a third person, not by what someone else says about Him, but them personally getting to know Him.

When getting to know someone, I think another level is always reached when you're alone with them. I believe the same goes for being alone with God. A lot can be learned about someone by what people who know them say, and by their reputation. You can learn about them by knowing some of their history. You can learn about them by observing their behavior at a distance; without involving yourself with them directly. However, I think all these methods of knowing about someone are not quite the same as being alone with them and getting to know them personally.

A person can talk with and hear God in any location. I find it easier to focus when I'm in a location that is free of distractions. Find a location that works for you and set aside a time to talk with Him there. Try to make it a habit. Speak to Him normally (in your head or out loud), and then be quiet and listen for His reply. It can be helpful to write down what you hear. Don't become discouraged.

As I do this, it can be a challenge to simply be quiet. Like, be quiet in my mind. It's one thing to keep your mouth shut but another thing entirely to keep the thoughts in your mind quiet. I'll be in the middle of being quiet and listening for His voice when I'll think about something totally unrelated like, "Oh, I have to make that phone call today," or, "What am I going to have for breakfast?" I must push away all those thoughts, calm myself, and really be quiet as I listen for His voice. At times this has been such a challenge that I feel somewhat successful if I'm able to simply have a quiet mind. It seems to get easier with time and practice. Often, it's when the chatter of thoughts in my mind is quieted that I can then hear Him speak.

It is helpful to get in a place mentally where nothing else in the world matters at that moment than you focusing on Him and letting Him speak or do whatever He wants to; there are no distractions or anything that is getting your attention more than Him.

Another obstacle I faced while praying was my trying too hard to hear His voice. My advice is to not try so hard. Let Him speak. Let His words come to you, don't try to make yourself hear Him. The most eager and straining ears will not hear Him if He isn't speaking, so wait and let Him speak.

I want to emphasize the point of being quiet and listening for His reply - if He has anything He wants to say. For most of my Christian life I did not do this. For years and years my prayers were a monologue of things I wanted, amen, done. I don't mean that we shouldn't ask the Lord for things, we should. What I mean is, I've discovered that prayer is more than me asking for things. In my opinion, when He speaks is the best part. It is important to ask for things, pray for others, and for anything He'd want you to, but hearing Him talk is the best part to me. Think of prayer as a conversation, not a monologue. For years I'd been completely missing that.

Again, don't become discouraged. When trying to hear God's voice, there will probably be times when you're mistaken. I've done that, and for me it feels pretty wretched. To me, it is a huge mistake: to think I heard God, but I didn't. Don't let mistakes keep you from continuing on. Frequently, even when I truly hear His voice there's something that makes me wonder if it's really Him. Like, am I really hearing Him or is it just me? I know it takes faith, but somehow knowing that doesn't really help me because I want to be sure it's Him. I guess that's the whole point of having faith – to be assured when based on human logic you're not sure. There have been many times I've heard Him and it was confirmed to me from an outside source. Yet, the whole time I had a slight doubt about if it was Him until it was confirmed. It was truly Him. It seems I sometimes have to get over the fact that I really do hear Him and it's not my imagination. I guess what I'm getting at is there can be times when you're unsure, or make mistakes in hearing Him and it's not abnormal. It's part of learning and growing.

I know that sometimes this "being alone with God" is rare, but it really shouldn't be. I think it should be normal. It can tend to happen at extreme times in a person's life. Like when they're stretched to their limit, feeling desperate in their circumstances, and so they fall to their knees and cry out to God for help. A person doesn't have to wait for a situation like this, and I hope they would not wait. Try to take the time now to develop this most important relationship in your life.

When a person makes a habit of being alone and praying to God, it won't feel so awkward. Because, it does feel awkward at first. Even now, sometimes I don't know what to say, or where to begin. At those times I might not say anything and wait for Him to say something. Or, I'll pray in tongues. Over time, He won't be like a stranger to you.

I wish everyone had a close personal relationship with God. I cannot really explain how important it is, other than it is invaluable and I feel like that doesn't explain it well at all. I can wish it for others and do what I should about it, but this issue is between a person and God, not anyone else.

Sometimes (and probably at times for the rest of my life), when I pray I realize my deficient ability to know God. It can be unsatisfying. On the other hand, I'm glad I am unable to know God completely, or else He wouldn't be God. I cannot really know God completely, nobody can. I catch a glimpse of the vast difference between myself and God, and even using the word "vast" to describe it is inadequate. The awe of God along with the insufficiencies of me inspires more awe of God. So, with all I can muster at that point to express myself I say, "God, Who are you? Who are you?" I mean, I know Who He is, but at the same time I don't know. It seems the more I know Him, the more I realize I don't know Him and how I can't know all of Him. It's kind of hard to explain. He's just so infinite, and sometimes I catch a glimpse of that. But, I am so very thankful that I (and we) can know Him to an extent. A very precious extent it is!

At times you will feel very close to Him, closer than you are with any other person. At other times you will experience the awe of Who He is and it's a little fearful. After all, you're communicating with the One Who has all power, created everything, and is accountable to no one. You're communicating with God, and sometimes that realization strikes me. And, I know I'm not fully grasping the magnitude of the fact. Makes me think of an aphid sitting on the palm of a person's hand and talking to them. In a moment the aphid could be squished dead. The difference between God and man is greater than this. I don't mean to say that a person should pray and be afraid of being "squished." I mean at times there is a feeling of deep reverence and awe toward God, in addition to the other times when He's like all the love and friendship you've ever experienced from other people rolled up into One.

This personal relationship with God is not just for me. When I say that I neither mean to suggest that my relationship with the Lord is all it can be yet nor that I have all the answers. My point is if the Lord has allowed Me to know Him as much as I do, He will surely do the same for you. And, He wants to. I am no more loved by Him than you are.

I would like to know Him more and more. I would like Him to be as real to me as any person. What I do know is, when you truly get to know Him you'll love Him. He loves you already, and will always love you more than you love Him. One thing that surprised me about Him is He has a delightful sense of humor. He always says the right things; He is wise. He's the best Teacher. He will help you. He's interested in every part of your life. He knows exactly how to deal with you. He's not impatient. Frequently He'll speak words that seem to dismantle your very soul and reveal what you're made of.

Sometimes, I believe the Lord just wants to be with His own people. He's always with us, but I mean setting aside a time to be with Him in a deliberate way. He doesn't want His people to do something all the time, but just wants to be with them. Because He loves them. He loves to speak with His own and talk about things. To be near. And, He wants this with you, too. Study, read, have fellowship with others, and listen to teachings. They are good, even necessary. But it is never the same as being alone with Him. When His own are alone with Him it is different than when any kind of third person is involved. The one-on-one times with Him are precious. He loves His own.

But when you pray, go away by yourself, shut the door behind you, and pray to your Father in private. Then your Father, who sees everything, will reward you. (Matthew 6:6 NLT)

Know that the LORD is God. It is he who made us, and we are his; we are his people, the sheep of his pasture. (Psalm 100:3 NIV)

And it is impossible to please God without faith. Anyone who wants to come to him must believe that God exists and that he rewards those who sincerely seek him. (Hebrews 11:6 NLT)

For if I pray in a tongue, my spirit prays, but my mind is unfruitful. (1 Corinthians 14:14 NASB)

Be anxious for nothing, but in everything by prayer and supplication with thanksgiving let your requests be made known to God. (Philippians 4:6 NASB)

supplicate: v. – cated, - cating. 1. To ask for humbly and earnestly by or as if by praying. 2. To make an earnest appeal. – supplication n.[1]

All heaven shall praise your miracles, O Lord; myriads of angels will praise you for your faithfulness. For who in all of heaven can be compared with God? What mightiest angel is anything like him? The highest of angelic powers stand in dread and awe of him. Who is as revered as he by those surrounding him? O Jehovah, Commander of the heavenly armies, where is there any other Mighty One like you? Faithfulness is your very character. (Psalms 89:5-8 TLB)

74

Just Say No to Comparing

They had an excellent job. They lived in a coveted (by some) location in the city. Other details I know about their life are nothing but exceptional, even admirable.

Then I compared myself to them.

The perilous round of thoughts began. I thought to myself, "They have a great job. I don't. They have their own upscale place to live. I don't. They're so active and able. I'm not. (That hit a sore spot.) How come I haven't achieved those things? They've accomplished things I haven't, and I'm older than they are. Why are other peoples' lives so simple, and mine is so complicated?" I did not measure up to them at all by these standards.

Then to console and elevate myself I thought of the good things I have that they probably don't. Which, at this point is basically and wholly my relationship with the Lord. I thought, "Well, they probably don't know the Lord as well as I do." I could have gone smugly on my way at that point, but it didn't end there.

That thought could not be accepted. It wasn't right. I thought, "My relationship with the Lord is something He's given me. I can't take any credit for that. Besides, I really don't know if they have a relationship with the Lord or not. If they don't, I want that for them. If they do, then they're like a sibling and I should be happy for them. Why am I comparing myself to them anyway?" Then I felt guilty and ashamed that I had even compared myself.

First of all, it is clear why they are in their situation and I am not. They made certain choices and worked hard for what they have. I did not make certain choices and have not worked toward those things. Second, I'm not them and they're not me. Third, I should not compare myself to anyone.

In this brief but tumultuous round of thoughts I learned quite a few things. The first thing I learned was rather humbling to see. Apparently, for a moment I had still valued wealth and position. If I didn't, I would have no reason to feel discontent about my situation vs. their situation.

As a result of the comparison I made, I felt less valuable as a person. As a result of that, I had to find something that elevated me and made me feel as valuable as they were, or more. The only thing I could find to serve this purpose was my relationship with the Lord. I'm disgusted by the fact that I would think of my relationship with the Lord in this fashion – in this unclean and conceited way. Of all things, can I keep even this treasured relationship free from being sullied by pride and worldly ambition? The depravity of the old nature is truly vile.

I learned that amongst Christians, there should be no competition. I knew this already, but the issue came up again through this experience. If someone knows the Lord better than another person it doesn't make them better. Christians are together a whole, and should help each other along. Each should be glad if one is honored and they themselves happen not to be honored. Everyone should be looking out for and wanting the best for each other, not competing with each other.

Finally, I learned about the guilt and shame I felt at the end of all these thoughts. The guilt and shame from comparing myself and from thinking of my relationship with the Lord in a prideful, competitive way. I learned that I will not accept these feelings at all! I do not need to feel guilty or ashamed of the behavior of my old nature, but I must not let it have its way in my life. I am glad that I'm disgusted by the ways of my old nature and its depravity, but the Lord has given me a new nature – a new life. The old nature is still with me, but it is not what I need to be ruled by or what I need to bear the shame of because of what Jesus did on the cross.

By God's grace, I feel that I ran through this obstacle course of thoughts successfully. I'm happy about that. The first obstacle was comparison. I suppose that was one hurdle I did trip over. But, I didn't get stuck in the obstacle of discouragement or depression. I didn't get stuck in pride or competition. I faced each thought/emotion, but did not get stuck in them. Since the devil couldn't catch me through all these thoughts, he gave one last try at the very end by trying to make me feel guilty and ashamed that I even thought them. Thank God his last try didn't work either.

Because a wrong thought came to your mind doesn't mean you've failed. Just don't let the thought make its home in your mind. Don't get deceived and trapped by it. Don't accept it, reject it.

I guess it's like facing an actual obstacle. A person has to recognize it as an obstacle to climb over it, or go around it. The is no guilt or shame in recognizing it. Recognizing it for what it is, is essential. A person has to see it, acknowledge it, and just because they do see it for what it is should not make them feel guilty or ashamed. They should be happy and grateful that they were able to see it, so they can deal with it properly. The fact that there was an obstacle at all does not mean the person failed, it's how they handle it. Will it be accepted or rejected? Often it's the devil who put the obstacle (wrong thought) in your path, so don't feel guilty or ashamed that you had to deal with it.

Don't compare yourself with others. Others' lives are not always as they seem. A photograph may be worth a thousand words, but it doesn't tell the whole story. About a year ago, I remember seeing a photo of myself that someone had taken. I had a smile and looked all right. But, I remember the moment that picture was taken and I was feeling drastically different than I appeared. Looking at the picture alone, a person would probably think I was blissfully happy and they would be so incorrect.

Beware of comparing; there are various dangers in it. Like, whining, complaining, feeling sorry for yourself, judging, anger, envy, and assuming things. I think the main dangers of comparing are becoming caught in either depression or pride.

I suppose a person could compare themselves with another, and then stop right there without a problem. However, I think that would be very difficult to do. It is very difficult to compare and then stop right there; being totally detached and unmoved by the comparison. Generally, a person compares and immediately uses the results of the comparison to make value judgements. That's the issue. And, one action (comparing) follows the other action (making value judgements) so quickly there is hardly time to stop yourself.

The harder a person tries to prop themselves up above others, competing and striving for importance by the world's standards, the more brittle and fragile they become. They're addicted to the very thing that is wearing them out. Let go of pride and find your worth in the Lord, as it was always meant to be. There is much rest to be found in doing this. So much dysfunction can grow out of the competition and ambition of the world. Leave those ways behind. A freshness and rest comes from being detached from the world.

The moral of my story is to not compare yourself with anyone in the first place. Try to make wise choices and focus on what you're dealing with in your life. I believe that's enough for anyone to deal with. There's always someone who is "better" than you, but no one is like you. Let go of competing. Your value is secure. Let other people be who they are, and you be who you are.

And he said to them, "Take care, and be on your guard against all covetousness, for one's life does not consist in the abundance of his possessions." (Luke 12:15 ESV)

Let your conversation *be* without covetousness; *and be* content with such things as ye have: for he hath said, I will never leave thee, nor forsake thee. (Hebrews 13:5 KJV)

Since we are living by the Spirit, let us follow the Spirit's leading in every part of our lives. Let us not become conceited, or provoke one another, or be jealous of one another. (Galatians 5:25-26 NLT)

Put to death therefore what is earthly in you: sexual immorality, impurity, passion, evil desire, and covetousness, which is idolatry. (Colossians 3:5 ESV)

But concerning the pure brotherly love that there should be among God's people, I don't need to say very much, I'm sure! For God himself is teaching you to love one another. Indeed, your love is already strong toward all the Christian brothers throughout your whole nation. Even so, dear friends, we beg you to love them more and more. This should be your ambition: to live a quiet life, minding your own business and doing your own work, just as we told you before. (1 Thessalonians 4:9-11 TLB)

Additional thoughts:

I was not envious of the specific things this person has. It is not my desire to live in the city, or to have the job they have. What I wanted, which they seemed to have, were answers. Answers to my unknowns. The unknowns of my life - like the how, when, and what of my future. Primarily, the unknown of how I will earn money. They seemed to have these answers for their life; they seemed to have it together. I do not yet have these answers. They seemed to know what they wanted to do in terms of a career, but I'm not sure I know what I want to do. Basically, I coveted the fact that they "knew" and I didn't "know." I coveted their "knowns" over my "unknowns." I disliked how complicated my life seemed to be compared to their seemingly simple and put-together life.

This is an issue that has plagued me since I graduated from high school. This issue of what I want to do in terms of a career, job, or way of earning money. I simply do not know. I'm trying to find out.

I've thought of trying countless things, seriously and not seriously. My thoughts have ranged from being a forensic pathologist to shipping myself off to Alaska to work in a fish cannery.

I've tried a few things. I've tried being a phlebotomist, floral designer, central supply tech (the person at a hospital who brings surgical supplies to the operating room), receptionist, and a library worker. Most of these I wasn't really interested in, I just tried them. Unfortunately, that sentence could be used to describe some people's romantic endeavors. I was fine with poking needles in people to draw their blood, but I didn't like the weight of the responsibility. Like, I'm literally sticking needles in people's veins and what if I messed up? It's not the kind of job where it's ok to say, "Oops." (Although, I've had my blood drawn before and the phlebotomist that was working on me could've said it a couple times and it would have been appropriate.) I didn't like it and in the long run I could not see myself doing that every day. I enjoyed working as a floral designer, but the work environment was horrible and the designs you would create were practically already planned. There was little room for creativity. That was one aspect that attracted me to working as a floral designer in the first place. Also, I realized that I hate customer service/dealing with the public. I tried being a central supply tech at a hospital. That was one of the worst jobs for me, because nobody trained me well and I didn't really know what I was doing. However, several times I did go into the operating room to deliver some supplies and that was interesting. I had never been in an operating room before. It's not as nice as I expected. In my imagination, I thought the inside of an operating room would look high-tech. Like a white and sparkling science lab or something. But, when I saw the room it wasn't like that at all. The tile floors reminded me of public restroom floors, and the rest of the room was so dreary looking. I saw the open belly of someone on the operating table. Since I felt I wasn't being trained properly I left that job. Working as a receptionist was probably the best job out of the things I tried and it paid the best. It was at a place that wasn't busy and the environment was peaceful. I had to answer phone calls which I hated, but there weren't many of them. The work I did there varied from time to time and I liked that. Some of it was unusual or unexpected. I liked that too. For example, sometimes my boss would ask me to draw something for her. Like, actually draw with a pen shapes and figures for this project of hers. Or, I'd be asked to work with the archivist and we went through historical photographs to organize them. I did many different things there and I liked the people I worked with. But, then I relocated so I had to leave that job. Finally, working at a library was ok. It was nothing special. I didn't enjoy it and toward the end of my employment there I absolutely hated it. It's interesting to me that I've never written the word "hate" so much as in this long paragraph of my job history.

At times, I have wished I could find something I'm truly interested in as a job so I could then be determined and ambitious to obtain it. I don't believe my not having found it yet is a matter of lacking determination. When I'm truly interested in something and want it, I have a great deal of determination, to a fault sometimes. I already went into the faults of this in a past chapter that touched upon idealism. When I am truly interested in something, I can get very determined to attain or accomplish it. To the point where common sense can be thrown out the window. I have put off eating, using the restroom, and other normal "distractions" when I'm really focused on something that interests me, like a project. Or, I have pushed myself too hard in other ways – usually sacrificing too much of me.

Anyway, ideally, I would like to find something that I don't hate doing as a job, and at the same time actually pays above minimum wage. In an attempt to help myself figure out what I want to do I've tried to imagine: if I could choose any sort of job in the whole world (without considering costs, abilities, or anything that would limit me), what kind of job would I like to have? And, I still don't know. Actually, in answer to this question I've posed to myself, I have selected certain occupations. But, then I add to them the other considerations (costs, abilities, common sense, etc.) and they don't seem plausible. Maybe it really is a lack of determination … or too much common sense. Or, maybe too little common sense and too many dreams/ideals. In achieving dreams, does one go with what makes sense and forgo the dream, or be determined enough to pursue the dream however nonsensical it may be and take the slim chance of winning and the high chance of losing?

This whole issue wouldn't be such a big deal to me and I wouldn't feel such pressure if it were not for the fact that I dislike how other people may think of me because of it. I don't like to be misjudged or misunderstood. For example, the possible misunderstanding that because I don't know what I want to do yet, I'm basically a failure at life. Like this person I compared myself to, they know what they want to do, and I don't, ergo they're winning at life and I'm not. The error I made in comparing (other than in comparing to begin with) is that I was using the wrong standard to compare my life with to determine if it is successful. Which brings me to this question. How do you determine if your life is successful? What is your standard, your criterion? I know my answer to that, but what do you use to decide if your life is successful or not? I think it is a very revealing question.

I don't want to care about what other people think of me, and I'm learning not to. It's certainly been a process. I don't want to care about expectations or what seems normal/usual. I don't want to care about how others judge me, and if they're wrong or right in their judgements. I don't want others' opinions or perceptions of me to influence what I do. I want to accept that it's ok if people don't understand me, or if they assume things, or get the wrong idea about me. I don't need to prove myself to them. If they don't understand me, it's ok. If they don't take the time to truly know me, then I should relax and let it be. I don't need to prove to everyone I meet that I'm a certain type of person. Let it remain a mystery if they do not wish to know, or let them assume what they will. Do I live for the opinions of others? Are they living my life, or am I? I'm learning that I do not need to have the approval of others to be comfortable with who I am. This has been easier since I've recently learned to value who I am. When you value who you are, you won't feel anxious for the approval of others.

I thank the Lord very much for this new perspective. Until recently, I'd never thought like this before. I always felt like I was indebted to others because I thought I was unpleasant to be around. Like, I didn't meet the "normal" standard of how a person typically behaves, so I understood that I was uncomfortable for others to be around and felt inwardly apologetic for that. I would want or feel like I needed others' approval because I was not "normal," therefore not worthy or valuable. If I got their approval, then I took that as an indication that I was really not so flawed. My issue was twofold - not valuing myself, and being too concerned with pleasing people. It isn't a good combination. It's a miserable way to live when other people's opinions determine your self-worth. There can be some awful consequences to this way of life.

Of course I want to find some work I like to do and be responsible in life. I think most people do. Not everyone gets there the same way and at the same time. I feel like I'm telling myself that more than anyone else. I need to shake off the shame of not knowing what I want to do with my life (career-wise), and focus on what I need to do - not on other people's opinions of me and be wrongly influenced by those opinions.

75

Doing Nothing?

There are times when the Lord is accomplishing things through you. There can be a regularity to it. Regularity in terms of frequency and manner. For example, perhaps once a month or once a week you've been used by Him in a specific or usual way. Whatever it may be, you're aware of it. Things are happening.

This particular rate and way of things happening with the Lord can become expected. I think there can be a tendency to assume that this is how it should and always will be. When things change, and are not being accomplished at this usual rate and way, a person could feel like something went wrong. They might think, "Did I lose touch with God?" Or, "Maybe it's me, maybe I'm being lazy. I'd better get motivated and do something." These reasons (or several others) may be true. They may be the reason why the Lord isn't using you in either the same way or as frequently as He used to. But, I would like to point out that there may be nothing wrong at all.

When I say "things happening" with the Lord, I don't mean a person's normal relationship with God. I mean when you know

He's accomplishing things through you.

I have been delighted to notice that there are many correlations between one's relationship with the Lord and dancing. This has helped me understand things better. I'm not very knowledgeable in dancing, but what I do know about it has helped me understand how I should be with the Lord.

In real life, (not to say that my life with the Lord isn't real) I have had the privilege of dancing with a good leader. When you know the person you're dancing with is a good leader, you trust them. Generally, you know that they won't lead you the wrong way and that they know what they're doing. As a result, you're willing to follow them.

I've thought of this in relation to the Lord. The Lord should be the Leader and I should be the follower. He's the best Leader. I should trust Him to lead me. He knows exactly what He's doing.

In addition, I should trust Him to teach me how to follow. To teach me to react properly to His cues. If He moves, I should move. If he doesn't move, I shouldn't move. The force of the lead, a hesitation, pulling toward, or letting go, He will teach me how to follow. He will teach me what He wants me to do.

If I notice a change in His lead, I should follow Him still. I must maintain my faith and trust in Him when things do change. I shouldn't be thrown off so much by the change, but remain steady and keep trusting in God. Again, He knows what He's doing and I should trust Him and follow.

It is understandable to wonder what is going on when something changes in His lead. If I were dancing with someone and had never felt the lead to do a twirl, I might wonder what in the world they were doing and what they wanted from me. I might wonder if I did something wrong, or be completely mystified, etc. Again, I must trust Him to teach me how to follow Him.

The day may come when He leads me to do something and purposely gives me no explanation. I believe in times like this He wants me to not need to understand, but trust and obey him regardless of that. He wants me to rely completely on Him. This may be easier to do if we've gone through the process of practicing obedience in smaller things that I understood fairly well, and incrementally worked on obeying Him in other ways with less and less of my own understanding of the matter involved. In that process trust in Him grows. By His grace, I will follow successfully even when I don't understand it all. If I don't follow successfully, I shouldn't despair. It's part of learning. With the Lord's help, I will learn to obey Him properly.

I want to let Him lead me. I don't need to understand every part of what He's asking me to do. He wants me to trust and obey. That is what He asks, not that I should understand every aspect of it. I believe sometimes He doesn't want me to understand every aspect of it so that I will learn to trust and rely on Him and not myself.

I've kind of experienced this in dancing. Someone led me in some way during a square dance (it was an optional move in square dancing) and I didn't know what it was. I did not know what it was; I just felt his hands turning my hands around in a certain way. I followed and it turned out fine. I didn't need to know what it was.

There was a second of thinking, "Ok. I don't know what you're doing, but I'll follow you." There was a small moment of trust. I say it was small because it was. In the scheme of things it was small. With the Lord, that trust may feel small or it may feel like your entire life is at stake.

Trust in the LORD with all your heart, and do not lean on your own understanding. (Proverbs 3:5 ESV)

In contrast, I can remember one time I was square dancing and I did not follow someone's lead. I was at a square dance festival. We were doing this call known as "Grand Square" and this guy reached out for my hands. But, his were intertwined as he reached for mine. I got the idea that he intended to initiate another one of those optional moves that I've seen people do. I did not know what it was. And, I wasn't feeling adventurous or like I wanted to trust him because I wanted to look out for my own physical well-being so I said, "I don't know how to do that." So, it didn't happen. I really don't care about this, but I bring it up as an example of what I don't want to happen between myself and God. I want to trust the Lord always.

This reminds me of another square dance. I was at a festival. This was some time ago when I was completely physically sound. I mention that to explain that I was completely able as a square dancer. So, again we were doing "Grand Square" and people were doing optional moves. At that time, I went along with whatever was going on. I didn't know what was going on, but I followed people's leads. I was doing all right until so much optional stuff had happened that I lost my place. I "got lost" as they say. The other people in the square did not get lost. It wasn't a big deal, and I blame no one but myself. However, I couldn't help but feel like the leading dancers were not uber-considerate.

I relay this story to say that I don't need to fear such a situation when trusting the Lord. I don't believe He asks people to trust Him and then when they do, lets them become lost. I'm not saying there won't be times when you feel lost, or times when you do something wrong. I mean the Lord is always with you and will not let you truly become lost. He will help you. He is always looking out for you. He knows perfectly all the limitations and shortcomings of a person.

In round dancing, when you're with your dance partner standing on the dance floor waiting for the music and the dance to begin, you're simply standing still in front of each other. You might have your hands together with theirs. Generally, you're not moving. There is no need to think you've lost touch with your partner or that you're being lazy and that's why things aren't happening. There's nothing wrong with the fact that you're standing still. It's just part of waiting for the music and the dance to begin. So, the same kind of situation can be going on with a person and God when it seems like He isn't accomplishing things through you as He used to. When you're standing still with God it may be completely all right. You haven't lost touch with Him. He's standing right in front of you, relax.

In square dancing, there's this call known as "Spin Chain

Thru." For most of the call, four of the dancers don't move. I remember our club's caller saying something like one of the hardest things to learn is to do nothing. In other words, just standing there can be difficult when you're used to dancing and moving around. However, that is exactly what needs to be done at times. In this call, if people start moving out of position when they're supposed to stand still, it can mess things up. Similarly, there may be times when the Lord wants you to not move.

I believe when it feels like things aren't happening, the Lord can be working on a person in other ways - in ways they may not be aware of.

At times, when you feel like you're doing "nothing" it is exactly what needs to be done. It is not actually doing nothing. There is obedience involved in this. You're being just as obedient when the Lord tells you to do something and you do it as when He tells you not to do something and you don't do it. This is a good lesson to learn, because it can seem like moving is always better than not moving. That is not always the case. I think knowing when to move is as important as knowing when not to move.

I am so grateful to have experienced this for myself. When the Lord has been accomplishing things through me in certain ways and then there seems to be a change in that, I have wondered what went wrong. As a result, I've gone on to try to do something we used to do together on my own because it seemed like the thing to do, to me. But, I learned that if He's not leading me to do it, I should not do it. I've tried, and thankfully it didn't work out. I tried, and I couldn't get anywhere without Him leading and being there with me. It didn't work. My endeavor was so lifeless and empty without Him. I could tell that something (Someone) was missing. I am so grateful to have noticed this. To have noticed the difference between doing something with Him and without Him. I thank God I wasn't able to make it happen on my own. If it did work through my own efforts, I might have thought I could keep doing things without His lead and presence. I might have thought I could basically do it on my own, without Him. It is a shocking thought. But, as I said it didn't work out so I understood that I need to wait for His lead.

In round dancing, sometimes one person will dance their part alone on the dance floor, without a partner. It is not uncommon. But, at no point does the dancer truly believe they are dancing with another person. It is completely obvious that they are dancing by themselves. They (and anyone who may be watching) notice the difference between them dancing with and without someone. It is unmistakable. I want the difference between doing something with God and without Him to be just as unmistakable. I wonder how many people truly believe they are accomplishing things with God/doing His will, but they are actually dancing by themselves. It is a frightful thought. I don't want to be like that; I don't want to be deceived.

I could easily get an idea in my mind of what I should do for God and run off in every direction with enthusiasm to do it. But, I need to wait for Him. He's the Leader, after all. And, what I think I should do may not be what He wants me to do.

A small detail I've noticed, that may have no bearing on the topic I'm writing about: waiting for whoever you're dancing with (the leader) is helpful. Waiting for the Lord is necessary. In round dancing, waiting for the leader is not that necessary, but helpful. Supposedly, in round dancing both the leader and follower know what they should do because the dancing is cued. So, there can be a tendency on the part of the follower to not follow. It's like it isn't necessary. Even though she knows what to do, it can make the dance go more smoothly if she waits for the leader and blends with how he's moving. If the cuer says, "left-quarter-turning-box" I know what to do. But, I try to wait and feel for who I'm dancing with to begin to move, then I move. It's like I'm a split second delayed because I want the leader to be leading. Often, I find myself jumping the gun because I already know what to do. As I dance I keep telling myself, "Wait for him…wait for him…" To me, it just seems to go better that way. I don't know, it's a small thing I noticed. I don't know how relevant it is to my topic. My point is it's imperative to be led by the Lord.

I have come to understand and appreciate this to the degree

that I believe if Holy Spirit (God) isn't leading it, I really shouldn't do it at all. I believe all my godly activities and good deeds are pointless without Him, maybe even harmful. It would be as if I were playing the "Christian" role and going through the motions without God. To me it would be meaningless. I believe He is the One that makes any of it worthwhile.

In round dancing, it's not unheard of that girl (the follower) will actually end up leading. It may be what works best for the couple. Perhaps the man (the leader) isn't leading properly. There could be various reasons for it. However, perish the thought of people attempting to lead God!

If during the time you're waiting for God's lead you become antsy, it may help to know that He has a good reason for it. You may be doing a Spin Chain Thru. He may be teaching a person to trust Him and obey when it means not moving.

I noticed something interesting in the book of Daniel in the Bible that kind of relates to the subject of this essay. Daniel became a captive of the Babylonian army when it attacked Jerusalem. Eventually he was made chief of all King Nebuchadnezzar's wise men. With God, he rose from being a captive to someone of influence in the king's administration. God gave him a special ability to interpret dreams and visions. He interpreted King Nebuchadnezzar's dreams; God accomplished things through him. So, it seems from chapter 1 to chapter 4 in the book of Daniel the Lord was doing things with Daniel, and he was well known by King Nebuchadnezzar. Though by chapter 5 it seems the current king (Belshazzar) did not even know who he was.

Between chapter 4 and 5 many years had passed, and we are told nothing of God accomplishing things through Daniel. Apparently, his importance in the king's court had faded during that time. However, later in chapter 7 it is revealed that things were indeed happening between God and Daniel, but not in ways that seemed to be recognized or influential to others at that time. The Lord was giving Daniel prophetic dreams during King Belshazzar's reign, when otherwise it seemed like he had faded into obscurity.

I think Daniel continued to have a very close relationship with the Lord throughout the time when it seemed like he was not important anymore; when he was not in a place of influence in the king's court. I wonder if Daniel ever thought about how much he was used by God in his earlier years, and thought about why he wasn't being used by God so much anymore.

After all those years with no record of Daniel being used by God (other than God giving him dreams), in chapter 5 Daniel was again used. He was called in to see King Belshazzar and interpret the writing on the wall. After that, in chapter 6 Daniel again held a high position in King Darius' kingdom.

This story and timeline of Daniel's life and how the Lord used him can be encouraging to anyone who may feel like they've been put on the shelf by God. The Lord didn't forget about Daniel, and He hasn't forgotten about you. He has His own perfect plan and timing.

I think about the faithfulness of Daniel. How he continued to trust the Lord despite when he may have felt his importance had decreased. He continued to trust the Lord despite the fact that he may not have understood why things had changed. He stayed connected with the Lord and was ready when God used him again. There are so many points to consider here. It could be that Daniel knew where true importance was: in the eyes of God and in his relationship with Him, not in the eyes of the king and Daniel's influence in his kingdom. He continued to follow the Lord regardless of change.

Again, things were going on between God and Daniel during his season of obscurity – when it may have seemed that outwardly, nothing was happening. He was being given amazing prophetic dreams by God. I like to think more than that was going on too.

There can be seasons in a person's life when they are being greatly used by the Lord, and other seasons when it seems like not much is going on. I would suggest to not become discouraged in the slow seasons. A person may ask the Lord why things changed, if they did do something wrong, but don't get in a panic by assuming something is wrong. Don't become depressed or discouraged by thinking the Lord has left you. Can you not move as well as move when the Lord wants you to? Sometimes one of the hardest things to learn is to do "nothing."

Throughout a slow season a person should still cultivate their relationship with and their knowledge of God. I think that's what is most important anyway. I believe that is where all the Lord may do through you stems from, and I believe that should stay constant.

Lord, lead me as you promised me you would; otherwise my enemies will conquer me. Tell me clearly what to do, which way to turn. (Psalms 5:8 TLB)

"My thoughts are nothing like your thoughts," says the LORD. "And my ways are far beyond anything you could imagine. For just as the heavens are higher than the earth, so my ways are higher than your ways and my thoughts higher than your thoughts. (Isaiah 55:8-9 NLT)

Preach the word; be prepared in season and out of season; correct, rebuke and encourage--with great patience and careful instruction. (2 Timothy 4:2 NIV)

So Jesus said to them, "Truly, truly, I say to you, the Son can do nothing of his own accord, but only what he sees the Father doing. For whatever the Father does, that the Son does likewise. (John 5:19 ESV)

I have not spoken on my own. Instead, the Father who sent me told me what I should say and how I should say it. (John 12:49 GWT)

So Jesus said, "When you have lifted up the Son of Man on the cross, then you will understand that I Am he. I do nothing on my own but say only what the Father taught me. (John 8:28 NLT)

"Not everyone who says to me, 'Lord, Lord,' will enter the kingdom of heaven, but the one who does the will of my Father who is in heaven. On that day many will say to me, 'Lord, Lord, did we not prophesy in your name, and cast out demons in your name, and do many mighty works in your name?' And then will I declare to them, 'I never knew you; depart from me, you workers of lawlessness.' (Matthew 7:21-23 ESV)

lawless: adj. 1. Without laws. 2. Unrestrained by law : disobedient.[1]

Wait on the LORD: be of good courage, and he shall strengthen thine heart: wait, I say, on the LORD. (Psalm 27:14 KJV)

For God is at work within you, helping you want to obey him, and then helping you do what he wants. (Philippians 2:13 TLB)

For all who are led by the Spirit of God are children of God. (Romans 8:14 NLT)

Next they traveled through Phrygia and Galatia, because the Holy Spirit had told them not to go into the Turkish province of Ausia at that time. Then going along the borders of Mysia they headed north for the province of Bithynia, but again the Spirit of Jesus said no. So instead they went on through Mysia province to the city of Troas. (Acts 16:6-8 TLB)

"If you love me, obey me; and I will ask the Father and he will give you another Comforter, and he will never leave you. He is the Holy Spirit, the Spirit who leads into all truth. The world at large cannot receive him, for it isn't looking for him and doesn't recognize him. But you do, for he lives with you now and some day shall be in you. No, I will not abandon you or leave you as orphans in the storm – I will come to you. (John 14:15-18 TLB)

For I am the LORD your God who takes hold of your right hand and says to you, Do not fear; I will help you. (Isaiah 41:13 NIV)

76

Seeking Holiness: Playing with the World

This struggle between holy and unholy is like a subtle game of tug of war to me, except it's no game. One reason why it's subtle is because I don't always perceive it clearly. Another reason why it's subtle is because I know which side is winning. Yet, the losing side doesn't give up; now and then it still pulls.

This tug-of-war is between my old nature and my new nature. It's between the desires of my old nature and the desires of my new nature.

At times the ways of the world have been alluring to me. This sometimes surprises me because I thought my interest in those things would be more dead by now. Every now and then it pops up, showing itself to still be there. Though it's not as strong as it used to be, thank God. It reminds me of a stubborn weed. You pull it up, but a small root remained in the ground and in a while it starts to grow again.

The ways of the world that I can identify as being alluring to me are the glamour, sparkle, and glory of the world. I will try to define that better. It's the desirable things the world can give like acclaim, regard, riches, and every kind of desirable object. For example, being known and applauded for something I'm good at; achieving great accomplishments that are admired by other people. Or sometimes it's something ridiculous like wanting to see and be seen. To see the bright city lights at night, going to exclusive venues, and experiencing fine and excellent things, rather than mediocre and common things. It's the flash and glamour vs. the dull and expected. Sometimes this is alluring to me and sometimes it isn't. The great majority of the time these things do not interest me. As I said, it goes back and forth like a game of tug of war, with my new nature on one side and my old nature on the other.

I know there is no lasting fulfillment in those things. But, my old nature will never be convinced. It must be made to submit – continually defeated – by my new nature and Holy Spirit.

I don't mean that a person shouldn't enjoy nice things and if they do they're living in the ways of the world. I mean that my underlying motives for wanting to have or experience these things is not right. My motives for wanting these things are to feel more important, fulfilled, and like I'm really living. To me, these types of motives are different than simply enjoying nice things. The wrong idea behind these motives is if I'm not experiencing or having these things, or promoting myself or making a name for myself, it's like I'm not really living. It's like I'm holding myself back from something good. Like I'm missing out.

I have wondered if it would be easier to find the ways of the world unappealing if I had tasted them to a greater degree than I have. To have personally experienced the things the world offers for fulfillment, realize they didn't fulfill, and then gladly go on my way living in the ways of God which do fulfill and bring life. There are many things I haven't experienced. So, I wonder if it's just the unknown of it that can be alluring. For example, I have not experienced feeling particularly self-satisfied in any of my accomplishments or abilities. I have not felt that I excelled at one specific admirable thing. I know a little about a lot of things. What is that phrase? Jack of all trades and master of none. Sometimes I want to excel at something, instead of being kind of good at a lot of things. Again, my motive for wanting this is not good. It is so I can be known by others as someone who excels at something, so I can feel like a "somebody." It's not simply to be really good at something for my own pleasure.

I haven't experienced other things the world offers for "real living" like being intoxicated, going clubbing, engaging in questionable activities of various sorts, or had the "fun" of getting in trouble. I just haven't. Liquor tastes so bad I doubt I could drink enough of it to get intoxicated. Going to clubs doesn't interest me because that basically requires being social in loud environments. Also, I don't like that kind of "dancing." Engaging in questionable activities or getting into trouble has not interested me either because I see nothing beneficial in doing so and I have a sensitive conscience. For the reasons I've described, I've been generally opposed to these specific activities from the start. They have not been appealing to me because of my own reasons.

However, the examples I gave of being known for something I excel at, and experiencing fine, upscale things have been appealing to me. So, it has been these things that have pulled the strongest along with my old nature in that subtle tug of war.

I wonder if this allurement toward the things of the world changes as one gets older. What I mean is, perhaps from years of experience with some of these things, or toiling towards achieving them, one understands that they are pointless. While, perhaps a relatively younger person is more likely to think there is still something worthwhile in them. It's true that old age does not equal wisdom, but I think when a person is older they must have gained some wisdom. At least, I would hope so.

After examining my thoughts toward the ways of the world, and my motives, I really dislike that I even bother thinking about the ways of the world. Figuratively, why do I even turn my head to look at these things, considering them at all? I know which way I want to go in life. I want to live in the ways of the Lord, in ways that are pleasing to Him. I want my desires to be about learning how to truly love others, growing in holiness, and living how God wants me to and being what He wants me to be. I don't want to care about the ways of the world. I want to have absolutely zero interest in those things.

I see that I am a foreigner here. I'm living in a world that values what I don't. We have nothing in common in that regard. We're at odds. It's just a fact. The ways of God and the ways of the world cannot be blended. They cannot compromise.

Dear friends, I warn you as "temporary residents and foreigners" to keep away from worldly desires that wage war against your very souls. (1 Peter 2:11 NLT)

I cannot live in both the ways of the world and the ways of God. I can't have it both ways. I could try, but in reality I think I would be living in either one or the other whether I realized it or not. Also, I might be at risk of being lukewarm.

"I know you well – you are neither hot nor cold; I wish you were one or the other! But since you are merely lukewarm, I will spit you out of my mouth! "You say, 'I am rich, with everything I want; I don't need a thing!' And you don't realize that spiritually you are wretched and miserable and poor and blind and naked. "My advice to you is to buy pure gold from me, gold purified by fire - only then will you truly be rich. And to purchase from me white garments, clean and pure, so you won't be naked and ashamed; and to get medicine from me to heal your eyes and give you back your sight. I continually discipline and punish everyone I love; so I must punish you, unless you turn from your indifference and become enthusiastic about the things of God. (Revelation 3:15-19 TLB)

I don't want to see how close I can get to living like the world, in some kind of pathetic attempt to live how my old nature wants and live how God wants me to at the same time. I don't want my affections to be divided. I don't want to attempt to play both sides. I don't want to play with the world. I want to leave the world's playground altogether.

Leaving the world's playground is not always easy. There are other people playing there and they look like they're having a good time. But, the playground is polluted to me. It used to be what would come naturally to me, but now it fights against my new nature. It used to be what I would desire without any inner opposition, but now a part of me is very much against it.

I feel like I'm living in two places simultaneously, but the values of each are not to be combined in my life. I'm living here in the natural world, where satan is the ruler at this time and it shows. It is shown by the ways of the world, what it values, and how it functions. Then I'm living in a spiritual place with God where there are His ways, a different set of values, and it functions differently than the natural world does.

At nearly every turn the values of the world are before me, waiting for me to conform to them. The scope of this is so broad. It could be something as small as a fad, to something as big as the purpose of life. It's what the world applauds, endorses, and holds up as something to pay attention to - "important" things.

One relatively small example is how to dress. I know Christians can have different opinions about this. People can dress however they want to and obviously, they will. Personally, I cannot pretend that how I dress does not matter. For me, I do not think it is appropriate to be dressed overtly and believe as I do. I just don't see how that is honoring to God. I'm not going to go down the rabbit hole of discussing what it can or cannot evoke in others. I'm talking about how it affects me. It is easy to see what the world values in how a woman should dress, but I don't share those values.

I think this particular example has to do with liberties we have as Christians. It's in issues like this that Christians can choose what they will do. I don't believe there exists in the Bible a list of appropriate clothing. I have not found a verse on what length skirt should be worn. A person has to choose what they'll wear and it can vary. I believe the Bible gives guidelines about a person's behavior and how their heart should be more than what is worn. I don't think if a woman dresses overtly it is a sin. Personally, I think it is not particularly appropriate and it might make me wonder what the motive behind it is. It's not particularly in keeping with 1 Timothy

2:9-10. It's just not for me. People's opinions on this vary. Also, I think it is wrong to think that what a person wears equals how righteous they are. Talk to the Lord about issues like this and find out what He says about them in regard to you.

Another example of how the values of the world are before me is in how I should live. If I were to guess, the world would say that a woman of my age should be actively dating people and go from one to another as I please without a backward glance because I'm an "independent" woman who is immune to being negatively affected by this. I don't agree that this is how I should live. Personally, I don't want to go around trying people like a person might test drive cars. I'm not saying getting to know someone and then realizing they aren't for you is wrong. I'm talking about becoming involved with people with no intention of any possible future commitment. I mean becoming involved with people like it's a sport.

Then there is the pressure to achieve and obtain certain things. These things which one should achieve and obtain are determined by the world. Achieving and obtaining these things determines your value as a person.

I suppose if you ask most people, "Does position, wealth, and possessions determine a person's worth?" their answer would be no. To me, it's not so simple. In some point in time and in one way or another, the idea of these things determining a person's worth will show itself to be held as true by every person because everyone has an old nature. It's held as true by a person for a moment or a lifetime. It's a natural inclination to a person's old nature. For instance, if a person has a great deal of money, has an excellent job, and drives a fancy car they are immediately considered more valuable than someone who doesn't have these things. It's an ugly thought, but it's true. If a person does not realize they make these judgements consciously, it's done subconsciously. It's an immediate, instantaneous judgement, and is kept in check only by the grace of God. By His grace, you have learned that these things do not make a person more or less valuable and you are choosing to avoid this type of thinking.

The features that make a person valuable by the world's

standards (and to our old natures) can differ depending on gender. It is very clear to me, and I'm sure to others as well. I will generalize and not elaborate. I will be blunt and grotesque. For women, it's being physically attractive. It's not really necessary to have any others virtues, and who will even mention her character? As long as she's attractive and reasonably cognizant it's good. For men, it's being wealthy. Bonus if he's physically attractive, but if he's wealthy that will make up for any lack of attractiveness. In fact, his wealth will probably make up for anything lacking in his character, behavior, beliefs, etc. So basically, anyone out there who wants to be valuable in the world's eyes: be attractive and/or wealthy. If you aren't attractive or wealthy, at least be talented or accomplished in something. And, you must be these things to a great enough degree. If you're not attractive, wealthy, talented, or accomplished enough, you won't cut it.

But the LORD said to Samuel, "Don't judge by his appearance or height, for I have rejected him. The LORD doesn't see things the way you see them. People judge by outward appearance, but the LORD looks at the heart." (1 Samuel 16:7 NLT)

I like this verse. That's a huge difference to take note of: people judge by outward appearance, but the Lord looks at the heart. It shows how different God is from man. It shows how He sees things and what He values. I thank God He's not like us. I want to see things like He does and value what He does.

I don't believe the Lord looks at the heart of a person because He's disconnected from the real world or because He's just being magnanimous toward a person's appearance. I believe He looks at the heart of a person because that's what is important. I hope I can take a cue from that and pay attention to what is important too.

A bit off-topic: the other morning I was praying. I believe the Lord asked me, "Who do you love?" I thought about it and I said, "You." Then I believe He asked me, "Why?" My answer came quick and I said, "Because you're so good." After I said that I realized what He was showing me. When people love, there is always a "because." "Because you make me laugh," "Because you're adorable," or "Because you're so smart." If it's not because of any of those things, it's because of a lot of other reasons. But with God, there is no because. He doesn't love you because anything. If your logical mind must have a because from Him, He loves you because He loves you. There is no other reason. He loves us because of Who He is, not because of who or what we are.

The generalizations I gave about people being attractive, wealthy, talented, or accomplished and that making them valuable may be as blatant as I described them in a person's view. A person may completely agree with those generalizations without apology and without shame; those things are what makes a person a "somebody." However, I think more people have subconsciously agreed with these generalizations at some point, me included. I dislike that. As I said before, I want to leave the world's playground altogether. I don't want a hint of its values to be among my values.

The fact that these values are pushed by the world to be conformed to is not ineffective. It can be very effective. Look at the effort and expense well-known companies put into advertising. I would think they wouldn't have to advertise so much because they're already profitable, well-known businesses. The reason why they advertise and promote themselves is because it works. People are influenced by advertisements. People are influenced by what they see and hear. And, look at how much effort the world puts into influencing others. There is pressure to conform. Night and day it tries to influence, and in nearly every way.

Set yourself apart from such things. Focus on the Lord and His ways – this new life. Don't try to live the old life when you have the new.

Sharing the values of the world creates problems. There are so many I hardly know where to begin. I think the world's values make it harder to love. Because its values make a person preoccupied with themselves too much. I will continue with this issue of appearances. When I see a woman who is more physically attractive than I am, I would like to be unaffected. Other than I would like to appreciate her as she is, how the Lord made her. I don't want to see her and immediately go down a nasty thought-road ridden with fault-finding, jealousy, critical judgements and thinking of anything that might make her less of a person in my mind and make me feel like more of a person. I really don't want to do that. I'm weary of it. So weary of it! I'm weary of all this competing and comparing. It disgusts me. Can I just love other people without making it personal? If someone, according to the world's values, is in any way better than I am, it is completely all right. It's fine. There is nothing I need to do about it. This issue is unpleasant for me to think about, but it really exists. I think it is fairly easy to avoid that nasty thought-road once one's personal worth in the Lord is known. When that is known, a person's worth is secure and there is no more need to compare or compete.

As a person finds their worth in the Lord, other people's opinions matter less. Even their own opinion matters less. They're not looking to others or themselves for validation, but to God. In God, each person's value is secure. He loves us individually and perfectly. Knowing this helps to eliminate the need to compare or compete.

Another factor that helps eliminate comparing or competing is being humble. When a person is proud, they are a "somebody" and they must keep up appearances for themselves. Whether that be literally their appearance, or other things like their position, abilities, reputation, etc. I think when a person isn't proud, there is no reason to compete. If others are perceived as better than they are, it makes no difference to them because they're a "nobody." I don't mean they're a nobody like they're worth nothing. I mean they're a nobody in terms of no longer feeling driven to be someone of importance. I think there is a lot of freedom to be enjoyed when a person isn't proud.

Yet another factor that helps to eliminate the need to compare or compete is when a person simply does not share the same values the world does. They don't have those values in their mind, so the thought of comparing or competing by those values is not there either. They're living in a different way.

How truly delightful it is to have every kind of trigger for comparing and competing shoved in your face, but you are completely free from being affected by them. They don't matter to you anymore. By God's grace you know your worth in Him, you're humble and are continuing to be, and you don't share the values of the world. What freedom!

Occasionally I've had the misfortune of seeing a commercial for a new movie. If it's an action movie, the images depict the strengths of man. There are images of people with tough looks on their faces and bulging muscles, wielding weapons that don't look real. There may be scenes of fighting where I assume the main character is soundly defeating all his enemies, with every kind of special effect employed to make it look awe-inspiring. Basically, the film is a lot about glorifying the strength and self-sustaining ability of man.

I thank the Lord that I look at all that and I am not moved; I am not impressed. Seeing all of it is kind of comical because to a degree I know how much greater God is than man. To a degree I know how utterly dependent man is upon God. This makes the strengths of man portrayed in the coming attraction look comical. I mention this because I think the strengths of man are good examples of what the world values.

If God were to take back his spirit and withdraw his breath, all life would cease, and humanity would turn again to dust. (Job 34:14-15 NLT)

By the blast of God they perish, and by the breath of his nostrils are they consumed. (Job 4:9 KJV)

A breath from God destroys them. They vanish in a blast of his anger. (Job 4:9 NLT)

Here it says how all life and humanity is dependent on God and would turn again to dust without Him. And, it says how easily God can destroy. With a breath, even the breath from His nostrils He can destroy. Seems to me that is very little effort (if you can call anything an effort to God). Can you blow air very strongly out of your nose? I tried it. I can blow air out of my mouth much stronger. Yet, that's all it takes for God. That's highly contrasted against all the strenuous efforts of man to overcome his foes in that action movie, where the main character almost lost his own life multiple times in the process.

The commercial I see for a new movie may not be an action movie. It may be a "romance" movie. There may be some sort of plot involved, but it probably doesn't matter because there's so much sexual immorality going on, who is paying attention to the plot? I guess I won't go into detail more than that. But again, I think this is a good example of what the world values.

I was watching an old black and white game show from the 1960s. I watched several episodes. Typically, the show features two celebrities from those days. There's usually a woman and a man. The announcer introduces them and says something like, "Here's the charming, popular, stage and television star, beautiful …" and then the lady's name. For the man the announcer says something like, "And the witty comedian, currently starring at the (some venue in those days) talented …" and then the man's name. When I was watching these shows I noticed these specific accolades. It wasn't enough to announce the celebrities names; they had to be built up first. I thought these accolades were excellent examples of what make people valuable and worthy in the world's eyes.

He said to them, "You are the ones who justify yourselves in the eyes of others, but God knows your hearts. What people value highly is detestable in God's sight. (Luke 16:15 NIV)

I like this verse too. Again, there is a huge difference to take note of: what people value highly is detestable in God's sight. I had to read that a few times slowly for it to begin to sink it. It shows how different God is from man.

There always exists a lure, irresistible to the old nature, of being loved, valued, and glorified by the world and people of the world. To be loved and valued by the world and people of the world, a person must meet their standards, and we know what those are. He calls His own away from the world; do not conform to it. It is even worse when teachers and leaders encourage integration of the church with the ways of the world. How can His own be holy when they play with the unholy things? Don't be mistaken between the holy and unholy. You cannot mask something unholy and make it holy.

Reasons that may come to mind for conforming to the ways of the world are various. For example, if you don't conform in some way you are uncool, self-righteous, or too uptight. Other reasons may be compensations for low self-worth. Like a person may feel they need to achieve certain things in order to be a worthy person. Or, it may be simple (or not so simple) peer pressure and the desire to be accepted.

While these reasons can be difficult to overcome, they do not matter when a person is committed to living a certain way. I want to be so focused on and in love with God that anything that is contrary to His ways is seen as nothing but the filth that it is.

My old nature is greatly interested in the world's values. It is eager to compete and attain them. But, my new nature is not; it couldn't care less. Furthermore, it is repulsed and disgusted by them. Likewise, my old nature is repulsed and disgusted by the ways of God. The ways of the world and the ways of God are not compatible with each other. They are opposed and cannot come to an agreement.

Not valuing what the world does goes a long way in keeping one from trying to find fulfillment in the wrong things. How many years and how much time and effort are spent chasing after the wind? It is a solemn thought. It's not about the things in life – circumstances, people, possessions, achievements – that bring completeness to your life. A person can have those things and not be satisfied. Know this now so you won't spend time searching in the wrong places or endeavoring in things for the wrong reasons. I believe no person has been completely untouched by this issue because each person has an old nature.

When I write like this I don't mean a person should not enjoy nice things. There's a difference between enjoying nice things and loving them; living your life for them. And, I'm trying to focus on a person's motives for desiring these things and what they expect to get from them.

I believe the Lord wants His own people to be His completely, not playing in the ways of the world and being His too. Why are the world's ways and values better than His?

I believe He wants a depth and strength of character in His own people. He doesn't want His own to be mistaken for sons and daughters of the world – shallow-minded, weak, and concerned with the fun and fancies of the world. He wants His own to be recognized as His because they are led by Holy Spirit and their lives show it. He wants renewed minds, and hearts that are set on Him.

Going back to what I wrote earlier about my wondering if I had experienced more of the ways of the world would it be easier to not be attracted to them. You could try everything in the world there is to try. Traveling, buying, owning, experiencing, achieving – everything the world has to offer you could try and still be missing what is most needed and important. You could try everything there is to try and still find only emptiness and longing for more. There is no lasting fulfillment or satisfaction in those things. He doesn't want His own to be deceived in this. Yes, to the old nature it's all so very attractive, but to the new nature there is no life there and this is clearly seen. Set your eyes and your heart on Him.

Must a person experience this personally to know it's true?

I thank God that when I think about my 1955 Cadillac, I know there is no true fulfillment of my life in it. It doesn't come close. The car has been taken to around 20 cars shows since it's been restored and has never failed to win in some class or category. Several times it's won multiple awards at individual shows. It could be called my dream car. I imagine in the eyes of the world, this possession is something of true value. It may even make the owner seem more of a "somebody." Thankfully, I do not see the car in that way. It certainly has monetary value, and sentimental value to me, but not the type of value that brings true fulfillment. Of course I enjoy the car, but it's not where my heart is. I don't connect my identity to it and I know it's just a car.

Actually, the things about the car that thrill me the most have to do with parts the Lord had something to do with. That's another story, but in this I can see for myself where my heart is.

I don't know if I can explain this well, but I've experienced this sort of detachment of feeling toward other nice things too. Possessions or experiences that my old nature would normally relish have lost their appeal. I know this may sound bad, but it's actually a good thing: I do not enjoy certain things as much as I used to. I enjoy them, but there is always a part of me that is looking away from the appeal of it and toward God. It's like my heart is not completely in those things anymore. How can I explain this better? Here's an attempt. You love someone. Your heart is with the one you love. Any other person who may seem nice or appealing is recognized as nice or appealing, but your heart is reserved for someone else. You just don't fully engage or become wholly involved with any other person because your heart is somewhere else. So, I've noticed this same type of thing when it comes to possessions or experiences I have in this earthly life. I enjoy them, but not completely because my heart is not in these earthly things.

Never think you've missed out on anything that the world offers for fun and entertainment. A person may observe how others live or what they've experienced, but if it is anything that the sinful nature desires, do not think you've missed out by having not experienced them. It is a blessing to not have experienced them.

See instead what the Holy Spirit produces in peoples' lives. Have you experienced them in your life? Are they growing and increasing in your life?

I believe the Lord wants His own to understand what is for them and what is not for them. There are simply some things you cannot put a Christian label on and make it good.

Remember not to judge yourself by the world's standards. His own do not live by them, why should they be judged by them?

Now and then when the ways of the world are alluring to me I remember who I am and Who I'm following. The fact that we're called foreigners in this world should mean something. Imagine a foreigner. They would not be like the others they're surrounded by.

They would be different.

This puts me in an introspective frame of mind. It makes me think of me. Am I like the world? Or, am I like a foreigner here? Do I feel at home in the world, or do I see how different my values and ways of living are from its values and ways of living?

In heaven a crown is waiting for me which the Lord, the righteous Judge, will give me on that great day of his return. And not just to me, but to all those whose lives show that they are eagerly looking forward to his coming back again. (2 Timothy 4:8 TLB)

In the past when I read a verse like this, where looking forward to Jesus' return was mentioned, I knew I did not feel that way. I just did not feel like I was looking forward to His return. I was having too good of a time to want the end of the world to happen. I wanted to keep enjoying everything here on earth and living this life for a while longer.

But now I do look forward to His return. There is nothing here in this world that I want to hold onto more than His coming back. If in a moment the Lord returned and the world changed I would not miss a thing from my old life. His coming back would be so much better than anything I could ever have on earth.

I think how a person feels about Jesus' return says a lot about where their heart is. And, where their home is. I think there should be a longing and a looking forward to going home. I don't mean that we should all just hold on for our lives and batten down the hatches until Jesus returns. He's given each of us things to do until then, but I think each Christian should sincerely look forward to His return.

It seems that more and more I'm realizing that living as a follower of Jesus will mean my life changes. My desires will change. My behaviors and thoughts will change because of Holy Spirit working in me. As a result of these changes I should simply be different from people who are not following Jesus. I should be different from the world, and not share its values. These changes in me should not be put on. They shouldn't happen because of my own sheer discipline and self-control. I could force myself and basically pretend changes had occurred in me and outwardly show it, but it wouldn't be true and I think it wouldn't last. There is discipline and self-control involved, but these changes start in a person's heart through the working of Holy Spirit and are shown outwardly simply as a result of it.

And so I say to you fathers who know the eternal God, and to you young men who are strong, with God's Word in your hearts, and have won your struggle against Satan: Stop loving this evil world and all that it offers you, for when you love these things you show that you do not really love God; for all these worldly things, these evil desires – the craze for sex, the ambition to buy everything that appeals to you, and the pride that comes from wealth and importance – these are not from God. They are from this evil world itself. And this world is fading away, and these evil, forbidden things will go with it, but whoever keeps doing the will of God will live forever. (1 John 2:14-17 TLB)

Don't copy the behavior and customs of this world, but let God transform you into a new person by changing the way you think. Then you will learn to know God's will for you, which is good and pleasing and perfect. (Romans 12:2 NLT)

Since you have been raised to new life with Christ, set your sights on the realities of heaven, where Christ sits in the place of honor at God's right hand. Think about the things of heaven, not the things of earth. For you died to this life, and your real life is hidden with Christ in God. And when Christ, who is your life, is revealed to the whole world, you will share in all his glory. So put to death the sinful, earthly things lurking within you. Have nothing to do with sexual immorality, impurity, lust, and evil desires. Don't be greedy, for a greedy person is an idolater, worshiping the things of this world. Because of these sins, the anger of God is coming. You used to do these things when your life was still part of this world.

But now is the time to get rid of anger, rage, malicious behavior, slander, and dirty language. Don't lie to each other, for you have stripped off your old sinful nature and all its wicked deeds. Put on your new nature, and be renewed as you learn to know your Creator and become like him. (Colossians 3:1-10 NLT)

So I say, let the Holy Spirit guide your lives. Then you won't be doing what your sinful nature craves. The sinful nature wants to do evil, which is just the opposite of what the Spirit wants. And the Spirit gives us desires that are the opposite of what the sinful nature desires. These two forces are constantly fighting each other, so you are not free to carry out your good intentions. But when you are directed by the Spirit, you are not under obligation to the law of Moses.

When you follow the desires of your sinful nature, the results are very clear: sexual immorality, impurity, lustful pleasures, idolatry, sorcery, hostility, quarreling, jealousy, outbursts of anger, selfish ambition, dissension, division, envy, drunkenness, wild parties, and other sins like these. Let me tell you again, as I have before, that anyone living that sort of life will not inherit the Kingdom of God.

But the Holy Spirit produces this kind of fruit in our lives: love, joy, peace, patience, kindness, goodness, faithfulness, gentleness, and self-control. There is no law against these things!

Those who belong to Christ Jesus have nailed the passions and desires of their sinful nature to his cross and crucified them there. Since we are living by the Spirit, let us follow the Spirit's leading in every part of our lives. Let us not become conceited, or provoke one another, or be jealous of one another. (Galatians 5:16-26 NLT)

So, dear brothers, you have no obligations whatever to your old sinful nature to do what it begs you to do. For if you keep on following it you are lost and will perish, but if through the power of the Holy Spirit you crush it and its evil deeds, you shall live. For all who are led by the Spirit of God are sons of God. (Romans 8:12-14 TLB)

Follow God's example, therefore, as dearly loved children and walk in the way of love, just as Christ loved us and gave himself up for us as a fragrant offering and sacrifice to God.

But among you there must not be even a hint of sexual immorality, or of any kind of impurity, or of greed, because these are improper for God's holy people. Nor should there be obscenity, foolish talk or coarse joking, which are out of place, but rather thanksgiving. For of this you can be sure: No immoral, impure or greedy person—such a person is an idolater—has any inheritance in the kingdom of Christ and of God. Let no one deceive you with empty words, for because of such things God's wrath comes on those who are disobedient. Therefore do not be partners with them.

For you were once darkness, but now you are light in the Lord. Live as children of light (for the fruit of the light consists in all goodness, righteousness and truth) and find out what pleases the Lord. Have nothing to do with the fruitless deeds of darkness, but rather expose them. It is shameful even to mention what the disobedient do in secret. But everything exposed by the light becomes visible—and everything that is illuminated becomes a light. This is why it is said:

"Wake up, sleeper,
rise from the dead,
and Christ will shine on you."

Be very careful, then, how you live—not as unwise but as wise, making the most of every opportunity, because the days are evil. Therefore do not be foolish, but understand what the Lord's will is. Do not get drunk on wine, which leads to debauchery. Instead, be filled with the Spirit, speaking to one another with psalms, hymns, and songs from the Spirit. Sing and make music from your heart to the Lord, always giving thanks to God the Father for everything, in the name of our Lord Jesus Christ. (Ephesians 5:1-20 NIV)

"If the world hates you, keep in mind that it hated me first. If you belonged to the world, it would love you as its own. As it is, you do not belong to the world, but I have chosen you out of the world. That is why the world hates you. (John 15:18-19 NIV)

We must not be like Cain, who belonged to the evil one and killed his brother. And why did he kill him? Because Cain had been doing what was evil, and his brother had been doing what was righteous. So don't be surprised, dear brothers and sisters, if the world hates you. (1 John 3:12-13 NLT)

You adulterous people! Do you not know that friendship with the world is enmity with God? Therefore whoever wishes to be a friend of the world makes himself an enemy of God. (James 4:4 ESV)

Command those who are rich in this present world not to be arrogant nor to put their hope in wealth, which is so uncertain, but to put their hope in God, who richly provides us with everything for our enjoyment. (1 Timothy 6:17 NIV)

"No one can serve two masters. For you will hate one and love the other; you will be devoted to one and despise the other. You cannot serve God and be enslaved to money. (Matthew 6:24 NLT)

But you are not like that, for you are a chosen people. You are royal priests, a holy nation, God's very own possession. As a result, you can show others the goodness of God, for he called you out of the darkness into his wonderful light. (1 Peter 2:9 NLT)

So think clearly and exercise self-control. Look forward to the gracious salvation that will come to you when Jesus Christ is revealed to the world. So you must live as God's obedient children. Don't slip back into your old ways of living to satisfy your own desires. You didn't know any better then. But now you must be holy in everything you do, just as God who chose you is holy. For the Scriptures say, "You must be holy because I am holy." (1 Peter 1:13-16 NLT)

So I tell you this, and insist on it in the Lord, that you must no longer live as the Gentiles do, in the futility of their thinking. They are darkened in their understanding and separated from the life of God because of the ignorance that is in them due to the hardening of their hearts. Having lost all sensitivity, they have given themselves over to sensuality so as to indulge in every kind of impurity, and they are full of greed.

That, however, is not the way of life you learned when you heard about Christ and were taught in him in accordance with the truth that is in Jesus. You were taught, with regard to your former way of life, to put off your old self, which is being corrupted by its deceitful desires; to be made new in the attitude of your minds; and to put on the new self, created to be like God in true righteousness and holiness.

Therefore each of you must put off falsehood and speak truthfully to your neighbor, for we are all members of one body. "In your anger do not sin": Do not let the sun go down while you are still angry, and do not give the devil a foothold. Anyone who has been stealing must steal no longer, but must work, doing something useful with their own hands, that they may have something to share with those in need.

Do not let any unwholesome talk come out of your mouths, but only what is helpful for building others up according to their needs, that it may benefit those who listen. And do not grieve the Holy Spirit of God, with whom you were sealed for the day of redemption. Get rid of all bitterness, rage and anger, brawling and slander, along with every form of malice. Be kind and compassionate to one another, forgiving each other, just as in Christ God forgave you. (Ephesians 4:17-32 NIV)

Put on your new nature, and be renewed as you learn to know your Creator and become like him. (Colossians 3:10 NLT)

Put on your new nature, created to be like God--truly righteous and holy. (Ephesians 4:24 NLT)

Wherever your treasure is, there the desires of your heart will also be. (Luke 12:34 NLT)

Jesus replied, "Anyone who drinks this water will soon become thirsty again. But those who drink the water I give will never be thirsty again. It becomes a fresh, bubbling spring within them, giving them eternal life." (John 4:13-14 NLT)

Then he said to them, "You like to appear righteous in public, but God knows your hearts. What this world honors is detestable in the sight of God. (Luke 16:15 NLT)

77

Raising Children

This is an essay that is not very cheerful to read. Please don't read it if you're feeling cheerful. It's not sad because of the subject itself, but mainly because of the observations I've chosen to share. I think this is important and I wanted to write about it.

Is there any subject in which opinions vary so widely? Is there any subject quite so sensitive to critique?

I don't have any children. I have no first-hand experience with raising them. The few times I baby-sat were less than unremarkable; I did not learn much from it. Any information I give on this subject may be met with an eye-roll and a smirk because I have no personal experience in the effort of raising children. Who am I to write about it?

I have observed and learned some things. I think a great deal can be gained from observation. Why not try to learn from observing others and then doing or not doing what they did? Some of the observations I will share come from when I was a child myself.

When I was around 10 years old I had a best friend. She was

my best friend; our names were rarely spoken in a sentence without the other's name included. They were spoken together so often they seemed to mesh together and become a strange new word. Kind of like when you try to repeat a phrase over and over as fast as you can and it becomes mushed together and unrecognizable. Or, like if you know an old married couple and when you hear of one of their names it is hard to think of it separately from their spouse's.

I will call her Jane. She was my age. I could tell her family life was not the same as mine. I felt sorry for her. I felt guilty about it too, because I felt mine was better than hers. She had no father to speak of. He was not in her life at all. I did have a father, so I felt sensitive to her situation every time I would mention my Dad. Father's Day was an unpleasant day because we both knew she didn't have one.

I distinctly remember once we were playing in her grandma's living room. Her mother was there. Jane went up to her, kind of hugged her and said, "I love you, Mom." I didn't think twice about it. I thought it was normal, and there was nothing particularly interesting to notice about it. But, her mother pushed her away, like Jane was bothering her and she did not say she loved her, too. Jane said it again, "I love you, Mom," this time with a little inflection in her voice that made it seem to me that she wanted a loving response from her mother. But, she did not get it and was pushed away. Come to think of it, I believe her mother said, "Jane, stop it." It may not seem like a big deal, but it was clear to me how much Jane was hurt by that. This was one situation I happened to witness. I don't know how her relationship with her mother was at other times. Although, I could guess.

Once her mother was driving us somewhere. She parked and we all got out of the car. In the process, the car door shut on Jane's fingers. She immediately began bawling and I imagine she was in pain. It seemed her mother was more irritated than being concerned about how Jane was. She was irritated by Jane's crying more than wanting to know how badly she was hurt. The lack of care by her mother (which I was apparently able to notice at that age), surprised me. I empathized with Jane and I hoped she wasn't really hurt.

Another time we were playing around in her grandma's home. We stopped playing for a moment and stood next to a window that overlooked a bay. It was a quiet, pensive moment as we gazed out the window. She asked me, "Were you a mistake?" I didn't know what she meant. She clarified herself. So I said, "No, my mom prayed for me." Then she talked about how she was a mistake. That her mother didn't really want her in the first place. It didn't shock me at the time. It disturbs me more now than it did then. To think someone as young as that labeled herself as a mistake. And, how did she learn that?

One day we were at her house. I was going to spend the night. Throughout the day we had a great time together, as usual. In the evening her mother's boyfriend came home. He and Jane did not get along.

It was dark outside now, and he called Jane into his and her mother's room. It was a small house. There was one cabinet in that room where Jane kept her stuff. I remember a doll that she liked was kept there, and other things like books, toys, etc. He called her into the room and I followed because we were friends and we tagged along with each other like that. He worked as a policeman or state trooper (I can't remember which) and was probably at least 6 feet tall. Being 10 years old at the time, he seemed quite formidable. He opened the cabinet Jane's things were in and began "talking" about how her cabinet was always messy and how she should reduce the number of things she had. I put "talking" in quotation marks because it was more like verbal abuse. He said if she didn't throw away some of her things he would dispose of her doll.

This was not normal scolding or telling a child what they should do. It was over the top. You would think Jane had committed a crime. He was so dramatic, harsh, and nasty in his manner. You could tell he didn't really care about improving Jane's organizational skills. He was being darn scary. He could've worked in a haunted house, or maybe he could've been an actor, or maybe a drill sergeant. Personally, I thought her cabinet of things looked orderly and there wasn't that much in there.

To me, the whole situation seemed so pointless and

unbeneficial and he was the one who made it that way. Jane looked miserable. There may have been tears, I cannot remember. Makes me angry now, thinking about this.

There were other behaviors of his toward her that were not kind at all, and I'm being nice with my descriptive word choices. Once she apologized to me for his behavior. She was often worried about a long list of chores that he had written out for her to do that had to be done. Sometimes I helped her with them.

Jane was a really sweet girl and I felt some of the people around her were bringing her down. People who I feel were in a position of responsibility for her, but who were careless with that responsibility. She had done nothing wrong. People around her created an unhealthy environment.

I lost touch with Jane a year or two later. About a decade or more after that I came to learn some things about her life that made me very sad. I'll just leave it at that.

When I was around 11 I had another friend who was about my age. I'll call her Hannah. She had a mother and a father. Here I will shift the focus a little from general parenting, to "Christian" parenting because they were professed Christians. We were pretty good friends. We went to summer camp together once and I'd go over to her house from time to time.

Sometimes Hannah seemed to act out. She would do things to draw attention to herself in an exhibitionist kind of way or would rebel against her parents.

I couldn't see why she did this. Her parents seemed normal and I thought Hannah was just being impulsive. I thought that was the way she was. But, one day I learned just a little of what was going on.

I'm thankful I didn't actually see it. Something had happened and Hannah and her younger brother were called upstairs to account for it. I just sat in a chair downstairs and waited for her to come back. I waited a long time. I heard her father yelling. It was loud. I felt uncomfortable and I wasn't even directly involved. I didn't hear her or her brother. I heard what sounded like someone being slapped. It may have happened more than once. A little later

Hannah came back to me. She did not seem like herself. I did not see her brother.

Some years passed and Hannah was sent away to live somewhere else, multiple places I think. I lost touch with her too. Again, many years later I came to learn some things about her life and it was terribly saddening.

I don't understand how someone can call themselves a Christian and treat their child in this way. Seems to me the hypocrisy would stick in their throats. Honesty begins with oneself. Also, whatever happened to fear of God?

Yes, Christians are far from perfect. Yes, they make mistakes, plenty of them. Yes, parenting can get messy. But to treat a child in this way is very hard for me to understand. I know there may be underlying issues that cause a parent to behave badly. There are possibly a multitude of variables and unknowns involved that I have no idea about. Perhaps I'm being too hard on "Christian" parents, but it bugs me. I'm afraid I have very little sympathy for people like this.

How can a person use the same hand to slap a child and then raise it up in praise to God? How can a person yell badly at a child and use the same voice to pray to the Lord? Who are these people fooling? Because they aren't fooling God.

If you must, if you cannot control yourself and nobody can stop you, treat your child the way you want, but don't involve the Lord in it. Don't say you follow Jesus and then treat your child badly. It makes it seem like He condones that behavior. Take the blame for your bad behavior yourself and don't let it somehow rub off onto God.

I know that Hannah is not a Christian now. I can only imagine how she feels toward Christianity and God. And, who is to blame her? If my Christian parents raised me that way, I think I would want to stay as far away from Christianity as possible. I would probably think of God in an unspeakable way.

There is a difference between scolding and verbal abuse. I believe a person can be disciplined without their soul being degraded.

There is a difference between being spanked and being physically abused, too. I hope we have enough common sense to know the difference. I was spanked as a child and it did me good.

To continually be in fear of one's parents, feel like you cannot communicate with them without being berated or not listened to, to feel like you don't want to be at home because it's so unpleasant there, etc. is not discipline. Not only is it not discipline, but I would say it is not normal. To know certain behaviors are not tolerated in the home, know that you're expected to listen and follow some basic rules sounds more like discipline to me.

I believe the home should be a place you want to go to, because there are people there who love you. It should be a place where people can communicate freely, and be honest and transparent. There is a big difference between love and force, between mutual respect and domination.

Because of my brief experience with Jane and her mother's boyfriend who was a policeman or state trooper, I have a slight distrust of men in law enforcement. Simply because of my experience with Jane and her mother's boyfriend. I figured maybe other cops are bad mannered and mean. I know that is a generalization and I am aware that not all men in law enforcement are like that. It depends on the individual, of course. Still, that's just how I feel. I have a slight distrust. Perhaps I will feel that way until I have an experience that is opposite of what I did experience.

This same kind of thinking could be used toward Christians. Hannah's parents called themselves Christians. A person could have adverse feelings towards Christians because of their personal experiences with such people. What's worse is their adverse feelings could be transferred over to God.

In my opinion, some people are just not good parents and they have no excuse for being that way. They've been negligent, unloving, and unwise.

I know that at a certain age each person is responsible for their own life and how they live it. At a certain age, their parents are no longer responsible for how they "turn out." I believe this is true, but it is not the whole story.

I think it's interesting that when you hear of a person's hellish upbringing and they turn out to be a healthy person it's like it's noteworthy. It's seen as something admirable. Why? It's because everyone knows they had to overcome a whole lot. Their upbringing obviously meant something, because it is acknowledged as something they overcame. So, how can the idea that one's parents/upbringing is not applicable once they reach a certain age be completely true? If it were so, there should be no acknowledgement that they had to overcome anything because at a certain age their upbringing would be meaningless.

I used to live in the city, where there is more pavement than exposed ground. Sometimes as I would walk, I'd see a weed growing through the smallest crack in the sidewalk. It almost looked like it was growing in concrete. The weed seemed to be growing in a most difficult place. It was amazing to see. It was noteworthy.

Also, to say that at a certain age a person's parents are no longer responsible for how they turn out, and that being the end of the story, seems to lower the importance of parenting. Let's say a person had great parents. But, at a certain age they no longer have any responsibility for how their child turns out. So, they were great parents and everything but that doesn't matter now? It had no lasting impact? Their parenting is null and void when the kid reaches a certain age? I think everyone who has had great parents will not hesitate to say how much they have positively influenced their lives. If a person were 90 years old and they had great parents, I believe they would still not hesitate to say how important they were to them and that they were thankful for them. I think good parenting should receive its proper respect.

Still, I think it is true that at a certain age each person is responsible for their own life. I just think parenting plays a much larger part in a person's life than this idea suggests.

I suppose it's possible a person could have great parents and still turn out to be unhealthy. I don't think it's right to put all the blame on parents for how their child turns out.

At the same time, I think the percentage of responsibility and influence over a child's life is higher for their parents than on the child themselves. I am trying to say that parenting is very important.

Let's imagine a person was given a fruit tree. They planted it in the right environment and it was growing and producing well. Another person was given a fruit tree. They planted it in a pot and kept it in their garage. It was not growing well. Let's say the person who gave person #1 a fruit tree asked them one day, "So, how's that tree I gave you doing?" They might respond, "It's growing fine and producing good fruit. I just need to prune it each year and keep the birds and bugs away." Now let's say the person who gave person #2 a fruit tree asked them, "How's that tree I gave you doing?" They might respond, "It's not doing good. I don't know why. I planted it and I'm keeping it sheltered, but it's leaves are falling off and there's been no fruit." When asked about how they planted it and the environment it's in, the person who gave it to them might say, "Well, what do you expect? You have to plant it outside, and don't keep it in a pot ..." Forgive my analogy, but I hope you see what I'm getting at.

Do not underestimate the influence a parent has on a child's life. I believe the Lord has given parents a great responsibility and He does not take it lightly if they are negligent. Who is more helpless than a child? I believe the Lord sees this, and does not take it lightly when they are misguided, mistreated, or taken advantage of in any way by those who are above them. Do you know how many tender, innocent souls have depended on and hung on the words of their parents, only to be hurt and dejected? Even adults experience this with other adults, but with a child it is different.

I have experienced times in my life when I asked my parents something and whatever answer they gave was going to mean a great deal to me. After I would ask them a question, there was a great deal of anticipation in what their answer would be. I hung on every word. Sometimes it decided whether I would choose to go one way or another. Like a signpost, "Go this way." To me, a signpost is a big deciding factor. It can change your route in life. It is a blessed thing to receive good guidance. And, a horrible thing to receive bad guidance.

As a person grows older the frequency of this changes. Over time, hopefully a person has gained common sense and can choose the right things without someone holding their hand. Thankfully, the Lord is always with me and I can ask for His guidance throughout my life.

It just really saddens me how the opportunity for good parenting is missed. As a parent you're helping to shape a life. To me, that is a great opportunity and a great responsibility as well.

As a Christian, I know that I am accountable to God. In a way, I can forget about being accountable to others or to myself, because I'm accountable to Someone with much higher standards and who doesn't overlook a thing.

I'm not saying let's all be perfect parents. There is no such thing. People are not perfect, and that's an understatement. Sometimes parents themselves had a poor upbringing and may not know how a normal family functions. Sometimes that motivates them to try to be better parents than their own were.

Once I had a pet bird. She was a Gouldian Finch. When she was a baby her mother abandoned her in the nest and stopped feeding her, which apparently can happen when there is only one baby bird instead of a clutch of around 5. So, I hand-fed the baby bird. It grew up and was very tame. Later on, it was housed with a male Gouldian Finch. They built a nest together and she laid around 5 or 6 eggs. Personally, I was excited because I loved that little bird and thought it would be nice for its lineage to continue. I monitored the timing of things, and knew when the eggs should hatch and when I might expect to hear baby birds chirping. When too much time had passed and I saw that the parent birds were not consistently sitting in the nest anymore, I investigated. I peeked in the nest and saw 5 or 6 tiny, pink, baby bird bodies. They were dead. It was so sad. Over the many years I've had finches that had not happened before. I chalked it up to the fact that the mother bird was not raised as a bird is normally raised, so it didn't know how to take care of its own babies.

I just see the examples of my childhood friends as parenting failures. To a small extent (which is not the full extent, but bad enough) I see how much they suffered as a result. What a sad thing to fail in. It affects more than your own life.

Fathers, do not provoke your children to anger by the way you treat them. Rather, bring them up with the discipline and instruction that comes from the Lord. (Ephesians 6:4 NLT)

Direct your children onto the right path, and when they are older, they will not leave it. (Proverbs 22:6 NLT)

Fathers, don't make your children resentful, or they will become discouraged. (Colossians 3:21 GWT)

"If anyone causes one of these little ones who believe in me to sin, it would be better for him if a large millstone were hung around his neck and he were drowned at the bottom of the sea. (Matthew 18:6 ISV)

78

A Writing from My Childhood

I didn't know this existed until it was found in one of my old notebooks the other day. I guess I was around 10 years old when I wrote it.

I think it's kind of funny and interesting. I don't know how I expected to save up money at that age. Dogs were a great interest of mine at the time. I would read books about dogs. I learned about the different breeds and enjoyed looking at the pictures. For me, watching national and international dog shows on TV was akin to how some take pleasure in watching the Super Bowl. Dogs were my thing. The writing ends abruptly, as if I did not finish it.

It was humbling for me to read this. It made me feel like I knew a few more things then, than I do now. Things I had forgotten about, but should know. I saw that back then I could recite some of the story of Jesus' life better than I could now. Also, is the part about being 30 years of age accurate? This is like new information to me. It kind of made me feel like I've not been diligent in reading the Bible.

Seeing how I thought about things at that age makes me not want to grow up. I mean that in two different ways. First, I mean that as I grow older and learn things through pleasant and unpleasant experiences, I don't want the unpleasant experiences to harden me in a bad way. I want to become stronger, but not stronger as in becoming jaded and cynical. The second way I mean it is in a spiritual way. Of course, I want to grow up spiritually, but not a bad way. By God's grace, I will learn things. But, I don't want any increases in knowledge to affect me negatively. I don't want to age badly. I don't want to think I know a lot. Also, I don't want to lose childlikeness and wonder toward God. I don't want to become strangely entrenched in knowledge and theology and fail to be childlike toward God. When I say childlike toward God, that can take many different forms: in my trust in Him, dependency, reliance, simplicity, innocence toward certain things, staying in awe of Him, taking Him at His word, and other ways.

A picture that comes to my mind is a head of lettuce in a garden. It's growing and at one point reaches its peak. It's mature and looks like what a head of lettuce should look like. Then it bolts as it endeavors to grow flowers and produce seeds. When it bolts it takes on a different shape, and in awhile it doesn't really look like a head of lettuce anymore. It has morphed into something else. Spiritually speaking, I don't want to become too grown up for my own good. I'd hate to look back and think I was in some way better in the past. I don't want to morph into something not as good. By His grace, I won't.

I want to see a butterfly and be delighted by the beauty of God's creation, rather than somehow be too absorbed in "higher knowledge" that I miss the wonderful simplicity of things. When I say simplicity of things, I mean that in other ways as well as in how I view nature. I want to always find joy in God Himself, and not be unduly focused on stuff He may want me to do. I want to grow up and learn new things, but also maintain a fresh and childlike perspective toward God no matter how old I get.

Jesus said, "Let the little children come to me, and do not hinder them, for the kingdom of heaven belongs to such as these." (Matthew 19:14 NIV)

Truly, I say to you, whoever does not receive the kingdom of God like a child shall not enter it." (Luke 18:17 ESV)

And Jesus called a little child unto him, and set him in the midst of them, And said, Verily I say unto you, Except ye be converted, and become as little children, ye shall not enter into the kingdom of heaven. Whosoever therefore shall humble himself as this little child, the same is greatest in the kingdom of heaven. (Matthew 18:2-4 KJV)

Here it is with all its amusing errors. (However, I went ahead and tried to create paragraphs because reading a single mass of text bothers me.)

I am going to save up money to buy a dog another one, a smaller one maybe a beggle or even maybe a chiwawa. I think I will save up money to get a beagle, yes, that is just the right size, perfect. But you know I still have Poppy my sweet German Shepherd. Ya know I'm starting to train her she knows how to sit, heel, stay, and catch! She is a very pretty dog the Lord blessed me greatly with her, she is so sweet, so is the Lord's grace.

I am very glad God made animals for us to take care of and for us and God to enjoy. I bet the Lord had fun making every feather on a beautiful peacock, and making every strip on a tiger and zebra. But remember God made us in His image and we have a spirit just like he does, unlike animals.

And God loved us so much he gave his only, Son that has been with God before, well, always was, with God, in heaven. He sent his Son to earth, through the virgin mary, as a little baby, but He did not just begin life just then, remember, he always was. So, He sent His Son to earth in that chosen way. And even before mary had the baby, God sent an angel to mary and the angle gave her God's message to her, "You shall name the baby, Jesus". When the baby was born she did call Him Jesus.

Jesus grew up, and there were some people called the Pharasus they believed in a way that was not of what Jesus was preaching about. Yeah, Jesus preached to the public, the law was that you had to be 30 years of age before you will be lit to preach, and Jesus met the standards of the law and he was 30 years old or older. But the Pharasees wanted to kill Him because he was preaching against what the believed in, and it was Satan in them because, remember, Jesus was God's Son and Satan hated God because even before God made the earth there was only heaven and Satan wasn't Satan then he was the highest angel, but he began to have thoughts and he wanted to be even higher than God the very God that created him so God cast him out of heaven and some more angels followed Satan and now the other "angels" that followed Satan are now his demons.

So that's why Satan made the Pharasees have evil thoughts in there heads because he hates God and God is good and Satan hates goodness and peace, and that why he put evil thoughts in the Pharasees heads to kill Jesus because Jesus was great and good.

So one day Jesus was preaching and the he went up to a mountain and was praying to God his father. Meanwhile the Pharasees and some roman soldiers went looking for Him and they went up on the mountain Jesus was on and they asked He asked them "who are you looking for" (But of course He already knew who they were looking for He was Jesus the Son of God He knew everything!) they replied "Jesus of Nazareth" they said "Nazareth" after "Jesus of" because Jesus, well, they thought He was born in Nazareth but, He was really born in Bethlehem, Anyway Jesus said, "I am He" and right at the moment He said that they all, Pharasees and soldiers fell to the ground! Then again Jesus asked them "who are you searching for? (But don't forget He already knew) and again they replied "Jesus of Nazareth" and Jesus replied "I told you I am He" So, they took Him.

During this whole time Jesus knew He was going to be killed, because God told Him. Jesus allowed the soldiers and Pharasees to take Him to be killed because He knew it was Gods will and it needed to be done. But before He was put on the cross the people of Jerusalem chose if a really bad theif and a really sinful person was to die or a sinless man was to die, which was Jesus. Now who would you choose to die? (of course I would chose the really sinful person, his name was Barabus. But of course Satan put thoughts in the people's heads that they should have Jesus killed. Unfortunatly Jesus now was going to die, they made Him carry the cross to a hill and then they nailed His hands and feet to the cross.

Later after He died they put Him in a tomb. A tomb is a place they put dead people in a long time ago in Jerusalem, it's kinda like a smaller cave and then they roll a big rock in the opening of the small cave so that the smell of the dead person won't spread in the town and be smelly.

A couple days later Jesus's friend Mary magdalene (not His mother) went to the tomb, but, when she looked in side the tomb the rock was rolled aside and Jesus' body was gone, and the only thing left was the garments He was wearing! Then she sobbed and sobbed because she thought that somebody had stolen His body. As she was sobbing she heard somebody call her, "Mary!" she turned and said to the man (which she thought was a gardener but was really Jesus)

79

One True Desire

Lately I've been thinking that the Lord Himself is my one true desire, whether I realize it at every waking moment or not.

There have been times, most of my life really, when I did not know this. It was not clearly identified for me. Or maybe it's not that I didn't know it, but He was simply not my one true desire at that time.

Do you ever consistently have certain things on your mind that you desire? They vary from person to person. I think it's usually attaining something. Like, getting healthy, getting an object you want, money, a promotion, a job, a state of life, achieving something, etc. For me, they are becoming physically whole again and finding a job I like.

My desire to become physically whole again I want so much, I can want it to the point of tears. But, it's been so long in coming that I've become better at not worrying about it, and just letting it come when it comes. I've made progress and that helps me to be patient, too. I desire to find a job I like, but I would prefer to become physically whole again first.

So, these have been the things I desire: becoming whole, and finding work I like.

Whatever it is that people desire, it can be like a constant weight upon their shoulders or like a constant hunger for something. These feelings can be severe or slight, but they're almost always there. These feelings generally aren't satisfied until the person gets what they want, or their wants change.

I have learned, and I'm continuing to learn, that it's not these things in my life that I want most of all. Though, at times it may feel like it. I've imagined attaining each of those things. I've imagined that if I did attain them, I would not be completely satisfied. I would not. They would satisfy me for awhile, but then I think I'd be right back to where I was before – wanting something more. While they would be exceedingly wonderful, they are not the purpose of my life. While I want those things – very much - they're not what I want most of all.

The Lord is the One I want. It is He alone who can satisfy this "wanting something more." I have mistaken this "wanting something more" for wanting other things. Like, I've thought that when I obtain these other desires of mine, then life will be rosy. But, I've seen that it's not my other desires that will truly satisfy.

I want to be satisfied being in His presence. I want to know Him better, love Him more, and please Him with my life. When I say this, I don't mean that I want to be a willing and obedient vessel for Him, doing all the external, outward things He may want me to do, exclusively. Although, I want that too. I mean that I want a direct and personal relationship with Him. I see that the outward works stem from a relationship with Him and are not a substitute for it.

A person could think, "That's nice, but how is that satisfying? Why would you desire that the most?" I cannot explain it. When you know Him personally, you will understand. There is something I cannot explain about Him that is more fulfilling to me than anything else, ever. I am so grateful to have learned this, even to the limited extent that I do.

I could attempt to explain why. I could say there is something otherworldly, fulfilling, and life-giving about knowing the One who created you, and knowing the One for whose good pleasure you were created. I could say there's something indescribable about knowing the One who knows exactly everything about you, and has far-reaching plans for your life that extend into eternity. I could say there is something enthralling about knowing the One who loves you the most (despite knowing everything about you), who cares about your life down to the smallest detail, and who will never leave or change. I could say things like that, but my explanations fall so short.

Is life with Him constant happiness? No. Is life with Him free of all trouble? No. But, life with Him is the only kind of life I want.

I feel like I'm beginning to see things more clearly than I ever have before in my life. Learning that the Lord is my one true desire has been an epiphany to me, except it's not been very sudden. It has come in increments. It's an epiphany that is so great I feel that I don't fully understand it yet.

Just think, the One I want most of all is already here with me. This "something more" that I desire is here, right now, not only somewhere in the future like my other desires are. I believe I will get to know Him more as time goes on, and I have more growing to do. However, there need be no anxiousness about it. We can be content together now, Him and I.

I have the Lord right now and He is enough. He should always be enough. I can be content with Him, and I'm realizing that nothing else could make me content quite like that. The Lord is my portion.

I have not come to this conclusion because of some kind of experience-induced cynicism. It is not my desire to become cynical. I have not thrown to the wind the appreciation for good things in life. (I'm not talking about the ways of the world.) I have not reached a new level of disenchantment, leading me to self-righteous rebellion toward life in general, leading me to proudly adopting "religion" as my new identity. I'm not thinking, "Well, real life didn't work out for me, I guess I'll become a religious fanatic." This is my real life. To me it's become more real than it ever has before.

Whatever I thought life was before seems like a charade now, but I know the Lord was working through all of it. I admit He has used certain life experiences to open my eyes, but in a necessary way. Many of those experiences were very painful, but I've seen the good that has resulted from them. Any disillusionment I've experienced has been to my benefit. Despite experiencing these things, I trust the Lord will keep me from being cynical. I want to appreciate the good things in life that the Lord provides. Physical wellness and work I enjoy would be wonderful; it's ok to want them. But, I have come to realize they are not what will truly satisfy.

To me, that is a great thing to understand. I will try to draw an illustration to show what I mean. It's like desiring cotton candy because you think it will satisfy you. Because you don't have any yet, you think about getting some all the time. You dream of it night and day. You want it badly because you feel it will satisfy and make your life so much better. So, one day you get cotton candy. It does satisfy; the sensation of it melting in your mouth and the visual appeal of it is delightful. Then suddenly it's gone. The satisfaction didn't last very long at all. You're left with sticky fingers and a tummy-full of liquefied sugar. Now you want something more. If you expected very limited satisfaction, then this situation would not be disappointing. However, my point is that most of the time people expect the fulfillment of certain desires to truly satisfy them, when in fact they will not. If a person understands this ahead of time, they can keep themselves from focusing the entirety of their life on the wrong things. Or, it can help them avoid unnecessary disappointment.

On a side note, as I alluded to before, my goal is not to be a religious fanatic, whatever that is. I feel it is a term often used to describe people who are misguided, unwell, and have turned to "religion" with wrong motives. I feel the term is used to describe warped people, although it could be used to describe sons and daughters of God as well. I don't care what I'm called, as long as I'm following the Lord's will. My point is, sometimes the term "religious fanatic" is used to describe people who are not following the Lord's will and so I don't want to be like that. My goal is to love the Lord, love others, do what He wants me to do and be what He wants me to be, while keeping a firm grip on truth.

I don't want to go through life always thinking, "When I get this, then it will be all right," or "When that happens, then everything will be good." Maybe it's not always consciously thinking these thoughts, but it's a kind of underlying feeling that it will indeed be all better when this or that happens. I feel like thinking in this way makes it very difficult to appreciate the present. It breeds discontentment. Also, I think this kind of thinking makes a person place wrong expectations on things. I see that nothing will truly satisfy me like a personal relationship with God.

I don't have to wistfully think, "Someday when ..." and be unendingly looking ahead. I believe a person could think like that all their lives and never comprehend that we're living right now. It's as if they're always living in the future. No, today is the day I have and the Lord is with me.

Learning that the Lord is my one true desire has had different effects on me. At first I thought, "Oh, so that's what I want." It has brought relief. It's made my other desires a little less important; the anxiousness to have them has decreased. I really shouldn't be anxious for anything (Philippians 4:6). The other desires I have are fine, but they are additions to something else that is most important. It has made me more content and at peace, and has given me clarity. Also, I'm still learning about this. It's not like I look ahead into the future and now I know what's going to happen and I understand it all. In fact, it has helped me to not look into the future so much, but focus on the present. When I do look ahead into the future, there are a lot of unknowns there. But, at least I know Who I'm aiming for and Who will always be with me.

I don't want to have such a strong and desperate grip on "things" that if they are taken away or do not happen it's like my world has ended. Keep a loose grip on "things" and hold tightly to the Lord. Don't hold too tightly to shakable things. Hold tightly to the Unshakable.

Perhaps I won't say this right, but I hope that no matter what I achieve or attain in life, I am not completely satisfied in those things. I hope I will not look at my physical health or job and think, "Now my life is complete." Doing so would show that I had been deceived. I want to fully understand what is most important. I want to be completely satisfied with the Lord.

I've already been there. I've already been deceived in that way before. I've already thought the "things" in life would satisfy me, but have realized they are not enough and never could be enough. It was wrong of me to think they would fulfill me in the first place. I did not realize this through my own intelligence. It had to be pounded into my head; like being hit on the head with a 2 x 4 multiple times. The Lord helped me realize it through events I would have never chosen to experience, but I'm very grateful for now. I only want the Lord to satisfy me. He's the only One who can.

My soul can say, 'The LORD is my lot [in life]. That is why I find hope in him.' (Lamentations 3:24 GWT)

"The LORD is my portion," says my soul, "therefore I will hope in him." (Lamentations 3:24 ESV)

[A [miktam] by David.] Protect me, O God, because I take refuge in you.

I said to the LORD, "You are my Lord. Without you, I have nothing good."

Those who lead holy lives on earth are the noble ones who fill me with joy.

Those who quickly chase after other gods multiply their sorrows. I will not pour out their sacrificial offerings of blood or use my lips to speak their names.

The LORD is my inheritance and my cup. You are the one who determines my destiny.

Your boundary lines mark out pleasant places for me. Indeed, my inheritance is something beautiful.

I will praise the LORD, who advises me. My conscience warns me at night.

I always keep the LORD in front of me. When he is by my side,

I cannot be moved.

That is why my heart is glad and my soul rejoices. My body rests securely because you do not abandon my soul to the grave or allow your holy one to decay.

You make the path of life known to me. Complete joy is in your presence. Pleasures are by your side forever. (Psalm 16 GWT)

Whom have I in heaven but you? I desire you more than anything on earth. My health may fail, and my spirit may grow weak, but God remains the strength of my heart; he is mine forever. (Psalm 73:25-26 NLT)

Whom have I in heaven but you? And there is nothing on earth that I desire besides you. My flesh and my heart may fail, but God is the strength of my heart and my portion forever. (Psalm 73:25-26 ESV)

Then I pray to you, O LORD. I say, "You are my place of refuge. You are all I really want in life. (Psalm 142:5 NLT)

After these things the word of the LORD came unto Abram in a vision, saying, Fear not, Abram: I *am* thy shield, *and* thy exceeding great reward. (Genesis 15:1 KJV)

I cry to you, O LORD; I say, "You are my refuge, my portion in the land of the living." (Psalm 142:5 ESV)

80

Thoughts on Marriage and Related Issues

Perhaps this will be entertaining to read. As with the chapter on raising children, I have no personal experience with this subject. But, of course I've thought about it. I've observed others and have contemplated the whole idea of marriage.

Sometimes I think about becoming married and sometimes I don't. The majority of the time it seems like it would be nice. It's certainly something to be honored (Hebrews 13:4). But, I am aware that being married isn't all fun and games. Getting married will not solve your problems. Also, the idea is that you'll be with this person the rest of your life and that's a big deal to me.

It's funny. I feel like when I say, "I think about becoming married," it sounds like it's a simple choice and is contingent only upon my choosing it or not. It's as if it were as simple as saying, "I think about getting a haircut." Getting married is a choice, yes, but it's not so simple. When you get a haircut the choice is primarily yours and yours alone. When you get married, there's a lot that depends on another person, obviously. Then add to that a multitude of other factors. If I think about it, I guess I'm glad it's not so simple.

If it was simple I might have made the choice a long time ago and regretted it. I think that sometimes things that seem complicated or challenging to obtain are best kept that way, in order to prevent someone from easily choosing it and making a big mistake. I'm sure I could recover from a bad haircut less painfully than from a bad marriage.

Occasionally I think about some of the unsavory parts of marriage and it puts me off. I think about the relatively small but real things. Like how I would be washing his dirty laundry, and how I'd probably be cleaning up various messes he made. I think about how I would be cooking particular meals day in and day out, rather than being concerned primarily with feeding myself at any regular or odd time I wish. I think about how I would have to wake up and see his face every day. I think about how I wouldn't even get to enjoy the peace and serenity of having the whole bed to myself. Already I see that I should work on being less selfish. And, what if he's extroverted and doesn't understand my needs as a non-extrovert? (Then it would be my own fault for marrying such a person.)

I suppose all the unsavory parts of marriage will be all right when I love the right person and they love me, and we both love God first.

Those things aside, what about the times when we're not getting along? Can we work together through hard times? Or, will one of us not be patient, mature, selfless, or understanding enough to handle it? Just like anyone else, I'd hate to get married and feel like I made the worst mistake of my life and feel stuck with someone I don't even like. I imagine being "alone" can suddenly seem like bliss when you're married to the wrong person.

Sometimes I really wonder if I am capable of living with another person. I wonder if I am capable of being lived with, too. I know I have my eccentricities. I don't feel I'm overstating it in the least when I say that sometimes it takes a truckload of patience and understanding to deal with me. That is rare to find in a person.

I often get tired of being careful with how I interact with men. Interacting with women is so much easier and less stressful to me. I sometimes get tired of being careful of how I behave toward men. I do it so often. Actually, I always do it, and it gets tiring. I have always done it because I have never felt I had the right to treat any man any differently than any other person. I feel like I've never had the right because nothing has ever been defined. Defined as in our being anything more than friends. If we're just "talking" or nothing has been communicated and defined, I feel that I have no right to speak to him differently than how I would to any other person because he is no different than any other person to me. It's as simple as this: if I'm waiting at a traffic light, I'm not moving until I get a green light. If it's red or yellow, I'm not going anywhere. In driving in real life, I might push through a yellow light, but not when it comes to how I interact with men. I get tired of being careful of not being too nice to someone in case they think I like them like that. I don't want to lead anyone on. I get tired of trying to walk this narrow line between too nice and not nice enough. I want to be nice, but I feel like people can misinterpret that. I don't want to seem cold and unfriendly, because I do care about people. I don't know … here I am yet again in my life mulling over appropriate or inappropriate social behaviors. For how much I've thought about it, I would think I'd be an expert at behaving properly by now.

Maybe this is one of the burdens of trying to be a lady. Maybe it's just a problem of mine. Or, maybe it's simple common sense and self-control, and actually being considerate of others.

The fact is no man (except one) has shown interest in me as a friend alone. Either it's no interest, or interest in something more than a friend. So, perhaps this history of mine makes me predisposed to being particularly careful when I interact with men.

If I had the right to show more-than-a-friend behaviors, it would come easily and there would be no guilt in doing so. It would be as easy as moving forward when I get a green light. This green light doesn't come from the other person alone. I have to get a green light from God first. And that hasn't happened yet. The more-than-a-friend behaviors I'm referring to are primarily manners of speech, although other things could fall into this category.

In the last paragraph I mentioned guilt. Yes, if I show more-than-a-friend behaviors without first having a right to do so I will feel guilty. Because I'm overstepping my bounds. Maybe I'm awfully old-fashioned. I respect myself and others. I just don't think it's right to play around like that.

If I didn't keep myself in check, I could easily say wonderfully appealing things that stroke the ego and lead a person on. If I didn't have a sensitive conscience, it would be easier than keeping myself in check. It could be like a game to me. Like some kind of shameless game that involves psychology, timing, and reading a person. It isn't difficult to know what men want to hear. I could play the part, say all the "right" things, lead them on and work them up, then leave them high and dry and think it was amusing. (Thank God He's done what He's done in my life and I have not and do not do those things.) Playing games with people's hearts is a bad business and a lot of pain can result. Also, playing like that with certain people would probably get me into trouble and then it wouldn't be amusing anymore. Besides all that, it is not my desire to live a depraved lifestyle.

I can easily cross that line and go into the "too nice" territory if I don't diligently hold myself back. When I say diligently, I mean diligently.

Definition of diligent: adj. Marked by persevering, painstaking effort : assiduous.[1]

Definition of assiduous: adj. Constantly attentive : diligent.[2]

I guess what I'm getting at is being careful in how I behave is just tiring. Being constantly attentive is tiring. But, I believe it's a good thing so it is worth the effort.

I believe people can get married with false expectations. They might be mistaken and think that when they get married everything will be so much better and maybe some of their problems will disappear. How sad to realize they may end up right where they were before – the same problems, the same insecurities, the same things that aren't right, except now they've got someone else along for the ride. Having someone else along for the ride could be helpful, but it could also make everything worse.

Furthermore, to me it is offensive to put those kinds of

expectations on another person. They're just another person.
They're not God. Go to Him if you want things to be better or if you
want fewer problems. Go to Him if you are insecure. Don't go to
other people thinking they're going to make you better. Don't use
me as a Band-Aid. Do you know what happens to a Band-Aid after
it's used? Especially if a person finds that it is not helping to heal
their wounds.

If a single Christian person is not content with the Lord, I hope
they do not go seeking contentment in any other person. Get your
foundation right first. I hope no person ever looks at me thinking I
can make them content because I can't. I'm telling you, I cannot
make a person content. Don't expect this from me, because I will
surely disappoint. Maybe for a moment I could make a person feel
content, or for some limited time, but I cannot really make them
content. Find the lasting and true contentment you can only find in
the Lord. I cannot provide this to anyone, and I hope I would never
expect anyone to provide this to me.

I detest when someone says to the object of their affection, "I
can make you happy." First of all, I feel like I'm being duped into
something. Second, no, you can't make me happy. In fact, you just
revealed to me how ignorant you are or how ignorant you think I
am, or both. And, don't expect me to make you happy. There is a
difference between love and happiness. First, loving someone will
not always mean you'll make them happy. Sometimes doing the
right thing will make others unhappy. Also, there is more depth to
love. If you love a person you will stay with them even when they
are not making you happy. My exclusion for this statement is if
you're being abused. Love for someone should not be contingent
upon what they're giving you.

Let me revise what I just said about when someone says, "I can
make you happy." I believe they can make me happy. I believe they
can make me happy for a small amount of time. Personally, I'm not
looking for that, exclusively. I don't want to build a marriage on
happy feelings. It seems so unstable. I think a marriage should
consist of this: first, both should know and love the Lord. Second,
there should be true love between the two people, not "I can make

you happy." I believe love provides stability, and confidence in knowing the other person isn't going to leave the moment unhappiness arrives. Of course, I don't want to be with someone who constantly makes me unhappy, but I'm not looking for moments of happiness. In love, happiness can be found. In happiness, love may not be found. Happiness can result from things other than love. Like, fulfilled feelings: someone making you feel important, getting attention, feeling wanted, etc. All these happy feelings can be experienced without love being present. It's sad to think that some people will settle for moments of happiness, and love is only a dream. I'm not looking for happiness alone. I would want much more than that. An ice cream cone can make me happy. I would like marriage to be comprised of something more than what ice cream is capable of in my life.

If a person must say something along those lines, I wish they would say something a bit more realistic like, "I'll try to make you happy." Even if someone says that and really means it, I know they will fail at times. I think I just dislike this emphasis on "happy." It seems so shallow. But anyway, to me, saying "I'll try …" vs. "I can …" is very different. At least the person who says "I'll try …" is more realistic, less ignorant, and arrogant than the person who says "I can …" in my opinion. I imagine the person who says, "I'll try …" is much more mature than the person who says, "I can …" And so, as I split hairs over these two words, perhaps I reveal one or more of my eccentricities. Truly, even a person who says, "I love you" and means it, will fail at times. Let us hope those failures are not major ones.

I read in the Old Testament how people carved idols out of wood or stone and worshipped them. Or, they made their idols in other ways. The idols were their gods. I don't believe it is very common to see carved idols being worshipped these days, but they still exist. Often, they are not seen; they are hidden in the hearts of people. I think these idols could be different things like money, a job, an object, achievements, activities, oneself, or anything that is loved more than God. I think a common idol is the idea of becoming married. For the sake of the era in which we live, I will downplay that and say a common idol is the idea of "being with" someone.

I digress, but I dislike how there are so many terms for it: being with someone, seeing someone, in a relationship, we're an item, etc. I dislike it because it makes something that in my opinion should be crystal clear, seem so ambiguous. I usually like some ambiguity, but I feel that these terms can confuse whatever it is two people are to each other. I may dislike it, but it is the business of others what they call their relationship, not mine.

Some people just need to relax about wanting to get married (or "be with" someone). It has become their idol. It's become a driving force in their life, an obsession. There are many reasons for this. It could be because it is expected. It could be because a person feels if they aren't married, they're not succeeding in life. Maybe it's to satisfying an underlying self-worth problem. There could be many reasons.

Fear is another reason. Fear of being "alone." Fear of the biological clock running out. Fear of the opinions of others and how they are perceived. It is sad. I hope no one is motivated to get married by fear. I don't know if it's worse to get married out of fear, or be the person married by someone who is motivated in that way.

I don't think it is right to be obsessed about getting married. It creates other problems. However fervently they may deny it, a person who is obsessed about getting married is desperate. Desperation can cause you to do strange and unhealthy things that hurt yourself and others.

1 Corinthians 7 contains a lot of information about marriage. I find this part interesting:

In all you do, I want you to be free from worry. An unmarried man can spend his time doing the Lord's work and thinking how to please him. But a married man can't do that so well; he has to think about his earthly responsibilities and how to please his wife. His interests are divided. It is the same with a girl who marries. She faces the same problem. A girl who is not married is anxious to please the Lord in all she is and does. But a married woman must consider other things such as housekeeping and the likes and dislikes of her husband. I am saying this to help you, not to try to keep you from marrying. I want you to do whatever will help you serve the Lord best, with as few other things as possible to distract your attention from him. But if anyone feels he ought to marry because he has trouble controlling his passions, it is all right, it is not a sin; let him marry. But if a man has the willpower not to marry and decides that he doesn't need to and won't, he has made a wise decision. So the person who marries does well, and the person who doesn't marry does even better. (1 Corinthians 7:32-38 TLB)

How do you feel after reading that? Was it a relief to read the part where Paul writes, "I am saying this to help you, not to try to keep you from marrying"? Perhaps the part that says, "it is all right, it is not sin; let him marry" was particularly comforting. Can you fathom not marrying so that you can serve the Lord better? Could you do such a thing? I think this can be a challenging issue for most people. It may put light on an idol in a person's life. Relax, you may not be one of the people who should stay unmarried. It may be God's will that you do become married. Probably you will get married. Is that more of a comfort to you than it should be? Be honest with yourself, however hard it is. Do you love the idea of getting married even if it decreases your ability to serve God the best you can? Throw away the idol, even if you're in tears when you do it and it pains your very soul. It's not so glorious as you may think it is, certainly not compared to the Lord. I am sorry if I'm sounding harsh.

I feel like this is a touchy subject. People don't like acknowledging that they have an idol in their life, and how that isn't right, because they love their idol. They love it; that's their god. I can speak from experience.

I was reading the parable in the Bible about seeds being scattered, and the various results of them falling on a path, rocky soil, among thorns, etc. and what they represent. I feel like I was one of the seeds that was growing among thorns. The cares of this life and other attractions began to stifle my growth in God.

I was convicted of the fact that I had idols in my life. I had more than one. But since this essay is supposed to be about my thoughts on marriage and related issues I will focus on that. I hesitate to give this story because I know there are obligations (like work, taking care of family, etc.) that people must give time to, and they spend more time in those things than in "spiritual" activities. I don't think there is anything wrong with that. Lord willing, people have to do what they have to do to live. If a person is concerned they may have an idol, I believe if they honestly examine their heart and ask for the Lord's help with this, they will know if something they spend time on is an idol or not.

So, I was convicted of people being an idol in my life. When I was convicted, I was sitting in an airplane. I was going on a trip to see someone. For this trip I had requested time off from work, spent around a thousand dollars, made plans, got a hotel room, rented a car, and now I was sitting in an airplane flying through the air on the way to my destination. I sat there and thought, "Here I am flying to a place I've never been, to get to know this person better. I don't even go to this much effort to know the Lord."

This is unpleasant for me to recall. I've seen that every idol will fail you. None come close to being worthy of holding that place in your heart that only the Lord should hold. They are not solid, sure, faithful, everlasting, and unchanging like God.

Am I saying I should not make an effort to get to know someone? No. I'm saying if the Lord is willing, it is fine, but don't value them or anything above God.

Do you, or have you, ever thought about who the ideal person for you would be? Your ideal significant other? Have you ever thought about what you want? What kind of appearance and personality? And that other small detail, what kind of character? I have thought about it. Years ago I came to the conclusion that I didn't really know what I wanted or needed. I thank the Lord that He granted me enough wisdom to even come to this realization. If it were up to me to choose someone, it would be very easy to come up with a profile: they'd be tall, dark, handsome, rich, and influential. But, I know that's probably not what I need or really want. A person could have all those attributes and be utterly lacking in other areas that are more important. And oh how well I know it. As I said, I came to the conclusion that I didn't really know what I wanted or needed. I am not intelligent enough to know what I truly need, when it comes to something this important. Also, there are so many people out there in the world. Do I really think I will be able to find the right one on my own? No. So, I talked to the Lord about it. I was praying that I wanted Him to choose the right person, because He knows what is best for me. He knows what I want and need better than I do. I said I wanted the union to bring Him honor and glory. Most of the time since then I have been at peace with it. He's taking care of it. I don't need to spend time worrying or thinking about it. I can spend my time on more important things.

Recently I was discussing with a friend what specific traits I would want in a partner. It made me think. For the sake of the conversation I came up with a list of what I think I would want, although as I said I'm leaving it in the Lord's hands. But, as I reflect on the list I made, I thought it was interesting that many of the traits I listed are attributes of God. I just thought it was interesting. It made me realize that I would like someone who's character is like God's character, though obviously not exactly as that is impossible and no one is equal to God.

If it is His will that I get married, then I will and that is what is best. If it is His will that I don't get married, then I won't and that is what is best. His will is always best. It's comforting to know that, and I want the best. Remember about being content with the Lord. Not getting married (or "being with" someone) only seems like the end of the world if the idea of getting married is your world.

81

Armor of God

A final word: Be strong in the Lord and in his mighty power. Put on all of God's armor so that you will be able to stand firm against all strategies of the devil. For we are not fighting against flesh-and-blood enemies, but against evil rulers and authorities of the unseen world, against mighty powers in this dark world, and against evil spirits in the heavenly places. Therefore, put on every piece of God's armor so you will be able to resist the enemy in the time of evil. Then after the battle you will still be standing firm. Stand your ground, putting on the belt of truth, and the body armor of God's righteousness. For shoes, put on the peace that comes from the Good News so that you will be fully prepared. In addition to all of these, hold up the shield of faith to stop the fiery arrows of the devil. Put on salvation as your helmet, and take the sword of the Spirit, which is the word of God. Pray in the Spirit at all times and on every occasion. Stay alert and be persistent in your prayers for all believers everywhere. (Ephesians 6:10-18 NLT)

I would like to stand firm against all strategies of the devil. His strategies can be blatant or crafty. If he can't get to you in an obvious way, he will try seemingly trivial ways to reach you. Whatever works. These verses from the book of Ephesians tell us to put on all of God's armor so we will be able to stand firm against all strategies of the devil.

The correlations between different pieces of armor and spiritual armor is interesting to me. There are reasons why specific pieces of armor are compared to specific spiritual armor. I think it shows how spiritual armor helps a person, like actual armor would. I will try to study each one.

Belt of truth: The verses from Ephesians tell us, "Stand your ground, putting on the belt of truth ..." When I hear "stand your ground" it makes me think of stabilizing myself in some way. As if I were steadying myself, or preparing to not move. What does a belt do? It supports the trunk and torso of the body. Some kinds of belts help a person with heavy lifting. So, knowing truth will do similar things for a person. Having a firm knowledge of truth will stabilize, support the core of a person, and can help them through heavy/difficult situations. Knowing the truth will help you to stand steady and not be shaken. This truth can be found in the Bible, and what the Lord Himself has told you. You won't be weakened by attacks from the enemy through deception when you know the truth and "put it on" as you might with a belt. In other words, bolster yourself with truth.

Body armor of God's righteousness (in some translations, "breastplate"): Again, we're told to stand our ground and put on the body armor of God's righteousness. What does body armor do? It protects the body from being pierced or wounded. It gives confidence to the wearer, and shields the heart. I believe this means that knowing how God is always right in what He does can give a person confidence and peace. Confidence and peace in how they live, when it's in accordance to God's will, for example.

Through our faith in Christ we are made righteous (Philippians 3:9, Romans 5:1). God's righteousness is compared to body armor for a person. It protects us from being wounded by past guilt or condemnation (which the devil will try to use against you). God's righteousness protects the heart, which I believe allows a person to come to God boldly.

Because of Christ and our faith in him, we can now come boldly and confidently into God's presence. (Ephesians 3:12 NLT)

Shoes from the Good News (in some translations, from the "gospel of peace"): We're told to, "… put on the peace that comes from the Good News so that you will be fully prepared."

Definition of prepare: v. 1. To make or get ready for some purpose, task, or event.[1]

What do shoes do? They protect the feet – parts that help you to stay upright, mobile, and help keep you balanced. Generally, if a person were outside without shoes, they would be uncomfortable. They'd probably not be confident or at peace in walking around. They would feel everything cold, hot, sharp, or wet. It is distracting to be without shoes. So, how can this relate to spiritual matters? When a person knows and believes the Good News, the gospel, it brings peace. Having a full understanding of what Christ accomplished brings confidence, too. His work is finished. Having this knowledge, and "putting it on" so to speak, will keep a person balanced and ready. It protects what you're using to stand with, your base. As Christians, we stand on the gospel. It is the basis of our hope and assurance. The efforts made by the devil to disrupt your joy or conviction of the Good News can be settled with the peace that comes from knowing that what Christ Jesus accomplished was the last word; it covers all and it is ultimate.

Shield of faith: "… hold up the shield of faith to stop the fiery arrows of the devil." What does a shield do? It provides protection and security. When you're behind that shield, practically nothing will harm you. It provides shelter while progressing/moving forward/advancing on the enemy. Practice using it.

I see fiery arrows of the devil as attacks; various things we encounter in life that would like to injure us or take us down. When we're safe behind the shield of faith, we're protected because strong faith will stop anything the devil tries to use against us. One of those arrows is discouragement and/or unbelief brought on by not seeing with our eyes what has been promised or what is true.

For we walk by faith, not by sight. (2 Corinthians 5:7 BSB)

Helmet of salvation: What does a helmet do? It provides protection to one of the most vital parts of the body, a place where it's hard to be badly wounded and live. It protects the back of the head, too. Going into battle without a helmet would leave a person badly exposed.

Salvation (like a helmet) is essential. If it's not able to be used in an offensive way, at least it is used defensively; it protects a person's life. Our salvation in Jesus Christ does this. It preserves our life, and we can go forward in the Christian life assured of this. It's interesting to me that a helmet protects the back, as well as other areas of the head. It makes me think that no matter what happens, like attacks by the enemy you may not have expected (like behind you), your life is kept safe through salvation.

Sword of the Spirit: "… and take the sword of the Spirit, which is the word of God." What does a sword do? It is used in offense and defense. Going into battle without a sword is almost as bad as going in without a helmet. It is a deadly weapon to an enemy. Keep it sharp for best use. Practice using it.

What do I expect to fight the enemy with? I can't very well fight him with the other pieces of armor listed here. They are all necessary, but they seem more like protective/defense items to me. A sword is not only used defensively, but offensively. That appeals to me. It says the sword of the Spirit is the word of God. The word of God is truth, everything about Him and His promises, and all that is in the Bible. I need to know the truth if I am to use it as a sword. I need to keep it sharp.

Let's recap.
- The belt of truth stabilizes, secures, and supports.
- The body armor of God's righteousness protects, gives confidence, peace, and shields the heart, allowing us to come boldly into God's presence.

- The shoes from the gospel of peace prepares a person. They provide confidence and peace.
- The shield of faith protects and provides a place of security. It helps you advance safely.
- The helmet of salvation protects your life. Make sure you have it.
- The sword of the Spirit is a deadly weapon to the enemy, and is used in offense and defense.

I observe that spiritual armor must be put on. This requires some action on the part of the wearer. Action in physical, mental, and spiritual ways. For example, to put on the belt of truth, the body armor of God's righteousness, the shoes from the gospel of peace, and the helmet of salvation I would want to gain knowledge in these areas. Knowing truth, God's righteousness, the gospel, and salvation would first require action on God's part (John 6:44, John 6:65). My actions (with Holy Spirit's help) would be learning about Him (and truth, righteousness, the gospel, and salvation) through the Bible. And, knowing Him and being taught by Him through the Holy Spirit, prayer, and time spent with Him. This all requires action spiritually, mentally, and physically. The shield of faith and the sword of the Spirit would require these actions too, but I see that there is the element of practicing involved with these. I think there is practice involved with the other pieces of armor too, but perhaps with the shield of faith and the sword of the Spirit there is more practice involved. I should practice faith. In difficult circumstances, or when the devil shoots those fiery arrows, I can practice using faith. I can practice using the sword of the Spirit (which is the word of God: truth, everything about Him and His promises, everything He has in the Bible). I can use this sword in a defensive way when I'm attacked by the enemy by swiping and jabbing away at his lies, or cutting away things that hinder/cloud/confuse my vision of truth. I can use the sword of the Spirit offensively, too. As led by the Lord, I can move forward, advancing on the enemy in areas he has occupied in myself, or in other people. If I can tell he's attacking another person in some way, with God's lead, I can move in and thwart his attack.

I think these verses from Ephesians can be meditated on for quite a while. There is a great deal to learn from them. Even as I write this, I see it would be beneficial for me to spend more time studying them.

I've focused primarily on the armor, but before all that we're told about how we don't fight against flesh-and-blood enemies. We fight against evil that is unseen - invisible authorities, rulers, powers, and spirits. If we are to fight against these things we need spiritual armor.

The difficulties we face are not what they seem. For example, if I have a day where it seems like absolutely everything is trying to bring me down like with discouraging thoughts, fears, feeling unqualified, etc. and nothing is "going right" I am aware that I am under attack. It's not just me, and it's not just certain circumstances. The devil will try to use your circumstances or introduce thoughts to your mind to bring you down. In such situations I must remember the truth, utilize the armor, and press on.

It is essential for Christians to realize who and what we are fighting against. How can a battle be fought if you don't even know who you're fighting against? Learn the devil's strategies. Be wise and learn his techniques. He often uses the same ones repeatedly. He knows what people's weaknesses are. Ask the Lord for help in understanding and discerning the devil's ways. That way we can be alert to them and avoid being fooled.

Be alert and of sober mind. Your enemy the devil prowls around like a roaring lion looking for someone to devour. (1 Peter 5:8 NIV)

in order that Satan should not outwit us. For we are not unaware of his schemes. (2 Corinthians 2:11 BSB)

I try to be aware of his attacks. I am aware that they can come in strange ways, and even from people who are very close to you. They may not be aware that they're letting the enemy have influence over their actions, but it can happen. For example, if a family member says something that is out of order and I know they know better, I will try to realize that it could very well be the enemy trying to get at me. I will try to look beyond the person, and at the source of the attack. Remember we're not fighting flesh-and-blood. Actually, the devil is rather clever at times. Let us be more clever than he is and not be fooled or affected by his attacks, in whatever way they come.

Sometimes if this happens with a family member, after some further discussion I realize they themselves were under attack. Like, they were dealing with a lot before they said something that was out of order. I have been there too. I hate that. I hate to allow the devil to influence me for his purpose in some way. Let us recognize when we're under attack and deal with the enemy directly before allowing it to bring us down and maybe a fellow soldier as well. An attack can have a domino effect. I imagine the devil thinks it's pretty hilarious when that happens. Let's be alert to his tactics. If you're a standing domino and another one falls against you, don't you fall too. Don't be weak, stand steady. Let's not be ignorant of this, so by God's grace we can prevent it from happening.

Other examples of how we fight against unseen evil, and not flesh-and-blood, are seen in various evils in the world. Social engineering, for example, has been used to break apart the family and what I believe are normal societal functions. Viewing the family/society through the results of social engineering, I'm not sure what the role of a man is today. What is he? A henpecked money earner? A disreputable animal that has lost its necessity? And what is a woman? The new man? The one that's supposed to do everything independently - support the family, raise the kids, and take over the world – all at the same time? And what are children? Things that are property of the state and are methodically indoctrinated and brought up by the government to become obedient, oblivious pawns? It all seems so very sad and grotesque, especially in light of God's ways. The unseen evil we fight against has influenced the world through people who agree with and serve evil.

Other than social engineering, there are other examples of

unseen evil working through people in parts of the healthcare system, the food industry, entertainment, various debased values the world has (wrong becoming right), and the general distortion of anything good, right, and normal. The general distortion and destruction of God's created order.

Resist evil and all the strategies of the devil by putting on God's armor. Let's be alert to what is going on around us, and hold tightly to righteousness and truth. Also, the last part of those verses from Ephesians tell us, "Pray in the Spirit at all times and on every occasion. Stay alert and be persistent in your prayers for all believers everywhere."

I know that the appeal of seriousness is very little. Many people don't want to get serious, they just want to have fun and let others deal with things. There is a time to have fun and a time to be serious. I think Christians should get serious. I know it may not be easy, but get serious. If you have trouble with this, ask the Lord for help in taking these things seriously. Let's not take an apathetic approach to this life. I don't want to be the fool that thinks the battle isn't serious so they're ill-prepared and are caught unaware. What would you think of a soldier who was irresponsible and didn't take their duty seriously? In the Bible, we're told what we're fighting against. We're told about the armor we've been given to use. So, let us be aware, be ready, and know the enemy. The comparison of armor to spiritual matters reveals the nature of what we're dealing with. We're in a battle, and the sooner we realize it the better.

The armor of God is given to each of God's people. It is expected to be used, and used wisely. They are necessary, not superfluous or extra. Know what they are and how they are used. If you are feeling weak in one area, strengthen the armor that pertains to that area for better protection.

Be strong in the Lord and in His mighty power. We are given this armor so that we will be able to stand firm against all strategies of the devil. So that we will be able to resist the enemy in the time of evil. Then, after the battle you will still be standing firm.

82

The Burn

We can rejoice, too, when we run into problems and trials for we know that they are good for us – they help us learn to be patient. And patience produces strength of character in us and helps us trust God more each time we use it until finally our hope and faith are strong and steady. Then, when that happens, we are able to hold our heads high no matter what happens and know that all is well, for we know how dearly God loves us, and we feel this warm love everywhere within us because God has given us the Holy Spirit to fill our hearts with his love. (Romans 5:3-5 TLB)

It has taken some time for me to be able to rejoice over problems and trials. It took more than time, too. It took God's grace. I had to learn why I can rejoice over them by seeing the benefits of going through problems and trials.

Depending on the type of problem or trial, it can be fairly easy or very difficult to see the benefits of it. It may take a long time to see the benefits of them. By God's grace, I can see the good in these unpleasant things more easily than I used to. If I cannot see it, I can use the patience, hope, and faith that past problems and trials have developed in me to trust God anyway. I am thankful for all this because it helps me deal with problems and trials better.

For me to rejoice when I run into problems and trials I must know that they're good for me. As these verses from Romans 5 tell us, it is the whole reason why we can rejoice in difficult circumstances: because we know they are good for us. They produce patience, which builds strength of character and helps us trust God more. Eventually, our hope and faith are strong and steady. We'll be able to know that all is well no matter what happens, because through the Holy Spirit in us we know how much God loves us. To me, that is a huge benefit to have in life.

I've titled this essay The Burn. The reason is because I've seen a correlation between the "burn" experienced when exercising, and a similar sensation when I go through problems and trials. This correlation helps me endure problems and trials when they come, by knowing that something good is being accomplished. It has helped me understand it better.

When I'm going through a difficulty of some kind, I feel an inner discomfort, turmoil, or pain. Or, it can feel like I'm pushing through resistance and must persevere - keep pressing on with endurance. In my mind, I've compared this to exercising, doing hard manual labor, or working out. Keeping this comparison in mind helps me handle problems and trials better.

There is some debate on whether "feeling the burn" is a good way to know if you're working out in an optimal and efficient fashion. Nevertheless, some people exercise with the goal of feeling the burn. It's like when their muscles start to burn they know they're on their way to desired results – building muscle and strength, for example. They work toward feeling the burn. It's actually something they want to feel.

In addition, micro tears can occur in muscles while exercising. Soreness is a result, but another result is muscle growth.

What I'm attempting to highlight is the fact that there is pain (or at least unpleasant feelings) involved in strengthening the body.

It can be the burn that some purposely strive to feel, or muscle soreness.

Again, I've compared these physical feelings to how I feel mentally and emotionally when I'm going through problems and trials. It's been awhile since I've been able to push myself physically, but I can remember when I would. When I pushed myself to a certain degree, everything hurt. Your chest is tense as you try to breath rapidly, you feel hot and sweaty (a.k.a. gross), your legs feel like they weigh twice as much, and it's just generally pretty miserable all around. I can feel similar ways when I'm going through problems and trials. Of course it's not exactly the same, but there is a definite miserable sort of feeling when enduring difficulties in life. I am able to endure it better when I know it's producing good results. I can be glad about it, as a person who endures physical exercise can be glad, because they are becoming stronger. And, the good results from problems and trials we go through are better than the good results from physical exercise.

There are moments when you're in the throes of intense physical exercise and you think, "I want to stop. I can't ..." Even your thoughts sound like they're gasping for air as you hear them in your mind. But, you just keep going and pretty soon the misery of it all drowns out your own thoughts. You persevere through it. Same thing with problems and trials. There are times when you can't take it anymore, but you persevere. There is something excellent in learning to persevere. In those verses from Romans we're told it produces strength of character. It certainly does.

Maybe when you think, "I want to stop. I can't ..." you do stop. Not only does your physical body stop, but so does growth. Strengthening stops. You will remain physically weak. Same thing with problems and trials. If you do not persevere you will remain weak in character, and how disappointing it is to be weak in character. It is more disappointing than being weak physically.

A factor in how well a Christian can rejoice in problems and trials is if they really want to become spiritually stronger or not. Do they desire to become stronger in patience, character, hope, and faith? There are people who desire to build up their body. It is their goal. There is no doubt that they want it because they work hard toward that goal. It is shown in how they exercise, eat, and in their whole lifestyle sometimes. They want to feel the burn when they work out. I wonder how many Christians desire to become stronger, to the point that they are willing to endure the spiritual burn and actually want to feel it. I think this desire (or lack of it) to become spiritually stronger points directly to how we are able (or not able) to rejoice in the problems and trials we face, because they are producing this spiritual burn and we know it is accomplishing growth.

Remember when the micro tears and soreness occur, the healing and results from that increase the muscle and increase its capacities.

Who welcomes the spiritual burn? People seeking to grow their muscles welcome the physical burn, even want it. People ask the Lord for growth, but are they willing to burn? Some are and some aren't. Imagine someone wanting to strengthen their body, but they're unwilling to endure taxing physical exercise. I believe sometimes the Lord takes people through spiritual burn (through problems and trials) and then they see how it was beneficial and then they learn to appreciate it, but not before having been personally brought through it (like in my case).

Don't fear the burn. The Lord is like your Personal Trainer, Who knows you better than you know yourself. He will not deal improperly with you. Don't despise the times of resistance when you have to keep pushing through. They build strength and trust. Delight even in difficulties, for they too produce something good.

I must say I do not purposely try to get myself into problems and trials to feel this burn, as an exercise-enthusiast might purposely go to the gym to feel the burn. (Problems and trials will come to each person without them purposely trying to get themselves into them, as I'm sure we all know.) However, times in my life when things are going smoothly, I sometimes think there may not be much growth happening. Kind of like if a person were lounging in a hammock they're probably not building up their muscles. There is a time for rest and healing. Nevertheless, I've seen the growth, strengthening, and benefits from the burn, despite the unpleasantness of it.

Personally, there are certain types of problems and trials that I have become accustomed to. I compare this to a person becoming accustomed to certain exercises, like, let's say, squats. By God's grace, I have become better at handling these types of problems or trials because I have become accustomed to them through repetition. Then one day, unexpectedly, comes a new exercise – a new type of problem or trial. Instead of your personal trainer instructing you to do your normal routine of squats, they tell you to do this other exercise to work on developing your triceps. A new exercise may be awkward and unusual at first. You may realize how weak you are in that area, and it's completely unpleasant to endure this new exercise. Trust in the Lord, endure, and you will become stronger in these new areas too.

I believe another way that Christians can experience the burn is when you surrender to God's will, and not your own self-will. Surrendering to God's will can happen in many ways, each day. When I have to deny my self, I recognize a feeling similar to the burn like when I'm going through problems or trials, and I know it's producing something good.

It is a very helpful, valuable thing to discern the burn. To know when you're feeling it, and to recognize it for what it is. If you do, you won't be so inconsolably distraught over the pain or suffering you're feeling, because you'll know that good growth is indeed happening through it.

I know it is incredibly difficult sometimes. It is not my intention to gloss over problems and trials like they're nothing. I believe those verses from Romans are not negating the difficulties we face, but are pointing us to a very real reason why we should endure them, and in fact rejoice over them.

I wrote this essay to try to emphasize this point: don't despise the spiritual burn. It is necessary for growth! Rejoice over it, as a fitness junkie would rejoice over feeling the burn.

And not only this, but we also exult in our tribulations,

knowing that tribulation brings about perseverance; and perseverance, proven character; and proven character, hope; and hope does not disappoint, because the love of God has been poured out within our hearts through the Holy Spirit who was given to us. (Romans 5:3-5 NASB)

Dear brothers and sisters, when troubles come your way, consider it an opportunity for great joy. For you know that when your faith is tested, your endurance has a chance to grow. So let it grow, for when your endurance is fully developed, you will be perfect and complete, needing nothing. (James 1:2-4 NLT)

83

Cup of Coffee

I was in the front passenger seat and she was in the back seat. Her cup of coffee was in the cup holder, near me. I took it and tried my best to hand it to her, kind of reaching behind me in an uncomfortable way. I had gloves on, which made me a little less sure of my grip.

Out of the corner of my eye I saw that she had grasped the bottom of the cup. But, I wanted to make sure she really had it because I didn't want it to fall and spill in the vehicle. I said, "Do you have it?" I heard a faint reply that I believed was affirmative, but I asked again, "Do you have it?" Then her reply was clearly affirmative. She said, "I've got it." So, I let go without a second thought.

In that moment I believe the Lord taught me something. I believe many times He's told me, "I've got you." Which basically means, I don't need to worry and I can completely trust Him. To me, it also means that He wants me to let go. To let go of myself, and give all of myself to Him.

Why are some things so easy to understand and do in this earthly life, but when the same actions are applied toward a situation between a person and God, it can become so difficult? It would be ridiculous if I kept asking her if she had the cup when she clearly told me she did. It would be ridiculous if I held out the cup of coffee to her and didn't let go. It belongs to her.

I wanted to be sure she had a grip on the coffee cup. Once I was sure she did, I easily let go. I had no distrust or fear in doing so. The act was so simple it's hardly worth describing any further. But, when the Lord tells me He's got me, suddenly it isn't quite so easy to let go. I should entrust myself to God infinitely more than entrusting a cup of coffee to any person.

By His grace I am learning to let go, and let Him have me. It can be as simple as handing someone a cup of coffee if there is trust. I have no need to fear. And, I belong to Him.

84

The Value of Wisdom

I'm very much a homebody. I don't enjoy going out often. I like staying home. If I do go out, and depending on my reason for going out, I'll give it my best shot and try to engage in whatever is going on. To do that, I prefer to have time to develop my plan of attack, fully prepare, and gear myself up for such an event. Then afterwards I've had enough social interaction to last me a week or more. Me being spontaneous is highly irregular.

If I go out, I like to do something either extravagant or simple. Extravagant as in some activity or event that is worth gearing myself up for. Simple as in being some activity or event that is rejuvenating, meaningful, or interesting to me. Going out for things that are not extravagant or simple often don't feel worth the effort.

Most of the time it's something simple, like going out to enjoy nature. I am frequently impressed by the textures and colors of tree bark. Re-reading that sentence almost makes me laugh at how pathetic it may seem to some, but it is not pathetic to me. It is genuinely interesting to me. Notice tree bark sometime when you're out. The rough bark of fir trees with that pale green stuff on it is very pretty. I especially like Madrona tree bark. Part of it is so smooth, and the color is lovely. It's strange how the bark kind of peels off, too. Actually, the whole Madrona tree is lovely to me. They're so graceful looking, in contrast to most of the evergreen trees, in my opinion. Have you noticed the color of Madrona leaves? They're dark green, but part of the stem is hot pink. At least, some I've seen are colored like that. I like seeing the things on the forest floor. Like leaves, moss, fungi, etc. Sometimes I will see a dead leaf on a path in the forest and it is comparable to a heavy flake, candy paint job on a hot rod. If someone is with me, I might point the leaf out to them because they've got to see it. I might take the leaf home with me. Although, I've yet to figure out how to keep the color in a dead leaf. It's like when it completely dries out it loses a lot of its color. I've also been known to bring home dead branches that have an attractive shape to them. I want them because they're pretty. What I will actually do with them I do not always know, though some of them I have definite plans for. Anyway, I enjoy nature. Its beauty is fascinating and soothing to me at the same time.

My life is not classically exciting. Or, maybe I should say it is not exciting in the world's definition of the word. I am intrigued by being taught by the Lord, and I'm intrigued with Him in general. This life with Him is exciting. I like learning new things through everyday occurrences. I like observing. I like learning from things that seem commonplace. When you see things in these ways, and the Lord teaches you through them, the most ordinary events are extraordinary.

One of the not-classically-exciting things I do is going to Costco. I sometimes take a detour over to where jewelry is kept on display. I think the jewelry is pretty, so I like to look at it. Keyword here is "look." The jewelry is exceptionally pretty under those bright lights. Probably in real life they'll never look so brilliant as they do in these display cases.

As I look over the different pieces of jewelry my mind goes on a little vacation. If I see a pearl necklace I think of what it would be like to find a pearl in an oyster. I wonder what the chances of that happening are. I see a fancy wristwatch and think about how I never wear a watch unless I'm working. I look at the earrings and practically all of them are for pierced ears and I don't have my ears pierced, but of course I'm only looking at the jewelry anyway. I see a diamond engagement ring and think of all the wonderful and horrible outcomes of a person presenting such a thing to another person. There's really so much to think about as I look at the jewelry.

The jewelry has some value, so the cases are kept locked. Normal precautions are taken because they have value.

I was thinking how in the Bible we are told that wisdom is more valuable than rubies, gold, and silver. Do we really know that? I thought about how jewelry is kept under lock and key because it is valuable. But, do we value wisdom even this much? Do we value it at all? Are we aware of the value of wisdom?

Receive my instruction, and not silver; and knowledge rather than choice gold. For wisdom *is* better than rubies; and all the things that may be desired are not to be compared to it. (Proverbs 8:10-11 KJV)

I don't hear wisdom spoken of often. Sometimes if I bring up the subject of wisdom I feel like I'm speaking on a foreign subject. Rarely do I hear the words "wise" or "wisdom" ever spoken. The world does not cherish wisdom, because it's a dampener on what the world values. It is kind of like an actual reason not to indulge in the things the world values. Rarely, if ever, have I heard someone describe another person as wise. It might almost seem like a backhanded compliment. Like, being wise is nice, but to me it has a connotation of being boring – an incorrect connotation.

Think of it. If you heard someone describe another person that you just met as "wise," what would your reaction be? At first I might wonder what they meant by that. I might be immediately turned off by it. I might have some kind of knee-jerk reaction and think, "Oh. They're the type that thinks they know everything." Or, I might think that was one of the most attractive traits a person could have.

What is wisdom? Here I will try to gather together some information I've found to build a definition of wisdom. Wisdom is knowing and doing right.[1] It is closely related to knowledge, understanding, good judgement, discretion, and prudence.

"I, wisdom, dwell with prudence, And I find knowledge and discretion. (Proverbs 8:12 NASB)

Wisdom and good judgement live together, for wisdom knows where to discover knowledge and understanding. (Proverbs 8:12 TLB)

Definitions of:

Discretion: n. 1. The quality of being discreet : circumspection.[2]

Discreet: adj. 1. Having or displaying caution and self-restraint : prudent.[3]

Circumspect: adj. Aware and heedful of consequences : prudent.[4]

Prudent: adj. 1. Handling practical matters judiciously. 2. Managing carefully : provident. 3. Behaving circumspectly : discreet.[5]

Judicious: adj. Having or exercising sound judgement.[6]

Provident: adj. 1. Showing prudent forethought.[7]

Wisdom: n. 1. Insightful understanding of what is true, right, or enduring. 2. Native good judgement. 3. The amassed learning of philosophers, scientists, and scholars.[8]

What does wisdom do? Wisdom gives a long, good life. It gives riches, honor, pleasure, and peace. It is a tree of life.[9] The Bible tells us happiness goes with wisdom:

… And happy are all who hold her fast. (Proverbs 3:18 NASB)

The man who knows right from wrong and has good judgement and common sense is happier than the man who is immensely rich! For such wisdom is far more valuable than precious jewels. Nothing else compares with it. (Proverbs 3:13-15 TLB)

Wisdom makes a man mightier than a strong man, because wisdom is mightier than strength:

A strong man knows how to use his strength, but a person with knowledge is even more powerful. (Proverbs 24:5 GWT)

The wise are mightier than the strong, and those with knowledge grow stronger and stronger. (Proverbs 24:5 NLT)

A wise man is mightier than a strong man. Wisdom is mightier than strength. (Proverbs 24:5 TLB)

Having wisdom brings safety, protection, and assurance, too:

My son, do not let wisdom and understanding out of your sight, preserve sound judgment and discretion; they will be life for you, an ornament to grace your neck. Then you will go on your way in safety, and your foot will not stumble. When you lie down, you will not be afraid; when you lie down, your sleep will be sweet. Have no fear of sudden disaster or of the ruin that overtakes the wicked, for the Lord will be at your side and will keep your foot from being snared. (Proverbs 3:21-26 NIV)

Get wisdom; develop good judgment. Don't forget my words or turn away from them. Don't turn your back on wisdom, for she will protect you. Love her, and she will guard you. Getting wisdom is the wisest thing you can do! And whatever else you do, develop good judgment. If you prize wisdom, she will make you great. Embrace her, and she will honor you. She will place a lovely wreath on your head; she will present you with a beautiful crown." My child, listen to me and do as I say, and you will have a long, good life. I will teach you wisdom's ways and lead you in straight paths.

When you walk, you won't be held back; when you run, you won't stumble. Take hold of my instructions; don't let them go. Guard them, for they are the key to life. (Proverbs 4:5-13 NLT)

Some other things wisdom does:

If anyone respects and fears God, he will hate evil. For wisdom hates pride, arrogance, corruption and deceit of every kind (Proverbs 8:13 TLB)

There is so much wisdom does, and all of them are excellent. The book of Proverbs is full of information about wisdom. I encourage you to read it because I am not going to include the entire book here. The more I learn about it the more I understand how important it is, and why it is more valuable than gold, silver, or precious jewels.

The sad results of lacking wisdom and common sense vary. It could be failing to prepare ahead for something and then finding yourself unprepared. It could be failing to take precautions and then finding yourself in a lot of trouble. It could be failing to see things clearly, and then being deceived which can lead to more problems. These failures could be avoided when a person has and uses wisdom.

Look at the examples of people winning the lottery. They gained so much wealth, but they can mismanage it and lose it all. They end up where they started, or worse. There is wisdom lacking there, and the results speak for themselves.

I have lacked wisdom, and the results are never good.

Sometimes people will tell me of some trouble they or someone they know are going through. They tell me some backstory and then what they're currently dealing with. As I listen, I sometimes see so clearly the lack of wisdom in the situation. It is the whole reason why they are in trouble. Then I realize the person I'm listening to is almost three times my age and I'm amazed that they are not wiser, or do not see the root of the problem. This reminds me of how older age does not equal wisdom. Though, being younger does not equal wisdom either. It grieves me to see the sad condition of being without wisdom, because I have seen how people suffer so much as a result.

It is actually alarming to me to think of being without wisdom. To think that a person could be living out their lives lacking something so valuable and important is alarming, because of the trouble and traps they could easily fall into. It's like they need someone to look out for them. Like they shouldn't be running around loose.

Even when a person has wisdom, they must use it and obey God. One cannot trust wisdom alone, for without God there is no wisdom at all. Also, there is no point in having wisdom if one doesn't use it.

There is earthly wisdom and heavenly wisdom. And heavenly wisdom comes from God. It cannot be earned and learned purely through man's own power. It cannot be bought, like an education. What does it take to obtain it? It takes God giving it to you. If you want it, ask Him for it. Maybe He's already given you a measure of it. If you want more of it, ask Him for more. Do Christians really want wisdom? They will ask Him for it if they do. And, how He chooses to give it to them is up to Him. He can impart wisdom in many ways.

I notice that for a person to ask for wisdom, they must first acknowledge their need of it. Then they must want it, and ask for it.

Again, the dictionary's definition of wisdom: n. 1. Insightful understanding of what is true, right, or enduring. 2. Native good judgement. 3. The amassed learning of philosophers, scientists, and scholars.[8]

I bring this definition up again because I think, while it is accurate, this definition refers in part to heavenly wisdom as well as worldly wisdom. The dictionary has mixed both kinds of wisdom in its definition.

There is a difference between worldly wisdom and the wisdom given by God. "The amassed learning of philosophers, scientists, and scholars" is worldly wisdom. Although God has given people the ability to be smart enough to be philosophers, scientists, and scholars, this kind of wisdom is worldly. By saying it is worldly I'm not saying it is bad, but it is able to be earned and learned through man's own efforts. The first definition of wisdom that the dictionary gives falls more into the kind of wisdom God gives. The first definition says, "Insightful understanding of what is true, right, or enduring." The ability to know what is true and right comes from God.

There is a way that seems right to a man, but its end is the way to death. (Proverbs 14:12 ESV)

Biblical evidence of there being a difference between the world's/human wisdom and God's/true wisdom:

Stop deceiving yourselves. If you think you are wise by this world's standards, you need to become a fool to be truly wise. For the wisdom of this world is foolishness to God. As the Scriptures say, "He traps the wise in the snare of their own cleverness." And again, "The LORD knows the thoughts of the wise; he knows they are worthless." (1 Corinthians 3:18-20 NLT)

So what about these wise men, these scholars, these brilliant debaters of this world's great affairs? God has made them all look foolish, and shown their wisdom to be useless nonsense. For God in his wisdom saw to it that the world would never find God through human brilliance, and then he stepped in and saved all those who believed his message, which the world calls foolish and silly. (1 Corinthians 1:20-21 TLB)

I can imagine a very book smart person. Perhaps they have several degrees, have a highly respected job, have written books or made new discoveries, and earn a lot of money, so that probably means they are wise by the world's standards. However, they can lack the wisdom that comes from God. This can be evident in different ways. Their life may be lacking some of those things that wisdom gives like peace, safety, and assurance. Or, they may lack these things:

But the wisdom from above is first of all pure. It is also peace loving, gentle at all times, and willing to yield to others. It is full of mercy and the fruit of good deeds. It shows no favoritism and is always sincere. (James 3:17 NLT)

In addition, we are told:

The fear of the LORD is the beginning of wisdom, and knowledge of the Holy One is understanding. (Proverbs 9:10 NIV)

Use logic here. The fear of the Lord is the beginning of wisdom, so how can a person who does not fear God be wise? I think this is another clue to whether someone is truly wise or not, because fearing God is the beginning of the wisdom He gives, as opposed to the wisdom of the world.

If all the excellent things wisdom is and does is not enough reason for one to want wisdom, maybe the results of lacking wisdom will motivate one to want it.

If you become wise, you will be the one to benefit. If you scorn wisdom, you will be the one to suffer. (Proverbs 9:12 NLT)

Wisdom is its own reward, and if you scorn her, you hurt only yourself. (Proverbs 9:12 TLB)

Wisdom speaking:

"Now then, my children, listen to me; blessed are those who keep my ways. Listen to my instruction and be wise; do not disregard it. Blessed are those who listen to me, watching daily at my doors, waiting at my doorway. For those who find me find life and receive favor from the LORD. But those who fail to find me harm themselves; all who hate me love death." (Proverbs 8:32-36 NIV)

Wisdom is beautiful. It is not boring. It is more brilliant than any faceted diamond under bright lights. It should be cherished and valued more than any precious gems. Cultivate a love for it. Prize it. The benefits of it are more valuable than jewels, silver, and gold. These things don't lead one to life, but wisdom does.

People adorn themselves with jewelry, but adorning yourself with wisdom is much better.

Obtaining valuable jewelry can be difficult. Yet, something more valuable is available to all who ask for it. If you could have that diamond ring displayed in the jewelry case by asking for it, would you ask for it? If you could have that gold watch by asking for it, would you ask for it? Wisdom is not available to all who have enough money to buy it, because it can't be bought. It is available to all who ask.

If any of you lacks wisdom, you should ask God, who gives generously to all without finding fault, and it will be given to you. (James 1:5 NIV)

For the LORD gives wisdom; from his mouth come knowledge and understanding. (Proverbs 2:6 NIV)

Cherish and treasure wisdom in a manner worthy of its value.

Can't you hear the voice of wisdom? She is standing at the city gates and at every fork in the road, and at the door of every house. Listen to what she says: "Listen, men!" she calls. "How foolish and naïve you are! Let me give you understanding. O foolish ones, let me show you common sense! Listen to me! For I have important information for you. Everything I say is right and true, for I hate lies and every kind of deception. My advice is wholesome and good. There is nothing of evil in it. My words are plain and clear to anyone with half a mind – if it is only open! My instruction is far more valuable than silver or gold." (Proverbs 8:1-10 TLB)

My child, listen to what I say, and treasure my commands. Tune your ears to wisdom, and concentrate on understanding. Cry out for insight, and ask for understanding. Search for them as you would for silver; seek them like hidden treasures. Then you will understand what it means to fear the LORD, and you will gain knowledge of God. For the LORD grants wisdom! From his mouth come knowledge and understanding. He grants a treasure of common sense to the honest. He is a shield to those who walk with integrity. He guards the paths of the just and protects those who are faithful to him.

Then you will understand what is right, just, and fair, and you will find the right way to go. For wisdom will enter your heart, and knowledge will fill you with joy. Wise choices will watch over you. Understanding will keep you safe.

Wisdom will save you from evil people, from those whose words are twisted. These men turn from the right way to walk down dark paths. They take pleasure in doing wrong, and they enjoy the twisted ways of evil. Their actions are crooked, and their ways are wrong.

Wisdom will save you from the immoral woman, from the seductive words of the promiscuous woman. She has abandoned her husband and ignores the covenant she made before God. Entering her house leads to death; it is the road to the grave. The man who visits her is doomed. He will never reach the paths of life.

Follow the steps of good men instead, and stay on the paths of the righteous. For only the godly will live in the land, and those with integrity will remain in it. But the wicked will be removed from the land, and the treacherous will be uprooted. (Proverbs 2 NLT)

85

Valuing You, Loved by the King, and a Girl's Worth

As the title may imply, this essay is directed to girls/women. Probably some aspects of its content pertain to men, but I cannot write from their perspective. I cannot understand it as well, either.

I suppose this is not applicable to every girl, but I think it is applicable to most: a better understanding of your value is needed. I think it is needed because some girls don't understand their worth.

Some time ago I was thinking about myself. I was thinking about how carefully I select things. If I'm at the grocery store and I pick out a dozen eggs, I will open the carton and make sure none are broken before choosing it. If I get a half gallon of milk, I'll glance at the expiration dates and pick the "newest" one. If I select some item off a shelf I might choose the one behind the ones displayed in front because somehow it seems better, although they're probably all the same. I spend time selecting fruit, trying to choose the best ones. Yet, when it comes to men, I wonder why I have not been so picky.

That sounds bad. It's not like I've really made bad choices

concerning men, thank God. What I mean is, I have noticed about myself that I can overlook flaws in men that I shouldn't overlook. Or, I might make up some excuse in my mind for an issue I see. I was thinking about this and I thought to myself, "Why am I scrounging around?" Why am I opening the carton of eggs, seeing broken ones, and having difficulty putting it back on the shelf when there are other cartons available with no broken eggs? As I thought about this, I saw that I should be more selective for my sake.

I wonder how many other girls do this. I wonder how many other girls see the flaws in a man and think it's ok. I don't mean imperfections or small flaws everyone has. I mean the ones that are like red flags waving frantically somewhere inside you, struggling to get the attention of your conscience. Your emotions may make excuses for them: "Red flags? What red flags? That flag is dark orange, and that one is maroon. There are no red flags here. Remember how sweet and thoughtful he was? Remember how that made you feel? Let's just think about that, magnify it out of proportion, and forget about these 'red flags' you keep seeing." However, in your heart you know they are serious issues.

All too often we're worth more than we think we are. Don't wreck your life choosing the wrong person. I don't care what excuses I make up in my mind for red flags, it would never do to choose the wrong person.

I don't expect to find a perfect person because there are none. I just mean I don't need to settle for something that isn't good.

Don't ignore the obvious. You know what I'm talking about. It's those things you know aren't right, but somehow you overlook them. If I was selecting fruit and part of it was rotten, I would not buy it. There is no need to ponder over it. There is nothing that will convince me to buy rotten fruit. I don't need to make excuses for it. I don't think that I can fix it and then it will be good fruit. It makes sense to at least be as selective as I am with fruit as with a potential life partner.

Don't feel the need to hold on to rotten fruit because you think you wouldn't or couldn't find something better. No fruit is better than rotten fruit.

An issue I would like to bring up here is the idea that a woman can "fix" a man. I'm aware that some women believe this. This notion of a man having a load of problems, and a woman coming along and making him all better by loving him or something. I do not think this idea is cute or romantic. Especially when I think about how many times this idea ensnares women. If a woman came along, saw a decrepit classic car poking through some blackberry bushes and decided to fix it, that would be one thing, but people are a whole different story. Let me just say, you cannot fix him. Only God can fix him; it's between him and God. You can't love him enough to fix him. You can't marry him and fix him. You can't have kids with him and fix him. You can't sacrifice your very life and fix him. You just might have to do so to find out it doesn't work. Let's hope not.

Also, you Christian women out there: don't get the idea that you will lead him to God through your more-than-a-friend relationship with him. Don't take him on as some personal project. This is really not something to trifle with, especially if your emotions become involved and interfere with your logic. You know who suffers the most in such a misguided undertaking. It must be God who does the work in his life. Again, it's between him and God. If you are led to, pray for him, and be a good influence as you should be in any circumstance. But, don't imagine that getting into a relationship with him will save him and bring him to God. And, don't use that as an excuse to justify your own feelings for him. You're not his savior.

So, why is there this issue to begin with? This issue of settling for men who are not good. I think there are many reasons, but one of them is that some girls don't know how much they're worth.

If nobody else on earth values you, know that God does. He values you more than anyone else could hope to. Live in accordance with the value He's given you. He loved you enough to die for you when you didn't care anything about Him. So, don't live like you're not valuable or worthy.

... you are precious to me, you are honored and I love you ...

(Isaiah 43:4 GWT)

Definition of precious: adj. 1. Of great value; not to be wasted or treated carelessly. 1.1 Greatly loved or treasured by someone.[1]

Finding someone who would die for a godly person is rare. Maybe someone would have the courage to die for a good person. Christ died for us while we were still sinners. This demonstrates God's love for us. (Romans 5:7-8 GWT)

Consider this: The Father has given us his love. He loves us so much that we are actually called God's dear children. And that's what we are ... (1 John 3:1 GWT)

Some women don't value themselves. People want and like to feel valued. Women can feel more valued if a man is interested in her. This is a big problem. If you feel this way, it can make you hang on to that carton of eggs that are broken because if you let it go it's like your value has decreased. Don't hang on to things that aren't good because you need an ego boost. There are a multitude of problems that can result from this. Your value is not contingent upon a man valuing you, or showing interest in you. Are you really going to allow some airhead dude's opinion of you to determine your worth? Are you going to allow any man's opinion of you to determine your worth? If you do, you're putting your confidence in the wrong things. Your value and future are not dependent on men.

There need be no striving to achieve or attain anything apart from God and His will for your life. You don't need to go running around proving this to that person, or earning this person's good opinion. There need be no earning of others' approval or good favor. You need no one's validation or approval but God's. And there is nothing you need to do to please others, as long as you're pleasing God. You don't need to strive to get anyone's good favor in order to gain anything. What good things can you get from anyone else that you can't get from Him? Who is richer, more influential, or more powerful than Him? Seek to please Him and Him alone. He loves you. Having the love of the King, and the favor of the King trumps any love or favor from anyone or anything else.

But seek first the kingdom of God and his righteousness, and all these things will be added to you. (Matthew 6:33 ESV)

For, At just the right time Christ will be revealed from heaven by the blessed and only almighty God, the King of all kings and Lord of all lords. (1 Timothy 6:15 NLT)

Imagine if you were loved by and had the favor of a king. Would you be very concerned with earning everyone else's love or favor, when the person above them all, the person with the highest place of authority already loves you? That in itself would give you peace, assurance, and confidence.

This was always an interesting detail to me in the book of Daniel in the Bible:

Now God had caused the official to show favor and compassion to Daniel, (Daniel 1:9 NIV)

It is interesting to me because it was God who, through a person in authority over Daniel, gave him favor. It wasn't the official himself. God caused him to show favor to Daniel. It may have seemed like it was the official himself who was showing favor to Daniel, but really it was God. Also, Daniel did not have to do things to earn favor from this official.

It is not pride to understand your value as God sees you. It is understanding fact. And understanding your value is not by way of comparison to others, it is the truth about you individually. I believe it is a tactic of the devil, especially toward Christians, to try to make them think that if they value themselves, they're being proud. Or, if you value yourself, you're thinking too highly of yourself. After all, we're supposed to be humble. Don't be proud, but don't let your worth be devalued at all.

Clothe yourself in love and humility. You can do this and still conduct yourself as a valuable person. Putting yourself in compromising or improper situations are ways of not valuing yourself. Giving too much of yourself is another way. Or, simply not viewing yourself as valuable. Don't stoop so low for things you shouldn't stoop for, but in His love, wash the feet of others.

I believe another tactic of the devil is the lie that it is selfish to not extend yourself to others. Obviously, the Lord wants us to love others, but He doesn't want us to be taken advantage of. Loving others should not destroy us. The devil preys on the kindness of people. I don't believe the Lord wants the love and kindness of His people to actually become a weak point, and a point of access for stealing, killing, and destroying. Guard your heart and be wise.

It's ok to say, "no." Not only is it ok, but sometimes it is right and very good. Many times it is good, and it should be used more often. Beware of the lie that saying, "no" is un-Christian or unloving. This is a great and successful trap for many people. In wisdom, know when to say yes, but know when to say no, too. Also, don't be afraid of missing out on something good by saying no. You may be saving yourself from something bad.

I've noticed something about myself, and I hope that noticing it will help me to alter my behavior. I imagine a friend of mine who is a girl. If she were to speak to me about some guy she was involved with, and how he had issues and was making her life difficult, I would probably speak right up and tell her to let him go. It depends on how bad the situation was. But, I would put up with very little from anyone who was mistreating her, or who wasn't good to her. Then I imagine myself in such a situation, and have seen that I would have much more tolerance for someone mistreating me or not being good to me. Why is that so? Why is it that I would be more protective toward a friend, than I would be toward myself? And so, as I said, as I notice this about myself I hope that it will help me alter my behavior concerning this issue.

I was thinking about this, too. Let's say a man is not honest with you. He's not truthful and forthright. Let's say you know that he isn't. It depends on the situation, but unless you're led by Holy Spirit to do otherwise, I see no need to do anything about it but to distance yourself from him. There is no need to confront him, or try to make him "pay" for it. You don't need to trouble yourself over his chosen behavior. He is accountable for his behavior to God, and that is a greater responsibility than being accountable to you. If he wants to behave that way, let him. He will have to answer to God for that. I think that keeping this in mind allows a girl to take herself out of the troubling equation, and eliminates an unnecessary burden.

As I learn to value myself, and learn about myself in relation to God, it has caused me to value others more. I've mentioned not getting involved with certain people for my sake. I have turned that situation around, too. What I mean is, I do not want to get involved with certain people for their sake. For instance, if someone is focused on God, has godly ambitions for his life, and is pursuing those things, I don't want to mess it up. I don't want to come into his life and somehow cause him to go off course, or get distracted. I don't want to mess up other people's lives because I value them, and what God is doing with them. I have some fear of God, too. I see here that God's timing is very important.

It saddens me to see that many women do not value themselves because of the fact that those around them do not value them. Perhaps their own parents and family do not value them. That is why it is so important for them to know and believe the truth that God loves and values them. Then, hopefully they will come to see themselves as God does, and will not have their value determined or validated by others.

I recall a gross conversation I overheard. I don't want to eavesdrop, but I was literally sitting a few feet away on the same couch as one of the two people who were talking, so I overheard their conversation. Both of them were men, in excess of 70 years old I'm estimating. I'll assign them names. One will be Jim, and the other one will be Harold. We were in a house, and a party was underway. There were about 10 to 12 people in total.

When I first got to the party, Harold (the host) introduced me to some people. One of them was this other guest. Let's call him Rick. I'm guessing he was around 50 years old. First of all, Harold introduced him by the wrong name, which immediately made me think he didn't know him well, but I couldn't be sure. Maybe it was just a mistake. However, later I found out Harold had just met Rick that evening. So, I was right. A feeling I had, immediately after being introduced to Rick, was that he was sketchy. Actually, it was even prior to being introduced to him. I got the feeling as he approached. I can't really explain it, but it was an immediate and strong feeling that he was sketchy. I don't usually get that feeling when meeting new people, but with this guy I did and it was a very strong feeling.

So, the party continues. I cannot help but observe that Rick is drinking a lot of wine. Not just a couple glasses. Another person pointed it out to me. It's difficult to explain in words, but other things I observed continued to support my initial feeling that he was sketchy.

Fast forward to when I was sitting on the couch, along with Jim. Harold was sitting in a chair next to Jim, and I overheard their conversation. We're all sitting there, kind of observing Rick who was still at the bar. Harold's daughter (in her early 20s) was also at the bar, next to Rick. Harold says something to Jim about how Rick and his daughter seem to be getting along well. Jim says something like how that would be good, Rick could, "… get her off your hands." Upon hearing that I was disgusted. I became more disgusted when Harold agreed with Jim, that it would be good. I was disgusted because I saw how Harold did not value his daughter. I could chalk it up to Harold simply lacking wisdom, which may be true, or various other shortcomings. Nevertheless, it disgusted me. It seemed to me that he did not value her, because he was practically saying it would be good if Rick got her off his hands (perhaps by marriage?) and to me it was written all over Rick that he was super sketchy. Furthermore, Harold didn't even know him. He met him that evening. So, how can you value your daughter when you are saying it would be good if this guy who you don't even know, who drinks excessively, and is behaving in other sketchy ways takes her off your hands? Strangely, I felt I valued Harold's daughter more than he did.

Minutes after overhearing this conversation, Harold gave a speech to the people in the party. He expressed his gratefulness, said he loved his wife, son, and daughter, and told a story which seemed to have no point to it. I only mention that he told a story that seemed to have no point to it because I was annoyed by it. The reason why I was annoyed by it was because I was listening intently to the story, really paying attention to it, and waiting for the moral of it. But, I never got it. There was no moral to it. It was so anticlimactic. I say there was no point or moral to it, because to me there was none. However, at the end of the story where one usually expects to find out what the moral of it was, he did utter a platitude. But, it was so dim, so very vague and indistinguishable that it was almost as bad as hearing no platitude at all. It was something like, if we all light a candle the world will be a brighter place. I was disappointed. I thought I was going to receive some words of wisdom from this aged man, yet I don't know why I thought that because I know age does not equal wisdom. I guess I was being overly optimistic. Or, I was expecting too much, which is so often the case. Also, I was already pre-annoyed/disgusted by the conversation I overheard. So, that probably made me prone to find other things annoying. Anyway, I couldn't help but feel it was insincere when he said he loved his daughter. If that is love, if that's what love between a father and daughter amounts to, it is not inspiring to me and I am disappointed again.

I would have had no reason to feel that his love for his daughter was insincere if I had not overheard his conversation with Jim. It's sometimes those things that are spoken in private that outweigh what is spoken in public. And, sometimes it's the differences (or lack of differences) between what is spoken in private and what is spoken in public that speaks the most.

There is some backstory to this. Harold's daughter is not his, biologically. In fact, she recently arrived to his household, and is his daughter through his marriage to her mother. Even so, his daughter being biologically his or not, it should make no difference when he says he loves her. But then, maybe that's what it comes down to – saying it vs. meaning it.

Perhaps I am being too harsh, or maybe too idealistic. But, I don't think so. It was totally disgusting to me. I would not entrust my dog to Rick. I care too much about my dog to do that. It totally disgusted me how someone would speak so carelessly of their daughter and Rick being together and how that would be good.

I won't go into detail, but I was told some things about Rick's history that only confirmed my initial feeling that he was sketchy. He is just not someone I would want any friend of mine to be tied to for life.

Unfortunately, I feel that until a person finds their worth in the Lord, and sees themselves as valuable because the Lord does, their worth is not secure. It is vulnerable. If their worth is found in others, it is not secure. If their worth is found in their accomplishments or abilities, it is not secure. If it's found in any other person or thing other than God, it is not secure because everything but God changes or can change. Learn what God thinks of you, and how He values you by reading what He says about you in the Bible, and by praying/spending time with Him.

Also, I feel that until a person finds their worth in the Lord they will want to find it somewhere else. Usually, in places that will disappoint.

People want to be loved unconditionally and they can only find that in God. People were created to have a relationship with God and when they don't, something integral is missing in their lives and they will find replacements for God, which don't compare to Him. They're filling the gap - the void - with something inadequate, whether they realize it or not.

I want to make another point about your value. It is a simple fact that you should fully understand. It is this: some people will not value you. Some people will not value you. Some people will not appreciate your value. They won't recognize it. I think this is a very simple fact. But, if it is not understood, it can cause problems for a person.

I'm not saying that you are perfect and everyone who doesn't recognize that is an imbecile. I'm not saying that there isn't anything about you that could be improved. No one is perfect. I think we all know that. I'm saying that you have definite value, but some people will just not value you. I think that understanding this can help a person to think about themselves in a clear and accurate way.

Try to look at it this way. Imagine a pile of gemstones are laid out on a blue velvet cloth upon a jeweler's bench. All the stones are clear; there are no colors. They look very similar in size and shape. However, this pile consists of rhinestones and one diamond. Let's say a customer of the jeweler is looking them over. He picks one up, looks at it, and puts it back down. He picks up a handful and lets them fall through his fingers like sand. The jeweler lets him choose one. He chooses a rhinestone. He has passed over the diamond and selected a rhinestone. The reasons for this are numerous. It could be because he is unknowledgeable. It could be because he likes rhinestones. Whatever the reason, it does not change the fact that the diamond has value. His passing over the diamond does not change its value at all. However, if the diamond had feelings it might wonder why this happened. It might wonder why it was passed over. If it was unaware of the point I made in the previous paragraph (some people will not value you) it might be distraught over not being chosen, and think that it did not have value just because it wasn't chosen – just because its value was not recognized.

Imagine the little diamond has arms and legs. When each new customer comes by the jeweler's bench it scrambles over the rhinestones toward the customer, with its arms waving, "I have value! I have value! Pick me! Let me prove to you that I have value!" It might do little dances to get attention, or try to coax customers to choose it. But, customer after customer choose a rhinestone. One customer scrutinized the diamond closely, but ended up choosing a rhinestone. None of them choose the diamond.

Now the diamond is depressed. Tears stream down its face, "Nobody wants me. I guess I'm not valuable. I guess I'm not really a diamond." It blots its face with the velvet cloth. The jeweler sees this and explains to the diamond that it really does have value. "You are a diamond. I carefully made each of your facets, and I know your worth. It was good that those customers didn't choose you. The one who chooses you should know and appreciate your value."

More customers come by, and now the little diamond does not scramble to prove its value. It does not do little dances, or coax anyone. It sits contentedly on the jeweler's bench and watches him at work. Now and then it glances up to see a new customer come by. When yet another rhinestone is chosen instead of it, it is not moved. It looks up at the jeweler, remembering what he said about its value.

One time a customer closed his eyes to choose a stone at random. He was about to pick the diamond. But, the diamond dodged his hand because it wasn't going to be chosen like that. It would rather stay on the jeweler's bench than go with someone who did not know its value.

There were some customers that the jeweler did not allow to choose any stone.

Let's say a final customer comes in. He looks over the pile of stones, too. He doesn't touch them. He just looks at them. The jeweler lets him choose one. He smiles at the jeweler, and promptly selects the diamond. "I want this one," he says. He knows the diamond's value.

Throughout this story the value of the diamond did not change. The main variables were the customers, and the diamond's perspective of its value. For various reasons, some people simply will not value things that are valuable. Don't let this fact negatively affect your perspective of your value.

I remember a bad experience I had. It was bad, but the Lord brought very good things out of it. It happened several years ago. This house that we're now living in was being built. At that time, we had a small group of construction workers working on the house. I'm guessing there were a group of 4 men. There is a backstory, but going further into detail is unnecessary. Basically, one day these 4 men, my Dad, and I were in the vicinity of each other. I was only there because I felt obligated to be at that moment. Typically, I would avoid hanging around because I'm not social like that, especially with men. I had nothing against them, I just had no reason to hang around them and it would be weird if I did. But, this day I was in the vicinity. I wasn't saying anything (no surprise there), I was just fulfilling my obligation in the vicinity along with my Dad. I will acknowledge, my Dad was under stress. I won't go into detail because it is unnecessary. It would become a long story and too involved. I will just try to get to my point. For a specific reason one of the construction workers asked my Dad in reference to me, "Isn't she worth $600 dollars?" And my Dad said, "No."

Nobody laughed because it wasn't said as a joke. I certainly did not laugh. It hurt. It hurt a lot, and on so many levels that I cannot define very well. It hurt in a way I had not experienced before. It hurt that one of the closest people in the world to me would not think I was worth $600. It hurt to hear that from someone I love. I wouldn't even say my dog wasn't worth $600 because I care about my dog more than that. Also, the fact that this was stated in front of 4 men made it so … I don't know the word for it … embarrassing, uncomfortable, demoralizing? I don't know the word for it. Would it have been different if my Dad said this to me alone or in front of a group of women? I have no idea. It just felt so strange to have monetary value placed on me by my Dad in front of men. It sounds sarcastic, but these are the kinds of things that went through my mind: So, is that my price tag? Anyone with anything less than $600 dollars in their pocket can buy me? No need to fear any retribution 'cause my Dad doesn't care. Be sure to pay no more than $600 dollars because if you pay more than that you're getting ripped off.

Another thought I had was that this was coming from someone who knew me well. He is one of the people who knows me best. So, I was thinking, when someone really gets to know me, is this their opinion of me? Is this what someone who really knows me would say about me? Maybe his statement was true. If anyone would be able to accurately know my worth, it seemed like my Dad would.

I tend to think that most fathers think their daughters are priceless. I don't know … the whole situation was bad. I felt like an unloved piece of trash.

Despite being hurt to my core, I found it interesting to notice the strange reaction I had to it. When I felt that my Dad didn't love me, and in fact thought I was worth less than $600, I wanted to hurt myself. This reaction came within minutes after the situation. I had never felt that way before in my life. I felt like I wanted to hurt myself and get in trouble. I felt like I wanted to do drugs, leave home, be promiscuous, and do anything that would hurt me. The thought of being promiscuous was the result of a deep hurt and a desperate desire to be valued. My Dad didn't value me so I needed to be valued by someone, and it was like that would be a way to be valued. (At that time, I had no real comprehension of God's value of me. The thought did not enter my mind. It meant nothing to me.)

All these reactions were because I was hurt and I didn't like myself anymore. I didn't value myself anymore. Perhaps I felt if I did those things it would hurt him back. It was such a strange, awful, and unexpected reaction to have. Suddenly I saw how the girls who do those things and hurt themselves must feel. I saw why they do those things. That was an eye-opener. What an awful way to live that must be. I cannot really imagine.

I saw how difficult it must be for people who have had bad parents to understand that God loves them. Often, I find myself more able to understand God's love for me by thinking about how my parents love me. After all, God is called our Father and we're called His children. What if someone had an abusive father? How could they fathom what it's like to have a loving One?

Something I learned out of this situation is that a person doesn't have to do anything wrong to be treated badly. At the time I truly wondered what I did wrong. What did I do to deserve that? I must have done something wrong, because my Dad wouldn't have said that otherwise, I thought. No, a person doesn't have to do anything wrong to be treated badly.

A healthy result of this situation was that my Dad was removed from the unreasonable pedestal I had put him on in my mind. It is good and fine to respect and honor one's parents, we're supposed to, but don't imagine that they are above being at fault.

Honor your father and mother. Love your neighbor as

yourself." (Matthew 19:19 NLT)

I saw how much I depended on my Dad valuing me. I should have really depended on the Lord valuing me. Also, I saw that my Dad's value of me was practically synonymous with my value of me, which is wrong. Your value of you should be synonymous (or as close as possible) to God's value of you, not anyone else's.

I would be remiss if I did not say here that my Dad apologized to me and I forgave him. We're good. I love my Dad, and I know he loves me. I appreciate his apology more now than I did then because I was so hurt then, and my forgiving him did not come easily.

Truly, it is not easy for me to share this story, and I deeply considered not including it here. I asked my Dad if he would be ok with it first. It is not my intention to depict my Dad in a bad light at all. It is not my intention to air dirty laundry for the sake of airing dirty laundry. I do not think that is a beneficial thing to do. When I share personal things, it is because I'm hoping that it will edify. I simply felt that this story, and what I learned from it, could be helpful to others.

I hope that every girl knows her worth, despite what any person says. I believe once she really knows her value in the Lord's eyes, no other person's opinion will matter. Since you are precious in God's eyes, who would dare to say that you are anything less than that? I would not want to contradict God. I would not want to mess with someone who is precious to the King. Hold tight to how God sees you, because there are plenty of people and things that want to take that away.

I think knowing your worth is a vital foundational element in life. It helps a person make right decisions because they see themselves accurately. They might make better decisions because they know their value, and not make decisions that are unworthy of them. They will not be trying to find their value in the wrong places or in the wrong ways.

Even if my father and mother abandon me, the LORD will hold

me close. (Psalm 27:10 NLT)

"Can a woman forget her nursing child, or have no compassion for the child of her womb? Even these mothers may forget; But as for me, I'll never forget you! (Isaiah 49:15 ISV)

Beloved one, God loves you. If no one else in all the world loves or values you, He does. And who is above Him? If no one else wants you, He does. These things will not change. You're His own, His very own. He loved you before you were born. He's seen every stage of your life – everything. Not only every stage up until now, but every stage – those that haven't happened yet. He loves you dearly. Never forget that. He is always faithful and true. He sees those the world does not see. He remembers the forgotten. His ways are not man's ways, and His thoughts are not man's thoughts.[2]

86

Christian Meme?

I was perusing the internet and saw this meme. The meme says, "When I see Christians post so many photos of themselves." Under that is an image that depicts a woman smiling and winking while taking a selfie. There is a thought bubble above her head. It says, "Wow, I'm so cute, pretty, fantastic, skinny, atractive, blessed .. etc. Must share my boastfulness .. I mean Thankfulness." (Misspelling and grammatical errors included.) It was accompanied by this verse:

For men shall be lovers of their own selves, covetous, boasters, proud, blasphemers, disobedient to parents, unthankful, unholy, (2 Timothy 3:2 KJV)

(Before I go any further, I just want to warn that this essay has grown to be quite long and is similar to a rant. Some may think I'm overreacting, missing the point of the meme, or that I'm being too severe. That's fine. I dislike the insinuation of this meme so much that I have chosen not to ignore it like I do with many other "Christian" memes. Sometimes something is so out of line that what may seem like an overreaction is appropriate. I could not care less about this meme. I'm interested in the principle of the matter.)

There are many "Christian" memes I disagree with. I think many of them seem to be some expression of inner aggression, impatience, or frustration. It's as if they want to provoke people into doing the "right" thing rather than teaching in a more forthright and mature way. I find that many memes do provoke or shock in some way. The meme may "hit hard" but does it hit the mark clearly? Is it teaching clearly? Another thing I don't like about some of them is that their message is short. Because it is short, I feel that not enough information is given, which can lead a person to conclude the wrong things.

When I say provoke, I mean that negatively. In teaching, I believe there should be some level of prompting someone to change, or at least I mean that when you're being taught it is not always warm and fuzzy. There is a difference between condemnation and being taught that change is necessary.

Going back to this meme. I was perusing the internet and saw it. It bothered me. I had to be honest with myself and truly think about why it bothered me. I wanted to get to the bottom of why it bothered me. I wanted to get to the bottom of it because it is my desire to please God. If I was bothered because the meme was convicting me of something wrong I was doing, I wanted to see that clearly, honestly, and make the appropriate change.

Examine yourselves to see whether you are still in the Christian faith. Test yourselves! Don't you recognize that you are people in whom Jesus Christ lives? Could it be that you're failing the test? (2 Corinthians 13:5 GWT)

Let us examine our lifestyles, putting them to the test, and turn back to the LORD. (Lamentations 3:40 ISV)

As I examined myself, looking for the possible cause for my being bothered by this meme, I asked myself some questions. Am I bothered by this meme because I have taken and posted selfies? Is it wrong to take selfies? Have I done something unbecoming of a child of God? Am I being stubborn to correction? Then I thought about how many selfies I've posted on my Facebook account. I thought, "Let me see … I think I have at least 9, no more than 20, probably around 15. Is that a 'safe' number?"

I really do not think I was bothered by this meme because I was being stubborn to correction. I've been stubborn to correction before and I know what it's like. I know what it's like to initially resist correction, and then submit to it. How can anyone who has experienced this forget it? It is a moment when your own self-will must die as you submit to God's ways, and the experience is distinct. It is death to your own will. It is the slaying of your own will. It is bowing your knee in surrender to God's will over your own. It usually doesn't feel good. So, I remember what it's like. But, it wasn't that way with this meme.

There are several reasons for why I was bothered by this meme. It assumes, and has directly correlated the number of photos a Christian may post of themselves with wrongdoing. It elaborates no further than that. In addition, I do not like what it is capable of stealing from people. I think this meme presents a prideful viewpoint that extends little grace to others.

Assuming that the creator of this meme is a Christian, I dislike that Christians should portray themselves in this manner, and/or that they should be trying to "teach" others in this way. This is my opinion. The teaching of whatever is trying to be taught in this meme is unclear. It actually brings confusion and can mislead. To me it was assuming, prideful, immature, and lacked grace.

I will explain my reasoning. First, I said I thought it was assuming. The first part of the meme says, "When I see Christians post so many photos of themselves." How do you know they are Christians? Also, you are assuming that because they post "so many photos of themselves" that it means their motives are wrong. Posting photos is wrong if one's motives are wrong, not solely because of the number of photos they post.

I said it was prideful. It seems to me that whoever created this meme thought they were a little bit better than other Christians because they don't stoop to posting "so many" photos of themselves on the internet. (However, I'm assuming that. If the meme's creator does indeed post "so many" pictures of themselves, they would be hypocritical. So, I have assumed they do not post "so many" pictures of themselves.)

To me, this pride I mentioned has resulted in assuming. It seems they have assumed the motives of Christians who post "so many" pictures of themselves are not good motives. That kind of assuming can speak about the person who created this meme. I think it is aptly written when it begins with, "When I see ..." That is exactly right; this is what whoever created this meme sees when they see Christians posting "so many" photos of themselves.

A person who is pure of heart sees goodness and purity to everything; but a person whose own heart is evil and untrusting finds evil in everything, for his dirty mind and rebellious heart color all he sees and hears. Such persons claim they know God, but from seeing the way they act, one knows they don't. They are rotten and disobedient, worthless so far as doing anything good is concerned. (Titus 1:15-16 TLB)

This makes me think of how some Christians are opposed to dancing. If it tempts you into sin, by all means refrain from dancing. However, other Christians may not be tempted into sin by dancing. What is unsuitable for you may not apply to everyone else. Also, so many different forms of dancing exist. Are we mature enough Christians to know there is a difference of propriety between dancing on a pole and dancing folk dances? Please, let us progress beyond these things!

The meme depicts a woman with a thought bubble above her head. It says, "Wow, I'm so cute, pretty, fantastic, skinny, at[t]ractive, blessed ..[.] etc. Must share my boastfulness ..[.] I mean Thankfulness." (By the way, I wish people who make the effort to create memes would proofread and correct.) Again, I think this speaks about the person who created this meme. I almost detect bitterness and jealousy. And again, there is assumption here. That may not be what Christians are thinking when they take and post pictures of themselves. Why must one assume the worst?

Love is patient, love is kind. It does not envy, it does not boast, it is not proud. It does not dishonor others, it is not self-seeking, it is not easily angered, it keeps no record of wrongs. Love does not delight in evil but rejoices with the truth. It always protects, always trusts, always hopes, always perseveres. (1 Corinthians 13:4-7 NIV)

If that is what someone thinks a Christian is thinking when they post their picture on the internet ("Wow, I'm so cute, pretty, fantastic, skinny, etc.), and they were motivated enough to create a meme and share it, to me it highlights their own problems and lack of extending grace to others. It seems immature, too.

Speaking of immaturity, a low blow that I see in this meme is the expression on the woman's face. It shows her winking.

A worthless person, a wicked man, goes about with crooked speech, winks with his eyes, signals with his feet, points with his finger, with perverted heart devises evil, continually sowing discord; (Proverbs 6:12-14 ESV)

Showing the woman winking in this meme would imply that Christians are posting photos of themselves in a similar manner. It paints them in a derogatory way. This passage from Proverbs indicates that winking is associated with a worthless, wicked person. So, I think it is a low blow.

I have rarely seen anyone post a selfie with themselves winking in it. I don't know why the creator of this meme just didn't go all out with the image they could have used of the woman. Why didn't they just use a picture of a woman scantily dressed, winking, and making a duck face? Could it be because that would be too un-Christian to put in a "Christian" meme? Could it be because it would be too blatant? So blatant that it makes the point of this meme seem absurd? So, to avoid absurdity a more subtle image was used, so as to make the point seem reasonable, even though it is still the same point trying to be made?

While this is a small detail it is worth mentioning to me. This meme depicts a woman, as if they are the only Christians with impure motives, posting photos of themselves. Men are just as capable of doing this.

I mentioned that I was bothered by the meme because of what it is capable of stealing from people. (If one takes to heart the meaning of this meme.) Honestly, posting photos of oneself is not much to have stolen in the grand scheme of things, but I don't want anything stolen that God has given me the liberty to do. It's not the action itself that means so much, it's the freedom to do it.

Let me backtrack a bit here and write about the meaning of this meme. What is your own impression of it? What is it really saying? What is it implying? One way of interpreting it is, if you are a Christian and you're posting "so many" photos of yourself on the internet it is not right. It's not good. So, change your ways. If you are a Christian, don't take "so many" photos of yourself and post them. Perhaps, if you want to be extra righteous, you will not post any.

Now going back to how this can steal from people. Why should a Christian with pure motives not post photos of themselves? If they have pure motives, and are so keen to please God that they take the meaning of this meme to heart, and stop posting pictures, their freedom to do so has been stolen. It was stolen because they saw the meme, and took its message to heart. It was stolen because they were really doing nothing wrong. This is similar to when a Christian who is not sinning while dancing could have the freedom to dance stolen if someone made a meme about, "When I see Christians dancing." If they took the meme's message to heart and stopped dancing, their freedom to dance would be stolen because they were doing nothing wrong in dancing.

I think this meme is disrespectful to Christians who do post photos of themselves. By God's grace, I have been conscious to the nature of the photos I choose to post. I think it is appropriate to be aware of their nature, whether someone is a Christian or not, but especially if they are a Christian. There are simply appropriate and inappropriate pictures. I have been picky enough about this that if I notice a selfie I took has a certain look in my facial expression I will choose not to share it. I am conscious of what I'm wearing in my pictures. Why? Because I care about what I do. I care about what I do because God cares about what I do, and I want to please Him. If it matters to Him, it matters to me. So, this meme that uses, "When I see Christians post so many photos of themselves" like a blanket statement - a generalization - it is disrespectful to those Christians who are thoughtful about the photos they post.

Say you watch T.V. Let's say you are aware or have been made aware by the Lord that when you watch certain shows it causes you to think impure thoughts. So, to help yourself avoid thinking impure thoughts, you choose not to watch certain shows, or refrain from watching T.V. completely. It is possible that other Christians do not have a problem with this, and are free to watch T.V. Am I saying that every Christian can watch R-rated movies without a problem? No, I don't think that Christians should watch R-rated movies, but they can and will do whatever they want. The change in their outward behavior must be motivated by their inner love for God, and as a result a disgust toward anything that is not pleasing to God. This is part of growing in holiness.

This same idea can be applied to posting photos of yourself. If you're aware or have been made aware by the Lord that when you take and post photos of yourself it causes you to think impure thoughts, or sin in some way, choose not to do it. It is possible that other Christians do not have a problem with this. Also, if the creator of this meme finds that they think impure thoughts or sin when viewing photos Christians post of themselves, perhaps they should not look at them.

"So if your right eye causes you to sin, tear it out and throw it away. It is better for you to lose a part of your body than to have all of it thrown into hell. (Matthew 5:29 GWT)

Continuing on, the meme says, "Wow, I'm so cute, pretty, fantastic, skinny, at[t]ractive, blessed ..[.] etc. Must share my boastfulness ..[.] I mean Thankfulness." Here is assumption again. There is the assumption that the Christian who posts photos of themselves is thinking these things and is boastful. Perhaps they are truly thankful. Also, to me it is implying that it is wrong to be these adjectives, and definitely wrong to think you are them. If these things are true about a person, what makes it wrong? I feel that it only becomes wrong if a person becomes prideful about it. And, what is wrong with acknowledging that God created someone who is physically attractive to you? Must one always take this observation to an impure place? I think a lot of people are attractive, but I don't lust for them. I suppose this can be difficult for some people.

In my opinion, it is some of these very adjectives that women should understand about themselves. It sometimes takes decades and a lot of difficulty for women to not hate how they look. I dislike that this meme is almost shaming women. It's as if when a Christian posts photos of herself, she's being boastful because she thinks she's cute, pretty, etc. Here again there is assumption. The photos someone chooses to share may actually be a step toward accepting and being content with how they look. To just assume they're being boastful is an example of not extending grace.

I don't know if I can explain this very well, but I'll give it a shot. When I say extending grace I mean when you extend love and consideration toward someone. It's when you extend good to others, whether they deserve it or not, because you choose to. The "good" that is extended is benevolence: kindness, compassion, goodwill. Probably someone will read this and think I mean the kind of "grace" that makes sin ok and acceptable. That's not what I mean.

I remember when I was in about the 4th grade in school. The school put together a yearbook. It was a fairly typical yearbook I guess. Part of it had pictures of students who were voted by other students into certain categories. Like, class clown, most likely to be successful, smartest in the class, most likely to watch cartoons as an adult, etc. I remember this one girl and I were voted into the category of, "weirdest smile." Up until then I never thought twice about my smile. What was there to think about? When I was put in that category it didn't kill me, it wasn't a big deal, but it created a slight insecurity about my smile.

Fast forward through the years, and now I'm in my 20s. I am still not super confident about my smile. So, I would not smile effortlessly because I wasn't confident about it. It might actually be weird. Again, not a big deal but not a pleasant thing either.

A couple years ago I had pictures taken of myself by a professional photographer. Still I was not confident, or even very content with my smile. Nevertheless, I smiled since I was encouraged by the photographer to do so and that's kind of what you're supposed to do when you get pictures taken. She told me I had a nice smile, or something to that effect. I didn't know if I believed her. Maybe she was just saying that since she was taking my picture. Later I saw the photos she took and I kind of liked my smile. Then I thought it was probably a fluke - somehow the pictures had turned out all right. Like, probably in real life my smile was still weird.

Shortly after that I was at a meeting at work. All the staff were there, about 12 people. We were going through some kind of training. I think it had to do with relations between people - how to deal with customers and coworkers alike. For some reason the instructor who was teaching us had pieces of paper with each of our names on a different piece. We were to pass the pieces of paper around, and depending on whose name was on it, we were to write something nice about them. It could be something nice in a personal way, or in how well they work, etc. So, at the end of the meeting each person received the piece of paper with their name on it, along with all the nice things everyone had written about them. I hesitated to look at mine. I don't know why. Maybe it's because I didn't know what to expect, and I didn't relish finding out what people thought of me. Anyway, I didn't look at it. I just took it home and gave it to my mom. I think she started to read the comments out loud and I stopped her. Hearing the comments spoken aloud was worse than me reading them privately. Eventually I did look at what my coworkers had written. Different things were written, but there were some definite common threads running through them. One common thread was about my smile. It was at that point that my perspective of my smile changed. It wasn't a 180 degree change, but it definitely changed for the better.

I am grateful for encouragement from others, whether they realize how encouraging they are being or not. I thank them, and I thank God for their encouragement too. It's especially nice when encouragement brings positive change for a person. And in truth, not because you're telling someone something nice that isn't true just to make them feel better.

I relay this story to supplement my earlier point that it is an assumption to think that when a Christian posts photos of themselves they are being boastful. It may be because they are beginning to be content with how they look. They may actually feel that they don't look weird, so they have enough confidence to share a picture.

Don't assume that every woman who posts photos of themselves, and who you (meme creator) apparently think is attractive ("Wow, I'm so cute, pretty, fantastic, skinny ..."), thinks they are attractive too. There can be many underlying issues and reasons for what people do. Extend some grace to others.

When I see photos posted by women who go for the sexualized corpse makeup look, or show themselves provocatively, I make an effort not to judge. It is easy to judge. It is harder to withhold judgement. It is an effort to extend grace. I do not want to conclude things about them. Am I flawless in this endeavor? Unfortunately, no, but I make a conscious effort. It is a discipline. While these types of photos (provocative, etc.) are unbecoming of Christians, even if I saw a Christian posting these types of photos I would feel sorry for them, not assume they are boastful. I would want them to understand better ways of presenting themselves – in ways that are appropriate to their worth. While there are exceptions, I believe many of the women who post these types of photos do not think they are pretty. They don't think they're fantastic. Their self-worth may be very low, and they want to be loved and valued. This may be their way of trying to obtain love and value.

Is it possible for a Christian to post photos of themselves and have pure motives? I believe the answer is yes.

There is an element of truth in this meme, or else I would not have taken the time to consider it. A discerning Christian would have no need to think about this meme if there were not an element of truth in it. It would be dismissed immediately. It's the element of truth in it that makes a person consider it, and consider themselves in relation to it. If there were not an element of truth in it, it would not have bothered me. I dislike things that are mixed – that contain both truth and something untrue. I dislike when the true part is used as bait to pull people into accepting the untrue part. Because I care about truth, I spend time trying to figure out these things that are mixed. Which part is true and which part is untrue? It's like a mess that should be sorted out.

The element of truth that I see in this meme is that some people do post pictures of themselves in a way unbecoming of a Christian. (Also, this thing about seeing Christians post photos of themselves: unless you know the person, how can you know they are a Christian? As far as I know, one cannot know if someone is a Christian by their photograph alone!) I hesitate to spell out how a Christian can post unbecoming photos, because sometimes when you spell things out people can take them as hard and fast rules. It's sad that it should even need to be spelled out. At risk of them sounding like hard and fast rules, I will spell it out. In my opinion, it's when women have applied their makeup in such a way that they look like a drag queen or a sexualized corpse. Or, when they are showing themselves in a provocative way. Need I say more? These are certain photos that are not becoming of saints.

To the church of God that is in Corinth, to those sanctified in Christ Jesus, called to be saints together with all those who in every place call upon the name of our Lord Jesus Christ, both their Lord and ours: (1 Corinthians 1:2 ESV)

But because the God who called you is holy you must be holy in every aspect of your life. (1 Peter 1:15 GWT)

The outward behaviors that are proper for Christians start in the heart - by the Holy Spirit working in them. It's from the inside out, not the outside in. Yes, there are outward choices to be made and disciplines to be kept, but it is by obedience motivated by love for God.

But whenever anyone turns to the Lord from his sins, then the veil is take away. The Lord is the Spirit who gives them life, and where he is there is freedom [from trying to be saved by keep the laws of God]. But we Christians have no veil over our faces; we can be mirrors that brightly reflect the glory of the Lord. And as the Spirit of the Lord works within us, we become more and more like him. (2 Corinthians 3:16-18 TLB)

Imagine a husband and wife. Let's say the husband works outside the home and the wife stays home and takes care of household things – cooking, cleaning, etc. She is very good at it. She's practically perfect at it. She makes plans, keeps things in order, and is never late to do anything. She greets her husband warmly when he comes home, maybe asks how his day went. Dinner is ready in minutes, and is excellently executed. But, she doesn't love him. When asked why she does all these things, she replies, "It's what I'm supposed to do. I really don't love my husband. I don't even know him that well, but does it really matter? I'm doing the things I should be doing as a 'good wife.' That's what matters." If the husband was a decent man, he would probably be upset about this. Don't you think he would want his wife to love him, and want her to do these household things because she loved him, rather than because it was simply something she is, "supposed to do?" Don't you think he would want her to care about knowing him, rather than being so focused on these things she should do? I might go so far as to say he would prefer that she wasn't practically perfect at all the household things, if it meant she loved him. And, if she loved him she would want to do well at keeping house to please him, not just because it's what she's supposed to do.

A person can do many right things even though their heart is far away from God.

Next, the verse that accompanied this meme:

For men shall be lovers of their own selves, covetous, boasters, proud, blasphemers, disobedient to parents, unthankful, unholy, (2 Timothy 3:2 KJV)

Again, I think there is an element of truth – accuracy - in this verse being applied to the attitudes of people these days, people who post photos of themselves included. I just think that tying this verse to the meme, suggesting that if a Christian posts "so many photos of themselves" it means they fall into the description of this verse can cause confusion, and can mislead.

If a Christian posts photos of themselves, it does not automatically equal wrongdoing.

Also, it says "so many" photos of themselves. How many is "so many"? Would you like to name a number, meme creator? I imagine not, because it would sound like a legalistic rule. It would not only sound like a legalistic rule, it would be one. The unclear "so many" is better because it leaves the number to people's imaginations and it makes the meme more acceptable. If the meme just blatantly said, "When I see Christians post 132 photos of themselves," it would smell too strongly of legalism. It would stink. Even if, "When I see Christians post 50 to 150 photos of themselves," was used, it would still be too smelly. The unclear "so many" is better. It cuts the smell of legalism down to only a whiff; it's nearly imperceptible. In this way, its message is more able to creep into acceptability.

The more I think about the usage of "so many" the more flaws I see in it. I may have already exhausted my point that using "so many" was a breaking point in the making of this meme. However:

It makes me imagine this ridiculous scenario. If a Christian posts less than 5 photos of themselves they're a gold star Christian, but if they post over 25 photos of themselves they are downgraded to a bronze star Christian. If they post over 100 photos of themselves their Christian faith is in question. If they post zero photos of themselves you can be sure they very pure, extra righteous, and surpass the ordinary star rank. So, now they are a supernova Christian. I am being grossly sarcastic here. But, it is only to match the carelessness and fallacy of this meme.

Furthermore, what if a Christian posts "so many" photos of their dog? Are they being boastful and proud? Or, do they like their dog? The posting of "so many" photos can be of things other than themselves. They could post "so many" photos of their car, boat, airplane, motorcycle, room, house, activities they're doing, things they like, etc. Why does this meme stop at photos of themselves? Why doesn't it go on and say, "When I see Christians posting so many photos?" I do not think it is wrong to be posting photos of any of these things as long as the person's motives are pure. To me, the meme is assuming that the person's motives are not pure.

Another thing I dislike about this meme is that it just implies what it implies, and that's it. It stops there. Whoever reads it is left to conclude what they will, and their conclusion may be wrong. One cannot control what people conclude, but the chances of wrong conclusions being made could be reduced if the meme provided some helpful direction. What I'm getting at is I see nothing in this meme that helps to instruct a person. Like, maybe teaching why it is not good to be boastful, why we should examine our motives, or why certain photos would be unbecoming of Christians. I see no effort to direct or teach people. I see very little, if anything at all, that is edifying. If a Christian who was posting photos of themselves in a boastful way saw this meme, they are provided with no redemptive direction. It's like the only thing they're told is, "You're posting 'so many' photos of yourself. You're being boastful. That's wrong." Actually, it doesn't even come out and say it's wrong, but it strongly implies it. It gives no reasons, no teaching, no direction.

I can compare it to being in an art class. Let's say you're learning how to paint portraits of people using oil paints. The teacher walks over and looks at what you're painting. He says, "You've got the eyes wrong. It's not good." Then he walks away without another word. Ok, so help me make them right. Please, tell me what's wrong with them.

I would get the feeling that the teacher doesn't care to help me, but just likes to point out what I'm doing wrong.

Here is that verse again, with some verses before and after it, (2 Timothy 3:1-5 TLB):

You may as well know this too, Timothy, that in the last days it is going to be very difficult to be a Christian. For people will love only themselves and their money; they will be proud and boastful, sneering at God, disobedient to their parents, ungrateful to them, and thoroughly bad. They will be hardheaded and never give into others; they will be constant liars and troublemakers and will think nothing of immorality. They will be rough and cruel, and sneer at those who try to be good. They will betray their friends; they will be hotheaded, puffed up with pride, and prefer good times to worshiping God. They will go to church, yes, but they won't really believe anything they hear. Don't be taken in by people like that.

It says that, " … people will love only themselves … " I think there can be an element of truth in this as it relates to some people who take selfies. But, I am not going to assume that when I see someone posting photos of themselves.

We are to love God with all our hearts, souls, and minds (Matthew 22:37). He is our God. We are not our god. We serve Him, not ourselves. As Christians, this should be true in our lives. This being true in our lives doesn't mean that we should then hate ourselves. Our love for God doesn't necessitate not loving ourselves. I know when I say that this verse may be brought up:

"If you want to be my disciple, you must hate everyone else by comparison--your father and mother, wife and children, brothers and sisters--yes, even your own life. Otherwise, you cannot be my disciple. (Luke 14:26 NLT)

Of course, I agree with this verse. Hating your life, as it says here, is hating what you can get out of this earthly life for yourself. It's putting your life aside - putting aside your own self-based desires and ambitions - to follow Jesus. It's to hate it in terms of counting it as worthless compared to following Jesus. It means you would forsake everything to follow Jesus. It is not saying hate who you are.

The Lord loves us. We should love ourselves, too. Not in a boastful or proud way, but simply and legitimately.

As I wrap up this chapter, I kind of feel like I've been writing one of those argumentative essays I used to like to write for my English class.

I kind of feel like I've been unravelling a knot.

Needless to repeat, this meme bothered me. It was for good reason. To me, it sank almost to the depth of those memes that you must "like" if you believe in Jesus or "ignore" if you're going to hell. What's worse is that some people may be influenced by memes like this.

As I read that last sentence, it spurred me to greater irritation. It is the ingredient of manipulation in some "Christian" memes that I really hate. I really hate when something as tender and heartfelt as our love for the Lord, and our desire to please Him, is used to try to manipulate. It is detestable. I think of the poor souls who see those memes that, if ignored, imply they must be going to hell because they didn't "like" it. I think of the poor souls who love the Lord, so they feel pressured to "like" the meme. It makes me mad and sad. Mad that some would use people's love for God to control them, and sad that it is sometimes successful.

I hope that Christians will become wise to these things and know that their love for the Lord, and His love for them, is kept as true and strong as ever even if they do not "like" a manipulative meme.

I wish that instead of throwing around "Christian" memes on the internet that can easily fail to communicate what may have been desired to communicate, we would take the time to be careful with what we try to teach. It is like an opportunity that is missed. Not only is the opportunity missed, but it may mislead.

If I take pains to find good in this meme, I can find it. I can take it as a reminder to be careful and thoughtful about pictures I take and post of myself to make sure they are not unbecoming of a Christian. It can be a slippery slope. I can take it as a caution to beware that excessive selfie-taking can possibly become detrimental. I can take it as a reminder for self-examination of motives, and as encouragement in my desire to grow in holiness.

In a backhanded sort of way, this meme has made me more diligent to not assume bad things about others. It has made me more careful of not being proud, in a self-righteous way. It makes me want to be more thoughtful and clear whenever I may try to teach someone something.

If these were the kinds of effects this meme intended to bring to people, then that would be good. But, it was not communicated well. If you want to teach and help people in these ways, say it clearly. Don't make it misleading, or difficult to find the good you're trying to convey.

This makes me think of a nice prime steak that you have to cook. So, you boil it, fry it, microwave it, then put it in the oven for 2 hours. It would take pains for me to find the good in this, except that it is possibly still edible. However, if you had prepared it appropriately, like maybe grilled it or something, it would have been much better. It's like the opportunity to enjoy a fine steak was missed because of how you prepared it to be served. Likewise, an opportunity to teach, share insight, truth, or wisdom can be missed when it is not presented well. It's a sad thing.

If the Lord wants you to create memes, and is leading you to do it, do it. If there is something spiritually nourishing in a meme and you feel moved to share it, share it. It is not my intention to put them down as a form of communication, or as something that the Lord can't work wonderfully through. I just wish that people would not create them carelessly, in a way that can create confusion, or in a way that can mislead. Also, I wish they were not so immature. When we as Christians are trying to help and teach others, I wish we would do so in a manner that is worthy of what we are trying to teach. And if we are Christians who are trying to learn from others,

I wish we were taught more carefully and clearly. It is easy to take a Bible verse and tie it to almost anything you want to say. It can take something more to teach or share insight along with Bible verses in a truthful, wise way.

I know that it is difficult to keep a message short, and communicate all you want to communicate. Even in my writings I feel that so much is unsaid. Though, I truly hope they are clear. A verse in the Bible is connected to so many other verses. A truth is related to so many other truths. It can be difficult to keep it brief and communicate clearly. It is not the brevity or length of the message that really matters, it is the truth and clarity of it. Clear, sound teaching is so valuable. A person could write a book on a subject and make it clear as mud. Another could write a page on the same subject and be completely clear about it. The reverse could also be true.

87

Tootsie Roll Pop

Do you remember those advertisements for Tootsie Roll Pops? The slogan was, "How many licks does it take to get to the Tootsie Roll center of a Tootsie Pop?" There was an animated owl in the ad, too.

This came to my mind as I thought about men. I believe it could apply to men and women alike, but since it came to my mind as I considered the ways of men I will continue with that theme.

(Before I go on, I just want to emphatically say that I don't believe all men are like this. I just mean that some men are. Some women are, too. I'm not a man-hater; some men are good and honest.)

When a man is interested in you, his initial behavior can be compared to the candy coating on a Tootsie Roll Pop. It's sweet and pleasant. If he happens to know what flavor you favor, he may adjust his behavior to suit it. For instance, if he knows you're a Christian and serious about it, his candy coating may include some quotation of Bible verses, a casual mention of going to church, or he may use some religious-sounding words in his conversations with you. This is part of the candy coating flavor you favor. He may voice some common Christianese sayings that are not actually Biblical. Like, "God helps those who help themselves." He may talk about God. But, who is he referring to when he says, "God"? You know Who you're referring to when you say it, but he may not be talking about the same God you know. Also, it is a flawed way of thinking to believe that when a person believes in God it is some indication of their character. Don't get all excited and go running home to your mother, enthusiastically telling her, "He believes in God!" as if it is something great.

You believe that there is one God. That's fine! Even the demons believe that and tremble with fear. (James 2:19 ISV)

It is the nature of the man's relationship with God, the condition of his heart, and his behavior that can give an indication of his character, not his belief in God.

If his candy coating is not Christian flavored, it may be adjusted to any other things you like. If you like certain activities, music, lifestyle choices, or anything like that, his behavior may be modified to suit you. Again, this is part of the candy coating that is sweet and pleasant to you.

In a way, this kind of strategy is logical. If he is interested in you, (or at the very least wants something from you) it would be best for him to be likeable to you.

But I am not surprised! Even Satan disguises himself as an angel of light. (2 Corinthians 11:14 NLT)

With wisdom and experience (and by God's grace) you can spot the candy coating quickly. It can be spotted quickly because it is essentially the same candy flavor you've tasted before. It isn't new. It's familiar. It may not be very sweet or pleasant anymore, because you know it's just the coating and not a reliable sign of what's on the inside. You yearn to finally get through it and find out what's at the center of this pop. It may not be Tootsie Roll. You may come to the point where you don't even want to taste the candy coating, you just want to get to the center already. Let us get past the preliminaries and get to what's real.

A reaction to the familiar-tasting candy coating may be this kind of cynical, not-very-hopeful reaction: I'll enjoy it while it lasts. It's like you've already concluded that the sweetness is limited, so you'll just enjoy it while it lasts. Then, when you get to the center you'll detach yourself from the situation. I can understand this, but if you already know the sweetness is limited and the center is not what you're looking for, I think it would be best to keep it moving and not hang around. I think it would be best because, for one, it's not nice to waste people's time. Secondly, you may enjoy the candy so much that when you do reach the center you will not want to detach yourself from the situation, even though you should. You'll be too attached to detach yourself.

One's reaction to the familiar candy coating may be harsh because of past experiences with it. When the taste of it brings back bad memories, one's reaction can be defensive and rather cold-blooded. Especially if the taste is extremely familiar. For instance, if some of the same lines are spoken they can touch nerves and can be met with an eye-roll, an instant rejection, a laugh, ignoring, or even a sense of violation or insult. If the same sort of lines are used, it can sting and this kind of thought process can ensue. "Yeah? You think you're clever, don't you? Nice try. Take your smooth talk and try it on someone else."

I dislike that this is part of reality. I prefer to take people at their word and I want to, but have painfully learned that a person is dumb to do that. I dislike the fact that good guys can be harshly rejected because of what bad guys have done. What bad guys have done can give the good guys a bad reputation.

One of my favorite movies is called The Heiress. It's from 1949 and stars Olivia de Havilland and Montgomery Clift. Basically, the character Olivia plays is heartlessly lead on by Montgomery Clift and they're supposed to get married and he practically leaves her waiting at the altar, but kind of worse than that. Her father in the movie was manipulative, too. So, later, after years have passed someone asks Olivia, "How can you be so cruel?" And she replies,

"I've been taught, by masters." This reminds me of why some women respond as they do to men's overtures. It's because they've had experiences and have learned how to be cruel.

In moments in my personal life I have reflected on the dialogue from this movie. It's like when someone uses the same lines or approaches on me, I think, "You came too late with those words. You came too late with those techniques. If you had come along before I was taught by a master those words would've worked on me." Basically, I reflect upon my past experiences with someone who I will call a master smooth talker. Since then, nearly everyone else who has come along have seemed like amateurs. I admit they were clever, but amateurs nonetheless. I'm not saying everyone who has come along since then was a smooth talker or misleading. Some were honest and real with me, and I appreciate that very much.

I have experienced this reaction to the familiar-tasting candy coating, too: tears and heartache. Bitter heartache. Heartache as you taste the sweetness of the candy coating, because you know it won't last. It's like you're tasting something you can't have, but you want. Or, it's like tasting something you like, but you know has no lasting substance. It's like something nice that ends in nothing, and you know it. It's odd how something so nice is laced with heartache. It is a horrible feeling. It's sad. I think, "Wow. You're so nice, but I know this isn't going to last." Or, "Wow. You're so nice, but you don't qualify. I wish you did." Or, "Wow. You're so nice, but I know that when you get to know me you'll lose interest. I wish I were who you wanted me to be. But, I can only be me." I can sense the end before it's hardly begun. Which is fine, but I don't like the teaser. I'd rather not taste it at all. I'd rather not taste something I can't have. I'd rather have no candy, than have a little taste of it and then have it taken away.

It's funny. In the previous paragraph I said something about "... you don't qualify ..." But, I don't think I've ever thought that about someone outright. To be more accurate, it's like I come to that conclusion by reluctant osmosis. Then, that conclusion is quickly followed by, "Well, I probably do not qualify for them, either."

I don't know why I have to be so nice about things. This polite banter isn't even verbal. It's in my mind. Why can't I just think, "He's a lousy good-for-nothing," and move on without a second thought? No, I tend to always reason things out in a nice, fair way. I feel ashamed of myself if I do otherwise, and I don't know if that's right. I tend to think that others are as good as I am, or better.

I am still amazed that other people would find me interesting. When or if that happens, I think, "What? Who, me? Please, don't waste your time with me. The world is full of women! I'm not what you're looking for." I will practically talk myself down and warn them that I'm different to the point that they will take my word for it and move on.

I don't know if this is right of me. I know I'm valuable. I know that in a relationship I would be devoted. I would try to be understanding, giving, compromising, loving, and respectful. I know that for the right person I would be one of the biggest blessings in their life. But, I also know that the impression some people have of me is different than what I am, and I hate to disappoint. The fact is, at some point in time I will disappoint, so I feel the need to let them know ahead of time.

One of my other problems is that I am an understanding person. I think that attribute is not generally considered a negative one. But, because I am understanding, I can understand the reasons for problems I see in people. Because I can understand them, they don't scare me off. I can find reasons for why they're that way, rather than just taking it at face value and rejecting them. Because I'm this way, I could like almost anyone. I could become fond of almost anyone. If they're not physically attractive to me, they were born that way. They were created by God that way. If they have emotional problems, there are definitely reasonable explanations for that. I may even end up feeling sorry for them. If they don't have their life together, I might chalk it up to them not having certain opportunities or anyone to help them. If they have made major errors in their past, I could say everyone makes mistakes. I am not perfect either. The list could go on. I think I have a hard time writing people off because I am understanding. Perhaps I create my own candy coating for people, through my being able to understand their problems. I want to be an understanding person, but not to the point where I become illogical.

Sometimes it takes months to get to the center. Sometimes it only takes days or weeks, and somehow I'm relieved when it only takes that long. I guess I feel that way because it seems like such a waste of precious time to spend months finding out who someone really is. On the other hand, I don't like to think that it is ever a waste to spend time with a person, but maybe it is. I'm not sure about this.

As I continue to think and write about this subject, I feel as if I'm discovering more instances of possible dysfunction in myself. This writing has taken a turn I didn't expect. This came to mind: as I'm working my way through the candy coating of someone, and I'm liking it so far, if I continue to like it I get uneasy. I get uncomfortable. I get distressed. I don't like that I'm continuing to like them, because I feel like I'm approaching future pain. If I'm working through the candy coating and something significant comes up that makes me dislike them, I am glad. I am relieved, and glad about it. I'm virtually thrilled about it. It's like I'm glad I found something I disliked about the person because it makes me less attracted. And, when I'm less attracted, my chances of ever getting emotionally attached, and then being hurt are less. I don't want to be hurt again. So, that's why I'm glad I found something about them I don't like. It practically eliminates them as a consideration, which in my mind equals not being hurt. What is that? Some kind of dysfunctional, yet effective way of self-preservation? However, it can keep me from ever really liking someone. The thought of liking someone again is disconcerting. I don't know if I could trust a man like that. I don't know if I could be vulnerable with a man and trust him to not hurt me. It amazes me how I was able to do that before, even in ignorance.

I know there are no guarantees in romance. That's one reason why it's hard to be vulnerable, because you can't be sure of not being hurt. I'm learning there is very little you can be sure of in this life. I absolutely hate the very real chance of getting so attached, where you would do almost anything for them, you do everything the very best you can, but then the other person walks away like you meant absolutely nothing. It's not even "like" you meant absolutely nothing. You were absolutely nothing to them the whole time. If you were something more than nothing to them, you were just their half-hearted attempt at maybe getting something. Maybe you were only an amusement. In their final this-isn't-going-to-work-out speech they nonchalantly said, "This has happened before" with them. That's great. To me that practically confirms that it was unimportant to you, and it makes me feel even dumber that I took it seriously. But, what about all those things they said? You replay the words over and over again in your mind, desperately trying to discover something you must have missed. But, nothing was missed. I guess the words just meant nothing. They were just careless, meaningless words that you – naïve, trusting, gullible you – took seriously. The trust you had seems more like stupidity. I feel like I'm always the one who cares more, who cares the most, who takes things seriously. The hopes and dreams you had evaporate. Then you wonder how you got to that place. Then you remember you weren't hog-tied and forced into that place, however you were most definitely lead there. But, because I'm the type of person I am, I blame myself most of all. Then you experience the misery of vivid memories, what ifs, guilt, shame, why am I not enough, what's wrong with me, what did I do wrong, for hellish months afterwards. If you want to add a little variety to that mix, there's seeing someone who resembles him in some small way and it grips your heart. Or, checking your phone repeatedly, thinking he might have tried to contact you. You hear someone say his name, or you happen to read it, and it means way too much to you. Then this is all worsened by realizing he probably doesn't think of you at all. He's probably on to the next one, and you're barely a memory. One person simply leaves, and the other person is left broken.

There was zero consideration of one's words involved. The things that were said were careless. Personally, if I said those things to someone, I would feel awfully guilty for leading them on. I'd feel very bad. I would never say those things to a guy, because I am aware that feelings can be stirred by them. I try to be considerate of others. The things that were said that I'm referring to were not, "I like you," "You're cute," or "We should go out sometime." It was much more than that. They were the kinds things that when spoken to a trusting girl, sink down deep into the heart and make a home there. Things that play with the emotions and the heart. Things that pull someone closer. Things that inspire a likely future together, or that make you really believe the guy is serious about you. Things that make you feel as if you are something special to them. Unnecessary things. I'm not making this up. I didn't walk down the garden path by myself.

If I can counsel anyone from all I've written here, it would be to be careful with your words. Be especially careful with your words toward people who might have feelings for you. Don't say unnecessary, premature things, or things that you know could unduly influence the heart. Don't say things you don't mean. Let the attraction grow from truth, respect, friendship, and trust, not smooth words.

That brings me to another subject I want to address: friendship. At least for me, I have got to be friends with a guy first, before being anything more than a friend. With this guy from my past there was no effort spent trying to be friends. It went straight from, "Hi, my name is …" to "I'm interested in being more than friends." This is too fast for me. How can you know if you want to be more than friends, when you aren't even friends - when you don't even know the person?

Furthermore, it makes trying to get to know someone for who they are more awkward, because relationship stuff is on the table right from the start. I want to get to know someone as they are first, in a more regular and simple way. When the idea of being more than friends is presented right off the bat, it can make it more difficult to know someone because relationship stuff is looming and can cloud good judgement. At least for me, it would be better to just spend some consistent time getting to know someone as a friend only. Then let things go, or not go, from there. When things move too fast, there is more stress and pressure, in my opinion. And for me, when there is too much stress and pressure I'm ready to move on. I didn't move on before, but I would now.

I am perfectly aware of the fact that some guys do not want to first spend time getting to know someone as a friend only, when they are interested in something more. It's too slow, and it's too much work for something that is not guaranteed. Hey man, if you want something fast go to McDonald's. Use the drive through if you can't be troubled to get out of your car. Pay for your meal with the loose change you find under your car seat. On the other hand, if you want Christmas dinner at the Four Seasons, you'll have to wait until it's Christmastime. Then you'll have to make sure you can afford it before you make dinner reservations with your last name. Then you'll have to fight through city traffic, park in the parking garage or get valet parking, make your way to the place, and wait to be seated.

I see that when I spend time getting to know someone, and I'm actually liking them as a person and some partiality is growing toward them, they can get impatient and then lose interest. I was getting there, but too slowly for them I guess. (I could go on to another subject here, the subject of not needing to like someone or be friends to obtain what some people are truly after, but I'll leave it alone.) Take your time getting to know them, and if they become impatient and lose interest because things are moving too slow, that can say a lot about their motives. In my opinion, this is one of the simplest ways to weed out the guys a girl shouldn't bother with. At the same time, I realize a guy can't wait around forever and there are many other reasons for why he may lose interest. To each his own.

Also, I personally do not need to spend time with a person every day 24/7 to stay interested. If there is meaningful communication or contact between us once in awhile that is satisfactory. I'm sure my needed quota of social interaction will almost always be less than anyone else's. Just because I do not communicate with someone doesn't mean I don't like them. I simply do not want to deal with being social very often, unless I really, really like you and I'm comfortable with you. Actually, I've noticed that when I have some time away from someone my partiality toward them can increase. So, I can be incommunicado and affection is growing on my side. Meanwhile, the guy thinks that I don't care. Then when I see him again nothing is wrong with me. Nothing has changed. I like him still. Maybe even more than before, but because I haven't communicated with him recently it's like he thinks I've lost interest, that I don't care, and he's standoffish. I just don't need or want as much social interaction as others do.

Since my experience, and carefully contemplating everything that happened in probably extreme and excessive detail, I feel like I've gotten to know that guy from my past much better than I ever did before. This has been beneficial to me. I've seen things more clearly. It's been enlightening.

I have seen and interacted with him a few times since. These places where I've seen and interacted with him could be compared to large parties. I've learned his style with women from personal experience and from astute observation. He's very charming, subtle, careful in his own way. Very light-handed, but exact. He doesn't show too much interest, but enough so that there is no doubt whatsoever that he is interested. He does not zero in on one woman. His style is not like shooting with a rifle, it's like shooting with a shotgun. The spread is broad. I've watched him work, and in some circles it must be considered an art form. For instance, in a group of 50 women, he has probably scoped out which ones are eligible within 15 minutes, and as I said he won't focus on one. (Unless he's decided there is only one present that is "worth" focusing on.) He'll work the room very well. He can manage multiple women at a time. He works his lean 6'4" frame as skillfully as a woman might work with her assets. A person already has to look up at him, but I've noticed that if he stands close enough to a girl while talking, he's towering over her and he knows it. I've seen his method repeatedly. He'll get close enough, then lean closer as he's talking as if he has to because of his height. This makes it feel like he's the dominant one and the girl is a delicate little flower beneath the protection of a tall oak tree. He'll turn to the girl, talking, flash a smile, and it works quite well I must say. Most of the girls he does this to seem to react positively, quite giddy, in fact. He's got his style down pat, and because he is good-looking, his methods are even more effective. I've learned that he is successful with women. He does not always need to be the initiator – they will approach him. Come to think of it, his appearance is probably 75% of his game. He really doesn't need to work that hard, and if he does, it's like he's not accustomed to it.

I've observed all of this with interest. It is fascinating to watch. It is fascinating to watch the preliminaries, when I know what actually comes later.

He may be successful with women in terms of catching them, but not in keeping them. When his center starts to show, it's very different from the candy coating and it can put a girl off fast. He is almost opposite of what he seems. He has issues, that is all. Ones you wouldn't expect, but I won't go into much more detail. Although, I could and I did, but I erased it. I feel like I would be sharing too much, and I've already shared enough on this particular subject in a past essay. He seems like a fine specimen of a man initially, in appearance and in his well-chosen words and manner, but later things really change.

It is important to learn the difference between personality and character, between appearance and the heart.

I know how he is. Despite his façade, he's a very insecure and immature person. The most insecure person I have ever met, even more insecure than me. Most of his issues seem to stem directly from his insecurity.

Because I'm the type of person I am, I feel sorry for him. This is so typical of me. I wish he did not have to suffer with his issues. I dislike that I have even a microscopic speck of sympathy left for him. Like, why? Why, after all? I dislike this about me. Why can't I just write people off, without an ounce of sympathy? Goodness knows I've been hurt badly enough to do so with him, but still I don't. I just feel weirdly neutral toward him, and sorry for him. I hope he has a good life. One reason for my remaining speck of sympathy is, I can understand the unfortunate reasons for why people have issues. That's one reason why I hung around him for as long as I did before he ended it. Because I was more understanding than some other girls might be, or dumber. I made the transition from his candy coating to his center like the hull of a boat pierces through a wave. It did not faze me. It probably should have. I made it through the candy, I saw the center, and I was still willing. I was willing to deal with all his issues, instead of just moving on. I was willing to settle in for the long haul with this guy, regardless. I don't think he understood me at all. Anyway, you can see how being understanding, or empathetic, can be a very negative attribute at times.

Now, I thank God that he ended it. To my knowledge, it was one of the most merciful things that have happened to me. Though, I did not realize that at the time. I realized it later. It was so profoundly merciful, that I attribute it to God, not to him at all. I wish he would've ended it sooner, instead of stringing me along for so long. Knowing me, I probably would have never ended it, would've gone all the way down the aisle for this guy, and spent the rest of my life with him. If I were the lucky girl – that was how I thought! That is embarrassing. I cared too much about someone who didn't care for me. Thinking of how I wouldn't have ended it scares me now. Thinking of how I would've been willing to spend the rest of my life with him is frightening now. I know I would have been disappointed and hurt, even more disappointed and hurt than when it ended.

I don't want to think I'm God's gift to man. I don't want to think more of myself than I should. At the same time, I would like to be with someone who thinks they're lucky to have me, too, not the other way around like before. I know I'd feel like the lucky one with whoever I liked. That's just how I am. Not everyone has to like me, not everyone will, but I don't want to be where I was before. Before, I felt like I was trying terribly hard to be good enough, and I never was. I want to feel like I'm more than enough just as I am.

By the way, coming out of a relationship where you never felt like you were good enough to begin with, and then being dumped to top it off, is a fantastic opportunity for the devil to take advantage of. He will not miss such an opportunity. He'll try to make you believe that there is something integrally wrong with you. He'll try to make you believe that you aren't good enough for anyone on the face of the planet. In fact, you should probably just do away with yourself and save everyone the hassle of your existence. This can be very difficult to overcome. If, by God's grace, you push through all of these attacks, when the time comes for another relationship, the devil will still try to beat you down. He won't let you go without a fight. He'll try to get you in the same rut you were in before of trying too hard to be good enough. This can really get you into trouble. Trying too hard can make a person do some unhealthy things. Or, he might try to make you feel insecure about every little thing you do, because it might be wrong. You might make the next guy leave you too. Lies! Be who you are, be true to how God made you, and know that that is enough. For some people, you'll never be enough. You can't make other people like you. The ones who like you should like you for who you are, as is. End of story.

I really don't care about the techniques men use to get women, except for when it's done in a way that is wrong, or can cause unnecessary emotional damage. Some of the emotional damage is completely unnecessary; it is avoidable. Some hurt feelings in romantic attempts are inevitable I think. But, by being careful and considerate, I believe a person can avoid hurting others in an unnecessarily damaging way. To me this is common sense.

I have an anecdote to share. I wasn't there personally, this was told to me by someone I know. This someone I know (a man who I will call John) was at a restaurant with this other guy who I will call Keith. Their waitress was apparently of Hispanic decent, probably Mexican. Keith notices this and when the waitress goes away, he informs John that Mexican women like it when you call them, "My strawberry." This is news to me. Anyway, so when the waitress approaches their table again, Keith says to John, "Watch this," and he goes on to speak to the waitress and call her his strawberry. The behavior of the waitress changes noticeably; there was an increase in friendliness. The words obviously had some impact. John (who had nothing to do with Keith's interactions with the waitress, but was a bystander) went back to the restaurant at a later date with other people. The same waitress attends to them. She remembers John, somehow relating him to that past interaction with Keith, and begins to treat him differently. In a very friendly way, let us say. So much so, that John stopped going to the restaurant because of it.

My point in sharing this anecdote is that words matter. They influence people. They affect people, and people know it.

Probably some men find it amusing that women can be manipulated with words. All I can say is if enough smooth words are used on certain women it can really tear them up. It can really mess them up. Especially if the words had no genuine or good motive behind them. If you find this kind of stuff amusing, let me check back with you when your sister, daughter, or a friend you care about is torn up over meaningless words that some smooth talker used her with, and I'll see if you find it amusing then.

There have been times when I have been tempted to lead someone on. To lead someone on when I have no real feelings for them. I am just tempted to play them. These temptations are considered for a second longer when I recall how I was lead on and how it hurt. It doesn't make sense, but it almost seems like a twisted way to "get even." Don't you think I could do it too? Yes, I could. I could say the right words, move the right ways, flirt like a pro, lead someone on. But, by God's grace I have resisted these temptations. It is a frightful thought to think that other people are tempted in these ways, but have nothing to hold them back from going through with it. I have Someone to be accountable to, and there is such a thing as right and wrong in this world. I'm not going to perpetuate wrong, just because something wrong happened to me. I won't be one to continue that behavior. It doesn't matter if I was hurt by it, that is no reason to spread the hurt.

Interestingly, when I met that guy from my past again recently, he seemed to have trouble looking at me directly. He'd look around the room or at the floor, but avoided my eyes. His irrepressible charm compelled him to compliment my appearance, but frankly he seemed uncomfortable around me. Very uncomfortable. He looked sheepish, but said nothing to indicate that. I just saw it in his manner. He was unusually quiet for someone who is very extroverted and gregarious. He wasn't so smooth this time. It was like he didn't know what to do. This behavior was so abnormal for him, and so noticeable, that it began to make me feel uncomfortable. This is extremely different from how he used to be with me. I wanted to say, "It's ok. Don't feel badly." But I didn't know if that was the right thing to say. Maybe I would be making too much of it. I've forgiven him. It's over and done – so much done. If anyone should bring up the past at all, he should, not me. I thought, maybe he thinks I still want something with him and is trying to show me no interest. Or, maybe he knows he blew it. Maybe he thinks it meant nothing to me, and I got over it in two days. Or, maybe he knows I was upset after I did not respond to him calling me, and after I would not give him my phone number when he "lost" it and wanted it again. Who knows? I'm tired of trying to figure him out.

He has no idea of what I experienced and how I felt. I have not spoken of it with him. What would be the point of telling him what I experienced? It would be pointless, completely pointless.

After my experience, I cannot say how attractive it is when a guy is mature, respectful, honest, and wants to be truthful with me. I think, "Are you for real? You're actually considerate? You're not playing games? You're being careful with what you say and want to be honest?" The guy who does this immediately becomes attractive to me. It's truly like a breath of fresh air and gives me much hope for mankind.

Still, because of my past experience, when a good guy comes along later and says some nice things, showing interest, I have almost no trust to give. I was dumb enough to believe what the other guy said and it made me the fool. I heard it all before, believed it, and it meant nothing. Why be the fool again? This good guy could be genuine, but that's what I thought with the other one. How can I move forward without trust? This lack of trust acts as a roadblock to any progress. It is so unpleasant to find myself in this kind of situation.

I feel as if I can control the boundaries in which I keep myself and my emotions, but those boundaries are restricted. At this time, it is difficult for me to imagine them being expanded enough to allow myself to like a man again (as more than a friend), but I want to. I do want to. Don't you think I want to? Of course I do, and I could – very easily. But, I won't let myself like I let myself before. Tears come to my eyes thinking about it even now. I remember how my liking someone wrecked me so badly in the past. And, that was the result of my only liking someone - not even loving someone. That was the result of many spoken words and minimal time together. In a way it was almost nothing, but it was incredibly meaningful to me. I feel like a fool writing that, but it is true.

To be afraid of liking someone is not right. I see that this is a problem. There must be some kind of proper balance to this. I really must discuss this issue with the Lord.

That thing I mentioned about being glad when I find something I dislike about someone. I've noticed this about me, too. When I'm working through the candy coating and I'm liking him so far, I have this inner, unspoken dialogue with him. They're only thoughts: "Please, please do something I don't like. Do something that really aggravates me so I don't like you anymore." What a backward way of thinking that is! Another dysfunctional means of self-preservation. It's like when they do something that really aggravates me, it provides to me the impetus to disconnect myself from them and future pain. It's like, something that really aggravates me about them = no attraction = no future pain. It allows me to jump ship. To jump a ship I believe will sink, even though it may not. To avoid future pain, even though in reality there may be no great pain in the future. Whether the ship will sink or not, and whether there is future pain or not, at this time I do not yet feel comfortable in sticking around long enough to find out. At least if I'm not on the ship, there is no chance of me going down with it. This writing has become so revealing to me.

You know, the more I think about this, I don't think I want to find something about them that I don't like for the sake of not liking them. It's for the sake of not being infatuated with them. I want to find something I dislike so my infatuation for them can be eliminated. According to Wikipedia, "infatuation or being smitten is the state of being carried away by unreasoned passion ... "[1] That's what I'm afraid of! I don't think I'm afraid of liking someone, I'm afraid of being infatuated. It's a horrible thing, being infatuated. Horrible. I hate it. It's like you're on some thrilling but frightening roller coaster that's going faster and faster and (in my experience) at the end you crash and nearly die. It has the feeling of being out of control. There is very little reason and good sense involved when one is infatuated. So, when I feel myself starting to like someone, and it starts to feel like infatuation, it's like a flashback to when I was on that roller coaster that crashed. I get the flashback and my reaction is like, "No, no, no. Not again! Get me off this thing!" It scares me. Perhaps when I simply like someone who has certain disagreeable things about them, there is no infatuation. I feel more stable that way. I feel safer that way. I can see things more logically because I'm not infatuated. It's a calmer version of liking someone, rather than the turbulent infatuation of someone.

Despite this unexpected epiphany about infatuation, there is still something in the back of my mind that is hesitant to even like someone. Probably because liking someone can lead to infatuation.

If you were on an actual roller coaster that crashed (rather than a figurative one) and you nearly died, I imagine you would feel resistant to ride one again. Even if you knew it would not crash this time. That seems normal, and warranted.

I already know I'm a sensitive person by nature. I don't like that an experience from my past has made me ultra-sensitive in terms of having feelings for a man. If I ever did like someone as more than a friend again, I would want them to feel like they could be themselves around me, and not feel as if they had to walk on eggshells at all times to cater to any unhealthy sensitivities I might have. I would want them to be considerate of my normal sensitive nature, but I wouldn't want them to have to deal with unhealthy, unnecessary sensitivities. In addition, I said I didn't know if I could trust a man, or trust him to not hurt me. I would want a man to trust me. But, how could I expect him to trust me, if I don't trust him? There should be mutual trust. Anyway, I wouldn't want to like someone, and possibly involve them with myself if I'm not in the right place. I'd like to be whole, not broken, when involving myself with others.

This is something I observed. When someone who is not careful, or is not healed or whole, involves themselves with another and ends up hurting them, it's like the cycle continues. It creates more hurt, unhealed people. Then they go off in search of something and hurt more people, and then there's just a whole bunch of hurt, dysfunctional people. The cycle continues; dysfunction is propagated. People must be more careful and considerate of others, if that is even possible. Am I expecting too much? People should take a step back, take a break, and heal before involving themselves with others. It can take time to heal. In addition, a person should go to the Lord for healing.

By God's grace, I will heal. I've already prayed about it many times. I've already made progress. God willing, someday I will step out and trust again, and I won't be afraid.

After my extensive departure from what was supposed to be the main theme of this writing (Tootsie Roll Pops and how they can compare to men, or women), I will try to get back on topic and salvage any further points I wanted to make.

I have seen the transition of going from the candy coating to the center. Now there are no more Bible verses, no more God talk, no more careful and persuasive speech. The veil is lifting. Observing the transition would be funny to me if it wasn't so sad. Perhaps someday reaching the center won't be disappointing. I'd practically prefer a sour Warheads candy type of man, if it meant he was initially sour and disagreeable but became sweet later. That analogy was insufficient; it doesn't say all I mean. But, I'll leave it here anyway. I'm interested in what's on the inside; what he's really made of.

At this point I have come up with some ways of getting to the center faster. Without doing anything I shouldn't, if I can get to the center in a more expedient way I think it is best to do so. It saves time and energy. However, you can sometimes scare people away with these methods. Even so, if they were scared away they were apparently not able to handle very much, so it saved even more time and energy. For example, I think one way of getting to the center faster is by seeing what he's like when he's angry. How does he behave when he's angry? Like an infant or with self-control? Seeing him when he's angry may be difficult to observe, kind of like catching a glimpse of a rare bird in its natural habitat. On the other hand, if it's not so difficult to observe him when he's angry because he's angry so frequently, then that can tell you something, too. If he asks you to go somewhere or do something, and you say, "no" pay attention to his response. Does he get an attitude? Does his demeanor become defensive, or does he complain? Or, does he receive a "no" answer gracefully? Another way to get to the center faster is to ask specific and revealing questions. If you know what you're looking for, the answers to some of these questions have a cross-sectioning effect and make a beautifully clean break of the Tootsie Roll Pop, exposing the center plainly.

Another method is to share something about yourself that is less than flattering, but true. You can show your own center. Sometimes the way he reacts to it can show you something about him.

Hopefully my methods are not coming off as manipulative. They're basically about observing, and asking questions. I'm not playing around when I say I'm interested to know what he's really made of.

Though you may use these methods, they are not everything. Try not to be too focused on getting to the center as fast as you can. I only say that because I have found that I can tend to want to know everything I can about a person as fast as I can and that is not very practical. If I could find a dark, empty room, place a desk and chair beneath a hanging light, and make an appointment to interrogate the guy that would be great. However, it is not practical.

As I write this I'm learning more about myself. Yes, I am guilty of this! Guilty of using observation techniques and questions in an attempt to find out who someone really is. And, wanting to find out who someone is quickly. I can look back at my past behavior and see that this is so true about me. Oh dear.

Naturally, there are the initial stages of getting to know someone when people generally want to make a good impression.

At least, they try to be somewhat agreeable in their behavior. The more you get comfortable with each other, some behaviors will change. You'll begin to see more of their true self. I think this is normal, and when I speak of the candy coating I'm not referring to this. Though some of his behaviors change, the integrity of the man's core (his character, beliefs, morals) should remain the same. When I speak of the candy coating, I'm referring to when whatever you're initially presented with is very different from what is at the center. They are not the same. Though some behaviors change when you get to know a person better, it should not change to the point where they are now a different person. If they portrayed that their character was one way, but now (as you've gotten beyond the candy coating) their character, beliefs, and morals have changed, something is wrong.

The possibility of this happening with someone is unsettling to me. The possibility of someone changing into a different person. It makes me think about when I used to live in the city and it was common to see pigeons walking on the streets and sidewalks. Once, I observed this man. He was feeding a small group of pigeons. He was squatting low to the ground, being quite still. He'd throw crumbs or something to the pigeons now and then. He coaxed a specific one closer to him. I wasn't so close that I could hear him, but in my imagination I like to think he was softly mimicking the sounds a pigeon makes to encourage it and make it feel comfortable in coming even closer. The crumbs weren't thrown so far away from him now, so the pigeon had to get closer to him to reach the crumbs. A little closer, a few more crumbs, a little closer, a few more murmured pigeons sounds, just a little bit closer … then bam! He snatched the pigeon with his bare hands. The other pigeons quickly flew away, but the one pigeon was gripped in his hands and at his complete mercy.

So, this is unsettling to me. The dumb pigeon trusted the man. It was being treated well, got some crumbs, was being softly spoken to (in my imagination). Then, when the man had it where he wanted it everything changed and now the pigeon was trapped and at his mercy. How I'd hate to be that pigeon.

Be wise and ask for Holy Spirit's guidance in your interactions with men. The candy coating may be covering a horrible center. Or, there may be no actual candy coating and the guy is good and honest all the way through.

As you work your way through the candy, be careful not to get attached to it. Don't be deceived by it. Don't get captivated by the candy, though it tastes very sweet. I mention this because you might like the candy coating so much, that by the time you get to the center and find out who the person really is you may not want to face facts. You might confuse the two, or not want to differentiate one from the other. You might be so charmed by the candy you've just experienced that when you hit the center you've become blinded by it. Work through the coating and wait to see what's at the center before thinking you know who they are.

It can be hard to let something go that was so sweet and pleasant. It can be hard to let something go on which you've spent time working through the candy layer. Thinking you're saving something, or saving your "investment" (time with the person, a relationship of some kind) by ignoring the center you've discovered is foolishness. You've discovered who they are. See it clearly, and completely separate from the candy coating. If the center is not good, cut your losses, let it go, and move on. You're saving something by moving on, not by sticking around.

I've noticed the layer of candy can vary depending on the person. Sometimes you'll hit a part of the center, then there's more candy beneath that, then you'll hit the center again. It's like it's layered. Sometimes there is no actual candy coating; what they portray is genuine. Sometimes the layer of candy is thick, and sometimes it's very thin. Regardless, it's what's at the center that counts.

Lord! Help! Godly men are fast disappearing. Where in all the world can dependable men be found? Everyone deceives and flatters and lies. There is no sincerity left. But the Lord will not deal gently with people who act like that; he will destroy those proud liars who say, "We will lie to our hearts' content. Our lips are our own; who can stop us?" The Lord replies, "I will arise and defend the oppressed, the poor, the needy. I will rescue them as they have longed for me to do." The Lord's promise is sure. He speaks no careless word; all he says is purest truth, like silver seven times refined. O Lord, we know that you will forever preserve your own from the reach of evil men, although they prowl on every side and vileness is praised throughout the land. (Psalms 12 TLB)

88

Beautiful Grace

The other day I read the book of Philemon in the Bible. It's in the New Testament. It has only one chapter. I had not heard much about that book. I think there is more than one thing to learn from it, but I wanted to write about what I saw.

What I saw in the book of Philemon were two good examples of grace. Two good examples of giving grace, or of grace in action.

It was interesting to me because it was very beautiful. Also, they were examples of a man extending grace to another man. Whereas, I feel that most of the time in the Bible we are told of God's grace to man.

Before I share the two examples, I want to try to get to the bottom of what grace is.

Definition of grace: n. 1. Seemingly effortless beauty, ease, and charm of movement, form, or proportion. 2. A charming or pleasing quality or characteristic. 3. Skill at avoiding an improper, inept, or clumsy course. 4. Good will : favor. 5. A temporary exemption, as from paying a debt : reprieve. 6.a. Divine love and protection given to mankind by God. b. A virtue granted by God. 7. A short prayer said at mealtime. 8. – Used as a title of courtesy for a duke, duchess, or archbishop.[1]

Definition of gracious: adj. 1. Marked by courtesy and kindness. 2. Compassionate : merciful. 3. Marked by good taste and elegance.[2]

Definition of mercy: n. 1. Kind and compassionate treatment : clemency. 2. A disposition to be benevolent and forgiving. 3. Something to be thankful for <a mercy no one was hurt>[3]

Definition of good will: n. 1. Benevolence. 2. Cheerful willingness. 3. A good relationship, as of a business with its customers.[4]

Definition of benevolence: n. 1. An inclination to do charitable or kind acts. 2. A charitable act.[5]

Definition of courteous: adj. Considerate toward others : polite.[6]

Definition of charitable: adj. 1. Generous in giving to the needy. 2. Lenient in judging others.[7]

Definition of charity: n. 1. Help or relief given to the poor. 2. A fund or institution that helps the poor. 3. An act or feeling of good will or affection. 4. Tolerance and leniency in judging others. 5. *Theol.* a. God's love for mankind. b. Brotherly love for others.[8]

Definition of lenient: adj. 1. Inclined to be forgiving and mild : merciful. 2. Not demanding : tolerant.[9]

With all of these various definitions in mind, I would say that grace is something that is not necessarily deserved. It is for the benefit of someone else. I would say it is loving and considerate favor and kindness. It is undeserved favor, kind of like a gift. It is merciful, not demanding, and lenient. I think essential ingredients of grace are compassion and consideration.

Definition of compassion: n. Actively sympathetic concern for the suffering of another : mercy.[10]

Definition of considerate: adj. Mindful of the needs or feelings of others.[11]

I think grace is amazingly beautiful! It is more moving than Chopin's Nocturnes, or the works of Debussy. I think grace is the type of beautiful that is fittingly compared to music, because it is so difficult to accurately portray its beauty in words alone. Music helps to cover the inadequacies of words. It is lovelier than the sweet scent of flowers on a summer breeze. It's more humbling than the skies at sunset, or the stars at night. What makes it more amazing is that it is not deserved. It's just given, because of love. Beautiful grace.

The two examples of grace I discovered in the book of Philemon were these:

Now I want to ask a favor of you. I could demand it of you in the name of Christ because it is the right thing for you to do, but I love you and prefer just to ask you – I, Paul, an old man now, here in jail for the sake of Jesus Christ. (Philemon 1:8-9 TLB)

I really wanted to keep him here with me while I am in these chains for preaching the Good News, and you would have been helping me through him, but I didn't want to do it without your consent. I didn't want you to be kind because you had to but because you wanted to. (Philemon 1:13-14 TLB)

Can you see it? Can you see the grace being given by Paul to Philemon? I saw it, and it was beautiful.

In the first example (verses 8 and 9), because of love, Paul preferred to ask instead of demand. Interestingly, he could have demanded it (in the name of Christ no less) but did not. The various aspects of grace are clearly shown in this example.

In the second example (verses 13 and 14), Paul is considerate of Philemon. I believe Paul could have very easily kept Philemon's runaway slave with him, but was considerate of Philemon. Judging by what Paul wrote about Philemon in the rest of the book, Philemon seemed like the kind of person who would have gladly allowed Paul to keep his slave if he were a benefit to Paul. I think Paul knew this about Philemon. One thing I like about this example is that there is a lack of assumption on the part of Paul. There's a lack of assumption on the part of Paul in regard to what would be ok with Philemon. Instead of assuming, he checks with Philemon and wants his consent. Also, Paul shows love and leniency by not wanting Philemon to be kind because he had to, but because he wanted to. To me this is profound. To me it is also rare.

It's so rare, I find it difficult to imagine finding this graceful quality in a person in real life, even with my robust imagination. When I have seen or experienced this quality in another person, it's striking to me. It seems unreal. It's practically perplexing. It pierces through my mind, my logic and reasoning abilities, and goes straight through and touches my heart. It's so beautiful, and unexpected, that it seems unreal. I wish it were not so rare.

What a strange and inexplicable thing grace is. It's just about as strange and inexplicable as true love. Its gentleness is delicate and yet its power is so overwhelming that it disarms a person. It disarms a person of a glib response to it. What is the appropriate reaction to something as marvelous as grace? What is the appropriate reaction to something as marvelous as true love? Personally, I would have no appropriate reaction, except to be without words and left completely humbled.

Such grace, such love, overwhelms me so that I feel as if I stand before it with nothing but empty hands in response. I have nothing in the face of such overwhelming grace. I have nothing to counter it with, nothing to offer in return. It was undeserved, after all. Kind of like when someone gives you an unexpected gift. I would feel surprised and slightly humbled. Then I'd feel like they were thinking of me and liked me enough to give me a gift. Then I might mumble a few words that fail to express how I feel. Like, "You didn't have to do that." Or, "Thank you. I didn't know we were giving gifts, or I would have given you something too." Basically, I'll feel kind of loved and special, and I really don't have anything to offer them at that moment but gratitude. This is my reaction to an unexpected material gift. But, what about gifts of grace that are not material? What about the greatest gift of grace, God's Way of salvation for mankind? What is my reaction to something like that?

I was thinking about grace, and it seems to me that it's kind of like the opposite of unfairness. Let me restate that. Grace and unfairness have similarities, but the result of each are different. Usually when I hear someone mournfully declare, "It's not fair" it's because some injustice (small or large) was done, or because the outcome to something was not even-steven. Usually when I've heard people say, "It's not fair" they are unhappy about it because the unfairness was negative in some way. But, I was thinking that grace isn't fair either. When a person gives grace, the outcome is not even-steven, and in a way it could seem unjust. But, instead of being unhappy about it because it was negative in some way, I think people should be generally happy about grace because it is a positive thing. The connotation of unfairness is that someone got short changed and didn't deserve it. Grace is like the opposite of that, where someone got something good but didn't deserve it. It was something that was not deserved, but given because of kindness, love, and consideration. It is at the expense of someone else, so that's a similarity between unfairness and grace. What was expended by someone in an unfair situation could be many things, like time, effort, heartfelt emotions, money, etc. What was expended by someone when they give grace is love and kindness. Yes, to give grace a person must give love and kindness. And, because of their love and kindness they will make sacrifices. That's what is given at their expense.

While grace is wonderfully beautiful, it takes great strength to give it. It is by God enabling us that we are able to give grace to others. I believe the ability to do this comes from Him. For a person to extend grace to others, it takes a kind of maturity, strength, and humility. A person cannot be selfish and give grace, that's for sure.

Grace – it is almost as elusive as wisdom in this day and age. But, it is easy to see who has it and who does not.

I will try to illustrate.

• Can you give grace to someone who has given you nothing, or has even hurt you? Small illustration: you're on the freeway. The traffic is heavy. Someone speeds by you in the outside lane, but it seems ridiculous because you know that lane will have to merge into your lane in a hundred feet. Somehow you have progressed fast enough in your lane that you caught up to the car that sped around you. Now they need to merge in front of you. So, you choose not to be a jerk and allow them space to merge easily, instead of squeezing them out. Bigger illustration: continuing to be kind to someone who has wronged you. Not in a way in which you allow yourself to be taken advantage of, but by showing them kindness that is not deserved.

- Can you give grace when it means your motives or intentions are misunderstood? There come times in life where you do good things for others, and you have no intention whatsoever to have strings attached. The thought of it is repellant. Although, to others it may seem that you're doing those good things with ulterior motives. I feel that you need not prove anything to anyone. You do not need to prove your motives are pure. Simply do what is good and right. Though, you may be misunderstood.

- Can you give grace when it means pain to you? For example, accepting the responsibility for something incorrect you did at work that your supervisor noticed was wrong, even though you were specifically told by a co-worker to do it that way. You choose to accept it as your own mistake, instead of saying, "Jane told me to do it that way." There is a bit of personal pain involved in accepting the blame and shutting your mouth, and not shifting the blame or throwing someone else under the bus.

- Can you give grace when it means you will have to step into the shadows and someone else gets to step into the limelight? For instance, you teach someone how to do something. Someone else sees what they are now able to do (because you taught it to them) and praises them because they are so able and talented. The person you taught accepts every bit of the praise, not mentioning the fact that you taught them at all - you have been clipped out of the picture. I think a way to extend grace in such a situation is to just let it be. Allow him to be the focus of attention. One does not need to say, "He's so good at it because I'm the one who taught him!" Just let it be. You might actually agree with them, since it is true, that this person you taught is indeed very adept. Let him have his moment.

- Can you give grace when it costs you something? Or, only when it is beneficial to you as well? Small example: seeing someone in the grocery store parking lot take the last bag of groceries out of their cart and put it in their vehicle. So, you ask if you can take their cart for them, because you're planning to use it anyway. Would you do the same thing if you weren't going to use it? Bigger example: you are deep into a discussion with someone. You want to say something really badly. You can barely keep yourself from saying it. You know you're absolutely right, too. But, you know it will only be beneficial to you. If you say it, it would make the person you say it to feel worse, or harm them in some way. It would not profit anyone or anything but you. It depends on the situation, but sometimes you must pay the cost of shutting your mouth for the benefit of someone else.

- Do you need others to see that you're giving grace? What is the motive of the one who needs to be noticed by others for something good they did? Possibly wanting to boost their value, a sign of their intentions, a mask for them, or pride. They may also be insecure. Beware of those who need others to see their good deeds. Small example: you're in a public place. You picked up that piece of trash off the floor (that wasn't your trash) and put it in the garbage can. Congratulations. Do you need people to notice, and stand around the garbage can and applaud you as you do this? Perhaps applaud is not needed, just one other person to notice you perform this huge and monumentally selfless deed will be sufficient. Mid-size example: you were working in the children's room of the public library. It is not within your job description to pick up the children's toys. However, this room that was tidy (thanks to you) the last time you were in the room 10 minutes ago now looks like a tornado passed through it. There are small and large toys alike all over the floor. The person who is actually in charge of the room is nowhere to be seen, and does not pick up the toys anyway. So, you choose to pick everything up (as usual), because it would be a good thing to do. Nobody will know you did it. Your pay will not be increased, you will not be thanked, and probably within the next hour it will be messy again. Final example: your supervisor at work is unkind to you. It has happened consistently, so you know it wasn't her just having a bad day or something. Unless, she consistently has bad days. You remember this verse in the Bible:

Bless those who curse you. Pray for those who hurt you. (Luke 6:28 NLT)

So, you actually do what it says. You pray for her. As you do it, part of you is really shocked at this strange behavior of yours: "Um, just what exactly do you think you're doing? You're praying for her? Stop that! You're taking this Bible stuff too literally. You really have become a religious fanatic. I don't understand you at all anymore! Fine. Go ahead and pray. It will make no difference anyway."

I will deviate from the main topic of this chapter for a moment, but I think it will be worthwhile: it's interesting how the devil or your own sinful nature resists obedience to God. The strategies that are used are fascinating. The dialogue I wrote above is telling. The first front of resistance is basically that you're doing something too bizarre. Yes, God's ways are very strange compared to my own ways, the devil's ways, and world's ways. Then, it's resistance in the form of not praying for her because she doesn't deserve it based on how she's treated you. This reasoning tries to placate and play upon your own hurt feelings. When all of this isn't successful in keeping you from praying, there's an attempt at bringing your human logic into the situation to work against you – "You're taking this Bible stuff too literally." Which kind of means, it doesn't make sense to believe or obey what it says. It's just a fact that pure human reasoning will often not align itself to spiritual matters and if a person must have them align, I'm afraid they have no faith. Then there is accusation and mocking: "You really have become a religious fanatic." Well, to me it doesn't matter what I'm called, as long as I'm doing what God wants me to, and what is right. If you've pushed through all this resistance so far, there is still more.

Now it's, "Fine. Go ahead and pray. It will make no difference anyway." First of all, it is a lie that prayer makes no difference. This lie encourages unbelief and tries to bring your faith down. Remember this verse:

Confess your sins to each other and pray for each other so that you may be healed. The earnest prayer of a righteous person has great power and produces wonderful results. (James 5:16 NLT)

Despite all this resistance, you exercise faith and obedience, and pray. Now, another part of you is quite pleased with yourself for being so gracious and generous that you prayed for someone who was unkind to you. Don't get proud! It is only because of God that you behaved as you should. I think a person can be glad that they obeyed, and be happy about that, but that's different than becoming proud in a wrong kind of way. Furthermore, you do not need to go to your friend and say, "You know, my boss was mean to me, but I was the better person and prayed for her. I'm really getting along well in this Christian life! Shake my hand and congratulate me, won't you?" No, you will most likely do this praying alone with God. You may feel like sharing your spiritual victories with others and I think that's fine, but check your motives first. (I'm thinking that this example is a mixed version of extending grace. Because, someone who hurt you does not deserve to be prayed for. That part fits my definition of undeserved grace. Yet, because we are Christians, it is only what we should do as instructed in the Bible. That part kind of makes it our duty, rather than the extension of grace being completely unwarranted.)

It takes a certain kind of maturity, strength, and humility to give grace to others. It is often a lonely and solitary undertaking. There will not be other people there to hold your hand as you give grace. It is a choice you make personally. As I say, it takes a kind of maturity. The strength you're exercising when you give grace is unseen. Actually, if one did not give grace in the examples I gave above, they might seem like the stronger person. Someone with more of a backbone. While, the person who does give grace in these examples seems weaker. But, it is not so. It takes more strength to give grace, much more. Sometimes what is flexible and giving is stronger than something that is rigid and unyielding. Even a backbone bends.

A person who gives grace may be perceived as stupid by others, or a pushover. Don't let this perception keep you from giving grace. I think anyone who has chosen to give grace knows very well what is going on. They are not ignorant. They know the position they're in, and the different ways they can choose to react. They know their "right" to not give grace. They know. It's just that they have chosen to behave differently.

Of course, the greatest example of grace being given is God's grace to mankind through His Son Jesus. It's because of His love and kindness shown through His Son that has saved me, and everyone else who has faith in Jesus.

But God is so rich in mercy, and he loved us so much, that even though we were dead because of our sins, he gave us life when he raised Christ from the dead. (It is only by God's grace that you have been saved!) For he raised us from the dead along with Christ and seated us with him in the heavenly realms because we are united with Christ Jesus. So God can point to us in all future ages as examples of the incredible wealth of his grace and kindness toward us, as shown in all he has done for us who are united with Christ Jesus. God saved you by his grace when you believed. And you can't take credit for this; it is a gift from God. (Ephesians 2:4-8 NLT)

But when the time came for the kindness and love of God our Savior to appear, then he saved us – not because we were good enough to be saved, but because of his kindness and pity – by washing away our sins and giving us the new joy of the indwelling Holy Spirit whom he poured out upon us with wonderful fullness – and all because of what Jesus Christ our Savior did so that he could declare us good in God's eyes – all because of his great kindness; and now we can share in the wealth of the eternal life he gives us, and we are eagerly looking forward to receiving it. (Titus 3:4-7 TLB)

Grace is a beautiful thing when it is seen in God's people - when His people show grace by the way they live. It makes them resemble Him very much.

You can tell who does not or cannot extend grace. It is very clear for one with eyes to see. If no one else does, God knows when grace is given. He is not blind or ignorant to it. So, know that He sees what you're doing even though you may feel alone when giving grace. It can seem like you're the only one in the whole world that knows you're giving grace (which can be very difficult and strenuous at times). But, you're not really alone. He knows, and He sees. Though no one else may see. And, it doesn't always need to be seen by others.

Grace is divinely beautiful, and it shows God's love. I believe He wants His people to extend grace as He does. Let us resemble Him in this way.

89

He Will Not Change

People change. People can change. I think this is both one of the most frightening, and one of the most wonderful things about people.

I'm going to set aside the wonderful part of it, and focus on the undesirable part.

The older I get the more I understand how unstable people can be. They can say one thing and do another. They can say one thing and mean another. One moment they're happy, and the next moment they're sad. They like you, and then they don't like you. They "love" you, and then they don't love you. They can make promises to you with utmost sincerity and then break the promises like they were nothing. Even serious commitments like marriage can be undone. And, people have a right to do so because there's this thing called free will. Though people have free will, obviously they will not always make the right choices.

So, I was thinking. Where in this mess of humanity does this leave me? Who can I trust? What can I trust? I feel like I can trust just a few people in my life, and even then I know they are not completely trustworthy because they are people. I can't even trust myself.

Basically, I can really trust no one. To an extent, and sometimes to a very great extent, I can trust people. But, because of the inseparable fact that they are people, I cannot trust them 100%.

I dislike this. I want someone I can trust 100%. But, if I try to find that in a person it would be unfair of me. I would be trying to find a perfect person. A faultless person. Someone who does not exist.

The realization that I can really trust no one makes it more difficult for me to love others. I think one reason for this is because I am not yet a completely secure person. It's hard to love others when I feel insecure. Because, when I'm insecure and I try to love others, my hope or expectation is that they would reciprocate. If they don't, I can feel even more insecure. It's like when I'm insecure I need some validation from others. I feel that an insecure person cannot really love to their greatest capacity. An insecure person will love, but to a lesser degree, and partly because they're needing to be loved back. It's like they love primarily in order to receive, rather than loving in order to give. They need others in an unhealthy way. People need love. I believe we all need others to a certain extent, but others should not be the equivalent of God in one's life. They should not be a replacement for God. Now that's a challenging thought. Are people, or a person, more important to me than God is?

I'm working on becoming a secure person. Knowing my worth in the Lord's eyes, building my relationship with Him through prayer/spending time with Him, being taught by the Holy Spirit, studying His character, and learning about Him through the Bible has helped a great deal. Continuing to understand that He truly loves me has been essential. I've simply prayed to the Lord to help me be secure as well.

I believe a secure person must have someone or something outside of themselves as their foundation, as their rock – a safe place. Someone or something stable. Someone or something that loves them all the time. Someone or something they can trust. People find many things to act as this in their lives, but any other than God is faulty because everything else is changeable. If they don't seem changeable, they can at least cease to exist at some point. That is a form of change.

I think about the things people find to act as their source of "unchanging" love or emotional security and it is sad. Sometimes people have been through so much pain and betrayal from others that they've decided it is they themselves who they must cling to for security and love. It's as if they themselves are the only person who cares about them, who won't hurt them. So, they forge ahead through life with themselves alone. Sadly, and yet understandably, they are unable to form close relationships with others. Sometimes people will frankly say they love their dog more than people. This may seem humorous, but to me it is awfully sad. To think that a person finds more love from a dog, and finds it more trustworthy than people is almost tragic. A common replacement for unchanging love and emotional security in a person's life is a romantic partner. While such a thing can be a blessing, it still should not be a replacement for God. A person need not have much experience in romantic endeavors to know that such love is far from unchanging. I hope I will never believe another person "completes" me as I've heard some people say. Only God completes me.

Perhaps those people who can rely on themselves alone as they make their way through this earthly pilgrimage are exceptionally strong. I am not one of them. I need someone I can completely trust and depend on if I am going to live in a decent way. To me, an indecent way of living would be to live like an abused and frightened animal who has now become hardened into something it was never meant to be. I don't want to be a pseudo-secure person who only needs themselves. I want to be secure, and able to love and give generously to others. I need an unchanging source of love that won't fail me if I am going to give love.

I have observed that in a marriage it is possible for one person to do everything right, but the other person can just change their mind and decide they don't want to be with them anymore. They can change, just like that.

I see that a person can become very jaded by how they've been treated by other people. Even the people who are supposed to love them the most have not loved them. This pain can morph into lifelong problems. I'm sure I have not personally experienced one quarter of what others have experienced in this regard. Still, there come times in my life when I do get jaded. My thoughts can run like this, "People come and go. They always go eventually. I think I'm getting used to it. They like you for awhile and then they don't. People don't really mean what they say. How can I believe what anyone says? Will there ever be anyone I can really depend on? Will there ever be anyone who loves me for me?" When I think that last thought it really hits me. If there never is anyone else who loves me for me, there will always be One I can be sure of.

God will always love me. Does that sound like a weak cliché of some kind? Maybe to some people it sounds that way. But, for me it is the strongest thing I have. It is something my life depends on at every moment. I need Him. His unfailing love will never change. He will never change. It has taken me a long time to understand this, and I'm still understanding it. He's the One I can trust 100%.

There is a reason He tells us in the Bible that He will not leave or forsake us, that His love is unfailing, and that He will not leave us as orphans. It is to assure us of His surety. He is the surest thing. Christians who are quite spiritually mature still depend and rely on these truths. In fact, I believe as a Christian matures, they will realize how much they truly depend on His love more and more. Many times, this is all His people have to depend on – His unfailing love.

Who else can boast of this, of having unfailing love? No one else. At some point the love of each person fails, in large or small ways.

Be strong and courageous. Don't fear or tremble before them, because the LORD your God will be the one who keeps on walking with you—he won't leave you or abandon you." (Deuteronomy 31:6 ISV)

Keep your lives free from the love of money and be content

with what you have, because God has said, "Never will I leave you; never will I forsake you." So we say with confidence, "The Lord is my helper; I will not be afraid. What can mere mortals do to me?" Remember your leaders, who spoke the word of God to you. Consider the outcome of their way of life and imitate their faith. Jesus Christ is the same yesterday and today and forever. (Hebrews 13:5-8 NIV)

Your unfailing love, O LORD, is as vast as the heavens; your faithfulness reaches beyond the clouds. Your righteousness is like the mighty mountains, your justice like the ocean depths. You care for people and animals alike, O LORD. How precious is your unfailing love, O God! All humanity finds shelter in the shadow of your wings. (Psalm 36:5-7 NLT)

"If you love me, obey my commandments. And I will ask the Father, and he will give you another Advocate, who will never leave you. He is the Holy Spirit, who leads into all truth. The world cannot receive him, because it isn't looking for him and doesn't recognize him. But you know him, because he lives with you now and later will be in you. No, I will not abandon you as orphans—I will come to you. (John 14:15-18 NLT)

It is important to keep your word. I have failed at this. I know people are not perfect. People make mistakes. But, I feel as if some people are not even trying to keep their word. In my opinion, it shows a lack of respect for themselves. Respect yourself by knowing when you say something you mean it. For me, when I cannot believe what someone says it destroys my trust of them. At that point, everything they say means nothing to me. I can't depend on it.

I was so accustomed to the undependable nature of what people say that I came to expect the same from God. Like, sure, God says things, but maybe there's that 0.001% chance of it not happening. I had learned to not trust people completely, and I was thinking the same way about God. Because I've lived around people all my life and I know how they are. But, God is not like people!

God is not a man, so he does not lie. He is not human, so he does not change his mind. Has he ever spoken and failed to act? Has he ever promised and not carried it through? (Numbers 23:19 NLT)

I will not violate my covenant or alter what my lips have uttered. (Psalm 89:34 NIV)

Keep in mind that the LORD your God is [the only] God. He is a faithful God, who keeps his promise and is merciful to thousands of generations of those who love him and obey his commands. (Deuteronomy 7:9 GWT)

This is a trustworthy saying: If we die with him, we will also live with him. If we endure hardship, we will reign with him. If we deny him, he will deny us. If we are unfaithful, he remains faithful, for he cannot deny who he is. (2 Timothy 2:11-13 NLT)

The Lord's promise is sure. He speaks no careless word; all he says is purest truth, like silver seven times refined. (Psalms 12:6 TLB)

God means every word He says. You can see how destructive it can be for people, especially Christians, to not mean what they say, do what they say, or keep their promises. It can happen so often that it becomes the norm. That is what people come to expect. Then people can expect God to be like that. It's often in a subtle, nearly imperceptible way which creates a soft unbelief toward God. Whether it be soft or blatant unbelief, the results are the same. Unbelief is destructive of one's faith and trust.

God is not like people. He means what He says and is always faithful. There is no 0.001% chance of Him going back on what He said. 2 Timothy 2:13 tells us that He remains faithful even when we're unfaithful, because He is true to Who He is.

Even when we are too weak to have any faith left, he remains faithful to us and will help us, for he cannot disown us who are part of himself, and he will always carry out his promises to us. (2 Timothy 2:13 TLB)

If we are unfaithful, he remains faithful because he cannot be untrue to himself. (2 Timothy 2:13 GWT)

Our faith may fail, his never wanes— That's who he is, he cannot change! (2 Timothy 2:13 ISV)

I know how I am. I'm different and I know it. I know my eccentricities. I might actually be an "eccentric." I know how difficult I can be. I know how odd I am. So, this has presented me with some problems. I tend to believe when a person really gets to know me, they will change their mind about me and not like me anymore. Because it has happened repeatedly. I show more of myself, and I can tell that it's too much for them. They cannot take me. I can be too much for people. I can't blame them, because as I said I know how I am. I am reserved and kind of average, but that's what people who don't really know me see. Maybe that's why when I show more of my self it can be a shock or something. I don't know.

When I'm with people I'm comfortable with, more of my true self shows. I'm even more reserved with them, and I'm happy that way. I am often alone, because I work best in those conditions, and I need to be alone sometimes to feel like myself again and process thoughts. I can be content to be with someone, but not necessarily be talking and interacting the whole time. I do need others, too. I am often blunt. I don't mean to be like that in a bad way. I just say things unfiltered when I'm comfortable with people. It can come across as blunt, although I thought it was just genuine and I didn't mean to be mean. Sometimes I am a glass-half-full kind of person, but more often I prefer to be realistic. That glass is half empty, too. I realize this is not what most people enjoy. That's fine. What I don't enjoy is when the half-full part of the glass is focused on so much, it's like the empty part doesn't exist at all. To me, this is unrealistic and annoying. I'm usually serious-minded. Then it's like I contradict that part of my personality and I like to dream. I like to dream about things that are unrealistic.

I rarely feel my age. I either feel like a child or a grandma. I feel like a grandma in terms of thinking logically, and sensibly. I can feel like a grandma when the people around me who are about my age are excited about something and I am not excited about it. I feel like a grandma when I have zero interest in "going out" and I'm content to stay home. Sometimes I feel like I'm 100 years old when I talk about deep, insightful things. Then sometimes I feel like a child because there are a lot of things I've never experienced. I'll feel like a child when I'm delighted in small things like sunshine and pretty flowers. I am genuinely interested in simple things, such as planting vegetable or flower seeds and seeing them grow. I can be playful in little ways, if I like you. For example, I'll be at home with my mom. Occasionally, out of the blue I'll suddenly say, "Mom!" with a tone of voice that purposely sounds like I'm slightly upset about something. She might be a bit bothered and say, "What?" Then I'll change my demeanor completely and ever so sweetly say, in a small quiet little voice, "I love you." And that is all. That's the end of my little game. I liked the unexpectedness of it and the initial unrest, followed by sweet reassurance. It's like a mini rollercoaster of emotions, one that lasts about 5 seconds. It's silly, but I'm that way occasionally. Sometimes my banter is childlike. I can talk about animals in practically the same way I did when I was a kid. Or, if I give a compliment to someone it can be very unrefined and frank. If I like someone I don't mind saying it directly. It would probably come off unsophisticated and with awkward timing, with a simple "I like you." I would really mean it, but I would probably have nothing more to say after that. I wouldn't have come up with anything to follow that up with, to make it sound more polished and put-together. It would just abruptly end there. Instead of something like, "You have an amazing personality and I just love spending time with you. You're so caring and considerate. I really like you." I am not that suave in real life. If silk fabric is what suave is, I am like cotton flannel.

Furthermore, I can switch from child to grandma, and from grandma to child quickly. I feel like I'm sometimes a contradiction.

I find it difficult to fake things. It is difficult for me to fake enthusiasm. I'm not one for superlatives because I feel like I'm being dishonest. I might understate things. Again, if I said "I like you" to someone, it is a very small thing to say but I would mean it more than it may seem. I mean, perhaps some people say that to others very easily, perhaps without much meaning behind it. For me to say that I would mean it. If I choose to say that to someone, I've been thinking about how I like them for a long time before I say it. Maybe this is one reason why I can take it hard if people don't mean what they say. Particularly if they say things that are supposedly expressing heartfelt emotions and feelings for you. Because if I say that mushy stuff to someone I mean it, and I subconsciously assume others are the same way. I remember when I was leaving a job I held for nearly 5 years. I liked my co-workers. We got along nicely and I couldn't ask for better ones. On one of my last days on the job one of my co-workers asked me if I would miss them. I responded in the negative, that I wouldn't miss them. I meant it, and they knew I meant it. I couldn't even fake saying I would miss them. I feel slightly bad about that, but not much because it was true.

Sometimes I won't speak for hours, and I like it very much. At one point, I wondered if my voice box would become underdeveloped from using it so little. Then sometimes I get full of thoughts and insights and that overflows into continuous speech that I don't want interrupted until I get to say everything I want to say. Usually these speeches are about deep things, and again I realize most people do not enjoy this, let alone appreciate it. It's unpleasant to express myself and talk about things that are meaningful to me and know I'm boring to death the person I'm talking to. If I'm not boring them, they probably don't understand what I'm talking about. So, I'll stay on certain topics of discussion for the sake of getting along with others better. I realize people don't want to discuss deep things all the time. I don't want to either, but a little more often would be nice. Also, I know there is a proper time and place for those types of conversations. If I'm in certain moods, people talking to me can seem physically painful. I don't blame them, it's just me. These certain moods are if I'm thinking about something creatively and I get interrupted, if I'm over-socialized and worn out because of it, or if I'm in physical pain. I like people, but in doses.

If I've been charged up with plenty of solitude, I can go out and socialize and do small talk, and perform like that. My performance will be passable. If I'm depleted of solitude, and then try to socialize and do small talk, my performance will be pitiful. If I'm depleted of solitude, I don't want to have anything to do with people. And, it's better for everyone that I don't, because I'm not myself and I can get irritable and easily aggravated. Talking becomes like nails on a chalkboard. I just want to retreat somewhere and listen to music and completely check out for a while.

Socializing is draining to me, except for those rare occasions when I find someone who likes to talk about deep things too. Other than that, socializing is one of the things I'm worst at. Most of the time, when I am socializing I feel like I'm not really being myself, because if I was being myself I probably wouldn't be socializing. I know it's necessary, and sometimes enjoyable. I know this difficulty of mine is hard for most people to understand. In a way, they should be glad it is hard for them to understand. Just imagine something that you're worst at, that is also draining, that often makes you and others feel awkward because you do it so badly, that can make you feel misunderstood, and is also something you have to do to be "normal." That's what socializing is to me.

Socializing is one of the first things you do with people. Sometimes I wish my first impression did not have to be something I'm the worst at.

My social abilities have improved. I do try. Even so, I feel like it's a game. Like I'm performing, and I'm not really being myself. Such is life, sometimes. Because, if I was being myself I'd probably be speaking 50% less than I do, and that is not socially acceptable. I'm barely in the socially acceptable range of talking as it is.

Furthermore, when I don't talk it can be interpreted in many different ways. Let me just say, if I'm not talking, don't jump to the worst conclusions. 90% of the time there is nothing wrong. I'm not upset, not bored, not angry, not stuck-up, not plotting something. Sometimes I'm just thinking about other things. Most of the time I just don't know what to say. If I think of something to say, I sometimes feel like I won't be able to say it the way I want to and that can keep me from saying it. Sometimes when I have to speak quickly and don't have enough time to think first, I end up saying something that I didn't really mean. I mean, I meant it, but it came off a bit wrong. I didn't choose the right words, so the meaning got twisted. I really dislike that, because sometimes I see that the person I was speaking to was wrongly affected by it, and I really didn't mean it that way.

Perhaps that's one reason why I like to write. Because I have time to think about what I want to communicate. I can take the time to sculpt my delivery with better word choices. I have a better chance at communicating accurately.

Because I am reserved and don't wear my emotions on my sleeve, it can be difficult to know me. I can have the same general expression on my face if I'm perfectly content and when I'm screaming inside. I guess I'm just difficult to know.

I am not a volatile and reactive person. For example, if I drop a plate of food all over the floor, or discover a mess that my dog Cooper made, I might not verbalize anything. I sometimes surprise myself at how unreactive I am. I feel some internal disappointment, of course. I might take a deep breath and sigh as I take in what just happened, but that's about it. Then I'll go and clean it up, or do what needs to be done. It is not worth getting excited about. Getting excited about things like that is boring to me. I'm not visibly flustered easily. I can get flustered, but it will be on the inside, not on the outside. Unless it is to an extreme and I cannot contain it. In that case, it will surface in an unattractive way. I have neither yelled at someone in anger, nor have I been yelled at. I have never been in an argument with my voice raised above normal volume. Actually, I cannot remember being in an argument. If I'm "arguing" it's more like playful disagreement. If it's a serious disagreement, of which I can remember having only one of, I will try to reason with the person and share my point of view while making it known that I care for them and I want us to come to a mutually favorable understanding. I remember it was very stressful for me, but it worked out well thank God. I remember trying to rehearse what I was going to say countless times before I even approached the person, and I could feel the effects of adrenaline and my heart beating in my chest during the whole discussion. It was miserable, but I disagreed strongly enough and cared enough about my relationship with the person to confront them. I dislike confrontations, but sometimes they are necessary.

It can take me a moment to process things. Often, I will understand what someone said a few seconds later than most people would. I'm not stupid, I just need more time to think. I've found that sometimes I'm slower because I'm thinking about it too much. Like I'm over-processing it.

I'm generally even-tempered. I'm not easily excitable. I rarely get visibly excited (in a positive or negative way) about anything, even things that are supposed to be exciting. For instance, if a meteorite fell from the sky and landed in my front yard, I'd be surprised but I wouldn't get very excited about it. If I do get excited about something, a person will probably not be able to notice unless they know me well.

There are a lot of things I really do not care about, and can take or leave. But, I can be intense about other things, like life and death things, right vs. wrong, life purposes, and God-related subjects. It's funny, one of the things I said I can be intense about is right vs. wrong. That can be applied to many areas. It can refer to moral issues, but it's funny because I can apply it to other things. For example, if I'm working on a project I can be intense about wanting it done right. If I'm selecting colors for a project, I will probably spend way too much time deciding on the right ones. I might spend a ridiculous amount of time choosing between two shades of blue. But, I don't really care because I want it to be right.

I try to be a considerate person, but if I reach a certain point I couldn't care less. For instance, I'll try to be considerate and reasonable with others, but if I find that someone is toxic to me I will cut them out of my life. I usually have some emotions and feelings in regard to people, even to strangers to some degree because I care about people. However, when certain things are done to me by another I will turn off my emotions toward them completely. It will be like they don't really exist to me anymore. They are a sad memory, as if they travelled to a faraway land and will never return. If it is unavoidable that I see them again, I will be civil, but my emotions will be turned off. It's like I'm an unfeeling robot at that point, just going through the motions of being civil. I can shut that emotional door very well, and I don't feel bad about it because they were given more than one chance. It is for my own self-preservation. It is done to protect myself from experiencing more pain. It takes a lot for me to get to this point.

Generally, if someone truly makes me angry and I see that I cannot do anything constructive about it, I will just go away. When I say I cannot do anything constructive about it, I mean I cannot do anything to change the situation for the better. If this happens, I'll just distance myself. Most likely I will not confront them or try to convince them of anything, unless it seems worth it. Most of the time it isn't. I may not say anything to them at all. I will just go away. I will just disappear. I do not care if they understand why.

I probably notice too much. Also, I'm very sensitive, which is often unpleasant. It is unpleasant for more than one reason, but one reason is because I can be hurt by rather small things. To help myself I try to keep in mind that this is just how I am, so that I do not lose proper perspective of things. Sometimes there is a benefit to being sensitive. I can pick up on how others may feel, or very subtle things. Mostly, I just feel like I notice too much. I will notice the slightest change in a person's voice and interpret that as them being sad or angry, or whatever emotion it suggests to me. I will notice someone hesitating. I notice when someone changes. I can tell when someone wants to say something, but isn't sure if they should say it. I will notice when someone is nervous, upset, or unsure. When I'm in a group of people it's as if I can feel a little bit of everyone else's current emotions. Maybe that's one reason why being around people is draining to me. I notice so much that it tires me out. It's like sensory overload. Sometimes I wish I didn't notice so much.

People usually aren't patient enough to know me. By the time I'm ready and feeling more comfortable with showing more of myself, they're tired of me. On top of that, when I do show more of myself, I'm too much for them. Sometimes I simply wait it out. I just wait until people get tired of me, because it's usually just a matter of time.

There are many other eccentricities about me, but those are the main points.

So, I know how I am. Again, I tend to believe when a person really gets to know me, they will change their mind about me and not like me anymore. I'm too much for them to handle. I tire them out. Maybe it's because they can't figure me out. I'm picturing it this way. I'm holding a weight in my hands. The weight represents my true self. Someone wants to know me more, or I want them to know me more. So, they put their hands out in front of them and I start to place the weight I'm holding into their hands. The weight I'm holding just makes contact with their open hands, and everything is ok so far. Then, I let the weight down onto their hands a little more. Still everything is ok. I let more of the weight down, and now they have to use their muscles a little to sustain the weight. They give me a funny look. I let down more weight, and they're struggling. It's too much for them and I have to pull the weight – the reality of who I am – off their hands because I'm too much for them.

I guess I go too deep. Maybe I'm too intense for people, but to me it's just being real. In conversation I can quickly go from talking about the weather to talking about some revelation that came to me earlier in the day and what I learned about it and how it's impacting my life and how it's changed my outlook and how I'm so enamored with God and all the things I'm learning and how I want to keep learning and growing. People's eyes can glaze over at that point, and I don't blame them. I try to control myself and only share such things with people who I think will understand. If I'm walking on a trail in the woods with someone, they might say something like,

"Look at how calm the water is over there. It looks like glass." Then I might tie their statement to how in the Bible it says:

As a face is reflected in water, so the heart reflects the real person. (Proverbs 27:19 NLT)

Then I might elaborate in what may seem like an overly-profound or dramatic way, but it doesn't seem that way to me. I just like talking about those things from time to time. I don't mean to be weird about it, or act like I'm more spiritual than I am. Also, it depends on who I'm with. I desire to talk about those things sometimes, but if I was with someone who I think will not understand me, I won't talk about it. I don't want to bore them, and I don't want to share thoughts that are meaningful to me with someone who won't appreciate them.

Actually, I feel like I frequently tie everyday objects or occurrences to a deep insight. I feel like I frequently tie everyday things to God. Like, if I'm with someone and we're looking at something like a bug, I might say something about how amazing it is that God made it, and how creative He is, and how detail-oriented He is, and how He must have had fun making everything. If I talk about this to the wrong person I feel like I'm being annoying or boring. They were just looking at a bug, and didn't want me to go so deep.

Yes, there is a time and a place for certain conversations. I don't want to talk about deep things 24/7. But do you know what bores me? Talking about what I think are superficial things. For example, I really do not care about the lives of fictional characters on a TV series. I find that some people can discuss this topic at length, as if the people are real and as if they are truly invested in their lives. This bores me to an almost painful level. I'm sorry. I'd rather live my own life, than spend it talking about or watching a fictional character act out their scripted lives. Talk to me about real things, not necessarily complex things. Talk to me about how you dug potatoes out of the dirt and how the soil smelled good and how it was like digging for buried treasure. Talk to me about how the sun sparkled on the water and how pretty you thought it was. Talk to me about how you bought a pair of shoes that you're happy with. Talk to me about something you aspire to do in the future. Talk to me about how you were disappointed today, or how something hurt you. Talk to me about anything genuine and real.

Yes, I guess I do relate everyday objects or occurrences to God frequently. Why shouldn't I? Let's say you are infatuated with someone, or you like someone, or you love someone. Don't you think of them often? Don't you see everyday objects and it makes you remember them? Or, if something fairly ordinary happens during your day, it can make you think of the one you love. The same kind of stuff happens with me, toward God.

Basically, I feel like I go through much of my life only showing others a percentage of myself. If I really opened up, it would be like opening up a floodgate and they would be washed away and/or drown. Or, I get softly rejected after opening up, and that's not enjoyable. As I talk with someone I find myself trying to judge if they're able to handle me or not. What is their breaking point? Sometimes I see that they can't handle me at all. I can't even go deep for like one millimeter. Other times, I am surprised by their strength. For example, I'll finish talking about some heavy stuff and they'll still be listening and it's a surprise to me. It's like I'll think, "Wow. Are you still with me? You weren't scared away yet?" If they've been able to deal with me for a while, the usual breaking point is when I start talking about God. And if they still haven't broken yet, I can go deeper about spiritual matters and then they will usually give up.

I've thought that when I get married (which will be a miracle), my husband will have a lot to handle, poor fellow. I would cost a great deal, and I believe most people are incapable of affording me. I don't mean to say that in a proud way, but simply as a fact. There are definitely some people I cannot afford, either. Because of who I am, I would cost a lot. Some of those costs: he would have to be mentally strong, grounded, patient, mature, and kind. He'd have to appreciate, or at least kindly endure, my eccentricities. He'd have to be mentally strong and grounded because I am not interested in trying to tame, strengthen, or corral the opposite of those characteristics. A man who does not have good sense or is mentally weak I am not interested in. I prefer to spend the rest of my earthly existence with someone who is stable in these ways. He'd have to be patient because I require it. I'm not asking for something I wouldn't give as well. I am a very patient person. He'd have to be mature. I am weary of immaturity, like stupid kinds of immaturity. And he'd have to be kind. I am not accustomed to being treated unkindly, and I do not intend on becoming accustomed to it. I am not accustomed to being disrespected either, and I do not intend on becoming accustomed to it. A gentleman would be nice - a real one.

I would expect him to earn enough money to afford a wife and any children that may follow. Is this old-fashioned? Then I'm old-fashioned. I would cost a lot, not just monetarily. Frankly, I feel that I'm not difficult to please as far as material things go. Also, I am not bored easily. I could probably not leave my house for a week and be happy. Give me a book, a notebook, and a pen and I'll have a field day. I like a lot of time alone by myself, so I've often wondered how that would work out.

If there were an argument between us and he decided to give me the silent treatment I would be satisfied. The silent treatment wouldn't be like punishment to me because I would welcome some solitude. I could easily outlast him in the silence game. It would be no contest. Punishment for me would be more like talking to me for hours about fictional characters on a TV series, or making me go out and socialize all day long.

Many people could go to a Honda dealership and purchase one. They are affordable, generally. Not many people can go to a Bentley dealership and purchase one. They are generally not affordable. Then after you get a Bentley they cost more to maintain than a Honda. Probably many more people visit Honda dealerships than Bentley dealerships because they know what they can and cannot afford. Probably a Bentley will sit on the showroom floor much longer than a Honda, because relatively few people can afford one. There are requirements to purchase and maintain a Bentley.

The main requirement is spiritual maturity. One of my worst

nightmares is to be married to someone who is a spiritual infant. Like, an immature Christian. It's not enough for me that he is a Christian. I feel as if there are a multitude of Christian men out there, but being a Christian isn't enough for me. A person can call themselves a Christian, and they very well may be one, but they're still a baby. They haven't yet grown up spiritually. They're about where they were when they first believed. I was there, too. At one point, every Christian was. But, I don't want a baby Christian for a husband. I cannot imagine it, and yet I have imagined it. I do not want to be that wife who has to be the spiritual leader of the family and who pushes the husband to grow in his personal relationship with God, to pursue God, pray, or read the Bible. That would get old very fast, for the both of us. I really don't want to push anyone to do anything. Encourage or help, yes, but not push. He's got to want God on his own. I can't make someone want God. He's got to want God for himself, and know Him personally. I'd want someone who knows God and cares for Him as much as I do, or more. Someone who has grown up (and is continuing to grow) and matured in their Christian walk. I don't really care about his church attendance record. I care about how often he meets with God in prayer and if he knows God personally. More importantly, does God know him? I don't want someone who allows me to try to live righteously, while he only does things that compromise righteous living. I've got enough opposition in my Christian walk with the world, the flesh, and the devil. I don't want someone who is supposed to be my partner doing things that try to bring me down too. We're supposed to be a team. I don't want to be the spiritual one, serving as some kind of mediator between the husband and God. Like, the husband just lets me be the spiritual one and that somehow seems to be good enough for the both of us while he has no personal relationship with God for himself. As if he's riding on coattails. That's not right. I do not want to be trying to follow God and trying to live a godly life, while the husband is apathetic about God and willfully dabbles in sin while claiming to be a Christian. I am not interested in lukewarm. I feel like he would hold me back, drag me down, and make life more difficult in every way. Like a ball and chain around my ankle. I do not want any part of that. I'd like someone who is actually a helpful addition to me in my Christian walk, and knows God for himself. Someone with some spiritual ambition. If for nothing else, to at least aspire to know God better and better (followed by the appropriate actions and not just talk). Actually, perhaps wanting to know God better and better is the greatest aspiration a person can have. I don't want a baby Christian husband who I must coax and take by the hand as they learn to walk. I would be willing to do that for some people. But, someone who would take the role of husband in my life should know how to walk already.

Ideally, he would know about spiritual warfare. He would know the authority he has in Christ, and know how to use it.

Perhaps you can begin to see what I meant when I said I would cost a lot. I have requirements and expectations. Will I get what I require and expect? I will answer my own question with another question. Does a person who buys a Bentley meet the requirements?

When I say he should "know" God, I don't mean he can quote Bible verses and tell me all about God. I mean he should have a personal relationship with God. I will try to explain. A person could quote John Wayne, and tell me all about him. They could say, "I know John Wayne ..." because they could tell me things he said, they know details about all his films, and they know his life story. But, John Wayne does not know them at all (assuming he was still alive). This person who knows all about John Wayne did not know him personally. They did not spend time with him, talk with him, or have any sort of personal relationship with him. I imagine this person amongst the crowds of fans waiting for John Wayne to appear. They proudly tell someone standing next to them, "I know John. I've seen all his films, and I know about his life. I really know him." John Wayne appears. The crowd is stirred and excited by his appearance. This person who knows him calls out, "John! John! It's me!" as they wave at him enthusiastically. John Wayne looks at them square in the face. There is that vacant, unfeeling look in his eyes that indicate this person is a complete stranger to him. He turns away, gets in his car and is driven away. The person standing next to them in the crowd says, "You said you knew him, but he didn't know you."

What a wonderful thing it is that God is not as hard to access as a movie star. Anyone can know Him if they want to, and He wants to have personal relationships with people.

This is not low self-esteem. It used to be that, but I'm growing out of it. I just understand that this is how I am, and it's ok to be odd. What bugs me the most about it is that people can misunderstand me, but I can't really blame them. How I am is often inconvenient, but I like how I am. Come to think of it, if I really scrutinize my own feelings toward myself, I've never disliked me. But, because I've experienced how other people have felt toward me since childhood, my feelings toward myself kind of turned into how I perceived others to feel toward me. Their perceptions and opinions of me became mine. I had felt inferior, since I was such an odd ball. As I've gotten older I've learned more about myself. I know that being an odd ball definitely has its cons, but it definitely has its pros, too. I like me, especially since God purposely created me this way – on purpose and for a purpose.

These last several paragraphs have been more than some kind of therapy session for me. I've said all this and described myself to make a point. I tend to believe when a person really gets to know me, they will change their mind about me and not like me anymore. Since this has happened with people, I have thought about this happening with the Lord and I. I've thought that He might get tired of me. That He might change His mind and decide I was too much work. I've thought there might come a day when He doesn't like me anymore. Yes, I know those Scriptures about the fact that He doesn't change, and about His unfailing love, but it has taken me time to really believe it.

The word "love" is said so often, but used to describe something that isn't really love, causing confusion.

It's from God that I'm learning what love really is. Love is not a distorted and ugly thing. It's not weak and unfaithful. It's strong and solid. I believe love is not this thing you fall in and out of based on how you happen to feel. Feelings are so changeable and feeble.

Love is more than feelings. It's being faithful and committed to someone even when you don't like them anymore. It's a conscious decision to stick with someone, and love them when they aren't lovable. To love them despite their eccentricities. Be serious and careful about who you choose to love, because with that choice goes a lot of responsibility. It is a commitment. Some definitions of commitment are 1. a promise to do or give something 2. a promise to be loyal to someone or something.[1] A person can break their promise to love someone, but this doesn't make it right. It makes me wonder if it was really love at all. God doesn't break His promises. Love isn't selfish. Infatuation or lust are often mistaken for love. But love is enduring, and it lasts. Infatuation and lust don't.

I highly dislike when love is described as this uncontrollable thing that overtakes a person: "It was bigger than the both of us!" or "It just happened one day! I fell in love!" This description sounds more like infatuation or lust to me. Makes me think of accidentally falling into a hole in the ground. "It just happened! I fell into a hole in the ground!" I don't want to be accidentally loved, as if the person had no choice in the matter. I want it to be on purpose, with the person's full consciousness and awareness intact.

Love is patient, love is kind. It does not envy, it does not boast, it is not proud. It does not dishonor others, it is not self-seeking, it is not easily angered, it keeps no record of wrongs. Love does not delight in evil but rejoices with the truth. It always protects, always trusts, always hopes, always perseveres. (1 Corinthians 13:4-7 NIV)

I think to really love someone is one of the most difficult things to do. I mean, to really, truly love someone, selflessly. It is one of the most difficult things to do. Just take the first thing love is from the verses above. It is patient. Already, this can be very difficult.

I wonder how many people have never truly been loved. Maybe more than I would expect. They might be loved for awhile. They might be loved for who they seem to be. They might be loved because they're useful for a time. They might be loved because of their abilities. They might be loved for what they look like. In each of these instances I'm using the word "love," but this isn't really love. When you're really loved it isn't for awhile, it's not for what you seem to be, not because you're of some use, not because of your abilities, and not just because of how you look. What a wonderful thing it is to have even one person who really loves you.

When I think about the gravity of the meaning of love, it makes me consider much more carefully the phrase "I love you." Do people really know what they're saying when they say that? Do they know the meaning of the word? Do they mean it if they don't know the meaning of the word? Perhaps, "I'm infatuated with you," or "I lust you" would be more accurate.

A slight departure from the main topic. Don't be infatuated or lustful and call it love. Learn the difference. I feel that infatuation and lust numb the senses. They numb logic. I know because it has happened with me and to me. Sense and logic leave the building when infatuation and/or lust arrive. And feelings are their best friends. They work together. I've found that I can be infatuated or lustful toward someone and not love them at all. At that point, it's as if nothing else matters, except for how I feel. This is so illogical. Feelings are not enough. Feelings are not enough to make it right. Feelings can be downright misleading. By the way, lust is not a good thing, so I try to extinguish it as soon as I'm aware of it. Also, I've realized that a person can be interested in me but it's like they've got glasses over their eyes and only see me through the lenses of infatuation and/or lust and the associated feelings. Again, this is so illogical. They've got to take off those glasses in order to know me for me. That is, if they care about knowing me. And if they do take off those glasses, most likely they will not like me at all.

I have never been "in" love, whatever that even means. I have not loved someone. At least I am aware of this, and have not mistaken infatuation or lust for love. If I ever loved someone, I really hope I would be logical about it, and not go purely by feelings. Going purely by feelings gets you into trouble. It's easy to get carried away with feelings. Love is not illogical. I may feel like jumping in the ocean because it's so delightfully blue and refreshing, but logically I cannot swim. It would be stupid for me to do so. Certain things have to be in place before I jump in the ocean, like wearing a life vest. I can't trust my feelings, and I've learned that lesson. Hopefully, I will never need to repeat it.

So, I return to my topic. My insecurities of not being able to trust people because they change, are made less important by knowing I can completely trust God because He doesn't change. Wanting to be loved for who I really am is satisfied by knowing God loves me for who I really am, and always will. This makes me feel relieved. I have found Someone I can trust completely. I have found Someone who will always love me for who I really am. He knows me the best, and still loves me with a perfect love. He's patient, and won't get tired of me. He's the security I need. He's my source of love, so by His grace I can learn to love others to my greatest capacity. I can't give something I don't have. I need a source of love. How can I truly love if I don't know Love?

God truly loves you. Remember what love really is. He will be faithful to complete what He has started with you.[2] He will be with you and bring you through this earthly life and home to Him. He won't fail to do this. Beloved, He really loves you. He's not changing His My mind about you, ever. His feelings toward you will not change. His love for you will never change. It will not even fluctuate in the smallest way. He's not going anywhere, ever. He's never going to leave you. He's never going to let you go from Him. He loves you very much, and He always will. You're His very own, and He loves you and wants you for Him, forever. You can be completely sure of this. It is not budging at all. It is solid and sure. Though everything else may change, this will not. He will not change.

Now I see why He is the refuge and security of His people. There is nothing else that is as safe and secure as He is, as His love is. He has matchless integrity. He is strong and never unfaithful.

Find your security in His unchanging love for you. True and pure and deep love. You can be sure of this. His unfailing, unchanging love for you. Though everything else may change, this will not. It won't age, it won't wear out or weaken. It will be as bright and strong as it ever was, ever will be, ever could be. Be sure of this. And this is not a general love for the masses – a vague "God's love" for a faceless crowd. I'm speaking of an intimate, great, personal, and individual love for each of His own - for you.

Dear friends, let us practice loving each other, for love comes from God and those who are loving and kind show that they are the children of God, and that they are getting to know him better. But if a person isn't loving and kind, it shows that he doesn't know God – for God is love.

God showed how much he loved us by sending his only Son into this wicked world to bring to us eternal life through his death. In this act we see what real love is: it is not our love for God, but his love for us when he sent his Son to satisfy God's anger against our sins.

Dear friends, since God loved us as much as that, we surely ought to love each other too. For though we have never yet seen God, when we love each other God lives in us and his love within us grows ever stronger. And he has put his own Holy Spirit into our hearts as a proof to us that we are living with him and he with us. And furthermore, we have seen with our own eyes and now tell all the world that God sent his Son to be their Savior. Anyone who believes and says that Jesus is the Son of God has God living in him, and he is living with God.

We know how much God loves us because we have felt his love and because we believe him when he tells us that he loves us dearly. God is love, and anyone who lives in love is living with God and God is living in him. And as we live with Christ, our love grows more perfect and complete; so we will not be ashamed and embarrassed at the day of judgement, but can face him with confidence and joy, because he loves us and we love him too.

We need have no fear of someone who loves us perfectly; his perfect love for us eliminates all dread of what he might do to us. If we are afraid, it is for fear of what he might do to us, and shows that we are not fully convinced that he really loves us. So you see, our love for him comes as a result of his loving us first. (1 John 4:7-

19 TLB)

90

Journal Entries from the Past

Recently I filled the last page of a private journal I've kept since 2010/2011. It has an assortment of things in it. There are a few actual daily entries, but mostly it is filled with bits of information that are meaningful to me and I didn't want to forget.

I flipped through the pages of the journal and found some entries from 2011 and 2013. They were generally interesting to me, and thought-provoking to look back on. The majority of them I wrote to the Lord.

Here they are, unedited, except for one name change.

April 28, 2011

After all this time I write again. First real entry in the journal I guess. I hope what I write is enlightening – helping me grow and mature into what God wants me to be. I want to be closer to Him, and yet must fight against my nature all the time. Sometimes it seems the greatest battles are against one's flesh – and the enemy, of course.

Not only do I hope to win battles against my nature, but against anything that is not good – anything that the Lord wouldn't approve of. I want to be more loving and kind – sometimes I feel that way inside, but it can have a hard time showing itself outwardly. I want to be full of grace, and be able to extend it always. To be humble too. Wise, humble, full of grace, loving, strong and mature spiritually, sensitive and intuitive – oh so many things. But I must not be anxious.

Help me to be more like You, Lord – the right perspectives and viewpoints, saying, doing, behaving how You'd want me to – making myself take the time and effort for You! Having a greater desire for all these things too.

You've/are so good to me, Lord. So very kind and loving and everything wonderful. So many blessings you've given to me, so many. Like I've said before I want to love You just as much as I do now (if not more), now that I'm surrounded with good things, as when/if I'm not, or if difficult times come along. I want to be content in any situation – like one of Your disciples said. I want to love You more, too. Please help me to do this. Part of me is aprehensive, and part of me wants to see and do new things, spiritually and otherwise. In either case, Lord, please help the aprehension to go away if it's the right thing.

Lord, You've created such beautiful and marvelous things! So beautiful.

I hope and trust that writing here, I will write with a purpose. Something – writing with a purpose somewhat unknown, but exciting and curious. In my old journals I would often say, "What will tomorrow bring?" but somehow I feel like – What will this year bring, or, the future? Growth, and a closer walk with You, my God.

Your beloved,
Daisy

June 20, 2011

I think there is nothing more heartbreaking or truly sorrowful than the conscious separation, or rather, the realization that one is distancing themself from God, when in their heart they don't want to. Or, when at least they feel less close to the Lord because of the things they've done, or continue to do. And, they don't really want to do those things. It's like the inner battle between one's spirit and flesh is in such a way that the flesh has been winning the battles so many times that one feels they have not done what is right, and what the Lord wants them to do, so then they feel like they are less close to the Lord. Maybe it's a fact that when one sins, it is like a distance has been made between them and God, - or, at least it feels like it.

I thought somewhere in the bible it said that if you're faithful in little you'll be faithful in much. I have to find where in the bible this is. I want to be faithful to the Lord in every seemingly-small thing. Why do I find this so difficult? I must be more on guard with myself, and not let anything go. When I start to think of the "little" things in my daily life that I should be guarding myself from doing, thinking, seeing, and hearing it is amazing how many things there are.

I don't want to be apathetic and asleep to the fact that I must stay/be faithful in even these things. I want to be refined and more mature spiritually, so I feel like these things – these seemingly small battles to be fought each day are important. I want the Lord to be pleased and honored by my conduct as His daughter. I don't want to be a disappointment, or not value all the things He's given to me and done for me by disregarding what He wants of me, and that is enough reason in itself, but I believe what He wants of me is what is really best for me too.

He's given me so much, and taught me so much, and helped me through so much, and helped me grow so much that I just cannot and must not let my flesh turn me away from what is right, and place a distance between the Lord and myself, or keep me from fulfilling His will. I want to be close to my Lord, to communicate with Him, and have Him guide me to do what I should do.

Maybe that verse in Hosea about sowing with a view to righteousness, and breaking up your fallow ground has something to do with what I must do – about being faithful in "little" things – daily things – and not letting the flesh win these battles. I think I would be doing these things with a view to righteousness, and the battles or maybe the things I know are not right – that I must overcome are the fallow ground.

It's like I have to break up the fallow ground in order to grow.

Lord, I thank you for answering my prayer the way I wanted, and first, according to your will, and letting me understand more about that verse in Hosea. Please give me the strength and fortitude to win these daily battles and not let any go by. Please help me to guard myself from any attacks and not be fooled by them.

Thank you Lord for forgiving me for my sins, and my wretchedness. For Your grace and mercy, and love. I hope I can learn to extend these things too.

Your beloved,
Daisy

February 26, 2013

Dearest Lord,

I have not written to You like this before, but in the past I wished that I could, and now I am. I can talk/pray with You anytime too, which is so wonderful, more than I realize. I thought/think it will be very good to write to You too. Thank You Lord for keeping us safe and well, for everything, for all the blessings You give to us and for taking care of us in so many ways – ways I'm not even aware of. I'm doing all right, thanks to You Lord. I'm learning that I shouldn't worry anymore, and I'm trying to do so too. I've been learning a lot from the videos we've been watching, and from reading Your bible, and from our talks also. I'm glad spring is coming soon. I can hear different bird sounds outside, and see many robins on the lawn. I've got things in the garden to work on – I hope I can do it all, but I will not worry about it. I hope some good, happy things happen this spring – I hope to have things to look forward to, too. Of course, knowing You more each day is something to look forward to. I am looking forward to warmer temperatures and sunnier skies too. Thank You Lord that spring is coming soon.

Your beloved,
Daisy

February 28, 2013

Dearest Lord,

Please forgive me for becoming discouraged so easily. I know You told me not to worry about a thing and that certain particular things would have a good outcome. Yet I get discouraged, and even worry. I guess it just shows how some things have become such a habit with me. I do hope to change these habits and ways though, with Your help of course. I will learn not to worry, and not be discouraged so easily because I will learn to have more faith and trust in You. Also, I do hope I will learn to pray/communicate with You better, Lord. I think I don't listen enough to You, and I talk too much. Please help me to do better with that too, Lord. I want to have more patience with myself as well. Not so much that I give myself too much slack, and yet not be so much of a perfectionist either. I must learn, and not just know how to do everything perfectly, after all. I should realize too that I will make mistakes – I have already, that's for sure. Sometimes I wish I did more things right, rather than more things wrong. Either way, I want to remain humble. Probably not doing things perfectly helps me to stay that way. Lord, I don't know how great of a letter this is to You/for You, but I thank You for understanding, understanding me more than I understand me.

Your beloved,
Daisy

March 1, 2013

Dearest Lord,

Bless You Lord, and thank You for everything, and for all of the countless blessings You've given to me. I'm glad You are God, and that You are the way You are. It was sure a nice, mild, almost warm day outside today. The first day this year so far that I can remember being able to feel a little warmth in the air. I bet the outdoor plants like it. Blitz and I walked on the power line road in the early evening. It was a nice walk, and I could hear some birds singing that I have not heard for so long. I hope someday soon we can take walks together, and go places together, and see things together. You could show me things in Your perspective – that would be the right way to look at things. It is kind of invigorating/refreshing to see that Spring is near. How much more invigorating/refreshing it is to hear from You, see and know Your ways, and so forth, Lord. Seeing life come back, or I should say, life reawakened in plants is always amazing. May the growth in myself and in my relationship with You be likewise, Lord. Tomorrow we will go pick up the mini – we'll see what happens next!

Your beloved,
Daisy

March 4, 2013

Dearest Lord,

It was a nice day today. It was sunny and clear, but cold. Thank

You for looking out for me, and taking care of me. Thank You also for leading and guiding, (and teaching) me each day. I think of You throughout the day. I'm not sure if it's really meditating (I think not), but I do think of You often each day. I think about how I will be closer to You in the future, and how our relationship will grow. I also think about how You may communicate with me, and how You already have/in the past. Sometimes I wonder what You think about me, but I don't want to draw great conclusions about that on my own, in case I'm thinking incorrectly. Also I think about Your other beloved children and how You must communicate with them too. When I look out onto the view here and the water and sky, and see its beauty, I often think of You then. I like that You are so vast/big and mighty/all-powerful, but are so full of details too. You are God. I'm so glad You're like You are, and not like man. I love You Lord, and thank You – more than that – that You love me too.

Your beloved,
Daisy

March 5, 2013

Dearest Lord,

It was a fine day today. It was cloudy and a little rainy outside. Thank You Lord for talking with me this morning. Is there anything greater than knowing You? I will try to remember the things I'm supposed to remember: that You love me, to not worry about a thing, and to trust You, and also to have patience and not be anxious. Those are all very good things that if I remember and do them, my life and mind will be better for them. Writing of my mind, I shouldn't lean/depend on my own understanding. We watched the last video in the course this evening, so we'll go through them again from the beginning. Thank You for those videos Lord – there is so much to learn about, and so much to grow in. My aquarium is doing much better now – the water tests showed the water is safe for fish. So, I'll think about what I should choose. The plants are doing so much better now that they have proper light. It's another picture of how without You we perish – like the aquarium plants decaying and declining in health those few days they were without proper lighting. Thank You Lord for Your creation(s).

Your beloved,
Daisy

March 6, 2013

Dearest Lord,

Thank You for another day – it was grey, cloudy, and raining today, but I really didn't mind. There were approximately 20 robins out on the lawn this morning. The pair of crows were there too, probably waiting for some bread. I did throw a little out to them – they took it pretty quickly. Please help me to do things, Lord. All of the good, fruitful, helpful, and right things. You know, even when I know of something I should do, it's difficult to do it. Most times, if I do actually do it, I find it wasn't as bad as I thought and I'm glad I did it. Occasionally, even if I do it, it feels like it was indeed difficult and I don't feel all that refreshed afterwards, but perhaps still glad it was done – or am I just glad it's over-with? In any case, please help me to do what I should do, and please help me to get over it feeling like a great burden to do so. I know doing the right things aren't easy all the time, but perhaps with some practice with seemingly smaller things, I'll get better at it and it won't seem like I'm struggling as much – like swimming upstream, or petting Blitz's fur in the wrong direction, or changing habits. Thank You Lord for taking care of me everyday, for looking out for me, and loving me so much.

Love,
Daisy

March 8, 2013

Dearest Lord,

I'm so glad You're unchanging. When I consider myself, I see that I'm changing a lot – even from minute to minute. I want to change in order to be better, but to stay in that place, and not change negatively. I wish I could do better at changing my habits – and have more self-control as well. Please help me with these things, Lord. I hope I will do much better at these things in the future – even tomorrow. It was sunny today. I could see those blue skies that have not been that common of a sight lately. Thank You Lord for everything, and for all of the blessings You've given to me each day. It's such a blessing to even have good, clean water to drink. We got an update on the mini today – so, it may be that we will get another update next Monday, or early in the week. Whatever the final outcome may be, I am expecting it to be good. So tomorrow the clocks are to be set forward one hour (in the evening). Happily, spring came quickly. I think it helped that winter was quite easy and mild. I am glad. Thank You again and again Lord for being Who You are – and the way you are. Thank You again and again for taking care of me and loving me so much.

Your beloved,
Daisy

March 11, 2013

Dearest Lord,

Thank You for teaching me. Thank you for caring for me each day, and communicating with me, Lord. I don't know if there is a thing comparable to being able to hear You, and talk to You/pray, and know You, Lord. Please continue to help me have a closer, more intimate relationship with You. Please help me to change my ingrained habits to foster or help that relationship, too, Lord. Thank You for continuing to work in me, Lord, and not giving up on me – I thank You for hearing my prayers and requests. I do hope I can/will make choices throughout my life and each day that are right, and honor and glorify You – and please You. Truly, if there is any good in me it's because of You. I do hope that I will change unproductive and counterproductive habits in my life as soon as possible (with, and only with Your help!). It is March – springtime soon. I hope it is filled with good and lovely things. I know I'll enjoy seeing plants grow new leaves, and maybe even some new blossoms. Milder temperatures and bird-songs are pleasant too. Lord You give me hope for the future. You are my hope. I'm glad You're with me, and leading me the right way.

Your beloved,
Daisy

March 12, 2013

Dearest Lord,

I see more and more how I cannot do anything without Your help. Please, continue to help me with all that I struggle with. It is disappointing to think that I'm lacking things. And, more disappointing to think about how I could ever obtain them. Perhaps I should not feel disappointed, but I do. I don't know what else I should write – I thank You Lord for loving me nonetheless, and for caring for me each day. Thank You for forgiving all of my many sins, and for continuing to work in me and not giving up on me. Thank You for everything, and for the many blessings You've given to me. I do hope I can do what pleases You. Please help me to overcome myself. Tomorrow it will be one week until my birthday. It's beyond my mind to think that You knew me before I was even born. It would be good to live a life that was worthwhile. One that honored You, and followed Your ways, and was faithful to You to the end. I'm hoping for those things in my life, Lord. Please help it to be that way – and maybe more could be added to that too. Please forgive my feeling disappointed – if I really should not feel that way, Lord.

Your beloved,
Daisy

March 13, 2013

Dearest Lord,

Thank You for another day, and for helping me and keeping all of us safe and well. Mom and I took the mini back to the dealership today. It was a long drive back and forth, but I'm glad that has been taken care of for now. It was a challenging drive here and there because of the rain and traffic – thank You Lord for helping me to drive and for keeping us safe! It was mild outside – not so cold like it has been. So it looks like Rebecca will have a lunch at her house this Sunday. It's her birthday too. I hope it goes well. On Friday Dad is meeting with a client, so he'll be driving into Seattle. I don't know if I'm going though. A kind of busy week. It's amazing to think of how much things that we do will not last. Eventually, they'll all pass away, even our own bodies, and the world. But, You go on forever – and our spirits too. I cannot contemplate forever very well, Lord. You're just so much more than I could ever think of. How wonderful You are, Lord. Wonderfully good, kind, powerful, and everything that is good. You understand everything, and nothing escapes Your notice. I'm so glad that You are God, Lord. I'm so glad You're God, and care to love me and know me. You're so much Lord, and I am nothing without You.

Your beloved,

Daisy

March 14, 2013

Dearest Lord,

Thank You for everything, and for all of the blessings You've given to me, and for keeping us safe and healthy. We went to Sequim and Port Angeles today to do some errands. It seems Dad will be going into Seattle on Sunday, and staying overnight for a couple nights until Tuesday, when he'll meet with his client. I don't know if Mom and I will go and stay that long, but we'll see. Lord, I still hope to do the things I should do – or at least, the things it would be good for me to do. Please continue to help me with doing this. Perhaps I should write out the things I should do/be doing. I will continue also, (with Your help), to not worry about a thing, and to not be anxious for anything. I think those are very good things to do, and I hope I will do them – strive to do it. I also want to change some habits of mine. Please help me to do this too, Lord. There really is plenty to do each day. If not only tasks and chores, and projects, then there are things to do about oneself. With everything I need Your help and guidance and wisdom and insight. You are very good Lord. Thank You for taking care of me each day, and showing me the right way.

Your beloved,
Daisy

March 16, 2013

Dearest Lord,

Thank You for another day Lord. Another day for growth and learning. There is so much to learn every day. I didn't do well in doing the things on the list I wrote. I did 2 out of 6. I want to do much better than that. I want to do 6 out of 6. I hope I will do them all tomorrow, and beyond. It is very disappointing to not do what I had the opportunity to do. Please help me to overcome myself and do what I should do, Lord. I am disappointed in myself. I am disappointed that I didn't take advantage in/of my opportunities – times during the day where the thought/decision came to me to do those things that I should do, and then I decided on doing other things, opposite things, instead. It's not even that I forgot to do them, but I was aware that I not doing them. It is disappointing. Of course, at the times I made my decisions, it seemed ok, but in the end I'm disappointed in my decisions. I want to do much better than this. In a way I feel that I can, but so far I'm not, which makes me feel some hope, and more disappointment at the same time. I do hope to see a noticeable change in my actions and habits sometime soon. I'm glad Lord that You're capable of anything, and You can do whatever You want to – all-powerful. Please help me to do these things that I should do.

Your beloved,
Daisy

March 21, 2013

Dearest Lord,

I know I haven't written for awhile, but I am again, now. I sure haven't felt very well the past few days, but I thank You Lord so much that it hasn't been worse – which I know it could be – a great deal worse. I hope to feel much better tomorrow. Then maybe I can continue to work on my flooring. A few days I've missed praying too, Lord. I will try and return to doing that, now that I think I'm going to feel much better now. Of course, I would like to pray even when I'm not feeling well, but I felt so unwell it was difficult to concentrate. I wonder if this is something that I need to work on, or is it something that changes as one matures? It's spring now. It felt cold outside, but it is spring. The sun sets just about right above the peak of the mountain now. Lord, please help me to continue to seek You, and not stop or give up in any way. Please help me to continue to do what I should do, and do what I should do, but haven't done yet, or haven't done consistently yet, or made new habits of. I want to make gains each day, to know You more each day, and grow each day – not regress or make useless mistakes. When I make mistakes, at least I could learn from them. And to obey and submit myself to You Lord. And resist my flesh. There's really so much Lord – but I will not worry or be anxious about anything.

Your beloved,
Daisy

April 17, 2013

Dearest Lord,

It's been nearly a month since I wrote last. You know, for awhile (longer than I have before) I was following my list of things to do somewhat well. Although, I didn't do everything, like I should have. But lately (past five days or so) I really began not following my list. It is disappointing to have to go back like this. Yet on one hand, I've been able to see how much better it is when I follow that list. I do hope, starting tomorrow, that I will follow that list more consistently again – and hopefully even better than I did before. I feel, with Your help Lord, that I will be able to do this, and in the future they will become habits that I will still need to keep, but they won't be as much of a struggle to keep. Mom has been in the Philippines for about a week and a half now. I do miss her, and I'm so glad that You're with her, Lord. Thank You for all of the mercies and grace You've shown Mom and her family, Lord. It sometimes seems like it will be a long time before she comes back, but perhaps it will go quickly. I certainly have enough things to do

– if only I would make myself do them! I'm glad You know me Lord, and love me still. I don't think anyone is quite like You.

Your beloved,
Daisy

Notes

CHAPTER 1 Appearance
1 Reference to Ecclesiastes 10:3

CHAPTER 6 He Loves to be Merciful
1 *Cambridge Dictionary,* s.v. "mercy," accessed June 18, 2019,
    https://dictionary.cambridge.org/us/dictionary/english/mercy.

CHAPTER 8 Meaning What You Say. Being True to What You Say.
1 *Cambridge Dictionary,* s.v. "esteem," accessed June 18, 2019,
    https://dictionary.cambridge.org/us/dictionary/english/esteem.

CHAPTER 10 Waiting
1 *Lexico Dictionaries,* s.v. "wait," accessed June 18, 2019,
    https://lexico.com/en/definition/wait.

CHAPTER 12 Attributes of God Part 1: Jealous
1 *Lexico Dictionaries,* s.v. "jealous," accessed June 18, 2019,
    https://lexico.com/en/definition/jealous; *Dictionary.com,* s.v.
    "jealous," accessed June 18, 2019,
    https://dictionary.com/browse/jealous.

CHAPTER 13 Personality vs. Character
1 *Wikipedia,* s.v. "persona," last modified April 30, 2019,
    https://en.wikipedia.org/wiki/Persona.
2 *Webster's II New Riverside Dictionary,* Revised ed., s.v.
    "personality."
3 "Difference between Character and Personality." *Difference
    Between.* Accessed February 29, 2016.
    differencebetween.info/difference-between-character-and-
    personality.

4 *Wiktionary*, s.v. "character," last modified May 25, 2019, https://en.wiktionary.org/wiki/character.

5 *Webster's II New Riverside Dictionary*, Revised ed., s.v. "character."

6 "Difference between Character and Personality."

7 "Difference between Personality and Character." *TheyDiffer.com*. Accessed February 29, 2016. https://theydiffer.com/difference-between-personality-and-character/.

8 "Difference between Personality and Character."

9 Lue, Natalie. "There's a difference between personality and character." *Baggage Reclaim* (blog). December 3, 2014. Accessed February 29, 2016. https://baggagereclaim.co.uk/theres-a-difference-between-personality-and-character/.

10 Lue, "There's a difference."

CHAPTER 14 Attributes of God Part 2: Omniscient

1 *Webster's II New Riverside Dictionary*, Revised ed., s.v. "omniscient."

CHAPTER 15 Broken Heart

1 *Webster's II New Riverside Dictionary*, Revised ed., s.v. "brokenhearted."

CHAPTER 17 Exploring Proverbs 15:16-17

1 *Merriam-Webster Dictionary*, s.v. "reverence," accessed June 18, 2019, https://merriam-webster.com/dictionary/reverence.

2 *Merriam-Webster Dictionary*, s.v. "revere," accessed June 18, 2019, https://merriam-webster.com/dictionary/revere.

3 *Webster's II New Riverside Dictionary*, Revised ed., s.v. "trouble."

CHAPTER 18 Attributes of God Part 4: Holiness

1 *Webster's II New Riverside Dictionary*, Revised ed., s.v. "holy."

2 "The Holiness of God (Paul Washer)," YouTube video, 54:49, "GoodTreeMinistries," April 6, 2012, https://youtube.com/watch?v=4sxAfl_OKxo.

3 "The Holiness of God."

4 Ibid.

5 *Dictionary.com*, s.v. "presume," accessed June 19, 2019, https://dictionary.com/browse/presume.

CHAPTER 20 New

1 *Webster's II New Riverside Dictionary*, Revised ed., s.v. "custom."

CHAPTER 24 Attributes of God Part 5: Omnipresent

1 *Webster's II New Riverside Dictionary*, Revised ed., s.v. "omnipresence."

CHAPTER 27 Attributes of God Part 6: Faithfulness

1 *Webster's II New Riverside Dictionary*, Revised ed., s.v. "faithful."

CHAPTER 28 Strong Enough for Patience?

1 *Webster's II New Riverside Dictionary*, Revised ed., s.v. "patient."

2 *Webster's II New Riverside Dictionary*, Revised ed., s.v. "endure."

3 *Webster's II New Riverside Dictionary*, Revised ed., s.v. "understanding."

4 *Webster's II New Riverside Dictionary*, Revised ed., s.v. "tolerance."

5 *Webster's II New Riverside Dictionary*, Revised ed., s.v. "persevere."

6 *Webster's II New Riverside Dictionary*, Revised ed., s.v. "steadfast."

7 *Webster's II New Riverside Dictionary*, Revised ed., s.v. "patience."

8 *Webster's II New Riverside Dictionary*, Revised ed., s.v. "longsuffering."

CHAPTER 31 Meriting Love

1 *Webster's II New Riverside Dictionary*, Revised ed., s.v. "merit."

CHAPTER 32 See or Believe

1 *Webster's II New Riverside Dictionary*, Revised ed., s.v. "contrary."

CHAPTER 39 Worse Than a Fool
1 *Webster's II New Riverside Dictionary*, Revised ed., s.v. "fool."
2 *Webster's II New Riverside Dictionary*, Revised ed., s.v. "conceited."

CHAPTER 40 Humility vs. Pride
1 *Webster's II New Riverside Dictionary*, Revised ed., s.v. "humility."
2 *Webster's II New Riverside Dictionary*, Revised ed., s.v. "humble."
3 *Webster's II New Riverside Dictionary*, Revised ed., s.v. "pride."
4 *Webster's II New Riverside Dictionary*, Revised ed., s.v. "conceit."

CHAPTER 41 Trust!
1 *Webster's II New Riverside Dictionary*, Revised ed., s.v. "trust."

CHAPTER 42 Worry
1 *Webster's II New Riverside Dictionary*, Revised ed., s.v. "worry."

CHAPTER 43 Beauty Is Vain
1 *Merriam-Webster Dictionary*, s.v. "vain," accessed June 19, 2019,
   https://merriam-webster.com/dictionary/vain.

CHAPTER 47 Hypocrisy
1 *Webster's II New Riverside Dictionary*, Revised ed., s.v. "hypocrisy."

CHAPTER 52 It's a Trap
1 *Webster's II New Riverside Dictionary*, Revised ed., s.v. "fear."

CHAPTER 59 Dangers of Idealism, Self-Worth, and Pleasing God
1 *Webster's II New Riverside Dictionary*, Revised ed., s.v. "ideal."
2 *Webster's II New Riverside Dictionary*, Revised ed., s.v. "idealism."

CHAPTER 60 Contentment
1 *Webster's II New Riverside Dictionary*, Revised ed., s.v.
   "contentment."

CHAPTER 62 Value Systems

1 Hereford, Zorka. "Have a Personal Value System." *Essential Life Skills.* Accessed May 11, 2019. https://essentiallifeskills.net/personalvaluesystem.html.

CHAPTER 66 Attributes of God Part 7: Mercy, Goodness, and Love
1 *Webster's II New Riverside Dictionary,* Revised ed., s.v. "mercy."
2 *Webster's II New Riverside Dictionary,* Revised ed., s.v. "clement."
3 *Webster's II New Riverside Dictionary,* Revised ed., s.v. "lenient."
4 *Webster's II New Riverside Dictionary,* Revised ed., s.v. "benevolence."
5 *Webster's II New Riverside Dictionary,* Revised ed., s.v. "good."
6 *Webster's II New Riverside Dictionary,* Revised ed., s.v. "love."
7 *Webster's II New Riverside Dictionary,* Revised ed., s.v. "affection."
8 *Webster's II New Riverside Dictionary,* Revised ed., s.v. "fond."
9 *Webster's II New Riverside Dictionary,* Revised ed., s.v. "immoderate."

CHAPTER 69 Attributes of God PART 8: Justice
1 *Webster's II New Riverside Dictionary,* Revised ed., s.v. "justice."

CHAPTER 72 Words You Speak
1 *Webster's II New Riverside Dictionary,* Revised ed., s.v. "power."
2 *Webster's II New Riverside Dictionary,* Revised ed., s.v. "life."
3 *Webster's II New Riverside Dictionary,* Revised ed., s.v. "death."

CHAPTER 73 Alone with God
1 *Webster's II New Riverside Dictionary,* Revised ed., s.v. "supplicate."

CHAPTER 75 Doing Nothing?
1 *Webster's II New Riverside Dictionary,* Revised ed., s.v. "lawless."

CHAPTER 80 Thoughts on Marriage and Related Issues
1 *Webster's II New Riverside Dictionary,* Revised ed., s.v. "diligent."
2 *Webster's II New Riverside Dictionary,* Revised ed., s.v. "assiduous."

CHAPTER 81 Armor of God
1 *Webster's II New Riverside Dictionary,* Revised ed., s.v. "prepare."

CHAPTER 84 The Value of Wisdom
1 Proverbs 3:21 TLB
2 *Webster's II New Riverside Dictionary,* Revised ed., s.v. "discretion."
3 *Webster's II New Riverside Dictionary,* Revised ed., s.v. "discreet."
4 *Webster's II New Riverside Dictionary,* Revised ed., s.v. "circumspect."
5 *Webster's II New Riverside Dictionary,* Revised ed., s.v. "prudent."
6 *Webster's II New Riverside Dictionary,* Revised ed., s.v. "judicious."
7 *Webster's II New Riverside Dictionary,* Revised ed., s.v. "provident."
8 *Webster's II New Riverside Dictionary,* Revised ed., s.v. "wisdom."
9 Proverbs 3:16-18 TLB
8 "wisdom."

CHAPTER 85 Valuing You, Loved by the King, and a Girl's Worth
1 *Lexico Dictionaries,* s.v. "precious," accessed June 19, 2019, https://lexico.com/en/definition/precious.
2 Reference to Isaiah 55:8

CHAPTER 87 Tootsie Roll Pop
1 *Wikipedia,* s.v. "infatuation," last modified April 30, 2019, https://en.wikipedia.org/wiki/Infatuation.

CHAPTER 88 Beautiful Grace
1 *Webster's II New Riverside Dictionary,* Revised ed., s.v. "grace."
2 *Webster's II New Riverside Dictionary,* Revised ed., s.v. "gracious."
3 *Webster's II New Riverside Dictionary,* Revised ed., s.v. "mercy."
4 *Webster's II New Riverside Dictionary,* Revised ed., s.v. "good will."
5 *Webster's II New Riverside Dictionary,* Revised ed., s.v. "benevolence."
6 *Webster's II New Riverside Dictionary,* Revised ed., s.v. "courteous."
7 *Webster's II New Riverside Dictionary,* Revised ed., s.v. "charitable."
8 *Webster's II New Riverside Dictionary,* Revised ed., s.v. "charity."
9 *Webster's II New Riverside Dictionary,* Revised ed., s.v. "lenient."

10 *Webster's II New Riverside Dictionary,* Revised ed., s.v. "compassion."

11 *Webster's II New Riverside Dictionary,* Revised ed., s.v. "considerate."

CHAPTER 89 He Will Not Change

1 *Merriam-Webster Dictionary,* s.v. "commitment," accessed June 19, 2019, https://merriam-webster.com/dictionary/commitment.

2 Reference to Philippians 1:6

.

Made in the USA
Lexington, KY
21 September 2019